ekklesia
(Ekklesia)

Ekklesia

(Ekklesia)

Indian Conversations

A Study of the Church

Edited by

Samuel George

H. Joseph Lalfakmawia

Ajungla Jamir

Christian World Imprints™

&

Master's College of Theology

First Published in 2015 by

Christian World Imprints™
Christian Publishing & Books from India
H-12 Bali Nagar, **New Delhi-110015**
info@christianworldimprints.com
www.ChristianWorldImprints.com
Phone: +91 11 25465925 Fax: +91 11 25173055

&

MCT Pustakaalayam
Master's College of Theology
(Senate of Serampore College)
Plot No. 5-7, Kommadi Road
Madhurawada, **Visakhapatnam** - 530048
mctvizag@outlook.com

ISBN-13: 978-93-5148-054-9 (HB) ISBN-10: 93-5148-054-2 (HB)
ISBN-13: 978-93-5148-055-6 (PB) ISBN-10: 93-5148-055-0 (PB)

Cover design: A. Devakrupa Varakumar

Type setting: H. Joseph Lalfakmawia & R. Satish Karun

Printed at Chawla Offset Printers

The Book

Jesus said, "… I will build my church, and the gates of hades will not prevail against it" (Mat. 16:18). What concept/metaphor/image of the church was he alluding to? What are its nature, character, and function? Is it a relevant institution today? Well, these and few other pertinent questions are not just raised but grappled with an Indian/Asian perspective by various authors in the book. The focus of the book is on church as *Ekklesia,* meaning "summoned or called out assembly of people." It can also mean a convoked community. Present day, Indian church needs to redefine her character and existence in such a way that it becomes meaningful and relevant to our society. This book, *Ekklesia: Indian Conversations* is a humble attempt towards that goal.

Foreword

Ecclesiology is one of the major courses in Theological Studies. The word Ecclesiology comes from two Greek words meaning "assembly" and "word" – combined together to mean "The Study of the Church." The Church can be broadly stated to as being the assembly of believers in the Lord Jesus Christ. I believe that a systematic study is crucial for those of us in Christian ministry and those being trained for Church ministry. Hence, Ecclesiology is a vital subject to understand God's purpose for believers in the world today. It helps us to appreciate both, the Church at large as well as the church as a local assembly of believers.

A Biblical understanding of Ecclesiology would go a long way to correct many of the common problems in churches today. Ecclesiology helps us to understand both the role of The Church as a corporate body of believers to each member, as well as our role within The Church. The Church is the Body of Christ and each of us has a specific function and role within that body. It provides us with the foundation to understand and appreciate church ordinances, church leadership: The selection and structure of leadership, and church interventions: what the church should be doing in regards to believers (worship and discipleship) and unbelievers (ministry and evangelism).

As this is a course prescribed by the Senate of Serampore College (University) the faculty members of the Master's College of Theology have compiled a book based on the syllabus.

I sincerely appreciate the efforts taken by The Principal, Dr. Samuel George and his team to put this module together. They have spent many hours in prayer and research to collect and present relevant, material in a very presentable and readable format. I believe that this is a vital reading that could be used as a textbook in Bible Colleges.

This book is not limited to theological students. I encourage every Christian who desires to be proactive in The Church, to read this and gain a better understanding, and appreciation of the functioning of the Church and his/her role within it. Encourage your friends as well, to get a copy of this book and read it.

It is my prayer that every person in the Body of Christ who reads this book will be blessed and be a blessing both to their local church as well as The Church, the body of Christ.

Yours in Christ,

Rev. Dr. **Arjuna Rao Chiguluri**
Director, Master's College of Theology
Visakhapatnam.

Contents

Notes on Contributors

Ms. **Ajungla Jamir** (B.Sc., B.D., M.Th.) is from Nagaland and belongs to the Baptist Church. She serves as the Assistant Professor (Christian Ethics) at Master's College of Theology (affiliated to the Senate of Serampore College (University)), Visakhapatnam. Some of her known writings are: "Sexual Orientation and Human Identity: Towards Recovering the Full Spectrum of Gender"; "An Inclusive Peace building through the Eyes of a Young Naga Woman: A Human Rights Perspective".

Email - jamirajung@gmail.com

Dr. **Atula Ao (Tsüdir)** (B.A., B.D., M.Th.,D.Th.) is from Baptist Church of Nagaland. She was awarded Doctor of Theology (Old Testament) from the Senate of Serampore College (University) for her research on Prophetic Oracles in the Old Testament. Currently she serves as the Associate Professor (O.T.) at Master's College of Theology (affiliated to the Senate of Serampore College (University)), Visakhapatnam, and editor-in-chief of *Master's Journal of Theology*. Some of her noted writings are: "Transgressing the Boundaries: Re-Reading the Story of Vashti in the Context of Quest for Women's Identity"; "Health and the Bible: Health in the Old Testament"; "Feminist Hermeneutics: A Few Methodological Reflections"; "Mission as Neighbourliness and Community Solidarity in the Context of the Margins: A Reflection from Isaiah 58: 2-7"; "Jubilee and Liberation: A North-East India Tribal Perspective".

Email – atulatsudir@gmail.com

Mr. **Gaikaolung Dangmei** (B.Sc., B.D., M.Th.) is from Manipur. He serves as the Assistant Professor (History of Christianity) at Master's College of Theology (affiliated to the Senate of Serampore College (University)), Visakhapatnam. Few of his published works are: "Gospel and Tribal Culture: Are They Complementary or Incompatible?"; "Historiography of Christianity in India: A North-East India Tribal Perspective".

Email - gdangmei2@gmail.com

Mr. **H. Joseph Lalfakmawia** (B.A., B.D., M.Th., (D.Th.)) is from Mizoram Presbyterian Church. Earlier he served as the Assistant

Professor (New Testament) at Master's College of Theology (affiliated to the Senate of Serampore College (University)), Visakhapatnam and also the Dean of Academic Affairs. Currently, he is pursuing his doctoral studies in NIIPGTS (Serampore). Some of his major works are: *Jesus in the Synoptic Gospels; Re-Reading the Gospel of John from Indian Perspective; New Testament: Its Historical Background and Content; General Introduction to Post Biblical Judaism, Basic Methodological Study Aid for Theological Students.*

Email: hjosephlfma@yahoo.com

Rev. Dr. **Jerome Sahabandhu** (BD, MA, PhD) is an ordained Methodist minster, and currently serves as the Principal of the Theological College of Lanka (Serampore University), Pilimatalawa, Sri Lanka. Many of his works are published in both national and international journals.

Email – sahabanj@tcd.ie

Dr. **John Alex** (B.Sc., B.D., M.Th., D.Th.) is from Kerala and serves with Jesus Mission. He was awarded Doctor of Theology (Christian Theology) by Serampore University for his research on Indian theologian – Pandipeddi Chenchiah. He also serves as the editor-in-chief of *Ebenezer Theological Journal*. He has written extensively in the field of Indian Christian theology in several theological journals published in India.

Email - bijuax@gmail.com

Rev. **John Basy Paul** (B.Sc., B.D., M.A., M.Th.) is an ordained minister of the Church of South India (CSI), Dornakal Diocese. Earlier, he taught in the department of Religious and Cultural studies at Master's College of Theology (affiliated to the Senate of Serampore College (University)), Visakhapatnam. Some of his known writings are: "Goddess Durga as *Mahishasura Mardhini*: A Homogeneous Image and its Relevance to Indian Feminist Theology"; "Masturbating Minds and Menstruating Bodies: Exploring the Religious Understanding of Menstruation and 'Blood – Pollution' Politics; A We-men's Approach".

Email – basypaul@gmail.com

Rev. Dr. **Origen Vasantha Jathanna** (B.D., Ph.D.) is an ordained minister in Karnataka Central Diocese of Church of South India (CSI). A well-known Indian Christian theologian, he earlier served as the Principal of the United Theological College, Bangalore. Some of his well-known writings are: *The Decisiveness of the Christ-event and the Universality of Christianity in a World of Religious Plurality*; "Religious Pluralism: A Theological Critique"; "The Meaning and Significance of the Trinity in the Indian Context"; "Conversion: Reflections on Select Issues from an Indian Christian Theological Perspective".

Email - ovjathanna@yahoo.com

Mr. **R. Lalruata** (B.A., B.D., M.Th., M.S.W.) is from Mizoram and currently serves as the Assistant Professor (Counselling) at Master's College of Theology, (affiliated to the Senate of Serampore College (University)), Visakhapatnam. Some of his writings are: "The Family Guidance and Counselling Center of the Presbyterian Church Synod with Special Reference to Pastoral Care and Counselling"; "Pre-Marital Counselling among the Urban Settlers with Response to Cohabitation".

Email - lalruataralte@gmail.com

Rev. Dr. **Roger Gaikwad** (B.A.-Hons., B.D., M.Th., D.Th.) is an ordained minister of the Mizoram Presbyterian Church. Earlier he served as the Director of SCEPTRE, and Principal of Aizawl Theological College, Mizoram. Since 2010, he serves as the General Secretary of NCCI. Many of his writings are published in both national and international publications.

Email - ncci@nccindia.in

Rev. Dr. **Roji T. George** (B.D., M.A., M.Th., D.Th.) is from Kerala, and currently serves as an Associate Professor in the department of New Testament studies at Luther W. New Jr. Theological College, Dehradun. He is also the Managing Editor of *Doon Theological Journal*. He has extensively written in various national theological journals.

Email – rojitgeorge@gmail.com

Mrs. **Rosy Baroi** (B.A., B.D., M.Th.) is from Nagaland. She serves as the Assistant Professor (Christian Theology) at Master's College of Theology (affiliated to the Senate of Serampore College (University)), Visakhapatnam. Few of her known writings are: "A Theological Understanding of the 'Ownership of Land' in the Naga-Tribal Context: A Feminist Critique"; "Paul, a Misogynist?"

Email – rosy.baroi@gmail.com

Dr. **Samuel George** (B.Com., B.D., M.A., M.Th., D.Th.) is from Jammu & Kashmir. Currently, he serves as the Associate Professor (Christian Theology) and Principal of the Master's College of Theology (affiliated to the Senate of Serampore College (University)), Visakhapatnam. Some of his known writings are – *Christology: An Introduction; The Historical Particularity of Jesus: A Dialogue with the Hindu view of History; The Gospel as Public Truth: An Indian Multi-Religious Perspective on Lesslie Newbigin.* Apart from these, many of his writings are published in both national and international journals. He also serves as the editor-in-chief of *New Life Theological Journal.*

Email – samueljammu@gmail.com

Rev. Dr. **Simon Pinto** (M.Th., S.T.D. - Rome) is an ordained Roman Catholic priest. Currently he teaches Mission studies at St. Peter's Pontifical Seminary, Bangalore. He is the author of: *Theology of Interreligious Dialogue for a Multi-religious Context in India.* Apart from it, many of his writings are published in reputed theological journals.

Email – peterssimon2010@hotmail.com

Mr. **Tinumeren Ozukum** (B.D., M.Th.) is from Nagaland. He serves as the Assistant Professor (Communication) at Master's College of Theology (affiliated to the Senate of Serampore College (University)), Visakhapatnam. Few of his writings are: "Life after Life: Implications from the Bible"; "A Study of the Political Economy of Mass Media, Towards Media and Education Among the Churches in India".

Email - tinumerenozy@gmail.com

Rev. Dr. **V. V. Thomas** (B.D., M.Th., D.Th.) from Kerala is an ordained minister of the Assemblies of God Church in India. He is the Head of Department of History of Christianity studies at Union Biblical Seminary, Pune. Some of his major works are: *Conciliar Ecumenism: The Beginning of the Former CSI-CNI-MTC Joint Council; Dalit Pentecostalism: Spirituality of the Empowered Poor; Understanding Subaltern History: Theoretical Tools.*

Email: vvthomas@gmail.com

Preface

Jesus said, "... I will build my church, and the gates of hades will not prevail against it" (Mat. 16:18). To which church was he alluding? What constitutes this church? What are the nature, character, and function of the church? Who operates the church? How relevant is the church today? How inclusive is the church today? Well, these and few other questions are not just raised but grappled with an Indian/ Asian perspective by various authors in the book.

In Christian theology, the branch of studying the nature and function of church is called – Ecclesiology. In its simplest sense it can mean, "Theology as applied to the nature and structure of the Christian church." Church derives from the Greek adjective *kuriakos,* meaning "belonging to the Lord." As such, it is "the Lord's house." However, church was always used in terms of another Greek word *ekklesia,* meaning, "summoned or called out assembly of people." In the English its equivalence is "convocation." Church therefore, is a convoked community. As such, the present day ecclesiology finds itself at a crossroad to redefine itself. The Indian/Asian context demands a reformulation, restructuring of *ekklesia* in our context. This book: *Ekklesia: Indian Conversations* (one of its kind in the Indian context) is a humble attempt towards that goal.

The book comprises of seventeen articles from various branches of Christian theology. A brief introduction is in order here.

General background of the term ekklesia – by H. Joseph Lalfakmawia is a pertinent and comprehensive introduction to the theme, which offers a clear guide to the reader to engage in a conceptual understanding of the term *ekklesia* that run throughout the Old Testament and the New Testament.

Egalitarianism in the socio-economic life of Israel: Implications for ekklesia in India – by Atula Ao examines the Biblical egalitarianism as found in the Old Testament. It offers both appreciative prospects and close-up assessments of the socio-economic life of Israel by analyzing major ideologies that underlines the biblical concept of egalitarianism. The writer concludes with a primary call of the church to radically redefine equality that would foster an unwavering *ekklesia* as a community of equals in contemporary society.

Origin and transition of the church in the first five centuries – John Alex's paper illuminates the socio-political aspects and historical analysis in the understanding of the church from a community guided by Holy Spirit to an organized state religion. This study is well illustrated with key themes ranging from early Christian ecclesiology to the church becoming the state religion.

The growth, development and structure of the church (kyriakon) in the Roman world from 1st to 6th century –The article by Dangmei Gaikaolung gives historical focus and perspective to ecclesiology by concentrating on the first six centuries, beginning with the founding of the Apostolic church and including treatment of the development of the church structure and the rise of the Roman bishop.

H. Joseph Lalfakmawia's second paper, *Confrontation of socio-religio-political oppressive powers in the ekklesia of God*, brings out the ministry of Jesus as a "ministry of conflict" against the demonic and dark forces. The aim is to enable the true *ekklesia* of God to turn towards the footsteps of Jesus and confront evils both within the church and the society at large.

Paul's vision for the ekklesia of God by Roji T. George – This article offers an overview of Paul's understanding of *ekklesia*, followed by an elaborate discussion on the fourfold character of the church that Paul envisioned. Prior to that, an introduction to the etymology of *ekklesia*, its origin and development in the early Christianity is undertaken.

Paul's understanding of ekklesia as "Community of believers": Ethical perspectives – by Ajungla Jamir attempt to obtain a fresh understanding of what constitutes community and to argue that *ekklesia* is inherently communal in structure. Considerable attention was drawn to Paul's understanding of *ekklesia* as a community of believers in the light of the Christian ethical perspectives.

Kalisiya – ek bharatiya sanskarika samudaya – In this article, Samuel George focuses his primary attention to an in-depth look at sacraments from a contextual perspectives and its implication for the Indian *ekklesia*. Through this unique lens, the reader will be able to re-formulate and re-define Indian ecclesiology as a *sanskarika samudaya* that spreads grace to others.

In the paper *Ekklesia – the body of Christ defiled in the church: A Christian Counselling perspective*, R. Lalruata discusses the inclusive and participatory dimension of the church with special reference to Paul's metaphor of the church as the "body of Christ". It is within this backdrop the writer explores the sociological reality as well as the theological relevance of Indian ecclesiology.

Ekklesia model or Kyriarchal model: Hermeneutical choice and the future of ekklesia by Rosy Baroi provide detailed study of the tensions and struggles between *ekklesia* model and *kyriarchal* model. The article concludes with a summary of the findings of these analyses and attempt to bring out a relevant hermeneutical choice in the shaping of the present church.

Ekklesia in the midst of Religious and Cultural Pluralism – by John Basy Paul offers a thematic overview that takes into account the architectural, cultural, historical, and theological issues. He discusses the significance of religious and cultural pluralism to the understanding of Indian ecclesiology, and broadens the understanding of the readers of *ekklesia* in relation with the kingdom of God and not related with any particular traditions of past history.

Ekklesia – The radical democratic assembly of equals: towards an Indian ecclesiology: A Pentecostal perspective – In his article, V. V. Thomas delves deep into the hearts of the Pentecostal perspectives in understanding Indian ecclesiology, offering readers helpful details such as overview of the modern Pentecostal movement, different types of Pentecostals, third wave revival movements, detailed analysis of the potentials of Pentecostalism, model church structure and many more significant themes.

Sociological perspectives for ecclesiology: towards a sociology of the church based on Francois Houtart's thoughts – Written by a distinguished Sri Lankan scholar, Jerome Sahabandhu, this study draws on the dialectical interaction of ecclesiology and society within a wider framework of religion and society debate. Significant part of his study is devoted to Francois Houtart's school of thoughts for fostering a relevant sociological perspective for Indian ecclesiology.

Renowned Indian theologian, O. V. Jathanna, in his thought-provoking article – *Ecclesiology in Context: Reflections from an Indian Perspective in the Light of Current Ecumenical Deliberations* seeks to define contextuality of the church in India in the light of current ecumenical thinking.

Towards 'People' (Laos) ecclesiology for Mission by Simon Pinto – This article examines and weighs the issues faced by the Indian churches and poses possible solutions by bringing forth a *'Laos'* ecclesiology which is fundamentally tilted more towards people, community, co-responsibility participatory working of the Church and the like.

Tinumeren Ozukum's article *The significance of communication in ekklesia* neatly outlines the correlation between church and communication. The focal point here is to shed light on communication as a subject matter of deep theological concern within the ecclesial milieu.

The major part of Roger Gaikwad's paper *Towards a new ecclesia: Re-reading the concept of 'Ecclesia' in the Bible: A few pointers* presents concise summaries of looking at *ekklesia* from an activist, ecclesial, and theological perspectives, while suggesting a need for a relevant understanding towards a true *ekklesia* in the present context – one that has secular-spiritual, religious-egalitarian, and compassionate-liberating implications.

Considering the dearth of relevant theological materials for studying ecclesiology in the Indian context, the *Pustakaalayam* (publishing branch of MCT) has undertaken this project to publish a book on the subject.

A project of this magnitude is impossible without the keen interest, and help of others. In this journey, many have contributed their energy, time, and help. We are extremely thankful to their contributions to make this dream true. A word of appreciation to Rev. Dr. Arjuna Chiguluri (Director, MCT); to all the faculty members of Master's College of Theology (Serampore University), Visakhapatnam for their wonderful contributions; to Dr. John Alex, Dr. Roji T. George, Dr. V. V. Thomas, Dr. Jerome Sahabandhu, Dr. O. V. Jathanna, Dr. Simon Pinto, and Dr. Roger Gaikwad for their thought provoking articles; and the innumerable hours of compiling, editing, and proof-reading of the documents by the Editors – Dr. Samuel George (Principal, MCT), Mr. H. Joseph Lalfakmawia (ex-Dean of Academic Affairs, MCT), and Ms. Ajungla Jamir (Asst. Professor, MCT).

It is our prayer and wish that this wonderful piece of theology would enlighten, and spark a fire to redefine *Ekklesia* in the Indian/Asian context, in a radical, relevant and meaningful manner. To that cause, we humbly dedicate this book.

Editors:

Dr. Samuel George
Mr. H. Joseph Lalfakmawia
Ms. Ajungla Jamir

Chapter 1
General Background of the Term *'Ekklesia'*

H. Joseph Lalfakmawia

When we talk about *church* the first image that pops up is either the 'church building' or 'denominations'. The association or council of churches instantly and implicitly means the association/council of various denominations. The general understanding of the term *church* is more and more particular and denominational. Liturgies and doctrines are more conspicuous than the vocation which is the true essence of the original church.

We will try to bring out the original conceptual understanding of the church from the Old Testament and New Testament and more importantly, the original intention of the very term used to mean 'the people of God'.

Root and Origin

The Greek root word for 'church' is *ekklesia* (ἐκκλησια) whose generally accepted root word is the verb form, *kaleô* (καλεω). *Kaleô* can be translated without hesitation as 'to call'. Obviously *ekklesia* is a combination of two Greek words in which scholars' opinions are divided, whether it is a combination of *ek* (ἐκ-from/out of) and *kaleô* (καλεω-to call) or *ek* (ἐκ-from/out of) and *laos* (λαος-people).

Generally it is accepted that the root word is *ek* (ἐκ-from/out of) and *kaleô* (καλεω-to call) to mean *ekkaleô* (ἐκκαλεω), 'to call out'; thus, *ekklesia* means 'the called out ones.' But this traditional idea is questioned by some scholars and assume that it is from the root '*ek-laos*' that means 'of the people'[1] may be because the verbal root *ekkaleo/ekkalein* (ἐκκαλεω/ἐκκαλειν – to call out) or its adjective, *ekkletos* (ἐκκλητος – the called out one) does not occur in the entire New Testament[2] though found in the OT.

The word *ek-laos* (of the people) or *eklêsia* does not occur even once both in the LXX (OT) and in the NT. Some of the most popular Greek lexicons such as Bauer's, Friberg's, UBS Lexicon, Louw and Nida, Liddell-Scott, J. Lust's Greek-English Lexicon of the Septuagint, Strong's Concordance etc. do not have these two words. So, definitely *ek-laos* is not a biblical word nor was used in the socio-religious context of Israel, even if this word was used in the secular field.

Meanwhile, we have many texts that sound like proof texts for *ekkaleô* (ἐκκαλεω) as the root word of *ekklesia*. It is found in Gen. 19:5 (in LXX - ἐξεκαλοῦντο) and Deut. 20:10 (ἐκκαλέσῃ) though in secular and general sense. The Hebrew word for this '*ekkaleô*' is *qârâ'* (קָרָא), 'to call' or 'call out' or 'recite'. Normally it denotes vocable.[3] It also means '*call unto someone*' which is applicable in Gen. 19:5.[4] So, it connotes 'calling someone audibly.' Bauer and Strong strongly affirmed that the word *ekklesia* (ἐκκλησια) is a compound word, derived from ἐκ (*ek*-from, out of) and καλεω (*kaleô*-to call).[5] Thus, *ekkaleô* (ἐκκαλεω) is translated as 'to call out' in the LXX too.[6] So, the assembly of those people that are 'called out' for specific purpose, whatever the reason/purpose is, is called the *ekklesia.*

More radically, though the detail discussion will be made below, the Hebrew word for *ekklesia* is *qâhâl* (קָהָל), whose root is a verb, *qâhal* (קָהַל) that means 'to call or to call together'.[7] The verbal root conveys an act of 'calling' together.

Hence, our conclusion now is that the root word of the term *ekklesia* is Greek *ekkaleô,* which is the combination of two words, ἐκ (*ek*-from, out of) and καλεω (*kaleô*-to call) but not *ek-laos* (of the people). Therefore, our ongoing investigation will be more on the Greek verbal root, καλεω (*kaleô*-to call).

Ekklesia (ἐκκλησια) in the Greek World

The term *ekklesia* (ἐκκλησια), in Greek, in its early usage, is purely secular. Right from the Athenian celebrities such as Thucydides (c. 460–396 BCE), Plato (428/7–348/7 BCE) and Xenophon (c. 430–354 BCE), *ekklesia* (ἐκκλησια) is 'the assembly of the citizens in Athens and in most Greek cities (*poleis*)'.[8] In those Hellenistic city-states, there used to be "a convocation of citizens called together by the 'herald' (keryx/κηρυξ) for the purpose of transacting official business,"[9] which is called *dêmos* (δημος). As it is seen from the explanation, this convocation of not mere people, but citizens (one must know that not all the residents of a polis/city-state are full-fledge citizens), is purely a secular meeting. This gathering/*dêmos* is called *ekklesia.* That *ekklesia* was the ultimate power in those Greek city-states (polis), whether it was a monarchy, oligarchy or democracy.[10]

While we say that the *ekklesia* of the Greek Polis (cities) was political/secular, we must also remember that the one who called them together (herald/keryx/κηρυξ) used to pray before the assembly was begun because every polis/city is considered to have its own god/goddess to whom prayer was offered.[11] So, this background reminds us that secular and religious tones are intertwined and are not easily separable.

What we try so say here is that the word *ekklesia* has, in the life setting of the Greek people, two characters: firstly and more significantly, it is a political and secular assembly. Secondly, it has a little religious flavour too. As we have just said, every meeting of the *polis'* assembly (*ekklesia*) was committed to the god/goddess by offering prayer. Therefore, though very political, its religious flavour is not completely absent. We can summarize that the former is more significant but the latter is not forgotten.

Ekklesia in the Old Testament and Judaism

1. Greek Judaism

a) LXX

The word *ekklesia* occurs about 100 times in the LXX. The Hebrew equivalence is almost always *qâhâl* (קָהָל).[12] According to Schmidt, in the LXX, this *ekklesia* is wholly secular term which almost always means 'assembly.' Thus, the most important is who assembles or who comprises the assembly. Sometimes those who assembled were prophets (1 Sam. 19:20) whereas the same seems to be riotous assembly in Sir. 26:5.

So, according to Schmidt, only the addition of *kuriou* (κυριου- of the Lord) makes *ekklesia* the people or congregation of God. Otherwise, the term *ekklesia* in LXX is only secular (cf. Dt. 23:2 ff.;

1 Chr. 28:8; Neh. 13:1; Mic. 2:5).[13] In other words, the term *ekklesia* itself does not simply mean religious assembly. Thus, the Greek word *ekklesia* was familiar both to Gentiles/Greek by political usage and to Greek-speaking Jews through the LXX because it occurs in their scripture.[14]

b) Philo and Josephus

There is not much difference between the LXX and the first century duo, Philo and Josephus. Philo added *theou* (of God) or *kuriou* (of the Lord) to mean religious assembly (cf. *Legum Allegoriae* 3:8, 81). The same treatment is found in Josephus' writings. Though he used this term, they are very secular.[15] So, secular tone is recurring in the works of Philo and Josephus.

2. Hebrew Texts

Schmidt is satisfied and affirmative to say that the two Hebrew words, *qâhâl* (קָהָל) and *'edâ* (עֵדָה) are the words translated into *ekklesia* in the LXX interchangeably that neither of them is intrinsically a technical term. Everything depends on the addition of Yahweh or Israel to mean religious, without which the *qâhâl* itself can mean any sort of assembly. Accordingly, he put the statistics that strengthen his argument. He pointed out that in Deut. (except 5:22), Jos., Judg., 1 & 2 Sam.; (apart from 1 S. 19:20), 1 and 2 Kgs., 1 and 2 Chr., Ezr., and Neh., *qâhâl* (קָהָל) is always translated as *ekklesia* (ἐκκλησια). But in Ex., Lev. and Num., *'edâ* (עֵדָה) is more common than *qâhâl* (קָהָל) to mean *ekklesia*.[16]

Lewis' study is also nearly like this. According to him, the verb *qâhal* (קָהַל that occurs 39 times in the OT) has the idea of assembling without regard to purpose. Similarly, the noun *qâhâl* (קָהָל that occurs 22 times in the Prophets) can be an assembly of any sort and purpose.[17]

To sum up, we can say that Schmidt does not see the special use of Greek *ekklesia* as a technical term to mean *religious congregation* in the LXX, Hebrew text and other Judaism. If this is right, then the term *ekklesia* alone, without the addition *kurios* or *Yahweh* or *Israel*, has no special meaning apart from mere *assembly*. Even if *ekklesia* (ἐκκλησια) is technical, it is still a political national assembly during the classical Greek period.

Moreover, even if *ekklesia* is derived from the verbal root *ekkaleo/ekkalein* (to call out) or its adjective, *ekkletos* (ἐκκλητος – the called out one), yet these two words do not occur in the whole New Testament[18] though found in the OT.

If the root word of *ekklesia* is *ekkaleo/ekkalein* (ἐκκαλεω/ἐκκαλειν – to call out) or its adjective, *ekkletos* (ἐκκλητος – the called out one), then there is a possibility that it connotes a specific sense; those, that are 'specially called out.' New Testament writers can also have this intention. But Schmidt is very doubtful and said that though not impossible, it is not probable.[19] So, this inference is not still applicable.

In one way, he is right because its occurrences, such as Gen. 19:5 (in LXX - ἐξεκαλοῦντο) and Deut. 20:20 (ἐκκαλέσῃ) are but pure secular and general usage. However, *qâhâl* (קָהָל) does not exclusively mean the secular assembly. Like the Greek *ekklesia,* it also represents religious assembly since the purposes of such assemblies sometimes were religious.

***Qâhâl* (קָהָל) as a Religious Assembly**

Though the verb and noun forms *qâhal* (קָהַל) and *qâhâl* (קָהָל) mean an assembly of any type for any purpose, Lewis' classification is quite persuasive as he quotes Lev. 4:13. In this verse, a clear distinction between *'edâ* (עֵדָה) and *qâhâl* (קָהָל) is found. The verse "If the whole **congregation** (*'edâ*-עֵדָה) of Israel errs unintentionally and the matter escapes the notice of the **assembly** (*qâhâl*-קָהָל)..." shows that "*qâhâl* (קָהָל) is the judicial representative of the community"[20] that differs from *'edâ.*

Thus, *'edâ* (עֵדָה) indicates the 'society' itself whether assembled or not while *qâhâl* (קָהָל) denotes only the actual assembly or meeting, not the people as a whole.[21] In the meantime, though used to mean a **religious assembly** – pagan or Jewish – but it did not become the title of any religious group, pagan or Jewish.[22]

This opinion is shared by lexical scholars such as Strong and Bauer. Strong believes that it means a *meeting,* **especially a religious congregation, either Jewish synagogue or Christian**

community.[23] Quoting some texts (Dt. 31:30; Judg. 20:2; 1 Sam. 17:47; 1 Kgs. 8:14; Hb 2:12 (Ps 21:23), Bauer affirmed that this *ekklesia* (in LXX) means 'people with shared belief'.[24] Though this is his third category, yet he accepts that the *qâhâl* or *ekklesia* carries a religious sense.

We must remember to ask why did the LXX translators translate the Hebrew *qâhâl* into the political and secular term *ekklesia* but not other religious term? A very good answer may be that since the Hebrew word *qâhâl* itself is not a religious term, so the counterpart, *ekklesia* is used to equate it. But the better answer is offered by Richardson who says that the LXX translators knew well that the congregation of God's people was unique and that no other Greek religious word can rightly represent the Hebrew *qâhâl*.[25] There too is a close and peculiar relationship between *qâhâl* and *ekklesia*. As we always said above, the Hebrew *qâhâl* is almost always translated into *ekklesia* in relation to Israel but not where it would mean a heathen *qâhâl*.[26] The Greek word *ekklesia* has more reservation than the Hebrew *qâhâl* to imply religious, especially Israelites' assembly for religious purpose.

Technical and Non-Technical Usage

From the information we have gathered, the Hebrew word *qâhâl* (קָהָל) or *'edâ* (עֵדָה) or the Greek word *ekklesia* (ἐκκλησια) itself does not strictly mean either secular or religious assembly. The context/purpose and the people involve, as well as the word attached to it (such as Yahweh, Israel, Lord etc.) determine whether it is used religiously or secularly. Otherwise, the term itself is neither exclusively religious nor secular but it can be both. One of the most important reasons is that they are used non-technically. Therefore, the context or the attached words are the deciding factors.

The technical usage, that is, *ekklesia* (ἐκκλησια) to mean exclusively the religious (Christian) congregation/assembly appears only in the New Testament. This is seen clearly in Pauline letters. Even when it was used in the OT non-technically, the contexts and the attached words tell us that the term is repeatedly used to mean religious assembly while many non-technical and secular gathering/assembly are there too.

The Called-Out Ones

Our resolution, as already clarified above, is that *ekklesia* is derived from the verbal compound word, ἐκ (*ek*-from, out of) and καλεω (*kaleô*-to call). So, the verbal root simply means 'to call out'. We must remember that our ongoing theme is not the verb but the noun form, *ekklesia.* So, people 'who are called out' are the 'called out ones', the assembly. In reality, in the Greek *poleis,* citizens were called out by the herald for mostly political purpose. The Septuagint usage of the *ekklesia* also connotes that people gathered/assembled for various purposes. But the outstanding feature is that those people were gathered because they were called. In other words, they were 'called out' from their respective homes/places and gathered somewhere. In fact, they were 'the called out ones' for specific purpose though differed. But the essence of this 'called out,' whether it tend to mean exclusive/separatist's ideology or inclusively and purposefully called out, will be dealt below.

The Peculiarity of *Kaleô* from the Other Greek Words for 'Call' in the New Testament

We have affirmed that *ekklesia* is rooted in the words *ek* and *kaleô* but not *ek* and *laos* because it involves 'calling' and the people 'who are called and gathered'. We are not tired off to repeat that the true sense, that is, CALL is the core subject both in Hebrew (as the verbal root קָהַל means 'to call/to call together' that carries an act of 'calling')[27] and Greek (καλεω). Interestingly, one of the English Bibles, The New Revised Standard Version (NRSV) uses the word 'call', 'calls,' 'calling,' 'called' and 'call for' for 289 times. NRSV translated various Greek words into 'call'. The Greek words for this and their placements are as follows:

1) λεγω (*legô* and its derivatives such as *epilegô,* for 50 times);

2) φωνέω (*phôneô* and its derivatives such as *prosphôneô* for 31 times);

3) καλεω (*kaleô* and its derivatives such as *epikaleô, proskaleomai, sugkaleô* and its noun κλησις and adjective form κλητος for about 172 times);

4) Some other Greek words are also translated into 'call' but not always. Such words are μακαριοῦσίν (*makariousin* – to call blessed - Luke 1:48), κοίνου (*koinou* – to make it common - Acts 10:15), αἴτεω

(*aiteô* – to seek - Acts 16:29), κραζω (*krazô* – to cry out – Acts 23:6; 24:21; Rev. 7:2; 18:2 etc.), ὄνομα (*onoma* – name – Mk. 14:32; Lk. 1:26) etc. for about 33 times. We will ignore this category since these words have no relationship with our ongoing discussion.

Legô (λεγω)

As we have mentioned above, there are about 50 times in which the word *legô* and its derivatives are translated as 'to call' and the like. Its usages can be classified as under:

1) To Name a Person or Place

For instance, Mt. 2:23 says, "There he made his home in a town called Nazareth." "Jesus was born, who is called the Messiah" (Mt. 1:16). This example and the following verses clearly mention that the *legô* and its derivatives are used secularly. Even though it concerns even the naming of Jesus, yet, the usage is still secular.

Such usages are found in the following verses: Mt. 1:16; 2:23; 4:18; 9:9; 13:55; 26:3, 14, 36; 27:16, 17, 22, 33; Mk. 15:7; Lk. 22:1, 3, 47; Jn. 4:5, 25; 5:2; 9:11; 10:35; 11:16, 54; 19:13, 17; 20:24; 21:2; 22:47; Acts 3:2; 6:9; Eph. 2:11; Col. 4:11; Heb. 9:2, 3; 11:24; Rev. 2:20, 24; 6:16 etc. In these instances, *legô* and its derivatives can also be translated as KNOWN AS. It almost always qualifies objects other than human beings. But human beings are also the object in certain cases. However, it can still be understood to mean 'known as'. For instance, John 21:2: "Gathered there together were Simon Peter, **Thomas called** (λεγόμενος) **the Twin....**"

2) To Address Others

Like the previous one, this is also secular and is used to address, mention or indicate persons or things. For instance, Jesus said to him, "Why do you call (*legeis*/λέγεις) me good?" (Mk. 10:18). Such usages are found in Lk. 18:19; Jn. 15:15; Acts 10:28; 24:14. It usually appears in a discourse.

3) To Call a Person (Audible)

For instance, "Come!" (Rev. 6:1). Other instances are John 5:18; 15:15; 20:24; 21:2; Rev. 6:1; 6:3; 6:5; 6:7.

In all these instances, *legô* and all the derivatives are used having **secular sense**.

Phôneô (φωνέω)

1) To Summon

In this usage, one person calls/summons the other to come to him/her (the caller). Such instances are Mk. 10:49; Jn. 1:48; 2:9; 4:16; 9:18, 24; Mk. 9:35; Lk. 6:13; 13:12; Acts 9:41; 10:7.

2) To address a Person

This is found when one asks or pleads to other; Mt. 27:47; Mk. 15:35; Lk. 16:24; 17:13; Jn. 13:13; Acts 10:18.

3) To Say/Speak Out

To speak out so that the audience will hear. Such instances are Mt. 11:16; 20:32; Lk. 7:32; 8:8; Jn. 10:3; 11:28.

4) To Command

Only some few instances are there such as Lk. 8:54; Jn. 12:17; Rev. 14:18.

One noticeable characteristic of the word '*phôneô*' is that it is always an audible call/saying by one person to another. The sense of this word too is purely **secular**.

Kaleô (καλεω)

1) To Summon

The sense of this usage is exactly same with the usage in *phôneô*, that is, secular, to summon the other to come to the caller. Such verses are as follows: Mt. 2:7; 15:10, 32; 18:2; 20:25; Mk. 3:23, 31; 6:7; 7:14; 8:1; 8:34; 10:42; 12:43; 15:16; Lk. 9:1; 15:6, 9; 15:26; 18:16; 23:13; Acts 4:18; 5:21, 40; 6:2; 10:24; 23:17, 18; 28:1; Rom. 4:17; Jas. 5:14. It almost always demands response towards the caller.

2) To Name a Person or Place

This usage is exactly same with *legô* as discussed above. Mt. 2:23b; 21:13; 27:8, 16; Mk. 11:17; Lk. 1:35; 1:60, 76; 2:4, 21; 6:15; 7:11; 8:2; 9:10; 19:29; 21:37; 22:3; 23:33; Acts 1:12, 19, 23; 3:11; 9:11; 10:1, 5, 32; 11:13; 13:1; 14:12; 15:22, 37; 27:8, 14, 16; 28:1; Heb. 3:13; Jas. 2:23; Rev. 1:9; 11:8; 12:9; 16:16; 19:11, 13. In this usage, there is a verse that talks about the baby Jesus who would be called 'Son of God' (Lk. 1:35). This, no doubt, concerns about God but the usage itself is secular. There is no difference between this and the new born baby to be called John (Lk. 1:60).

3) To Call a Person to Hear

1 Pet. 3:6.

4) To Address a Person

This usage is secular in its sense. Mt. 5:9, 10:25;19; 22:43, 45; 23:8, 10; Mk. 12:37; Lk. 1:32; 15:19, 21; 20:44; 22:25; Jn. 1:42; Acts 8:10; Rom. 9:25, 26; 2 Cor. 1:23; Heb. 2:11; 11:16; 1 Pet. 3:6; 1 Jn. 3:1; Rev. 19:11.

5) Invocation

When *kaleô* (καλεω) is used concerning human calling God, it is closer to mean 'invoke' as in Acts 2:21; 22:16; Rom. 10:12-14; 2 Tim. 2:22. This is a 'human-God call'.

6) Divine Call

This is exclusively a call by either Jesus or God. The usage here is not like the secular sense 'call' as described above because the contexts are completely different from them. It is neither to summon nor demand nor communication between two or more persons but divine communication to human. This is a 'God-human call'. For instances, Mt. 4:21; 9:13; Mk. 1:20; 3:13; Lk. 5:32; Acts 2:39; Rom. 8:30; 9:12; 9:24; 1 Cor. 1:9; 7:15, 17, 21, 22, 24; 15:9; Gal. 1:6, 15; 5:13, 8; Eph. 1:18; 4:1, 4; Col. 3:15; 1 Thes. 2:12; 4:7; 5:24; 2 Thes. 2:14; 1 Tim. 6:12; 2 Tim. 1:9; Heb. 5:4; 9:15; 11:8; 1 Pet. 1:15; 2:9, 21; 3:9; 5:10; 2 Pet. 1:3; Rev. 17:14.

7) Those who are Called/Adjectival Usage (*kletos*-κλῆτος)

Those that are called by God are referred to as being 'called'. The caller is not mentioned though obvious, God. Mt. 22:14; Rom. 1:1, 6; 8:28; 1 Cor. 1:1, 2; 24; Jude 1:1.

8) The Call Itself/Noun Usage (*klesis*-κλῆσις)

Rom. 11:29; 1 Cor. 1:26; 7:20; Eph. 1:18; 4:1, 4; Phil. 3:14; 2 Thes. 1:11; 2 Tim. 1:9; Heb. 3:1; 2 Pet. 1:10.

The first four points (to summon, to name a person or place, call a person to hear and to address a person) have not much difference from the other terms (*legô* and *phôneô*). In fact, they are sometimes interchangeably used as if there is not much difference. However, the last four (invocation, divine call, adjectival and the noun usages) are purely God-related call. No other Greek words such as *phôneô* and *legô* are used in this sense. Though *kaleô* and its derivatives are also used secularly yet this word is exclusively used to mean the call of God/Jesus for the divine concern.

To be precise, this 'call' has the sense of 'particularity' or being 'specific', therefore, it has a sense of 'vocation'.[28] The special use of *kaleô* as God's call of human for the divine purpose is comparatively less in the Gospels. The verb form, that is, 'divine call,' is equally distributed throughout the Epistles except in James, Johns and Jude, save other missing Pauline letters. The noun form (*klesis*) is most frequent in Pauline letters but K. L. Schmidt's statement regarding the noun *klesis* as "a technical Pauline or deutero-Pauline term"[29] is proved wrong as it is also found in the other letters though less in number and size.

Reasons for Using *Ekklesia*, the Secular and Political Term

Though we repeatedly say that the *qâhâl* (קָהָל) and *ekklesia* (ἐκκλησια) proper (without the added word such as Yahweh, Israel, Lord etc.) were not technical terms to mean religious gathering, yet we too painstakingly say that the religious connection is always found. However, it is an undeniable fact that they, especially the Greek *ekklesia* (ἐκκλησια), are obviously secular and political terms. If so, then why did the Jews, the translators of the LXX use this secular word? Why did the early Christians, who were very Jewish in their socio-cultural and religious traditions, retain this secular and political term rather than some Greek religious terms or Jewish more religious terms such as *synagoge* to denote the congregation? Some answers are offered:

1) A very good answer may be that since the Hebrew word *qâhâl* itself is not a religious term, so the counterpart, *ekklesia* is used to equate it.

2) To affirm continuity with Israel through use of a term found in Greek translations of the Hebrew Scriptures. [30] This is likely because of their early traditions (such as circumcision, Sabbath observance etc.).

3) To alleviate any suspicion, especially in political circles, that Christians were a disorderly group.[31]

4) Richardson's opinion is noteworthy as he says that the LXX translators knew well that the congregation of God's people was unique and that no other Greek religious word can rightly represent the Hebrew *qâhâl*.[32]

5) The term *ekklesia* was chosen but not any individual name even Jesus or Christ. The followers or Jesus did not individualize their community like other cults. In the meantime, it is not possible

to know who began to use *ekklesia* instead of the Jewish counterpart, *synagôgê* (συναγωγή). It is also suggested that it might be from the Greek-speaking Jewish Christians who used LXX but stopped using *synagôgê* then adopted *ekklesia.*[33] Thus, they did not try to individualize the community. They too did not try to discover new religion. Therefore, they did not use other religious terms too.

6) Though they maintained continuity from the parent socio-religio-cultural tradition, they wanted to identify themselves from the Jewish religious congregation, that is, synagogue or temple based congregation. They slowly cut off their ties with the Jews due to many reasons which we cannot give space here due to its length. Therefore, they intentionally used the other secular term, that too has some religious essence.

The True Nature of the True *Ekklesia*

The *ekklesia,* in its true sense in the primitive church, has wonderful natures. Some of the characters of the unpolluted *ekklesia* are:

1) Community of Equal and Democratic

As we have said above, the *ekklesia* in the Greek *polis* consisted of the *citizens* of that city. In that *ekklesia* (assembly), "Every citizen had the right to speak and to propose matters for discussion... A decision was only valid if it won a certain number of votes."[34] The *ekklesia* has democratic nature in which equality was maintained. It was not monopolized by a certain wealthy leader/citizen, but the majority in number determined decision of any proposal.

In the *ekklesia,* every individual has real significance. Keeping that characteristic, the leaders of the Koinonia community of the early believers listened to the congregation and examined themselves (Acts 6:1ff.). No one claimed private ownership of any possessions, but everything they owned was held in common (Acts 2:44; 4:32).

2) Inclusive Community

We translated the Greek root as 'called out ones'. But some scholars do not accept this and claimed that this is not the intention in the New Testament times, as well as in its earlier usage.[35] Louw and Nida do not support *ekklesia* to mean the 'called out ones' that too is to mean "total separation from worldly behaviour."[36] This is undoubtedly a right interpretation. Nevertheless, by 'called out ones,' we do not mean a total separation from the world or to form a sectarian group or to seclude from the mass of the people. As the citizens were called out/gathered together for specific purposes during the classical Greek period, the early Christians selected this Greek secular term *ekklesia* to mean those who are called by God for God's mission, a specific goal/mission of God. 'Being called' does not mean 'an exclusive call' to rule out the uncalled or ordinary people. Unlike the classical Greek *ekklesia,* the New Testament/early Christian *ekklesia* did not make boundary line to demarcate the 'full-fledge' citizens[37] and the mere residents. Anyone who wanted to be the members were welcome, irrespective of gender (Acts 5:14) and identity (Jewish or Gentiles).

3) Praxis Gathering

The two Hebrew words for *ekklesia* as we discussed above are *qâhâl* (קָהָל) and *'edâ* (עֵדָה). As it has already been explained, *'edâ* (עֵדָה) mostly means the people of God (Israelites) whether assembled or not while *qâhâl* (קָהָל) denotes the actual assembly/meeting. Those *qâhâl* (קָהָל)/assemblies were always for some specific purposes, as assembly in action. Those assemblies were assemblies for actions, sometimes for war, sometimes for worship etc. In fact, they were praxis assemblies. Such nature was found also in the early Christian community. Apostles did many wonders and signs, tirelessly and earnestly taught, preached, healed others and supervised the community.

4) Strengthening Community

Acts 9:31 tells us that the church (*ekklesia*) throughout Judea, Galilee, and Samaria had peace and was **built up**. The word for *build up* here is *oikodomeô* (οἰκοδομέω). This word can be translated as *strengthen* or *build up* or *make more able*. It means to help improve ability to function in living responsibly and effectively.[38] The early *ekklesia* community built up itself and strengthen the members to live responsibly and effectively. It is a member-oriented community. The same verse too says that the number of the community was multiplied. But this is not the main emphasis here. Rather, the *ekklesia* community gave emphasis on the so-called lay people, the members. It strengthened and made them more able. Thus, the community as a whole could live responsibly and effectively.

5) Mission Oriented Assembly

As the Jerusalem church heard that they were in need in Antioch they sent Barnabas there (Acts 11:22). Barnabas and Saul (Paul) were also sent out from Antioch according to the call of the Holy Spirit (Acts 13:2f). Likewise, Apostles were sent out to various places to reinforce their missionary works. One strange fact was that the leaders of the *ekklesia*, the Apostles and teachers, who were the deciding factors, were the real people who spearheaded the spreading of the word. They were not cowering themselves or sit idly at peaceful areas, enjoying the harvest of the commoners, rather they were at the frontiers of the mission of the *ekklesia*. To be precise, the *ekklesia* was not only a missionary-sending-*ekklesia*, but also a community practically led by the leaders in terms of its missionary endeavours.

6) Sharing Community

No one claimed private ownership of any possessions, but everything they owned was held in common (Acts 2:44; 4:32). They sold their possessions and goods and distributed the proceeds to all, as any had need (Acts 2:45). There was no accumulation of wealth or goods for one's own benefit. The rich shared their possessions with the poor.

7) Poor-Loving Community

Acts 4:34, 35 tell us that there was not a needy person among the members of the *ekklesia* (Koinonia community) because the haves sold their lands or houses, and those proceeds were brought to the leaders (Apostles) and were distributed according to their own need. It is the wonder of the wonders that there was 'not a needy person' within that community because the haves became the benefactors, at their own expense, for the have-nots, which actually is contradictory to the worldly standard of the present day CHURCH.

Endnotes:

[1] J. W. Roberts, "The Meaning of *Ekklesia* in the New Testament," *Restoration Quarterly* 15, no. 1 (1972): 28.

[2] Karl Ludwig Schmidt, "καλεω, κλησις, κλητος κτλ," in *Theological Dictionary of the New Testament*, vol. 3, ed. Gerhard Kittel (Grand Rapids: William B. Eerdmans Publishing Company, 1964-1976), 530.

[3] Leonard J. Coppes, "קָרָא," *Theological Wordbook of the Old Testament*, ed. R. Laird Harris, Gleason L. Archer and Bruce K. Waltke (Chicago: Moody Press, 1999), 810.

[4] "קָרָא," *The Brown-Driver-Briggs Hebrew and English Lexicon* (Peabody: Hendrickson Publishers, 2004), 896.

[5] "καλεω," Walter Bauer, *A Greek-English Lexicon of the New Testament and Other Early Christian Literature* (hereafter this Lexicon is cited as *BDAG*), 3rd ed. (Chicago: University of Chicago Press, 2000), 303; Strong-2564, James Strong, *The Exhaustive Concordance of the Bible: Showing Every Word of the Text of the Common English Version of the Canonical Books, and Every Occurrence of Each Word in Regular Order* (Nashville: Abingdon Press, [1894] 1965), 39.

[6] Johan Lust, "ἐκκαλεω," *Greek-English Lexicon of the Septuagint* (Stuttgart: Deutsche Bibelgesellschaft, 2003) (ebook).

[7] "קָהַל," Wilhelm Gesenius & S. P. Tregelles, *Gesenius' Hebrew and Chaldee Lexicon to the Old Testament Scriptures* (Bellingham: Logos Research Systems, Inc. 2003), 726.

[8] Schmidt, "καλεω, κλησις, κλητος κτλ," 513.

[9] "δημος," *BDAG*, 223.

[10] Roy Bowen Ward, "Ekklesia: A Word Study," *Restoration Quarterly* 2, no. 4 (1958): 164.

[11] Schmidt, "καλεω, κλησις, κλητος κτλ," 514.

[12] Ibid., 527.

[13] Ibid.

[14] Ward, "Ekklesia: A Word Study,"168.

[15] Schmidt, "καλεω, κλησις, κλητος κτλ," 528.

[16] Ibid., 529.

[17] The purposes are varied such as for evil counsel or deeds (Gen. 49:6; Ps. 26:5), civil affairs (I Kgs. 2:3; Prov. 5:14; 26:26; Job 30:28), or war (Num. 22:4; Judg. 20:2, etc.); the assembled armies see the fight between David and Goliath (I Sam. 17:47); an assembled multitude of nations (Gen. 35:11), peoples (Gen. 28:3; 48:4), and even the dead (Prov. 21:16); the returning exiles (Jer. 31:8; Ezr. 2:64), etc. Cf. Jack P. Lewis, "קָהַל," in *Theological Wordbook of the Old Testament*, ed. R. Laird Harris, Gleason L. Archer and Bruce K. Waltke (Chicago: Moody Press, 1999), 790.

[18] Schmidt, "καλεω, κλησις, κλητος κτλ," 530.

[19] Ibid., 530.

[20] Lewis, "קָהַל," 790.

[21] Ward, "Ekklesia: A Word Study," 166.

[22] Ibid., 168.

[23] Strong 1577.

[24] "ἐκκλησια, ας, ἡ," *BDAG*, 303.

[25] Alan Richardson, *An Introduction to the Theology of the New Testament* (London: SCM Press Ltd., [1958], 1969), 284.

[26] Rudolf Bultmann, *Theology of the New Testament*, vol. 1 (London: SCM Press Ltd., [1952], 1959), 38.

[27] "קָהָל,"Gesenius & Tregelles, *Gesenius' Hebrew and Chaldee Lexicon*, 726.

[28] Schmidt, "καλεω, κλησις, κλητος κτλ," 487.

[29] Ibid., 492.

[30] "ἐκκλησια, ας, ἡ," *BDAG*, 303.

[31] Ibid.

[32] Richardson, *An Introduction to the Theology of the New Testament*, 284.

[33] Schmidt, "καλεω, κλησις, κλητος κτλ," 516f.

[34] Lothar Coenen, "Church," in *The New International Dictionary of the New Testament Theology*, vol. 1, ed. Colin Brown (Grand Rapids: Zondervan Publishing House, 1975), 291.

[35] J. P. Louw, & E. A. Nida, *Greek-English lexicon of the New Testament: Based on Semantic Domains*, vol. 1 (New York: United Bible Societies, 1989-1996), 125.

[36] Eugene A. Nida and Johannes P. Louw, *Lexical Semantics of the Greek New Testament: A Supplement to the Greek-English Lexicon of the New Testament Based on Semantic Domains*, ed. David E, Aune (Atlanta: Scholars Press, 1992), 57.

[37] One must remember that not all the people lived in the Hellenistic polis/city were automatically the citizens of that polis. That made the non-citizen residents of that polis insignificant person/s.

[38] "οἰκοδομέω," *BDAG*, 696.

Chapter 2
Egalitarianism in the Socio-Economic Life of Israel: Implications for *Ekklesia* in India

Atula Ao

Introduction

The terms "equality" and "egalitarian" are employed in the intra-scriptural discussion without a common or consistent meaning. One scriptural meaning of equality, endorsed by Forrester, is that each person is of inûnite worth and needs to be treated as such, "independently of their ability, contribution, success, work, or desert."[1] Bauckham discerns a narrower biblical meaning of "egalitarian:" that no person is "entitled to status and privilege above others."[2] These two definitions of equality corresponds to the fact that God regards each person as worthy of equal love, coexist with status differentials in a Christian institution such as a church. On the other hand, Elliott is of the opinion that, egalitarianism demands the elimination of status, rank, position, control, and power relationships.[3]

The economic aspects of equality are also highlighted by Forrester and Bauckham, which are specific concern of particularly the distribution of wealth, as manifested in the Mosaic Law.[4] In the same way, Grudem focuses on material possessions in assessing equality, arguing that while "some inequality of possessions is fundamentally good," "some extreme inequalities are wrong in themselves".[5] This is a qualified form of economic egalitarianism. The secular literature has long pointed out that equality can be constituted by diverse attributes. For instance, equality of opportunity in some attribute, such as education, might be offered as a criterion for "egalitarian," but so could equality of outcome.

The characteristics specifying each of these states may be contrary to the other. A variety of approaches can be taken to measure seemingly constrained variables relating to equality, such as those of interest to economics, like income and wealth. Nagel suggests that given "complete equality among persons being impossible, the real meaning of the idea is reduction or amelioration of inequality."[6] This specification characterizes egalitarian as the enhancement of its opposite, without defining either polarity. Other secular discussions of "egalitarianism" do not provide a definition of egalitarian or equality that can be followed consistently. One summary of the secular debate is that "there is no agreed answer to the question in what respect should people be judged more or less equal," a judgment applying also "to the question of measurement."[7] No single meaning of "egalitarian" is able to capture all of the dimensions of equality across the various arenas in which it applied. That is, "there are multiple dimensions to inequality".[8] The indeterminacy occurs because "equality" and "inequality" are socially constructed terms, not natural kinds.

Etymology

The term *Egalitarian* is derived from the French word *égal*, meaning "equal." Thus, it involves affirming, promoting, or believing in equal rights for all people. Egalitarianism is a trend of thought that favors equality for all people. Egalitarian doctrines maintain that all humans are equal in fundamental worth or social status. According to the *Merriam Webster Dictionary* the term is either defined as a political doctrine that all people should be treated as equals and have the same political, economic, social and civil rights or as a social philosophy advocating the removal of economic inequalities among the people or the decentralization of power.

Biblical Egalitarianism

In recent Christian discussion on the pre-monarchical implications of the Mosaic Law.[9] The Law has been interpreted as promoting more equal distributions of wealth and income between Israelite families (and others in the society) than would occur without the Law, and compared to distributions that existed in other contemporary Ancient West Asian societies. This implies that the ancient Israel embodied non-egalitarian structures as well—patriarchy within the extended family, unequal rights for resident aliens, and the use of slavery. Nevertheless, it is advocated for the continuing applicability of the principle where wealth and income should be distributed more evenly and the basic material needs of each person should be met. Blomberg calls this the principle of moderation. According to him, the modern extension of this argument is that adequate wealth/income is such a good thing that each person and family requires sufûcient levels to participate fully in the social, economic, and religious life of the community in which they live.

In ancient Israel, owning land (except for the Levites) was the necessary and sufficient condition for participating fully in Israelite society.[10] This understanding of economic egalitarianism can be related also to the scriptural analysis of Graafland. He identiûes a needs principle, and puts forward the idea that households should receive what they need to participate fully in the life of their community in exchange for contributing according to their ability. The capabilities of all people are to be optimized, but inequalities may persist.[11]

The argument suggests that the Mosaic Law's effects in the aggregate would be similar to effects of the needs and capability principles. The Mosaic Law overall sought to reduce unequal outcomes between extended families (and other persons), preserve equal opportunities, and allow the basic needs of people to be met. It did not seek to generate totally equal outcomes. Biblical egalitarianism shares many of the complementarian beliefs in spiritual equality, in submission, in servant leadership, and in good and useful differences between the sexes. It disagrees, however, with the idea of male headship and female submission, rejecting the assertion that there are certain leadership roles that should be denied to women and arguing instead that we should consistently apply the Biblical principles of spiritual equality and mutual submission. In looking at the Biblical data and arguing for egalitarianism, one must remember the words of John G. Stackhouse, Jr.:

> The task of Christian theology is not to arrive at the one, timeless, seamless answer that fits everything nicely into place without strain and without remainder. The task instead is to formulate an interpretation that does the best job, relative of other options, of explaining most of the important data and as much of the remainder as possible.[12]

Judaism posits that all humans are essentially created equal and in the image of God (Gen. 1:27). This recognizes that regardless of gender, ethnicity and race all humans contain the spark of the divine within them and as a result must be treated with human dignity.

Egalitarianism, within Christianity, is a movement based on the theological view that not only are all people equal before God in their personhood, but there are no gender-based limitations of what functions or roles each can fulfil in the home, the church, and the society. It is sometimes referred to as biblical equality. Egalitarians understand the Bible as teaching the fundamental equality of women and men of all racial and ethnic groups, all economic classes, and all age groups, based on the teachings and example of Jesus Christ. It should not be confused with secular political, economic, social egalitarianism.

In this paper the writer attempts to survey the ideological agenda of egalitarianism presented in the *Torah* especially in the distribution of land and in the sabbatical and jubilee year. Egalitarian tendencies are reflected often in the Mosaic Laws and in the writings of the Old Testament. Even though those tendencies are not equivalent to all contemporary understanding of equality yet we cannot undermine the fact that the ideology of egalitarianism was presented in the lifestyle and teachings of the people of God in the Old Testament. Some of the underlying ideologies can be discussed as follows:

1. Egalitarianism and Archaeology

Faust argues that ancient burial customs in Biblical Israel reflect the ideology of an egalitarian society in which simplicity and equality are highly valued. Israelites used simple inhumations to distinguish themselves from surrounding cultures that tended to bury their dead in elaborate tombs, accompanied by more ostentatious displays of wealth and burial goods. This emphasis on simplicity is found in other aspects of the material culture of Biblical Israel as well. The undecorated, utilitarian pottery so typical of Israelite settlements, for example, stands in marked contrast to the elaborately painted wares of the Canaanites and Philistines.

Similarly, the characteristic Israelite "four-room house" offers easy access between rooms and lacks an obvious hierarchal arrangement, which is another sign of the ideology of an egalitarian society. It must be stressed, however, that Biblical Israel was far from a pure egalitarian society. There is no such thing as a truly egalitarian society, and the kingdoms of Israel and Judah were quite hierarchical, as demonstrated by history, archaeology and the Prophets. Biblical Israel, however, appears to have had an egalitarian ideology in which people were expected to live by a code of simplicity and equality, even if the social reality was quite different.[13]

This same ethos of simplicity and egalitarianism was noticed by a number of scholars from various schools of thought, in works written generations ago up to the present day, and by scholars as prominent as William Foxwell, Albright, Frank Moore Cross and William Dever. As Dever has puts it, "There does appear to be a kind of primitive democracy reflected in the settlements and the remains of their material culture."[14] This is an echo of a sentiment articulated by Cross: "There is a strong patriarchal-egalitarian anti-feudal polemic in early Israel, which appears to be authentic, grounded in history."[15]

While many of these studies especially the earlier ones were naïve and simple, it is clear that something in the data drove all the scholars to the same conclusion, that ancient Israel had an egalitarian ethos. Though ancient Israel was not an egalitarian society but it had an egalitarian ideology.

2. Egalitarian ethos in the *Torah* corpus

The Pentateuch eschews (avoids) the divide between a class of tribute imposers, which controls economic and political power, and an even larger class of tribute bearers. In its place, the Pentateuch articulates a new social, political, and religious order, the first to be founded on egalitarian ideals and the notion of a society whose core is a single, uniformly empowered, homogenous class.[16]

The first political philosophy to rise up against this anti-egalitarian consensus, thus generating the ideals that are today considered the cornerstones of an enlightened society, emerged in the sacred writings of ancient Israel. It was composed in the literary, theological, and legal corpus known to us as the Pentateuch, or *Torah*—the Five Books of Moses, which narrate the stories of creation, the Patriarchs, the exodus from Egypt, the wandering in the desert, and the laws God gave to Moses on Mount Sinai.

The *Torah*—primarily considered a religious text—revolutionized social and political thought in ways that still influence us today. Indeed, when seen against the backdrop of ancient norms, the social blueprint found in the Pentateuch represents a series of quantum leaps in a sophisticated matrix of theology, politics, and economics.

The Pentateuch mentions multiple classes of individuals within the Israelite polity, an order that cannot be termed egalitarian in the full sense of the word. It speaks of those with entitlements and privileges, such as the king, priests, and Levites.

Most significantly, the *Torah* rejects the divide between the class that imposes tribute, and thus concentrates economic and political power in its hands, and the larger class of those who pay the tribute. Instead, it calls for a new social, political, and religious order, founded upon egalitarian ideals and the notion of a society whose core is a single, uniformly empowered, homogeneous class.[17]

Although the account of the revelation at Sinai is usually conceived in religious terms, its political implications are no less dramatic and constitute the bedrock of the Bible's egalitarian theology. Elsewhere, the gods allegedly communicated only to the kings and had no interest in the masses. At Sinai, God spoke to the entire people, without delineating any role whatsoever for kings and their entourage. In fact, in light of archaeological findings, we can grasp how the Sinai narrative transformed the entire people of Israel into a collective of king-like individuals. The covenant between God and Israel displays many elements reminiscent of Ancient West Asia "vassal treaties."[18]

The story of Mount Sinai copies the idea of the vassal treaty and applies it to the relationship between God and his chosen people. The Israelites, having been saved from Egypt by God, make a covenant with their heavenly sovereign and pledge their loyalty to him and his laws. From a socio-political point of view, this is a ground breaking development. In fact, there is a case to be made that biblical theology's most impressive innovation was not the idea of one God, which had already been formulated by the Egyptian pharaoh Akhenaton in the fourteenth century B.C.E., but the epochal change it wrought in the status of the masses: The common person was raised to a new height, while nobles, royals, and the like were nowhere mentioned.[19] The Pentateuch portrays the entire people as a party to the covenant, thereby elevating the common people from the status of a king's servant to a servant-king.[20]

Against this background, the anti-elitist stance of the Bible becomes starkly apparent. Indeed, it is telling that the Bible never depicts priests or scribes as jealous or protective of their writing skills, as was common in neighbouring cultures.[21] Although the number of early Israelites who knew how to read and write was probably quite low, the sacred text that served as the focus of their religious existence was accessible to as many of them as possible—and if they were unable to read it, it could always be read to them.

Just as Moses had read the covenant to the people at Sinai, the people were commanded to gather at the Temple on a regular basis to hear public readings of the *Torah*. The biblical faith, and rabbinical Judaism after it, were developed as a tradition of "open knowledge," whose legal criteria were, as Amos Funkenstein and Rabbi Adin Steinsaltz have noted, "public, known to all, and open to criticism from all who shared in this knowledge."[22] This egalitarian notion was explicitly expressed by Moses: "Would that all the Lord's people were prophets, and that the Lord would put his spirit upon them (Num. 11:29)."

Because of the desire to share the divine word with the entire people, the *Torah* strove to establish a community whose members adhered to high intellectual and moral standards. This paved the way not only for the uniquely literate culture of Judaism, but also for a new political agenda that promotes equality as a lofty ideal.

The *Torah* also strove to establish egalitarian norms in spheres outside of theology. Its stance in regard to the exercise of authority and political power provides an excellent example of this approach. In several essential ways, it is closer to the spirit of modern democratic governance than it is to ancient monarchism. The *Torah* does not specify any political entity whose role is to appoint leaders or representatives; instead, it addresses the entire people in the second person—the collective "you"—and charges it with assigning a king (Deut. 17:14-20).

The biblical concept of authority is also distinctly egalitarian in regard to social mobility. The allocation of political offices by class and kinship was widespread in almost all pre-modern societies. The *Torah*, however, perhaps for the first time in history, recommends a distribution of power—or a substantial part of it, along lines of institution and instrument without regard to social standing. The same is true with regard to the judiciary. Theoretically, the *Torah* allows any Israelite to become a judge; and no less important, it appears to expect all members of the community to participate in the process of nominating judges.

Deuteronomy uses the second-person collective "you" in this case as well: "Judges and officers shall you make for yourselves in all your gates, which the Lord your God gives to you, throughout your tribes: and they shall judge the people with righteous judgment." The *Torah* does not hand over this authority to the king, and it does not prescribe a precise mechanism for the appointment of judges. Deuteronomy does not say anything about which representative bodies should make the decision, how many judges are to be appointed, or the hierarchy of the different levels of the judiciary. No doubt, such apparatuses existed; but had the *Torah* enshrined them in law, those bodies would become the focus. In omitting the precise mechanisms, the Pentateuch retains its focus on the citizenry as a whole—"you."

3. Egalitarian Tendencies in Land Allocations in the Agrarian and Tribal Society

The *Torah* envisions an economic system that seeks equality by encouraging respective households to assist one another and by granting relief to those who have fallen into hardship.[23] It is an association of free farmers and herdsmen, subsumed within a single social class.[24] In contrast to the systems that served the narrow interests of an elite, biblical law placed a premium on strengthening social bonds.[25] According to Daniel Snell, it is likely that in ancient Israel, "free peasants must have constituted the largest group in any period."[26]

The *Torah's* economic laws encourage an egalitarian agenda in several ways. The first concerns the distribution of land which is the main source of income in ancient times. In other parts of the ancient world, most of the land was the property of the palace and the temple.[27] The Pentateuch, in contrast, posits that the ultimate owner of the land is God, and he has turned it over to the people as a whole.[28] It is important to stress that the Pentateuch speaks of collective ownership of the land. In the society to which it refers, extended families functioned as protective associations, subsumed under the further backing of the tribe.[29] The ties of family solidarity that maintained associations of this kind allowed the individual to sacrifice for others while being confident that, in a time of need, the same would be done for him/her.

On entering the Promised Land, the book of Numbers suggests the land was allocated by God to the tribes of Israel on criteria that embodied elements of equal opportunity and outcome, and of meeting the economic needs of each Israelite family. Num. 26:54 instructed that "to a large tribe you shall give a large inheritance, and to a small tribe you shall give a small inheritance," with the word "tribe" becoming "clan" in Num. 33:54. The territories allocated to each of these groups were determined by lot, as were the location of the land plots for farming to the heads of extended families within the territories (Num. 26:55-56, 33:54). Since area was proportional to tribe/ clan/family population, "the principle of distribution was equitable," as was the allocation by lot, held to reflect God's determination.[30] Equi-proportional principles governed the area, if not the fertility, of land allocated to each household head. Milgrom expressed in this regard and says, "The location of the tribal territory is determined by the lot, but the size of the tribe's territory as a function of the tribe's census count."[31] However the land allocations in Joshua 13-21 entails some problems because here the areas are not proportional to tribe, clan, or family size, but are distributed by lot only. Economic egalitarian tendencies might not be operative in this scenario.[32] In the land distributions we can clearly see that the land areas were proportional to tribe populations, and farm sizes were approximately equal, but not in fertility.[33]

Mott and Sider claim, "The criterion of the division was thus equality,"[34] and extended to the time of the Judges when the society was made up of "small land holdings of equal size," "a relatively egalitarian society of small landowners."[35] Archaeological evidence backs this view: 'in the early days of settlement ... excavations in Israelite towns bear witness to this equality in standards of living.' These 'towns' were little more than clusters of extended farming families of the same clan, but for one excavation, houses were 'all of the same size and arrangement,' and families 'lived in the same way as its neighbours.'[36]

This rough equality on the same site had disappeared by the eighth century BCE. Wenham makes a similar point, "Standards of house-building have lead archaeologists to conclude that early Israel was a relatively egalitarian society."[37] In sum, "with a few exceptions ... the archaeological record indicates that the socio-economic relations of the Iron Age villagers was relatively egalitarian."[38] This might not be surprising, since "most members of the Israelite league were drawn from the lowest and most abused strata of society and were desperately poor,"[39] descendants of state slaves in Egypt.

The benefits of farmland allocation did not extend to all members of the Israelite community. Resident aliens and Levites received no share, although the Levites were granted towns and pastureland. It is sometimes claimed that Israelite orphans and widows also would have been disadvantaged in the land allocation. However, orphans and widows would likely have been part of an extended Israelite family and would have lived and worked on the farms of their kin.

Division of land done by using a lot raises some additional problems because of the way it was distributed. Nevertheless, it is reasonable to assume that there existed some more sophisticated method for measurement, as the agriculture soil apparently is not homogenous for the production purposes. Soss suggests that the land was divided to give some of its inhabitants an equal market value per capita.[40] It is obscure about the exact valuation methods employed, but the grounding aim of the procedure was nevertheless to be as equal as possible. The initial division of land is commanded to be permanent and is based on equalitarian rule.

4. Egalitarianism in the Sabbatical and Jubilee year

The Sabbatical and Jubilee year demonstrates the egalitarian ethos by asserting the rights of the poor in the society. The "forgotten" sheaves and fruit were "deliberately intended for the poor."[41] Nelson asserts that 'the poor have a legal right to access to this food.'[42] Rambam[43] rules that the highest form of charity is to step in with help to prevent a person from becoming poor. The responsibility for caring of the poor is defined geographically, whoever happens to be near a poor person, must help.[44] The help includes food support, but any individual is not required to bring a poor into his/her household, which would mean a forming of involuntary enslavement.[45]

The law also asserts that ten percent produce tax be available to the poor every third year, as well as to its yearly Levite recipients (Deut. 14:28-29, 26:12-13). Craigie points out that, "those without regular means of subsistence ... were thrown onto God,"[46] and would have their needs partly met by the tithe. Such laws alludes that "giving to the poor is just as sacred as giving to the priests."[47] The 'concern for the poor and powerless (including the earth and animals) is indeed in the very soul of the law,' toward 'giving the poor special upward movement.'[48]

The manifesto of sabbatical year, also affirms the egalitarian ethos.[49] The new temporal order based on a cycle of seven served the Bible's egalitarian agenda. The commandment of the Sabbath, which requires everyone to rest on the seventh day, temporarily bridges the gap between the haves and have-nots. Declaring the seventh year to be a "Sabbatical" serves a similar function. The fields lie fallow, their produce is available free of charge to all, and all debts are relieved. Time itself is used as an instrument of equality.[50] The sabbatical year was rotated between land areas, so that the poor would be able to gather food each year. The idea underlying these laws was "that all members of the covenant society have rights, in principle, to a share in the blessings of the land, which is ultimately Yahweh's gift to the people as a whole.... This principle overrides all other economic and property considerations."[51] This as such would ensure more economically egalitarian outcomes than without them.

The economic utopia of Pentateuch is especially suited for the Jewish nation and maybe not intended for any use among the gentile economies. Nevertheless, it offers interesting alternative view of seeing the basic economic fundamentals in a society, as taxation, labour leisure decision, social care, economic institutions, financial market, economic growth and private property. The loan laws "seek to rob debt of its tyrannical power, to limit human misery, and to avoid a paralysis of economic life that would stunt the blessings of productivity".[52] The loan requirements would have helped meet the material needs of the poor, generated more equal outcomes than would have prevailed otherwise, and enhanced equality of opportunity for the recipients to meet their material needs.[53] Therefore, "biblical law is unique in the ancient West Asia in imposing an absolute ban on lending and borrowing with interest."[54]

If interest were to be charged to a poor farmer, the probability would increase that the farmer would be pushed into further poverty.[55] It might sound inconsistent to say that loans were given to prevent debt, but the loans were more akin to grants. One aim of the loan (grant) provisions was to prevent the occurrence of debt, "the greatest internal threat to the social foundation of the equality of all the Israelites."[56]

Brueggemann observes, "debt cancellation by itself would send the poor person back on the street without any resources."[57] Alternatively, these bondservants could stay with their employer forever in relative economic security. Noth points out that "Hebrew" does not refer to an Israelite but to different nationality underprivileged strata within Israelite society. Nevertheless, the provisions pushed in the direction of greater egalitarianism in economic outcomes than would occur without them.

The sabbatical year was proclaimed as the year of liberation where the land remained fallow, debts were cancelled, and Israelite slaves were freed. For Israelite families who were the recipients of the fifty-year redistribution, the Jubilee was economically "egalitarian" as that term is used here. The Jubilee aimed to reinstate equal opportunity, aimed to enable each family to meet its material needs from its farm, and pushed in the direction of more equal outcomes than would exist without the Jubilee. In these senses, the Jubilee had economically egalitarian orientations. The Jubilee had other aims as well, such as preserving family unity and maintaining "the solidarity of the various clans in Israel by keeping alive the ideal of the equality of all Israelite citizens under the covenant."[58] The jubilee would have restored some semblance of equality between the Israelites, thereby recapturing something of the relationship that existed between them at their creation.[59]

The Jubilee was of course not totally egalitarian in direction since particular groups, such as resident aliens, had received no initial land and therefore no land at the Jubilee. Schneider claims that, 'the principle of redistribution' of the Jubilee 'was certainly nothing like an egalitarian one,' because certain groups were excluded from the initial and fifty-year land re-allocations. Despite these omissions, the Jubilee did have egalitarian effects on those at whom it was directed, the majority of Israelite society. It cannot be claimed that 'the poorest people in society were unaffected by it' because resident aliens received no benefit from the Jubilee.[60] The Jubilee occurred simultaneously with the Sabbatical Year, and the economically egalitarian provisions of that year applied. Some of the poorest might well have included Israelites who would benefit from both the Sabbatical Year and the Jubilee. Evidently, the Jubilee's egalitarian tendencies were to be extended in the new eschatological exodus by Israel. Ezek. 47:14 asserts that at this point the land is to be divided "equally" between the tribes, and resident aliens are to share in the allocation.

The aim of the initial land allocations and the regulations given for Jubilee and sabbatical year was to prevent poverty from occurring, especially through debt. Their purpose was to enable each able-bodied member of Israelite society, native and alien, to earn via work a sufficient living to provide for their basic needs. This sufficiency was to be liberal enough for them to participate fully in the economic, social, and religious life of the society. In this sense, the Law's effects pushed in the direction of greater economic egalitarianism, as defined here, than would have existed without the measures. Inequalities in varying economic and other dimensions would exist within the society, but the Law purposed to ameliorate them, and push toward greater economic equality.

De Vaux summarizes the safety nets as aiming "at preventing pauperism and restoring a certain equality between Israelites,"[61] while Mason expresses it that the Mosaic Law aimed "in the direction of economic equality,"[62] seeking to mitigate characteristics of economic inequality by emphasizing an "egalitarian bias." Similar variants of the economically egalitarian orientation in the Mosaic Law intentions have been proposed by Meyers. According to him, "the social structure of pre-monarchical Israel as hierarchical, in which lateral egalitarian tendencies would exist between different groups, such as tribes."[63]

McNutt doubts that an egalitarian social structure was achieved in ancient Israel, even though 'ideally, land would have been evenly distributed among families.'[64] It is unlikely, however, that there was a truly egalitarian socio-economic structure in Iron Age, as Gottwald argued. Ethnographic studies indicate that even in societies with an egalitarian ideology, there is some differentiation in status, power and wealth.[65] Schaefer and Noell suggest the Law as aimed at ensuring "equal access" and limiting "the redistribution of wealth from the poor to the wealthy." They see the Law as providing "the property less with sustenance they would otherwise not have in an agrarian economy."[66] All these judgments conform to the definition employed here of economically egalitarian tendencies contained within the Law. Notwithstanding its non-egalitarian features (e.g., slavery), Bauckham describes the sought pre-monarchical structure of Israel as "an economically realistic form of egalitarianism, recognizing that, since power and privilege come from the accumulation of wealth, real equality must have an economic base."[67] Whether pre-monarchical Israel actually achieved an economic egalitarian bias or not, most of the commentators above suggest this was the intention. Both the sabbatical release of debts (Deut. 15) and Jubilee (Lev. 25) would if practiced served the basic equality of opportunity.

Implications for *Ekklesia* in India

Today the approach perceives the natural equality between human beings as a basis for entitlement. Since all members of society are naturally equal, they are entitled to equality of outcome, such as wealth distribution, or equality of opportunity for social status, political power, and the like. The *Torah* took measures to allow earlier and more moderate forms of this kind of equality. The need for an equal acceptance of responsibilities is seen in its careful use of the second-person "you," it addressed the entire Israelite collective and, simultaneously, each individual member personally, placing heavy religious and moral obligations upon them. The dual principles of the responsibility of the community to its citizens as well as the responsibility of citizens to the community is not merely an important aspect of the biblical legacy, but also something that our current political and ethical discourse urgently requires.

How do we apply today in the Indian *ekklesia* in a context of unjust distribution of wealth and in a context where gender inequality has dominated the scene? It is assumed that cases and circumstances will differ, but if the principle is being properly applied, then it will be possible to recognise the pattern of the paradigm. In this sense, the social life of Israel-their laws and institutions are to be taken as paradigmatic. We know that our circumstances and context differ greatly from those ancient Israel. But as we study them we are able to form objectives and the policies and to initiate action in our day which recognizably display the shape of the biblical paradigm.[68]

At the very heart of the Jubilee is the divine demand for equality for all. On the one hand, it is recognized that human life always has an economic and communitarian basis, and that this basis is the same for all members of society, without class, race or gender distinctions. This recognition is implicit in the initial distribution of the land among the tribes of Israel, during the period of conquest, according to the number and size of the clans and families in each tribe (cf. Num. 26:52-56; Jos. 13-19). On the other hand, it emphasizes on liberation from all oppressive structures that binds human beings from being freed. As Hartley aptly affirms, "The goal of Jubilee was to maintain the solidarity of the various clans in Israel by keeping alive the ideal of the equality of all Israelite citizens under the covenant."[69] The year of Jubilee is the year of liberation. The liberation during the year of Jubilee gives every person the freedom to live like a human being, according to God's purpose. It is not an act of generosity on the part of the powerful, but rather a gift from God who expresses his own justice, which is instituted in his law.

Jubilee year was a divine endorsement of egalitarianism. The fact that, under certain condition land would revert to the family of original owners every fifty year supports the kind of egalitarian distribution in the society. Such interpretation of the text and its possible applications to cultural settings appears to support an egalitarian redistribution of holdings. How relevant are principles originally given to a large agrarian people to totally different socio-economic and cultural situations of contemporary Indian church?

The task of applying this paradigm to contemporary society is not an easy one yet we can draw out some paradigms. What would equality of economic opportunity at least for the resources necessary to be an active participant in one's community mean in our contemporary world? It would mean that the basic resources needs to create enough wealth for a decent life would be available to all.

Economic freedom is a necessary condition for personal and political liberty. No one can be free in the political sense if he/she lacks economic freedom. Economic freedom aids the existence and growth of political liberty by helping to check the concentration of too much power in the hands of too few people. As long as large number of people in a society exercised ownership control, the economic egalitarian aspect will be diffused. No one can be free when he/she is dependent upon others for the basic economic needs of life. The biblical social vision demands equality before the law and economic equality. It amounts to at least to the point of equal opportunity to earn basic necessities for a decent life. In Israel's social vision, land, the basic capital in that agricultural economy was shared with everyone in such a way that every family had the resources to earn the means to be an active participant in the community.

The Israelite society though had a limited status for women especially in the distribution of land and property. While women had a lesser position legally, this was not the case in religion or divine commission. Though women's position and roles in the ancient Israelite society was limited yet there are many laws in which men and women are given equal status.[70] The women in Israel had a status found among few other people. Therefore while her roles as a woman was restricted to home legally she could on occasion have an extraordinary impact on community life. It was in later Judaism that the reactionary movement against women took place.

If Biblical egalitarianism is to satisfy the heart as well as the head, then egalitarians must show how a church and family are to live out the message of gender equality. By implementing egalitarianism, the church can finally stop inviting the unnecessary contempt of a culture that recognizes the gifts of the bright, intelligent, and talented women the church sometimes bypasses.

The church needs to embrace an egalitarian community. Communitarian living and fellow feeling is possible only when there is a strong feeling of egalitarianism. If this egalitarian aspect of life is understood in terms of structural justice and equality for all women then the ideology of jubilee will not remain an utopia.

About half of the world population is constituted by women, but yet they have not treated equally as men or they have not enjoyed equal rights in the society. Gender differences, customs, traditions, social attitudes etc., are mainly responsible for the inequality between men and women. Women in traditional patriarchal society have always been considered as weaker section or inferior section of the society. Today, all the members of the society have an equal right to live, to enjoy equality, to be treated justly and to live in peace.[71]

The Indian church being the patriarchal church have gone through a long process of discrimination and injustice. Discrimination is the exclusion or restriction of women from realizing, enjoying and exercising their human rights in political, religious, economic, cultural, civil or any other area. Women are completely denied access to social, economic, political, religious and other resources. Rather than mitigating the plight of women, it has multiplied the cycle of injustice. Despite some progress, women continue to be economically, socially, and politically disadvantaged or discriminated against.

The church which is supposed to safeguard the identity of women is a place where women are given less importance in terms of partnership in ministry. So, churches suffer from the structural evil of patriarchal sexism and racism in various degrees.[72] The hierarchy of the church has allowed patriarchy to influence its interpretation of God's word and has similarly sanctioned male dominance in its governance of the people of God. Patriarchy articulates structural and institutional relations of domination. It also assumes absolute gender domination and sexism in the church.[73] Thus, women have been denied their right to fully participate and contribute to the life of the community and to develop their full potential because of the oppressive ideology of patriarchy and male dominated church structures. Analysing from a perspective of gender, we can perceive that the church needs to be more embracive and reflect a process of egalitarian aspect rather than exclusion of women from the ecclesial arena.

The above discussion may be a minimal demand to posit egalitarianism in a higher standing. However, it calls the church to redefine equality in contemporary society where gender bias, caste and class distinction, unequal distribution of wealth and power becomes the domain of the church. The Egalitarian ideologies presented in the *Torah* demands a more radical understanding of equality that would foster an unwavering *ekklesia* as a community of equals.

Endnotes:

[1] Dunncan Forrester, *On Human Worth: A Christian Vindication of Equality* (London: SCM Press Ltd., 2001), 30f.

[2] Richard Bauckham, *God and the Crisis of Freedom* (Louisville: Westminster John Knox Press, 2002), 116.

[3] John Elliott, "Jesus Was Not an Egalitarian. A Critique of an Anachronistic and Idealist Theory," *Biblical Theology Bulletin* 32 (2002): 76.

[4] E. C. Beisner, *Prosperity and Poverty* (Westchester: Crossway, 1988), 57-73; E. C. Beisner, *Where Garden Meets Wilderness* (Grand Rapids: Acton Institute, 1997), 51f.

[5] Wayne Grudem, *Business for the Glory of God* (Wheaton: Crossway, 2003), 51.

[6] T. Nagel, "Equality," in *The Oxford Companion to Philosophy*, ed. T. Honderich (Oxford: Oxford University Press, 1995), 248.

[7] D. Miller, *Principles of Social Justice* (Cambridge: Harvard University Press, 1999), 249f.

[8] L. Osberg, "Inequality," in *Encyclopedia of the Social and Behavioral Sciences*, ed. N. Smelser and P. Baltes (Amsterdam: Elsevier, 2001), 73-76.

[9] Cf. Christopher J. H. Wright, *Walking in the Ways of the Lord: The Ethical Authority of the Old Testament* (Leicester: Apollos, 1995); S. Mott & R. Sider, "Economic Justice: A Biblical Paradigm," in *Toward a Just and Caring Society*, ed. D. Gushee (Grand Rapids: Baker Books, 1999), 15-45; C. Beed and C. Beed, *Alternatives to Economics* (Lanham, MD: University Press of America, 2006).

[10] C. Blomberg, *Neither Poverty nor Riches* (Leicester: Apollos, 1999), 240.

[11] J. Graafland, "Market Operation and Distributive Justice: An Evaluation of the Accra Confession," *Journal of the Association of Christian Economists U. K* 38 (2008): 3f.

[12] Stackhouse G. John, *Finally Feminist: A Pragmatic Christian Understanding of Gender* (Grand Rapids: Baker Books, 2005), 75.

[13] Avraham Faust, "Early Israel: An Egalitarian Society," *Biblical and Archaelogoical Review* 39, no. 4 (July-Aug 2013): 49.

[14] G. William Dever, "How to Tell a Canaanite from an Israelite?," in *The Rise of Ancient Israel*, ed. Hershel Shanks (Washington: Biblical Archaeology Society, 1992), 54.

[15] M. Frank Cross, "Reuben, First Born of Jacob," *Zeitschrift Fur Die Altetstamentliche Wishenschaft* 100 (1988): 62.

[16] Joshua A. Berman, *Created Equal How the Bible Broke with Ancient Political Thought* (New York: Oxford University Press, 2008), 6f.

[17] Joshua A. Berman, "The Biblical Origins of Equality," *Azure* 37 (2009): 57f.

[18] Noel Weeks, *Admonition and Curse: The Ancient Near Eastern Treaty/Covenant Form as a Problem in Inter-Cultural Relationships* (Edinburgh: T & T Clark, 2004), 6-10.

[19] Yochanan Muffs, *Love and Joy: Law, Language, and Religion in Ancient Israel* (New York: Jewish Theological Seminary of America, 1992), 45.

[20] Joshua A. Berman, "God's Alliance with Man," *Azure* 25 (Summer 2006): 79.

[21] Miriam Lichtheim, *Ancient Egyptian Literature: A Book of Readings*, vol. 1 (Berkeley: University of California, 1975), 155.

[22] Amos Funkenstein and Adin Steinsaltz, *The Sociology of Ignorance* (Tel Aviv: Ministry of Defense, 1987), 22.

[23] Norman K. Gottwald, "Social Class as an Analytic and Hermeneutical Category in Biblical Studies," *Journal of Biblical Literature* 112, no. 1 (1979): 6; Edward L. Greenstein, "Biblical Law," in *Back to the Sources: Reading the Classical Jewish Texts*, ed. Barry W. Holtz (New York: Summit, 1984), 96; Shalom M. Paul, *Studies in the Book of the Covenant in the Light of Cuneiform and Biblical Law* (Eugene, Ore: Wipf & Stock, 2006), 44.

[24] Jon D. Levenson, "Poverty and the State in Biblical Thought," *Judaism* 25, no. 2 (1976): 232. The biblical worldview rejects feudalism, which gives excessive rights to a small portion of landowners, as well as statism—as practiced by centralized bureaucratic states such as Egypt, which relied on revenues in the form of labour and taxes collected from their subjects.

[25] Norman K. Gottwald, "The Prophetic Critique of Political Economy: Its Ground and Import," in *The Hebrew Bible in Its Social World and Ours*, ed. Norman K. Gottwald (Atlanta: Scholars Press, 1993), 362.

[26] C. Daniel Snell, *Life in the Ancient Near East: 3100-332 B.C.E* (New Haven: Yale University Press, 1997), 87.

[27] O. David O'Connor, "The Social and Economic Organization of Ancient Egyptian Temples," in *Civilization of the Ancient Near* East ed. J. Sasson, vol. 1 (New York: Scribner, 1995), 319; C. Gregory Chirichigno, *Debt-Slavery in Israel and the Ancient Near East* (Sheffield: Journal for the Study of the Old Testament Press, 1993), 35.

[28] Jeffrey A. Fager, *Land Tenure and the Biblical Jubilee: Uncovering Hebrew Ethics through the Sociology of Knowledge* (Sheffield: Journal for the Study of the Old Testament Press, 1993), 88.

[29] Norman K. Gottwald, *The Tribes of Yahweh* (London: SCM Press Ltd., 1979), 613.

[30] R. Harrison, *The Wycliffe Exegetical Commentary: Numbers* (Chicago: Moody Press, 1990), 349f.

[31] J. Milgrom, *The JPS Torah Commentary: Numbers* (Philadelphia: The Jewish Publication Society, 1990), 227.

[32] Clive Beed and Cara Beed, "Economic Egalitarianism in Pre-Monarchical Israel," *Faith and Economics* 54 (2009): 86.

[33] Kurt C. Schaefer and Edd S. Noell, "Contract Theory, Distributive Justice, and the Hebrew Sabbatical," *Faith and Economics* 45 (Spring 2005): 6.

[34] Stephen Charles Mott and Ronald J. Sider, "Economic Justice: A Biblical Paradigm," *Transformation* 17, no. 2 (2000): 57.

[35] Ibid., 58.

[36] Roland de Vaux, *Ancient Israel: Its Life and Institutions* (Grand Rapids: William B. Eerdmans Publishing Company, 1967), 72f.

[37] Gordon J. Wenham, *The Book of Leviticus*, ed. R. K. Harrison and Robert L. Hubbard, Jr., The New International Commentary on the Old Testament, vol. 3 (Grand Rapids: William B. Eerdmans Publishing Company, 1979), 317.

[38] Paula M. McNutt, *Reconstructing the Society of Ancient Israel* (London: SPCK, 1999), 72.

[39] John Bright, *A History of Israel*, 4th ed. (Louisville: Westminster John Knox Press, 2000), 177.

[40] M. Soss Neal, "Old Testament Law and Economic Society," *Journal of the History of Ideas* 34, no. 3 (July-Sept., 1973): 325.

[41] Ian Cairns, *Word and Presence: A Commentary on the Book of Deuteronomy* (Grand Rapids: William B. Eerdmans Publishing Company, 1992), 214.

[42] Richard D. Nelson, *Deuteronomy: A Commentary* (Louisville: Westmnister John Knox Press, 2002), 293.

[43] Acronym for Rabbi Moshe ben Nachman, also known as Nachmanides (1194-1270) of Gerona, Spain. Author of numerous basic works of all aspects of Torah and a successful defender of Judaism. Cf. Rambam, *Hil. Matanos Aniyim*, 10:7.

[44] Neal, "Old Testament Law and Economic Society," 333.

[45] Nelson, *Deuteronomy: A Commentary*, 293.

[46] Peter C. Craigie, *The New International Commentary on the Book of Deuteronomy* (Grand Rapids: William B. Eerdmans Publishing Company, 1976), 234.

[47] Philip S. Johnston, *Deuteronomy: The People's Bible Commentary* (Oxford: The Bible Reading Fellowship, 2005), 184.

[48] John R. Schneider, *The Good of Affluence: Seeking God in a Culture of Wealth* (Grand Rapids: William B. Eerdmans Publishing Company, 2002), 77f.

[49] John D. Currid, *A Study Commentary on Exodus*, vol. 2 (Darlington, NY: Evangelical Press, 2001), 118.

[50] Benjamin Uffenheimer, "Myth and Reality in Ancient Israel," in *The Origins and Diversity of Axial Age Civilizations*, ed. S. N. Eisenstadt (Albany, New York: State University of New York Press, 1986), 142f. The laws of tithes in the book of Deuteronomy better the lot of the general public. They stipulate, for instance, that two out of every three years, the recipient of the tithe is none other than the Israelite producer herself/himself, who is mandated to consume the tithe at the site of the central sanctuary. This practice enabled pilgrims to the Temple to undergo a unique religious experience at the place of worship, but it also served a very earthly purpose: As the tithe constituted a tenth of her/his produce, the farmer could hardly consume it alone. They had to share it with members of her/his household and, most likely, with others in the community who were not as fortunate as he. Moreover, the *Torah* commands that every third year, the tithes should be given directly to the needy—Levites, aliens, widows, and orphans. This appears to be the first known programme of legislated taxation specifically serving a social purpose.

[51] J. Gordon McConville, *Apollos Old Testament Commentary: Deuteronomy* (Leicester: Apollos, 2002), 364.

[52] Nelson, *Deuteronomy*, 190.

[53] Schaefer and Noell, "Contract Theory, Distributive Justice, and the Hebrew Sabbatical," 5. The purpose of the loans was to enable the disadvantaged to attain a state where they could exercise their economic capability to ensure that their basic material needs were met. These loans (produce and money) were interest free to native Israelites, and probably to resident aliens, part of the Israelite covenant community as distinct from foreign temporary residents in Israelite localities. The *Torah* mandated that debt relief should take place automatically every seven years, independent of the will of the king or any other source of authority: At the end of every seven years you shall make a release. And this is the manner of the release: Debt

relief, usually a political tool in the hands of rulers who wanted to consolidate their status, is presented in the *Torah* as the common person's legislated right.

[54] Nahum M. Sarna, *The JPS Torah Commentary: Exodus* (Philadelphia: Jewish Publication Society, 1991), 139.

[55] Johnston, *Deuteronomy*, 170.

[56] John E. Hartley, *Word Biblical Commentary: Leviticus*, vol. 4 (Dallas: Word Book Publisher, 1992), 434.

[57] Walter E. Brueggemann, *Abingdon Old Testament Commentaries: Deuteronomy* (Nashville: Abingdon Press, 2001), 166.

[58] Hartley, *Word Biblical Commentary: Leviticus*, 443.

[59] Wenham, *The Book of Leviticus*, 317.

[60] Schneider, *The Good of Affluence*, 83.

[61] Vaux, *Ancient Israel*, 73.

[62] John Mason, "Biblical Teaching and Assisting the Poor," *Transformation* 4 (1987): 7.

[63] Carol Meyers, *The New Cambridge Bible Commentary: Exodus* (Cambridge: Cambridge University Press, 2002), 35-45.

[64] McNutt, *Reconstructing the Society of Ancient Israel*, 74.

[65] Gottwald, "Social Class as an Analytic and Hermeneutical Category in Biblical Studies." 6.

[66] Schaefer and Noell, "Contract Theory, Distributive Justice, and the Hebrew Sabbatical," 5-7.

[67] Richard Bauckham, *God and the Crisis of Freedom* (Louisville: Westminster John Knox Press, 2002), 120.

[68] Christopher J. H. Wright, "The Use of the Bible in Social Ethics," *Transformation* 1 (1984): 10.

[69] Hartley, *Word Biblical Commentary: Leviticus*, 443.

[70] For example, the equality that is expressed in Genesis 1, that both men and women were created in the image of God. In the Jewish law striking or cursing both father and mother were a capital offence (Ex. 21:15; 17; Lev. 20:9). Personal experiences of God are enjoyed as much by women as men. The women take part with men in important national occasions like the return of the Ark of the Covenant to Jerusalem (2 Sam. 6:5) women could swear oath's in God's name (Rut. 1:17) the law basically applied to both men and women though only men were its interpreters and teachers.

[71] Jogesh Das, "Women's Human Rights in North-East India," *Journal of Humanities and Social Science* 3, no. 4 (Sep.-Oct. 2012): 34.

[72] R. L. Hnuni, "Patriarchal Cultures and Traditions in the Bible," in *Feminist Hermeneutics*, ed. Lalrinawmi Ralte and Evangeline Anderson Rajkumar (Delhi: ISPCK for IWIT, 2002), 82.

[73] Elisabeth Schüssler Fiorenza, *Wisdom Ways: Introducing Feminist Biblical Interpretation* (Maryknoll: Orbis Books, 2001), 116.

Chapter 3
Origin and Transition of the Church in the First Five Centuries

John Alex

Introduction

The church should constantly reflect upon its roots to think over the present and the existence in the future. What constituted the church? What was the nature and call of the church in its origin? To constantly reflect upon its origin does not mean simply a literal following of the early church but to follow "the real essence of the real church"[2] expressed in the historical form. Jesus movement was a group of wandering charismatics. It was a fellowship of pneumatically guided community. The early followers never developed the doctrine, the office or the exercise of authority of the church. However, by fifth century the church became the state religion highly institutionalized, having well defined doctrine and supreme authority. What were the factors that led to such a change? What were the shifts occurred in the understanding of the church in the first five centuries. This chapter is a socio-political and historical analysis in the understanding of the church from a community guided by Holy Spirit to an organized state religion.

1. Early Christian Ecclesiology

1.1. Terminology and its Usage in the Bible

In the New Testament the Greek term *ekklesia* is usually translated as "church."[3] The word *ekklesia* is derived from the verb *kalein* (to call) and its compound form *ekkalein* (to call out). In classical Greek literature, the citizens of a city are called out by a herald, who summons them to come together. Thus the term has an official connotation, since the people were to assemble for officially sanctioned purposes.[4]

In the LXX translation of the Old Testament the term *ekklesia* occurs about hundred times. Most often *ekklesia* is translated from two common Hebrew terms for the gathering of the people – *qahal* and *edhah.*[5] The word *qahal* has much the same basic meaning of a convoked assembly. *Qahàl* is the assembly of Israel convoked by God (Deut. 5:19; 23: 2-9; Num. 16:3; Mic. 2:5). Thus the term has more theological significance and is used for important events like receiving of the law (Deut. 5:22), the dedication of Solomon's temple (1 Kings. 8:14ff) and the reading of the book of law by Ezra (Neh. 8:2).

The primary reference of ekklesia in the New Testament is to the actual assembly meeting for worship (1 Cor. 11:18, 14:19, 35), prayer instruction or deliberation (Acts 11:26; 12:5). However, very quickly the term extended to refer to the community of the faithful in any given place, to the local community (Acts 5:11; 8:1, 3; 13:1; 15:22; Rom. 16:1; 1 Thess. 1:1), Christians in a province (Galatia; Gal. 1:2) and is used in plural to denote a wide area (Asia: 1 Cor. 16:19; Rev 1:4, 11). Thus, in the New Testament the term *Ekklesia* is described for congregations of Christians who by their relationship are united with Jesus Christ.

1.2. Ecclesiology of the New Testament

Sociological studies of the primitive Christianity points to the fact that the early Palestine Christianity was developed around the wandering charismatics.[6] However, after first two decades of Pentecost the early Christian community became organized and structured. In the gospels seldom we see the term church but in the Pauline thought there are constant references to church. In the New Testament we do not find a single unique ecclesiology. R. E. Brown rightly points out: "there was no evidence in these works [NT books] that a consistent or uniform ecclesiology had emerged. Rather writings addressed to different New Testament communities had quite diverse emphasis."[7] Thus in the New Testament we can find different models of Church.[8] This chapter further analyses the Lucan and Pauline writings. [9]

1.2.1. Luke/Acts

Luke writes the Book of Acts as continuity to the Gospel of Luke.[10] Thus Lucan ecclesiology is a sense of continuity to what went before.[11] The distinguishing feature of Lucan ecclesiology is the overshadowing presence of the Spirit. The term *pneuma* occurs

70 times in the Acts, which is almost one fifth of the total New Testament usage of the word.[12] The *ekklesia* was born on the day of Pentecost when the disciples experienced the outpouring of the Holy Spirit, which was prophesied by the prophets (*cf.* Acts 2 & Joel 2: 8- 29).[13] Emil Brunner rightly asserts: "The outpouring of the Holy Ghost and the existence of the *Ecclesia* are so closely connected that they may be identified."[14]

Another feature of the Lucan ecclesiology is the intervention of the Holy Spirit at crucial moments when the help is needed even to the leaders. The courage-lacked apostles were empowered by the Spirit to speak (Acts 2:33; 4. 8, 31). Reception of the Spirit marked the entry into the group of believers attracted by this preaching (Acts 2:38; 8:5-17; 9:17; 15:8; 19:5-6). The Spirit directed missionaries to promising areas (8:28; 39), especially to Cornelius' house and the baptism of the first gentiles (Act 10 & 11). The Spirit separated Barnabas and Paul for the mission to the gentiles (13:2, 3). At Jerusalem council, Peter, Paul and James agreed to admit Gentiles without requiring circumcision. It is phrased in these terms; "For it has seemed good to the Holy Spirit and to us not to burden you" (Acts 15:28). Paul was prevented by Spirit in taking a detour in Europe and was resolved in the Spirit to go to Rome (16:6-7; 19:21).[15] Thus, Lucan ecclesiology is a pneumatological ecclesiology.

The Spirit first came to Jewish believers, then to the Samaritan believers, then to the gentiles and finally to a small group of disciples of John the Baptist (Acts chapter 2, 4, 10, 19). George E. Ladd points out: "these four comings of the Spirit mark the four strategic steps in the extension of the *ekklesia* and teach that there is one *ekklesia* into which all converts, whether Jews, Samaritans, Gentiles, or followers of John are baptized by the same Spirit."[16]

The earliest ekklesia consisted in the free fellowship of Jewish Christians who had in no way broken with Judaism. There was neither an organization nor appointed leaders. The only authority was apostles whose authority was spiritual than legal (Acts 1&2). The first formal leadership was chosen when an internal problem arouses between Hebrew speaking and Greek speaking Jews (Acts

6). A group of elders appears very soon into the scenario (Acts 11:30).[17] Along with the apostles there were prophets whose authority was basically in the area of teaching (Acts 11:28; 21:10; *Cf.* 1 Cor. 14:4, 28; Eph. 4:11).

1.2.2. Pauline

Paul uses the term *ekklesia* to the local churches.[18] Each local congregation is considered as a church. The church is conceived not numerically but organically. The church is not thought of as the totality of all local churches rather "each community however small, represents the total community, the Church."[19] Paul uses metaphors to bring out the theology of the church.

The Church as temple or Mt. Zion signifies the indwelling of the spirit. Paul speaks the body of each believer as the temple (1 Cor. 6:19), each local congregation as the temple of God (1 Cor. 3:17), and even the whole church as the temple (Eph. 2: 19-22).[20] It proclaims the closest possible identification of the church with Christ.[21] The church as the body of Christ is the most distinctive image applied to the church. Paul uses the imagery of church as body in his undisputed correspondence, especially in overcoming the jealousy of gifts at Corinth. As different parts of the body function differently, the difference in gifts functions make the body of Christ whole. The body image has moved to a corporate understanding with Christ as Lord over that body (Eph. 4:4-5).

On the other hand as R. E. Brown points out: "Despite corporate understanding, the church as the body of Christ does not become a corporation."[22] The church as the body of Christ is a growing entity living with the life of Christ himself. "We are to grow in every way into him who is the head, that is into Christ from whom the whole body joined and knit together by every joint ... grows bodily and build up in love." (Eph. 3:15-16; *cf.* Eph. 4: 12-13; Col. 2:19). The theme of love is very strong in this approach. Paul wishes to present the Corinthian church to Christ as pure virgin[23] and is more expanded in Ephesians. He takes the pattern of the love between husband and wife to show the intense love of Christ and the church. "Christ nourishes and cherishes the church" (Eph. 5:29). "Christ loved the church and gave himself up for her" (Eph. 5:25).[24] The goal of life and death of Christ has become church.

Holiness and fellowship are the other important features of this imagery. Christ died to sanctify the church and to cleanse the church so that she might be a radiant bride without spot or wrinkle or any such thing so that she might be holy and without blemish (Eph. 5:27). The church is the fellowship of the saints or the sanctified (1 Cor. 1:2). Almost never is *hagios* used in the singular referring to the individual members of the church.[25] G. E. Ladd points out, "the term carries primarily a *Heilsgeschichte* rather than an ethical connotation."[26] The fellowship of the saints is created by the Holy Spirit (Phil. 2:1). The life of the saints is at every point circumscribed by the Holy Spirit, determined and empowered by it.

Pastoral Epistles: Pastoral epistle is a post Pauline heritage[27] and we see further development of an institutional structure. In the New Testament *episkopos* (overseer, guardian) is once applied to Jesus Christ (1Pet. 2: 25). Paul appointed elders in all his churches (Acts 14:23) but in writing to the Philippians he also mentions bishop and deacons (Phil 1:1). Here elders and deacons probably refer to the same persons who exercised functions of oversight and care (Acts 1:20; 20:28). We see further development in the Pastoral Epistles by the appointments of presbyters, bishop and deacons to maintain the apostolic heritage of the church. R. E. Brown points out that in the Pastoral Epistles presbyter-bishops are to be the official teachers of the community, holding to the sound doctrine that they have received through Titus and Timothy and rejecting any novel or different teaching.[28] Thus the movement associated with Christ guided by the Holy Spirit became enough organized as a society to be called as a church.

Summary: In the New Testament we can trace of a change of the concept of the church as a movement guided by the Spirit slowly moving towards a structured community. In other words, there is a development of the imagery of Peter from "fishers of men" to "tending of the sheep,"[29] or from an egalitarian society towards two/three tier system of hierarchy. In the following sections we discuss further shift towards institutionalization of the church as it expands.

2. The Factors for the Shifts in the Understanding of the Church

The church has moved from its historical origin. After the first generation, Christianity was forced to adopt into different circumstances of external and internal pressures. Gnostic, mystery religions and other philosophical traditions raised the internal threat. The fellowship community now needs a self-definition, which led to the doctrine of apostolic succession and the fundamental traditions.[30] The external threat was the constant persecution from the Roman Emperors. The believers were scattered and local churches were also formed. It was necessary for the church to maintain its unity. The above factors contributed for the bishop-centered Christianity and later on a hierarchal institution. The shifts cannot be fully ruled out as evil[31] but the product of the context. Once when the church became the official religion of the state the theological shift also got political overtones. These shifts were not a sudden but the changes take place in tiny and continuous stages. We shall briefly sketch the shifts that the churches had undergone in the first five centuries.[32]

3. Towards Bishop Centered Church

The early Christian community was an egalitarian society. Ministerial office developed in the Pastoral Epistles and later it further developed into a hierarchal office.

3.1. Apostolic Fathers

There was a shift in the functions of the ministerial offices by the second century. Clement of Rome was the first to claim authority based on apostolic succession. Clement calls the persons who are in charge of the church as bishops and deacons. He interchangeably uses the terms bishops and presbyter.[33] This shows there was no fixed distinction between bishops and deacons. Further development is visible in the writings of Ignatius of Antioch. He writes: "In like manner, let all reverence the deacons as an appointment of Jesus Christ, and the bishop as Jesus Christ, who is the Son of the Father, and the presbyters as the Sanhedrin of God, and assembly of the apostles. Apart from these, there is no Church."[34] Ignatius underlined the importance of the bishop in the local church and he was actually the first witness to the existence of a monarchical episcopacy.[35] For Ignatius, without the consent of the bishop, it is not lawful to celebrate Baptism or the Eucharist and also advised that marital union take place with the consent of bishop.[36]

3.2. Irenaeus

Irenaeus writes his view of the church in the context of the rise of Gnostic teaching. The Gnostics claimed to possess a secret tradition of truth passed down from apostles. Irenaeus has counter argued that the church possesses the true apostolic tradition, which is not secret but available to all in the Scriptures. It is in this context Irenaeus calls Church as "the mother of all Christians." For Irenaeus, work of the spirit is in the church. He writes, "where the church is there is the spirit of God; and where the spirit of God is, there is the Church and all grace; and the spirit is the truth."[37] Else where he says,

> It is within the power of all, therefore, in every Church, who may wish to see the truth, to contemplate clearly the tradition of the apostles manifested throughout the whole world; and we are in a position to reckon up those who were by the apostles instituted bishops in the Churches, and [to demonstrate] the succession of these men to our own times; those who neither taught nor knew of anything like what these [heretics] rave about.[38]

3.3. Cyprian of Carthage

By the time of Cyprian[39] we see further institutionalization of the office of the bishop. According to Cyprian the unity of the church is in the episcopate. The bishops are the successors of the apostles, and their authority, which derives from that succession, is the same that Christ granted to the apostles.[40] The bishop is in the church and the church is in the bishop, and where the bishop is not there is no church.

Though Cyprian is from the Carthage of Africa, he exalts the primacy of Peter among the apostles and thus the importance of Roman Church for the Universal church. The Roman church is "the chief church whence priestly unity takes its source."[41] However, refuses to grant the bishop of Rome, as "the bishop of bishops", the priority of authority of Peter to other apostles does not mean that Peter is superior to the other apostles. Similarly the priority to Rome does not grant priority of authority over other bishop.

For Cyprian in every bishop the totality of the episcopate is represented. He writes, "The episcopate is one, each part of which is held by each one for the whole. The church is also one, which is spread abroad far and wide into a multitude by an increase of fruitfulness."[42] Therefore, each bishop is to govern his diocese independently of a monolithic hierarchy. The unity of the episcopate is such that bishops should consult with one another in matters of importance. Thus, Cyprian has a federated view regarding the episcopate. It was because of this reason Cyprian opposed Pope Stephen when he tried to intervene in the decision of the African Church. He writes:

> For neither did Peter, whom first the Lord chose and upon whom He built His church, when Paul disputed with him afterwards about circumcision, claim anything to himself insolently, nor arrogantly assume anything; so as to say that he held the primacy and that he ought rather to be obeyed by novices and those later come.[43]

Thus, for Cyprian the unity of the church is in episcopate, of which all bishops share as if it were a common property. He maintained a balance between the autonomy of each bishop in his own church and the authority of the body of bishops acting as a group. The ecclesiology of Cyprian produced a shift of authority from people to bishop. The bishop became supreme in a metropolitan area, ordained to proclaim and preside at the Eucharistic celebrations surrounded a group of presbyter and deacons. Paul Tillich criticizes the Spirit of succession from the early apostles (apostolic succession) as the "greatest triumph of the office, that now the spirit is bound to the office and the spirit is called the Spirit of succession."[44] In the course of the history of Christianity, we see Peter as the symbol of the unity of the church used as the theoretical justification for the unique authority of the Roman Pope.[45]

4. Towards One Universal Church

From the very beginning of the Christian community the unity between believers was emphasized. The Holy Spirit came upon those who were one in mind. However, this unity was only a unity of faith and not a unity of administration. Each local congregation was fully independent.[46] There was only a network of relationship between the local churches. J. N. D. Kelley points out, "Looked at from the outside, primitive Christianity has the appearance of a vast diffusion of local congregations each leading separate life with it own constitutional structure and office and each called a church."[47] Adolf Harnack points out, "Originally the Church was the heavenly Bride of Christ, the abiding place of the Holy Spirit; and its Christian claims rested upon its possession of the Spirit...."[48] However, in its later development, "The church ceased to the sure communion of salvation and of the saints and became the condition of salvation. This conception of the church, which represents the development of the churches into one definite church."[49]

The idea of "One, Holy, and Catholic Church"[50] was a later development in the theology of the church. The adjective "catholic" first appears attached to *ekklesia* in Ignatius of Antioch about 109 CE.[51] Ignatius suggests that Christ's standard rallies His followers everywhere, whether Jews or Gentiles, in one body of His Church.[52] As Polycarp faces death he prays for the entire Catholic Church throughout the world.[53] Justin Martyr speaks of all those all those who believe in Christ as being united:

> [B]eing one soul, and one synagogue, and one church, as to a daughter; that it thus addresses the church which has sprung from His name and partakes of His name (for we are all called Christians), is distinctly proclaimed in like manner in the following words, which teach us also to forget [our] old ancestral customs, when they speak."[54]

Though Irenaeus affirms church as one universal on the other hand he stood for the local expression of the church. In the quartodeciman controversy[55] Victor, the bishop of Rome, proposed to excommunicate the Asian churches for not coming into line with all the others, he was constrained to desist by a firm protest from Irenaeus.[56]

4.1. Cyprian of Carthage

Cyprian wrote extensively *On the Unity of the Church*. Cyprian was expressing the conviction of the church catholic from the beginning. Heresies and schisms violate the unity of the church. The ideal Catholic Church has to pursue the purity. Cyprian's understanding of the holiness of the church come from his controversy with the Bishop of Rome over the cogency of baptism outside the church and the reentry of the lapsed. According to Cyprian the presence of a sinful member will not nullify the holiness of the church.[57] However this does not mean the church could tolerate sinful clergy. Cyprian writes, "This sacrament of unity, this bond of a concord inseparably cohering, is set forth where in the Gospel the coat of the Lord Jesus Christ is not at all divided nor cut, but is received as an entire garment."[58]

The early teachers till the time of Nicaean Synod used "holy Catholic Church" in a sense that church is directed by Christ with local churches presided by the bishops.[59] In the synod of Nicaea one holy Catholic Church got a new turning point.

4.2. The Synod of Nicaea

The Fourth century turned a new epoch in the history of Christianity. The emperor Constantine turned the persecuted church into a tolerated religion. The emperor Constantine called the synod council of Nicaea to settle down the disunity within the church. The synod was called in the context of Arian controversy. Arius was a presbyter in the church of Alexandria who was in clash with the deacon Athanasius also from the church of Alexandria.[60] The systems were opposed to each other and could not be compromised. The threatening division of the church would divide the whole empire into pieces. Thus the dogmatic statements got a political dimension that they had not previously had.

Though the emperor did not command the content of the dogma, he exercised pressure when there were two different opinions. The politics of the emperors is now involved in the theological decisions of the church. Thus the imperial protection, which he gave to the Christianity, also implied the possibility of imperial condemnation to one theological position. The Empire needed unity in the church. Justo L. Gonzalez rightly points out "Constantine's ecclesiastical policy consisted in turning the church into the Cement of the Empire."[61]

The synod of Nicaea produced the famous Nicaean creed.[62] Prior to the Nicaean creed all creeds and summaries of faith were local in character. The creed of Nicaea was the first formula to be published by an ecumenical synod. It was the first creed, which claimed a universal authority. J. N. D. Kelly points out "Its [Nicaean] anathemas excommunicating, in the name of the Catholic Church, those who dissented from its definitions sounded a new note in the history of Church as an institution."[63]

It is in the Nicaean creed we see the formula "We believe in one holy catholic and apostolic Church."[64] C. H. Turner writes, "The old creeds were creeds for catechumens, the new creed [Nicaean] was a creed for bishops."[65] The episcopate needed a stronger unity, which would make schism and division on questions of doctrine and worship impossible. In the earlier statements of faith the meaning of unity was a sharing unity, standing together against the threats of heresies and persecutions. Now the Nicaean Creedal definition advocated a hierarchical unity having political tones. Thus, the one holy Catholic Church under one episcopate is a shift from community oriented life to bishop-centered structure. Now the episcopate becomes the source of authority.

5. Church as an Institution of Salvation

The early Christian community considered itself as the communion of saints. Though salvation happens in the church it has never considered itself as an institution, which provides salvation. In the course of history we see that the church has become an institution that provides salvation. The development of a structured doctrine took several centuries. In the Latin Christianity, the writings of Cyprian mark a clear shift of the understanding of church towards an institution of salvation.[66]

Cyprian sees church as the indispensable ark of salvation.[67] During the time of Noah, no one outside of the ark could be saved and only those who are in the ark be saved. Similarly now those who are only within the church can be saved. Cyprian writes, "There is no salvation out of the church"[68] (*extra ecclesiam nulla salus*). Elsewhere he writes,

> If you abandon the Church and join yourself to an adulteress, you are cut off from the promises of the Church. If you leave the

> Church of Christ you will not come to Christ's rewards, you will be an alien, an outcast, an enemy. You cannot have God for your father unless you have the Church for your mother.[69]

The church is now the institution in which salvation is attained. This represents a radical shift from the early Christian period in which the church was a community of saints not an institution for salvation. Cyprian adopts an uncompromising attitude against the baptism received from the schismatics and the so-called heretics because it is the institution of salvation. For Cyprian these are not the church and there is no salvation within their community or forgiveness of sins or direction of the Holy Spirit or true Eucharist or true baptism. To accept schismatics and the so-called heretics baptism as valid would be to recognize that their group is ecclesiastically valid. Therefore it is necessary to affirm all the actions of them including their baptism, are the work not of Christ but of Antichrist.[70] Cyprian writes,

> Let none think that the good can depart from the Church. The wind does not carry away the wheat, nor does the hurricane uproot the tree that is based on a solid root. The light straws are tossed about by the tempest, the feeble trees are overthrown by the onset of the whirlwind.[71]

The clash of Augustine with the Donatus and his followers is a major theological turning point of the institutionalization of the church. Adolf Harnack points out "It [Donatist] was the last remnant of the old demand that in the church not only the institution, but above all the persons must be holy...."[72] The central doctrinal clash between Donatist and Augustine was: What is the causal connection between the unity of the church and the holiness of the church? Donatists demanded that the church must be purged of those among its clergy and bishops who had been betrayed of guilty of betraying the faith under persecution. The mortal sin of apostasy nullifies the sacraments they perform. Augustine on the other hand points out; the holiness of the church was not the holiness of its members of clergy but holiness of grace dispensed in its sacraments. For Augustine the one sin that threatening the church is not adultery or apostasy of a bishop but schism. Ernst Troeltsch points out, "The problem [sect type contrast church type] first appears clearly in the opposition between the sacramental conception of Augustine and the Donatists."[73]

We see a shift from personal holiness to institutional holiness. It was only after the conflict between Augustine and the Donatists the Western theology began to construct the theory of nature and number of the sacraments.[74] In the Medieval Catholicism the church has become the institution that provides salvation through the grace that administered through sacraments. Later on the church began to control the state in the medieval period.

6. The Church became the State Religion

In the New Testament there were contrasting tendencies towards the state. Obedience and appreciation (Rom. 13) is contrasted with divine judgment upon the worshipper of idols and the persecutor of the saints (Rev. 13). However, basically in the pre-Constantine period relationship between the Church and State was negative.[75]

The emperor Constantine was converted to Christianity. Constantine himself considers as the thirteenth apostle and as bishop ordained by God to oversee whatever is outside the church.[76] The Edict of Milan in 313 CE gave Christianity equal status with traditional pagan state religions. The church except the Syrian Christian community has become the state religion.[77] The martyrdom at the hands of State was no longer possible. This condition had far reaching consequences. There were mass conversions to the church that inevitably detracted from the depth of conviction and the moral life of the church.[78]

In 380 CE Theodosius I made Christianity the sole state religion. In the Eastern Byzantine empire there was only a close parallel relation between the secular and the spiritual kingdom. This tradition persisted till the fall of Byzantine. However in the Latin Christianity, the Papacy tried to become supreme over the empire. The writings of Ambrose, Augustine and Gelasius I paved the way for the supremacy over the empire.

Bishop Ambrose

Bishop Ambrose was the son of a praetorian perfect of Gaul. As a son of government official he had a rich knowledge of the state. According to Ambrose, "The palaces belong to the Emperor, the churches to the Bishop. Authority is committed to you over public, not over sacred buildings."[79] He defended the right of the church to autonomy and liberty in the matters of faith and ecclesiastical jurisdiction. He insists that the emperors were subject to the moral law as interpreted and practiced by the church. He does not hesitate to confront imperial rulers and call them to submission when occasion wanted it.[80]

Augustine

Augustine started writing on the city of God after the Roman Empire fell in 410 CE. The first ten books are on the reason for the fall of Roman Empire the earthly city. The remaining eleven books are on the present world condition where he portrays the conflict between the divine city and earthly city. The heavenly city also has earthly manifestations and one of them is the One Catholic church. There will be an end ahead when the kingdom of this world would become the kingdom of God.[81]

Bishop Gelasius I:

Gelasius I developed the doctrine of two swords in 494 CE. He writes, "there are two powers by which this world is chiefly ruled; the sacred authority of the popes and of the royal power. Of these the priestly power is much more important because it has to render accounts to the kings of men themselves at the divine tribunal."[82] Thus, Gelasius I made the priestly power above the kingly and the imperial, and that from the decisions of the chair of Peter there is no appeal. In the medieval Catholicism thus chair of Peter was the center of political decisions.

Summary: The church in its real essence was an egalitarian community guided by the Holy Spirit. Each congregation was independent. Ministerial offices developed after the period of apostles. The persecution and the threat to the Christian faith made the church to center around bishop. The local congregations unified and became one universal church by third century. The church was the communion of saints in the beginning and has become an institution, which provides salvation. Once the church has become the only official religion of the state, it began to exercise political power. In the medieval Catholicism the church controlled the entire politics.

7. Reflections and Conclusion

In the New Testament we see the Holy Spirit guiding the church, each local congregation was fully independent in its administration and was basically a movement. However, no movement remains the same forever and it is true to Christianity also. The "sect type" Christianity in the first century has become the "church type" Christianity by fifth century.[83] When those shifts became universal and permanent the church lost its vibrancy and freedom. In these shifts the church became institutionalized and the Holy Spirit has become the Cinderella of the fellowship of the church. Martin Luther rightly calls it as "the Babylonian captivity of the Church." Paul Tillich writes, "The traditional hierarchy was confined against the prophetic spirit. This meant that the prophetic spirit was more or less excluded from the organized church and had to flee into the sectarian movements."[84]

One of the Faith and Order document states: "The Church belongs to God. It is the creation of God's Word and Holy Spirit. It cannot exist by and for itself."[85] Therefore, it is "One Holy Apostolic and Catholic Church." This unity of the church does not imply a one unified church, which could produce only a "new distortion of the church image."[86] On the other hand acknowledging each other's faith and sharing each other is the need of the hour. The comment of R. E. Brown is much relevant at this context: "in a divided Christianity, instead of reading the Bible to assure ourselves that we are right, we would do better to read it to discover where we have not been listening."[87] True unity comes through acknowledging the plurality of the expression of the Christian faith. Dietrich Bonhoeffer writes, "The Church is the Church only when it exists for others."[88]

Endnotes:

An earlier edition of this article was published as John Alex, "Origin and Transition of the Church in the First Five Centuries," *New Life Theological Journal* 2, no. 1 (Jan.-June, 2012): 41-56. Reprinted with permission.

[1] Hans Küng, *The Church*, trans. Ray and Rosaleen Ockenden (New York: Shed and Ward, 1967), 5.

[2] K. L. Schmidt, "καλεω, κλησις, κλητος κτλ," in *Theological Dictionary of the New Testament* ed. Gerhard Kittel trans, Geoffrey Bromiley vol. 3 (Grand Rapids: William B. Eerdmans Publishing Company, [1965] 1976), 504. The term ekklesia is not found in Mark, Luke, John, 2 Timothy, Titus, 1 Peter, 2 Peter, 1 John, 2 John and Jude.

However, we see parallel expressions for the church in the New Testament. For details see *Theological Dictionary of the New Testament* 3, 517.

[3] Ibid., 516.

[4] *edhah* is usually translated as synagogue. After exile this become the regular term for Sabbath day meeting of Jews for prayer and study of Torah. Thus it had technically started using it for the building in which the meeting took place. This may be the factor for the primitive Christian community that took over *qahal* for *ekklesia*. See further Edmund Hill, "Church," in *New Dictionary of Theology*, eds. Joseph A. Komonchak, Mary Collins and Dermot A. Lane (Bangalore: Theological Publication in India, 1996), 185f.

[5] For details of Jesus Movement as wandering Charismatics see Gerd Theissen, *Sociology of Early Palestinian Christianity*, trans. John Bowden (Philadelphia: Fortress Press, 1978). Also, there are studies which interpret Jesus Movement as Women's movement. However to go into the details of such research is beyond the scope of this research. For further details see, Elisabeth Schüssler Fiorenza, *In Memory of Her: A Feminist Theological Reconstruction of Christian Origins* (London: SCM Press Ltd., 1983); Gillan Cloke, "Women, Worship, and Mission: The Church in the Household," in *The Early Christian World*, ed. Philip F. Esler, vol. 1 (London: Routledge, 2000) (422-451).

[6] Raymond E. Brown, *The Church Apostles Left Behind* (New York: Paulist Press, 1984), 146.

[7] The work of Cardinal Avery Dulles, *Models of the Church* (Garden City, N.Y: Doubleday and Company, Inc., [1974], 1987) is a thoughtful reflection on the theme from a more systematic perspective. For Dulles, Church is a theological mystery therefore it can be portrayed only through models. He brings out six different models of Church as Institution, Mystical, Communion, Sacrament Herald and Servant. In the revised edition he adds one more model: church as Community of Disciples. Paul Minear, *Images of the Church in the New Testament* (Philadelphia: Westminster Press, 1960). He provides a shrewd summary of models of the church in the New Testament. He brings out 96 models of the images of the church in the New Testament.

[8] The relationship between kingdom of God and Church, Johannine understanding of community, though important the specifics are beyond the scope of the paper. Looking into the details of the date, authorship and theology of each literature is beyond the scope of the research paper. For a detailed introduction to the New Testament books see, W. G. Kümmel, *Introduction to New Testament* (Nashville: Abingdon Press, 1975). R. E. Brown writes that Post Pauline strains can be detected in Luke/Acts and Pastoral Epistles.

[9] R. E. Brown calls it as a bold ecclesial step since Luke putting together the story of the proclamation of kingdom by Jesus and the story of the proclamation of Jesus by Peter and Paul on the same level. Brown, *The Church Apostles Left Behind*, 63.

[10] Ibid.

[11] Ibid., 65.

[12] Discussing on the Baptism of the Holy Spirit and speaking in tongues are beyond the scope of the paper. For an excellent summary see J. D. G. Dunn, *Baptism in the Holy Spirit* (London: SCM Press Ltd., 1977), 55-68.

[13] Emil Brunner, *The Misunderstanding of the Church*, trans. Harold Knight (London: Lutterworth Press, 1952), 11.

[14] Brown, *The Church Apostles Left Behind*, 67f.

[15] George Eldon Ladd, *A Theology of the New Testament* (Grand Rapids: William B. Eerdmans Publishing Company, [1974] 1993), 384.

[16] We do not know when and how they were chosen. The elders shared the role with the apostles in the Jerusalem council (15:2). Also when Paul established churches in Asia he appointed elders (14:23).

[17] See New Testament usages of the term.

[18] Schmidt, "καλεω, κλησις, κλητος κτλ," 506.

[19] Minear, *Images of the Church in the New Testament*, 96-98. Majority of the critical scholars consider Ephesians and Colossians as post Pauline letter See Brown, *The Church Apostles Left Behind*, 47f. Ephesians/Colossians is a post Pauline heritage. However in this research the ecclesiology of Ephesians/Colossians is not treating separately. Ephesians/Colossians presents a one universal church whereas Paul speaks of local congregations also as the church of God.

[20] Minear warns us not to produce one single inclusive definition of this image, since it carries various meanings in different contexts in which Paul uses, Minear *Images of the Church in the New Testament*, 174.

[21] Brown, *The Church Apostles Left Behind*, 50.

[22] For the metaphor of the church as virgin; see Minear, *Images of the Church in the New Testament*, 54.

[23] This understanding may be a later development because in Pauline understanding "Christ died for all" (Rom. 5; 2 Cor. 5:14).

[24] Minear, *Images of the Church in the New Testament*, 136.

[25] Ladd, *A Theology of the New Testament*, 544.

[26] See Brown, *The Church Apostles Left Behind*, 31.

[27] Ibid., 34.

[28] "Fishers of men" is a missionary imagery whereas "tending of the sheep" is a pastoral imagery.

[29] The New Testament is the product of this self-definition in its written form.

[30] There were constant dangers, which manifested visibly in the course of the history of Christianity.

[31] Brunner, *The Misunderstanding of the Church*, 74.

[32] Justo L. Gonzalez, *A History of Christian Thought*, vol. 1 (Nashville: Abingdon Press, 1970), 65.

[33] Ignatius of Antioch, "The Epistle Of Ignatius to The Trallians," in *The Ante-Nicene Fathers: Translations of the Writings of the Fathers down to A.D. 325*, ed. Alexander Roberts, and James Donaldson, vol. 1 (Buffalo, NY: Christian Literature Publishing, 1885), 67. Hereafter *ANF*.

[34] Gonzalez, *A History of Christian Thought*, 77.

[35] Ibid.

[36] Irenaeus, "Against Heresies 3:24:1," *ANF* 1, 458.

[37] Irenaeus, "Against Heresies 3:1:1," *ANF* 1, 415.

[38] Cyprian was the first to write on the theology of the church. The treaties *On Unity of the Church* and *On the Lapsed* are the first writings on the ecclesiology. During 250 CE many believers left the faith due to persecution of Decius When the edict appeared that required all the inhabitants of the Empire to offer sacrifice to the gods, and to obtain a certificate stating that they had done so. Some give away their faith and some others obtained false certificate and avoided martyrdom. When the persecution passed away many wished to return to the Christian faith. The problem of

restoration of the lapsed led to the schism of the church. It is at this context Cyprian called a synod, which was attended by sixty bishops. In order to make his position clear to the synod and to the church Cyprian wrote the famous treatises *On Unity of the Church* and *On the Lapsed.* The plague that developed in 250 CE and the controversy regarding baptism with Pope Stephen of Rome gave occasion to Cyprian to produce the best of his theology.

[39] Cyprian, "Epistles 33," *ANF* 5, 312- 314.

[40] Cyprian, "Epistles 59:14," *ANF* 5, 344.

[41] Cyprian "On Unity of the Church," *ANF* 5, 423

[42] Cyprian, "Epistles 70:3," *ANF* 5, 377.

[43] Paul Tillich, *A Complete History of Christian Thought*, ed. Carl Braaten (New York: Harper and Row Publishers, 1968), 100.

[44] Innocent I (406-17 CE) considers Roman bishop as the "head apex of the episcopate." When Leo's tome was read in the Council of Chalcedon the cry went up "Peter has spoken through Leo." Emperor Valentinian III (423-55 CE) decreed by "perpetual edict that it shall not be lawful for the bishops of Gaul or of the other provinces... to do [anything] without the authority of the venerable pope of the Eternal City." Through the middle ages Pope was consider as the Vicar of Christ and "above peoples and kingdoms."

[45] See the section NT usage of Church.

[46] J. N. D. Kelly, *Early Christian Doctrines* (San Francisco: Harper & Row, [1948] 1978), 189.

[47]Adolf Harnack, *Outlines of the History of Dogma*, trans. Edwin Knox Mitchell (Boston: Beacon Press, 1959), 97.

[48] Ibid

[49] In the ecclesiological controversies notes of holiness and unity are of immediate relevance, for by their intimate and intrinsic association with the doctrine of the sacraments. Jaroslav Pelikan, *The Emergence of Catholic Tradition (100-600)*, vol. 1 of *The Christian Tradition: A History of the Development of Doctrine* (Chicago: University of Chicago Press, 1971), 156.

[50] Ignatius of Antioch "The Epistle to Smyrna 8," *ANF* 1, 90.

[51] Ignatius of Antioch "The Epistle to Smyrna 1," *ANF* 1, 86.

[52] "The Encyclical Epistle of the Church at Smyrna," *ANF* 1, 39.

[53] Justin Martyr, "Dialogue 63," *ANF* 1, 229.

[54] Victor of Rome tried to unify the practice of the whole Christian world in the matter of celebrating Easter, and so he called for meetings of bishops in different places to report on the practice of their localities. The answer from every other place except that of Polycrates, Bishop of Ephesus in the last decade of the second century, was that the feast of our Lord's Resurrection was celebrated only on Sunday. Polycrates, however, speaking for the bishops of Asia, stated that they had preserved unchanged the tradition of celebrating only on the fourteenth day of the month of Nisan, the day when the Jewish people put away their leaven, whatever day of the week that might be. Thus, they were often called Quartodecimans.

[55] Eusebius Pamphili, *Ecclesiastical History*, Books 1-5, trans. Roy J. Deferrari (Washington: Catholic University of America Press, 1953), 333-338.

[56] Cyprian, "Epistles 67:3," *ANF* 5, 370.

[57] Cyprian, "On Unity of the Church 7," *ANF* 5, 423.

[58] J. N. D. Kelly, *Early Christian Creeds* (London: Longmans, Green & Co. Ltd., 1964), 384f.

[59] Arius belongs to the Anitochian School and Athanasius belongs to the Alexandrian School.

[60] Gonzalez, *A History of Christian Thought*, 280.

[61] It is to be noted that the creed now popularly used as Nicaean Creed is the revised creed of the council of Nicaea adopted by the council of Constantinople in 381CE.

[62] Kelly, *Early Christian Creeds*, 207.

[63] Before the Nicaean Creed, in the Apostolic Creed (its origin is unclear, however it was used in the 3rd century) also we see "...I believe in the Holy Spirit, the holy catholic church, the communion of saints, the forgiveness of sins...."

[64] Cited by Kelly, *Early Christian Creeds*, 205.

[65] Eastern theologians (Cappadocians, Cyril of Alexandria, John of Damascus and others) consider salvation as deification which comes closer to the biblical understanding. However to deal with the eastern theologians is beyond the scope of the paper.

[66] Cyprian, "On Unity of the Church 6," *ANF* 5, 423.

[67] Cyprian "Epistles 72:21," *ANF* 5, 384.

[68] S. L. Greenslade, ed., *Early Latin Theology: Selections from Tertullian, Cyprian, Ambrose, and Jerome* (Louisville: Westminster Press, 1956), 127f.

[69] Cyprian "Epistles 70," *ANF* 5, 377.

[70] Cyprian, "On Unity of the Church 5," *ANF* 5, 423.

[71] Harnack, *Outlines of the History of Dogma*, 333.

[72] Ernst Troeltsch, *The Social Teaching of the Christian Churches*, trans. Olive Wyon, vol. 1 (New York: The Macmillian Company, 1931; reprint, 1949). Troeltsch makes distinguish between the sect type and church type. According to him, "the church is that type of organization which is overwhelmingly conservative, which to a certain extent accepts the secular order and dominates the masses." The sects "are comparatively small groups; they aspire after personal inward perfection, and they aim at a direct personal fellowship between the members of each group" (331). Augustine belongs to the church type whereas Donatists belongs to the sect type.

[73] Pelikan, *The Emergence of Catholic Tradition (100-600)*, 171.

[74] The development in the church and state relationship after 3rd century see Troeltsch. *The Social Teaching of the Christian Churches*, 209ff.

[75] E. Glenn Hinson, *The Early Church: Origins to the Dawn of the Middle Ages* (Nashville: Abingdon Press, 1996), 197.

[76] Other than Latin (Western) Christianity and Byzantine (Eastern) Christianity there was a third stream of Christianity – the Syrian community. The Syrian Christian community developed in the Persian Empire. The Syrian community under Persian Empire is different in many ways from the Christianity under Roman Empire From very early period Syrian community remained as a missionary community. There was neither official relation nor persecution from the empire. Thus the Syrian Christianity does not have political theology. For details see: Wolfgang Hage, *Syriac Christianity in the East*, Moran Etho (Kottayam: St. Ephrem Research Institute, 1997).

[77] Gonzalez, *A History of Christian Thought*, 269.

[78] Ambrose, "Epistles 20:19" *Nicene and Post-Nicene Series II*, vol. 10, ed. Philip Schaff and Henry Wace (Edinburgh: T&T Clark, ND), 425

[79] Louis J. Swift, "Ambrose," in *Encyclopedia of Early Christianity*, ed. Everett Ferguson (New York: Garland Publishing Company, 1990), 30-32.

[80] Cf. Hinson, *The Early Church: Origins to the Dawn of the Middle Ages*.

[81] Cited by Gerd Tellenbach, *Church, State and Christian Society*, trans. R F Bennett (New Jersey: Humanities Press, 1940; reprint, 1970), 33.

[82] Classification by Troeltsch, *The Social Teaching of the Christian Churches*, 331ff.

[83] Tillich, *A Complete History of Christian Thought*, 41.

[84] "The Nature and Purpose of the Church: A stage on the way to a common statement Faith and Order Paper No. 181 - November 1998" http://www.wcc-coe.org/wcc/what/faith/nature1.html [online document] (accessed August 20, 2006).

[85] Wolfhart Pannenberg, *The Church*, trans. Keith Crim (Philadelphia: Westminster Press, 1983), 153.

[86] Cf. Brown, *The Church Apostles Left Behind*.

[87] Dietrich Bonhoeffer, *Letters and Papers from Prison*, ed. Eberard Bethge (New York: Macmillan Publishing Co., 1972), 382.

Chapter 4
The Growth, Development and Structure of the Church (*kyriakon*) in the Roman World from 1st to 6th century

Gaikaolung Dangmei

Introduction

Christianity was one of the fastest spreading religions of its time. Jerusalem as its centre, the growth of the church spread extensively to the Jews and also to the non-Jews. The great promoters of the spread of Christianity were the **Apostles**, acting in obedience to **Christ**'s commandment to proclaim the gospel to all the nations. According to Acts 8:1 & 4, the believers were scattered throughout the region of Samaria and Judea and went about preaching the gospel. By the end of the first century, Christianity has reached in the most of the important cities and town in the Hellenized Roman Empire. Churches: at Philippi (Acts 16:40), Corinth (Acts 18:7), Rome (Rom. 16:5; 14-15), Ephesus (1 Cor. 16:19), etc. The house-churches were the only churches that Christians had, not only in the New Testament period, but also through most of the second century.[5]

From Jerusalem, churches were founded throughout Samaria (Acts 8:14 & 15) and Antioch (Acts 11:22). By the end of the first century churches were planted in most of the important cities and towns of the Roman Empire. Among the Apostolic churches, the church of Jerusalem and the church of Antioch were the two main important centres for the Christians.

1. Church in the Antiquity

1.1. The Church at Jerusalem

The growth of the Jerusalem church was truly exceptional. Starting with 120 people, they received 3,000 new members on the day of Pentecost. Later, the number had reached 5,000 (Acts 4:4) excluding women. The church became large (Acts 21:20) and included even priests and Pharisees in its membership (Acts 6:7; 15:5). It included also many Hellenists, Greek-speaking Jews of the Dispersion who came as pilgrims to feasts or various reasons were staying in Jerusalem.[6]

Their distinctive practices included a baptism in the name of Jesus, regular attendance at instruction given by the apostles and a fellowship on a household basis as being in breaking of bread and in prayers. The first leadership of the church was by the twelve apostles, especially Peter and John, but soon gave away to that of elders in the regular Jewish manner, with James the brother of Jesus as leader.[7] At the same time, it was a voting church. The Deacons were elected by the church and appointed by the Apostles (Acts 6:3, 5-7).

The congregation of Jerusalem became the mother church of Jewish Christianity, and gradually of all Christendom. The apostles were assisted by a number of presbyters, and seven deacons or persons appointed to care for the poor and the sick. But the Spirit moved in the whole congregation, bound to no particular office. The preaching of the gospel, the working of miracles in the name of Jesus, and the attractive power of a holy walk in faith and love, were the instruments of progress.[8]

1.2. The Church at Antioch

Antioch was at one time the third largest cosmopolitan city in the Roman Empire. The Antioch church was founded by Hellenist Jews and it was a mixed Jewish and Gentile group. Here the disciples/believers were first called *christianoi*, 'Christ-people,' by their Gentiles neighbours (Acts 11:26). Antioch became the launch pad for the expansion of the gospel throughout the Levant.[9] Barnabas was the first key figure and besides him Simeon who was called Niger, Lucius of Cyrene, Manaen who had been brought up with Herod the tetrarch and Saul were the important prophets and teachers (Acts 13:1). The names of these leaders represent several ethnic and social backgrounds, thus the leadership reflected the cultural diversity of the church. The order of the names of the prophets and teachers proves no special ranking or hierarchy of importance, nor is the specific title attached to them of the utmost consequence.

Antioch and Jerusalem were in constant fellowship with each other. Some prophets came down from Jerusalem to Antioch and Antioch sent generous funds to help the Jerusalem church in time of famine (Acts 11: 30). Though Jerusalem was the mother church of Antioch, however she did not overextend her control in a way that tended to subvert the message of the Gospel. The Church of Antioch had commissioned Paul and Barnabas to preach the gospel throughout the Roman world.[10] Therefore it was the first missionary church.

1.3. Pauline Churches

Apostle Paul following his conversion until his death, he made three extensive missionary journeys. He founded churches on the Antiochene pattern in the southern provinces of Asia Minor, in Macedonia and Greece.[11] Hultgren states, "Paul can be considered the founder of the churches in Galatia, Ephesus, Corinth, Thessalonica, and Philippi. He may have founded churches elsewhere, but it is these congregations that can be investigated on the basis of Paul's letter."[12] In due course, however, a separate *Ekklesia* – the word must sometimes have had the flavour of *synagogue* – of Jewish and Gentile converts came into being, each with its own elders appointed by the apostle or his delegate from among the responsible senior believers. There was no organizational link between Paul's churches, though there were natural affinities between churches in the same province. Local administration and discipline was autonomous. No church had superiority over any other, though they all acknowledged Jerusalem as the source of spiritual blessings.[13]

1.4. The Church in Rome

The church in Rome appeared to have been the result not of missionary activity but rather of the immigration of Christians from Palestine and Syria, who joined together to form a community.[14] Traditionally, the Church in Rome claimed to be founded by two apostles – Peter and Paul.[15] However, history is almost silent as to the origins of the Roman Church, without evidence that it was of apostolic foundation, there is some interesting evidence for the early planting of Christianity at Rome. In 51 CE, Claudius expelled Jews from Rome because they were indulging in constant riots at the instigation of Chrestus (*impulsore Chresto*).[16] Aquila and Priscilla were among the Jews expelled and were apparently already Christians (Acts 18:2).

By the middle of the third century, Christianity in Rome had been fully Latinized and the Latin elements had gained full control of the Roman Church.[17]

2. The Development of the Church Structure

The Apostolic Church is never an "institution," but it is simply "the people of God," the true Israel.[18] The emergence of some forms of structure in the book of Acts appears to have been necessitated in the light of the church ministry for the orderly conduct of worship, the collection and distribution of charity, the administration of the Sacraments, communal/social fellowship, and the arbitration of disputes.

In New Testament times a charismatic ministry of Apostles, Prophets and others endowed with gifts of the Holy Spirit played an important part in the spread and building up of the Church, but the beginning of the second century the *Didache* played an important part in the life of the Church.[19] William G. Young quotes the *Didache,* "Elect ... for yourselves bishops and deacons worthy of the Lord, men meek and not covetous, and true and approved: for they minister unto you the ministry of the prophets and teachers.[20] The Apostles also made arrangements for a settled, ordained ministry among congregations of converts.[21] Over the centuries the structure of the Church developed progressively.

2.1. The Order of Ministers

The terms "bishop" or "overseer" *(episkopos),* "elder" or "presbyter" *(presbuteros)* and "pastor" (*poimen*) are synonymous (Acts 20:17, 28; Tit. 1:5, 7; 1 Pet. 5:1, 2). These terms are used interchangeably. Never did one bishop/elder/pastor lead a church; these leaders were always plural in number,[22] and they led as servants by way of example rather than as worldly lords (1 Pet. 5:1-5; cf. Mt. 20:25-28; Mk. 10:42-45).

In the second century the charismatic type of leadership was slowly replaced by the ordained ministry and with the elected and ordained ministers, the local church organization of the second century emerged. Ignatius mentioned a three-fold ministry of the local church. Henry Bettenson quotes the writing of Ignatius, "

> All of you follow the bishop as Jesus Christ followed the Father, and follow the presbytery as the Apostles; and respect the deacons as the commandment of God. Let no man [*sic*] perform anything pertaining to the church without the bishop."[23]

Bishops administered the appointment and training of presbyters and deacons, ordaining them into service by laying on of hands at the same time presbyter and deacons assisted bishops in leadership in worship. New bishops were selected by the people of the particular churches in which they were to serve but were consecrated to their positions by other bishops from surrounding towns and cities through a ceremony of laying on of hands. Deacons were both male and female and mostly they assisted those undergoing baptism.[24] As the ordained ministers arose, distinction between ministers and members of the congregation who were called the laity became more separated. As the clergy continued to drift apart from the laity, the church's hierarchy continued to evolve. Earle E. Cairns observes,

> It was but a short step to the recognition that the monarchal bishops of some churches were more important than others. The exaltation of the monarchal bishop by the middle of the second century soon led to the recognition of the special honour due to the monarchal bishop of the church in Rome.[25]

By the third century each city had one recognized episcopal leader or senior bishop. The bishop of Rome was believed to possess an important spiritual role in the Mediterranean world however there was no single administrative head over the Church.[26]

2.2. Episcopal Hierarchy

By the end of the third century a clear pattern of Episcopal hierarchy is emerging though it is by no means uniform or universal.[27] Cyprian, bishop of Carthage and an important early Christian writer, writes on the Episcopate,

> ... [T]hence age has followed age and bishop has followed bishops in succession, and the office of the episcopate and the system of the Church has been handed down, so that the Church is founded on the bishops and every act of the Church is directed by these same presiding officers. Since this has been established by divine ordinance, I am astonished that certain persons have been rash and bold enough to choose to write to me in such a manner as to send their letter in the Church's name, when the Church consists of the bishop, the clergy and all the faithful.[28]

In the course of the years the bishops in the larger cities began to exercise authority over the bishops in their surrounding area. In 341 the Council of Antioch ordered that in each province the bishop in the chief city, or metropolis should have precedence over the other bishops in the providence, and that the other bishops should do nothing extraordinary without him. The metropolitan or archbishop was to take no common action without the occurrence of the other bishops in his province. Each bishop had authority in his own diocese, namely, the whole district which is dependent upon his city; to ordain presbyters and deacons; and to settle everything with judgment. But he was not to undertake anything further without the bishop of the metropolis, nor was the latter to undertake anything further without the consent of the other bishops of the province. Any bishop might have under him what were called *chorepiscopoi*, appointed by himself, to supervise the church in villages and rural districts. The *chorepiscopus* had been ordained to the episcopate and could ordain those in the subordinate ranks of the clergy – readers, sub-deacons, and exorcists – but not presbyters or deacons. The bishops in the chief cities of the Empire had positions of outstanding prestige. Especially prominent were those of Jerusalem, because of its historic association with the beginning of Christianity, Antioch, and the chief city of Syria, Alexandria, Constantinople, and particularly, Rome.

The bishops of these sees were eventually known as Patriarchs.[29] The name patriarch was at first, particularly in the East, an honorary title for all bishops, and as not till the fourth century exclusively appropriated to the bishops of the three ecclesiastical and political capitals of the Roman Empire, Antioch, Alexandria and Rome, and also to the bishop of Jerusalem *honoris causa*, and the bishop of Constantinople or New Rome. In the West the term papa afterwards appropriated by the Roman bishop, the Patriarch of Rome came to be known as the Pope; in the Persian Empire often called the *Catholicos*.[30]

Church and bishop were more and more identified as one, belonging to each other. Cyprian says, "Now above all we bishops who preside in the Church must adhere firmly to this unity and defend it, to demonstrate that the authority of bishops itself is one and undivided.[31] So, the church is in the bishop and the bishop is in the church. Therefore the idea that the whole Church met when the bishops met was widely held by the end of the third century.

2.3. The Great Councils

The four great councils of the Church were the Council of Nicaea (325), Council of Constantinople (381), Council of Ephesus (431), and Council of Chalcedon (451) in which the majority of participants were bishops. Important decisions on matters of doctrine and church discipline were taken by these councils.[32] These councils made the church law and its creeds were authoritative, on the other hand Christians who did not conform to it were called heretics.

2.3.1. At the Council of Nicaea, 325:

The Council of Nicaea affirmed the privileges of the four great Sees – Rome, Alexandria, Antioch and Jerusalem. Among these Antioch, Alexandria, and Rome were most prominent, because they were the capitals respectively of the three divisions of the Roman Empire, and centers of trade and communication, combining with their apostolic origin the greatest political weight. To the bishop of Antioch fell all Syria as his metropolitan district; to the bishop of Alexandria, all Egypt; to the bishop of Rome, central and lower Italy, without definite boundaries. William G. Young quotes canon 6 and 7 of the Council of Nicaea:

> Let the ancient customs hold good which are in Egypt and Libya and Pentapolis [Cyrenaica], according to which the Bishop of Alexandria has authority over all these places.
> For this also is customary to the Bishop of Rome.
> In like manner in Antioch and in the other provinces, the privileges are to be preserved to the Churches. But this is clearly to be understood, that, if anyone be made a bishop without the consent of the Metropolitan, the Great Synod [Council of Nicaea] declares that he shall not be a bishop . . .
> Since custom and ancient tradition has held good, that the Bishop of Aelia [Jerusalem] be honored, let him have his proper honor, saving to the Metropolis [Caesarea] the honor peculiar to it.[33]

2.3.2. At the Council of Constantinople, 381:

The Council confirmed Gregory of Nazianzus' appointment as bishop of Constantinople, rejecting the rival claimant backed by Alexandria. Anti-Western feelings were strong, and the schism at Antioch went on. Alexandria's interference in Constantinople and Antioch was clearly in mind when the Council drew up its canons. The second of these adopted the dioceses in the eastern Empire as regions for church purpose, and forbade intervention in the affairs of another diocese.[34] The third canon read, "The bishop of Constantinople shall have the primacy of honour after the bishop of Rome, because Constantinople is new Rome."[35] Rome based her supremacy on religious grounds, claiming to be founded by Peter, the apostle. The new ruling would leave Rome's future position uncertain instead of unchangeable supreme on the basis of history tradition. The Roman church repudiated it – delaying Western recognition of the Council as ecumenical until the sixth century.[36]

2.3.3. At the Council of Chalcedon, 451:

The council also reaffirmed the decision of the Council of Constantinople, 381 regarding the privileges of Constantinople, New Rome. The canon 28 (B.) of the Council declares:

> . . . [W]e also determine and decree the same things with regard to the privileges of the holy city of Constantinople, New Rome. For to the throne of Old Rome, the Fathers gave privileges with good reason, because it was the Imperial City. And [the Council of Constantinople], with the same consideration in view, gave equal privileges to the most holy throne of New Rome; judging with good reason that the city honoured by the monarchy and the senate, and enjoying equal privileges with the old imperial Rome, should likewise receive equal rank in matters ecclesiastical, holding the second place after her.[37]

Eventually, among the great Sees, Rome and Constantinople, the two capitals became the most prominent sees. From the middle of the fourth century the new patriarch of Constantinople or New Rome, arose to the primacy among the eastern patriarchs, and became a formidable rival of the bishop of old Rome.[38]

3. The Rise of the Roman Bishop

The development of the doctrine of apostolic succession and the exaltation of the Lord's Supper were important factors in the rise of the Roman bishop to power. The Roman church claims not only human but divine right for the papacy, and traces its institution directly to Christ, when he assigned to Peter an eminent position in the work of founding his church.[39] William G. Young recorded that in 251 Cyprian spoke of the authority of the bishops acting together (the collegiate episcopate) and its relation to the authority of the Bishop of Rome, as the successor of Peter.[40]

The first example of the exercise of a sort of papal authority is found towards the close of the first century in the letter of the Roman Bishop Clement (d. 102). This epistle, full of beautiful exhortations to harmony, love, and humility, was sent, as the very address shows, not in the bishop's own name, which is not mentioned at all, but in that of the Roman congregation, which speaks always in the first person plural. It was a service of love, offered by one church to another in time of need.[41] Between 313 and 590 the bishop of Rome won the primacy over other bishops.[42]

Pope Leo I, 440-481 C.E., really laid the foundations of the Papacy. He became Bishop of Rome at a critical time in the history of the West. The Empire was slowly breaking up; in the East the Church was engaged with schism and heresy. Both church and State needed a strong man at the head of affairs, and Leo was undoubtedly a strong man, both brave and able. He was ambitious to extent the jurisdiction of the Bishop of Rome, and in 445 C.E., Valentinian III, acknowledged to his urgencies and further enlarged his authority.[43] But, the accession of Gregory who is usually called the Great, to the episcopal throne in 590, the Roman bishop began to claim his supremacy over other bishops.[44] The historical factors which favoured the ascendency of the Roman see were:[45]

(1) The high antiquity of the Roman church, which had been honoured even by Paul with the most important doctrinal epistle of the New Testament. It was properly the only apostolic mother-church in the West, and was thus looked upon from the first by the churches of Italy, Gaul, and Spain, with peculiar reverence.

(2) The labours, martyrdom, and burial at Rome of Peter and Paul, the two leading apostles.

(3) The political pre-eminence of that metropolis of the world, which was destined to rule the European races with the sceptre of the cross, as she had formerly ruled them with the sword.

(4) The executive wisdom and the catholic orthodox instinct of the Roman church, which made themselves felt in this period in

the three controversies on the time of Easter, the penitential discipline, and the validity of heretical baptism.

Concluding Remarks

In scrutinizing the growth, development and structure of the Church, over the centuries various level of structure can be seen vividly. During the first century, none of the churches were governed by monarchial bishops (traditional one-man pastor) nor was the episcopate considered the upper rank of a clerical order which governed the laity. In the later centuries, Clerical Order surfaced as distinguished from the laity. The elevation of monarchial bishops within local churches came into light while the Great Councils acknowledged this development and hold into it by further making the church law and its creeds. This advancement of the church finally led to the supremacy of the Roman bishop.

Our model of church is basically the result of the third and fourth century church. The monarchial bishops possess the highest rank within the church. Lay people may often take lower church offices and work their way up through the ranks. The pastor is the Omni-competent administrator, teacher, evangelist, theologian, and counsellor, the paternalistic authority figure in the church; almost all of them are seminarians. Do we find a democratic form in the structure of the church?

Endnotes:

[1] D. W. B. Robinson, "Church," in *New Bible Dictionary,* ed. J. D. Douglas, 2nd ed. (Wheaton: Tyndale House Publishers, Inc., 1988), 205.

[2] Albert James Dager, "What Is 'The Church?' With Whom Did God Make His New Covenant?" *Media Spotlight: A Biblical Analysis of Religious & Secular Media,* http://www.mediaspotlight.org/pdfs/What%20Is% 20The%20Church.pdf (accessed March 23, 2014).

[3] Ibid.

[4] W. P. Hares, *A History of the Christian Church of the First Six Centuries,* 2nd ed. (Madras: The Christian Literature Society for India, 1952), 14.

[5] Bradly Blue, "Acts and the House Church," in *The Book of Acts in its First Century Setting,* ed. David W. J. Gill and Conrad Gempf, vol. 2 (Grand Rapids: William B. Eerdmans Publishing Company, 1994), 189.

[6] Robinson, "Church," 206.

[7] Ibid.

[8] Philip Schaff, *History of the Christian Church: Apostolic Christianity; A.D. 1-100,* vol. I (Grand Rapids: William B. Eerdmans Publishing Company, 1985), 247.

[9] Robinson, "Church," 207.

[10] Arland J. Hultgren, *The Rise of Normative Christianity* (Minneapolis: Fortress Press, 1994), 50.

[11] Robinson, "Church," 206f.

[12] Hultgren, *The Rise of Normative Christianity,* 42.

[13] Robinson, "Church," 207.

[14] Schuyler Brown, *The Origins of Christianity: A Historical Introduction to the New Testament,* Revised ed. (Oxford: Oxford University Press, 1993), 131.

[15] Henry Chadwick, "The Early Christian Community," in *The Oxford Illustrated History of Christianity,* ed. John McManners (Oxford: Oxford University Press, 1992), 35.

[16] L. E. Elliott-Binns, *The Beginning of Western Christendom* (London: Lutterworth Press, 1948), 92.

[17] George La Piana, "The Roman Church at the end of the Second Century: the Episcopate of Victor, the Latinization of the Roman Church, the Easter controversy, consolidation of power and doctrinal development, the Catacomb of Callistus," *Harvard Theological Review* 18, no. 3 (July, 1925): 275.

[18] Emil Brunner, "One Holy Catholic Church," *Theology Today* 4, no. 3 (October 1, 1947): 319.

[19] William G. Young, *Handbook of Source Materials for Students of Church History* (Delhi: ISPCK, 2009), 149.

[20] Ibid., 150.

[21] Ibid., 149.

[22] Acts 11:30; 14:23; 15:2,4,6,22,23; 16:4; 20:17,18; 21:18; Philm. 1:1; 1 Tim. 5;7; Titus 1:5; Heb. 13:17; Jas. 5:14.

[23] Henry Bettenson, *Documents of the Christian Church,* 2nd ed. (Oxford: Oxford University Press, 1967), 63.

[24] Dale T. Irvin and Scott W. Sunquist, *History of the World Christian Movement: Earliest Christianity to 1453,* vol. I (Bangalore: Theological Publications in India, 2004), 103.

[25] Earle E. Cairns, *Christianity Through the Centuries* (Grand Rapids: Zondervan Publishing House, [1954] 1977), 124.

[26] Ibid., 107.

[27] Young, *Handbook of Source Materials for Students of Church History,* 153.

[28] Bettenson, *Documents of the Christian Church,* 73

[29] Kenneth Scott Latourette, *A History of Christianity* (New York: Harper & Row Publishers, 1953), 185.

[30] Young, *Handbook of Source Materials for Students of Church History,* 153.

[31] Ibid., 154.

[32] Ibid., 154f.

[33] Ibid., 155.

[34] Tim Dowley, *The History of Christianity* (Oxford: Lion Publishing House, 1990), 176.

[35] Young, *Handbook of Source Materials for Students of Church History,* 155.

[36] Dowley, *The History of Christianity,* 176.

[37] Young, *Handbook of Source Materials for Students of Church History,* 156.

[38] Philip Schaff, *History of the Christian Church: Ante-Nicene Christianity; A.D. 100-325,* vol. II (Grand Rapids: William B. Eerdmans Publishing Company, 1985), 155.

[39] Ibid., 155.

[40] Young, *Handbook of Source Materials for Students of Church History,* 153.

[41] Schaff, *History of the Christian Church: Ante-Nicene Christianity; A.D. 100-325,* 157f.

[42] Cairns, *Christianity Through the Centuries,* 169.

[43] Hares, *A History of the Christian Church of the First Six Centuries,* 193.

[44] Cairns, *Christianity Through the Centuries,* 169.

[45] Schaff, *History of the Christian Church: Ante-Nicene Christianity; A.D. 100-325,* 156.

Chapter 5
Confronting Socio-Religio-Political Oppressive Powers in the *Ekklesia* of God

H. Joseph Lalfakmawia

Introduction

The Fourth Gospel says that the light shone in the darkness, but the darkness did not know it. So, the ministry of Jesus, from the beginning, is a ministry of conflict with the dark and demonic forces. As a light, his mission is to let the dark know that he is the light. If fact, it was the ministry of the light against the dark. The devil took control over all aspects of life, even to the extent of religious life. Since the work of Jesus was to overcome the demonic kingdom and to establish the Kingdom of God, the two forces encountered each other in every phase of life. As a result, Jesus did not leave any part of life untouched. He counteracted the work of the devil directly and indirectly by means of healing and casting out demons from the demon possessed. He challenged and argued against the religious authorities, conflicted against the existing culture and political authorities. His conflicting ministry can be summarized as follows:

1) Jesus Conflicted Against the Religion and the Religious Authorities

Jesus challenged the existing religious tradition in various ways. He criticized against the manner of prayer, fasting, almsgiving etc. as hypocrite. Two outstanding challenges made by Jesus over against the religious authorities and traditions will be discussed and applied in our context here:

a) Violation of Sabbath law

Sabbath is a sacred day for the Jews. Stern prohibitions were made in order to observe it satisfactorily. Such prohibitions are clearly seen in the *Book of Jubilee*. It (2:17, 18) says,

> And He gave us a great sign, the Sabbath day, that we should work six days, but keep Sabbath on the seventh day from all

> work. And all the angels of the presence, and all the angels of sanctification, these two great classes—He hath bidden us to keep the Sabbath with Him in heaven and on earth.[1]

Jubilee 2:25-28 says that those **who work on Sabbath shall die and whoever defiles shall surely die**. They were not allowed to do their own will, to prepare anything to eat or drink, to draw water, to bring in or out of their doors anything that has to be carried, which they have not prepared in the six days of work in their dwellings.[2] In the midst of this uncompromising rule, Rabbis discovered certain detour to serve their purpose so that they would observe but not as strict as it was recorded in the book of Jubilee. In fact, there were certain cases in which the sabbatical laws were superseded by certain inescapable obligations. For instance, if 'a Jew' was in mortal danger he could break the Sabbath.[3] Mishnah also permits this, "And any matter of doubt as to danger to life overrides the prohibitions of the Sabbath" (Yoma 8:6).

Four Sensitive Things should be Marked Here:

Firstly, according to the book of Jubilee, death penalty is awarded to anyone for any form of breaking Sabbath law.

Secondly, that strict rule can be bent/superseded on account of certain inescapable obligation such as mortal danger. If there is no acute danger to the life or if the sick person can wait for the next day, this supersession is not applicable.

Thirdly, if the victim is a Jew (in case of mortal danger).

Fourthly, intentional desecration of Sabbath was to be punished by stoning to death (Sanhedrin 7:4).

When Jesus healed on Sabbath, not one of them suffered from life-threatening sickness who cannot wait for the next day (Mk. 3:1–6; Lk. 13:10–17; 14:1–6). According to the Jewish law, he should not have to heal on the Sabbath. "Doing good" for his opponents meant keeping the Sabbath, and keeping the Sabbath meant not healing the cripple. In other words, the sabbath was more important than the well-being of a person.[4]

When Jesus healed them on the Sabbath day, the synagogue leader angrily scolded them to come on the other six days and get healed but not on Sabbath. They blindly wanted to observe

Sabbath that they did not have compassion on their fellow human who suffered. Jesus intentionally violated Sabbath by healing the sick. He challenged the existing religion and its understanding because the way they worshipped God and the observance of the Sabbath were not from divine, but from human. He conflicted against the blind religion which was influenced by the demonic power, and instead he established the Kingdom of God in which God is worshipped from within. Jesus uncovered the fallacy of their legalism.

The condition, 'if the victim is a Jew,' (even in case of mortal danger) is an irritating fact. This exclusivity is particularly for the Jews. This makes us curious to know what would happen if the victim is a non Jew while the healer is the Jew. This interpretation can mean a provision for the Jew that he/she can be healed on Sabbath if the sickness is deadly. If this is a provision then it also implicitly implies that the non-Jew/Gentile would not be treated on Sabbath even if his/her sickness is acute danger for life since the healer is a Jew. This is, in one way, a curse for the non-Jews.

Take the crippled woman (Lk. 13:10-17) as an example. As she had been suffering from that sickness for eighteen-year long time, it was obvious that the synagogue congregation would know very well that she could wait for the following day for her cure so that she and the healer would not violate Sabbath law.

Two questions can be asked then:

1) Firstly, Jesus undeniably violated the Sabbath law. According to the sabbatical law, he should be put to death. Why the synagogue leader did not accused him of that fatal offence to the Sanhedrin and put Jesus to death? How could they let Jesus escape from death?

Certain laws were not only superseded but also were bent in order to suit their purposes and conveniences. Sabbatical law prohibits one to draw water because they have to tie a rope to the bucket and draw it from the well. Rabbi Eliezer ben Jacob interpreted and justified that 'A woman ties (1) the slit of her shift, (2) the strings of her hairnet and of her belt, (3) the thongs of a shoe or sandal, (4) [leather] bottles of wine or oil, and (5) a cover over meat, and 'they tie a bucket with a belt but not with a rope.'[5] According to this, they can draw water from the well if they tied bucket with their belt because it is not a rope but part of a woman's cloth. This interpretation is nothing but bending the law according to their convenience.

Jesus' Sabbath violation and that kind were not pursued because sabbatical laws were reinterpreted milder from time to time. This can be learnt from the comparison between the strict sabbatical law of the *Book of Jubilee* and the Mishnaic interpretation as we have seen here. These revisions held their hands to immediately sue Jesus from his violation. If this is the case, why did not they revise the law in order to care for the poor and weaker sufferers? In fact, they were harsh and quick to the weaker whom they could audaciously exploit but were passive to whom they feared or respected.

2) Secondly, how did they differentiate between 'mortal illness' and 'a little less mortal illness'? Was the sickness of that woman, which lasted for eighteen years due to which she was bent over and could not stand up straight, less severe than any other so-called mortal sickness of that time?

Any religion that condemns the healer of that bent over woman on ANY DAY, sacred or ordinary, due to religious fundamentalism is nothing but devilish. Any religious leader that legitimizes such fundamentalism is but devilish. Religious leaders who do not bother the devilish work in the church uphold the devilish work within the church.

Just like Sabbath law was legitimized and unchallenged even by the religious leaders during that time, Indian Christianity in some states, for instance in the south India, legitimized certain covert evil within the church. Caste discrimination are still practiced in some churches though lesser in the Protestant church. In the Catholic churches in some of the south Indian states, separate seating for caste and Dalits are still reserved. Separate burial places in catholic cemeteries, inferior role in the mass, as well as in the festivals are still practiced in the Catholic Church in the south India.[6]

I have heard the real life testimony from the members of the Syrian Christians of certain Pentecostal church in Kerala that the Dalit Christian converts are not welcomed within the 'caste' church, causing the outcaste Dalits struggling to establish their own churches. Similarly, the aggressive and unsolvable tension between the Mala and Madiga Dalit Christians of Church of South India (Andhra Pradesh) is but reluctantly legitimized because the people within the church are happy with this system. They agree that they cannot share cups in the Holy Communion not because of hygienic issue but due to caste difference. These issues are real and current, and they are in contrast to the socio-harmonic teaching of Jesus. However, it is extremely difficult to address even for the church leaders/theologians because the ongoing system (largely by lay people) more or less legitimizes it. Any attempt otherwise, can backfire the one who will propagate against it.

But this reminds of us the mission of Jesus when he knowingly violated the formidable Sabbath law. In spite of his clear knowledge about the probable outcome against him, Jesus broke Sabbath law in favour of the weak and sufferers. For Jesus, love and passion are prior to legalism; service to human is prior to tradition.

b) Woe Pronouncement

Jesus also pronounced 'woe' to the high profile religious leaders and authorities: Pharisees, Scribes and lawyers (Mt. 23:13-29; Lk. 11:42-52). The Pharisees were zealous to make converts (their ministry), they fulfilled the regulations for purity extraordinarily by giving tithe and ritual purification (ritual washing their hands etc.). They were outwardly good and pious, but Jesus pronounced woe to them and called them hypocrites because they were unclean within whereas inward cleanliness is what God demands. The scribes were the theologians who wanted respect, and strived for places of honour. They relied on their theological knowledge; they knew and preached the will of God, but they did not fulfill it. In other words, the religious leaders were also under the direct influence of the devil, and their works were condemned by Jesus.

Jesus' woe pronouncement against Pharisees is on three issues:[7]

1) Giving meticulous care to legal details but neglecting God's justice and love;

2) Coveting attention and pride of place;

3) Being hidden contaminators of the nation's life, like buried graves.

The Pharisees were giving 'mint, rue and herbs of all kinds' as tithe, the ritual debt to God. In fact, tithing referred to here is from Lev. 27:30–33 and Deut. 14:22–29. However, Mosaic Law does not say any word about tithing these. The Pharisees overdid it.[8] Matthew records a very interesting exaggeration by Jesus saying, "You cross sea and land to make a single convert" (Mt. 23:15)! After all these outward zeal, Jesus rightly called them as Hypocrites. The Kingdom of God is not about the traditional sanctity or ritual elegance but justice and the love of God (Lk. 11:42).

Woe to the Present Day Church

Generally speaking, most of the denominations share similarity in the fundamental teachings of the Bible such as virgin birth, passion, salvation, parousia, justification by faith etc. However, there are some significant differences among the denominations such as liturgies and medium or mode or style of some of the rites such as baptism. Theological difference too plays an important part such as Trinitarian debate. No radical church leaders or members can compromise in these issues. Every denomination claims superiority in its own doctrines and liturgies and estrange other denominational members just like the then Jewish leaders were lost in the custom and religious traditions. The true and earnest worker of the Kingdom of God must pronounce WOE to these church leaders and members because the true church of God is not about doctrines or liturgies or traditions but service to God by serving human, especially the neglected ones of the society.

Three woes were also pronounced against the lawyers (Lk. 11:46-52) concerning the following:

1) burdening others while exempting themselves;

2) honoring dead prophets while involving in the causes of their deaths;

3) leading astray people from the truth.

This is a challenge to every church leaders, pastors and theologians. The true characteristic of the true church is not stern demand from the church members or interpreting the Bible in such a way that lay people will give while the church leaders will enjoy.

Joshua, on the verge of Jordan, gave instruction to both the people and the levitical priests that the distance between the people and the priests should be of about two thousand cubits (Jos. 3:4). The narrative says that the priests must go before the lay people two thousand cubits ahead. When they did that, the overflowing Jordan River stood still and the Israelites were crossing over the dry ground! Joshua also said that the lay people had never passed that way before, which is also true.

The church leaders must go ahead of the members. It may be on the verge of danger or losing wealth just as the priests never knew if they might be drowned. Still, the duty of the church leaders is to lead the members. The true *ekklesia* of God must be led by the true leader who must go ahead of the members. Jesus condemns such leaders who put burden on others while exempting themselves.

2) Jesus Confronted the Existing Socio-Cultural Setting

Jesus could not fit himself in the existing socio-cultural setting because he did not want to conform himself to the 'legitimized socio-cultural sins'. We call it 'legitimized' because those lifestyles that we are going to deal with were well accepted as if they were the socio-cultural standard of life. We too call it 'sins' because they were oppressive. People, especially the elite groups, enjoyed their lives at the expense of the oppressed. They oppressed the weaker section of the society in the name of God and People of God's culture! They did not stand against those undisclosed sins. On the contrary, they brought into the temple and were handed from generation to generation. Jesus did not tolerate these that caused him his life, though preordained. Some of the areas are as follows:

i) Male Chauvinism

The Jews before and during the time of Jesus practiced patriarchal cultural set up, in which men oppressed women. Woman is openly despised.[9] Some few examples clarify this:

a) All ought to rest on Sabbath but women did not rest (Ex. 20:8ff).[10]

b) Husband is the lord of wife (Gen. 3:16).

c) In Mishnah, Rabbi Eliezer says, "Whoever teaches Torah to his daughter is as if he teaches her sexual satisfaction."[11]

d) To differentiate between man and woman, Mishnah says, "The man sells his daughter, and the woman does not sell her daughter [Ex. 21:6]."[12]

e) The man arranges for a betrothal of his daughter, and the woman does not arrange for the betrothal of her daughter [M. Qid. 2:1].[13]

f) The wife should neither bear witness, instruct children, nor pray at table; she is not even bound to keep the whole Torah.ÿþ[14]

g) In the synagogues, wives did not actually come forth out of their inner chambers, and unmarried ladies (virgins) were kept in the strictest privacy, shunning the eyes of men, even of those who were their nearest relations, out of modesty.[15]

h) Woman's honour lies on bearing children. Barrenness/ childlessness is accurse of God.[16]

Oepke rightly said that woman was legally more a moveable property than a person in Israel.[17] In today's word, we can say that men spoiled the women's life and violated their rights. This set up was legitimized both by society and religion. Amidst this context, Jesus did not reject women as the society did. He takes the side of the poor and oppressed women always. He even protected the prostitute from the mob who tried to stone her. He not only protected her, but also counteracted against the people who thought themselves righteous by letting them know that they were the sinners.

Women in India today

According to the UNICEF report on women and children 2009, avoidable complications during child birth results in the death of 78,000 women in India every year. The maternal mortality rate of India stands at 301 per 100,000 births. It is highest in Uttar Pradesh at 517 and lowest in Kerala at 110. In India more than 2/3 of all maternal deaths occur in a few states like Uttar Pradesh, Uttarakhand, Bihar, Jharkhand, Orissa, Madhya Pradesh, Chhattisgarh, Rajasthan and Assam.[18] The comment of the UNICEF about of death of 78,000 women is extremely ridiculous; "avoidable complications during child birth!"

Some of the (few selected) sad cases reveal the tragic fate of women in India:

Domestic Violence

Globally speaking 1/3 of women faces violence at the hands of their husbands, fathers, or brothers and uncles in their homes.[19] This is extremely rampant in India among every culture, religion, class and ethnicity. The National Crimes Bureau, Ministry of Home Affairs, Government of India reported 71.5% increase of torture and dowry deaths from 1991 to 1995. In 1995, torture of women constituted 29.25% of all reported crimes against women. More than 9, 5000 women are killed every year in India over dowry. According to the same report, there were over 32,000 murders, 19,000 rapes, 7,500 dowry deaths and 36,500 molestation cases against women during 2006.[20]

In India, girls are still less likely to enroll in school than boys; in 2005, for upper primary school (Grades 6-8) girls' enrolment was 8.8 points lower than boys, for Scheduled Tribes (ST) the gender gap was 12.6 points and 16 points for Scheduled Castes (SC).[21]

Physical suffering from family:

1) Murder: Mr. Simhachalam in Andhra Pradesh killed his two daughters and wife Lavanya on 9th November, 2012 as his wife did not give birth a baby boy.[22]

2) Suicide: Ms. Mopada Vijayalakshmi committed suicide on 30th August, 2012, by jumping into a well along with her two-and-a-half-year-old son at Chettupalli village, Andhra Pradesh due to additional dowry harassment.[23]

3) Dowry Harassment: A newly married woman hanged herself on August 31st, 2012 due to dowry harassment by her husband and in-laws in Lingapur village, Karimnagar district, Andhra Pradesh.[24]

A 24-year-old woman, Ashwini Sonawane, filed a dowry case against her husband and mother-in-law at the Vartak Nagar police station, Thane, Tamil Nadu, on 6th October, 2013 (Sunday).[25]

Jesus' Response to these Issues

In the midst of these past and present suffocating facts, Jesus' words and cautious actions are really interesting.

1) Jesus used woman and her domestic chore (preparation of leaven, Mt. 13:33) as a parable for the Kingdom of God. This parable is not a plain old interesting story, but about the Kingdom of God, his main message and ministry! He did not use the proud men here.

2) He willingly speaks to woman (Jn. 4:27 etc.).

3) Unlike Rabbi Eliezer, he taught woman (Lk. 10:39).

4) He calls a woman the daughter of Abraham (Lk. 13:16). Jesus boldly equates men and women and given the celebrated title, 'daughter of Abraham.'

5) He speaks on behalf of women (Mk. 12:40 and parallel).

6) He breaks the 'unbreakable' Sabbath law On behalf of a sick woman (Lk. 13:10 ff.).

7) He is not hesitate to contact even unclean women (Mk. 5:27ff.; Lk. 7:38ff.).

The true Ekklesia of God must follow Jesus, the owner and founder. If the church is found against Jesus' teaching and life example, then that is the time and place to stand up and proclaim the Kingdom of God and Jesus' interpretation of it.

ii) Religiously Sinners were Culturally and Socially Estranged

Some of the trades/professions, according to Mishnah, were religiously despised and were culturally estranged. Abba Gurion of Sidon instructed, "A man should not teach his son to be an *ass driver, a camel driver, a barber, a sailor, a herdsman, or a shopkeeper*. For their trade is the trade of thieves."[26] These trades were suspicious trades because temptation was great for the goods entrusted to them.[27] Contrary to this, Rabbi Judah considered camel drivers and sailors are decent and saintly. But to him physicians and butchers are sinners. He said, "The best among the physicians is going to Gehenna, and the best of the butchers is a partner of Amalek."[28]

Rabbi Judah was very harsh to the physicians because they were considered to favour rich people as they could pay well while they neglected the poor as they could pay little.[29] Butchers were considered cheating people by selling flesh of animals with some fatal physical blemishes.[30]

Generalizing such trades and condemning all the people involving there is nothing but sheer prejudice. Unfortunately the whole society was absorbed into that teaching. In the midst of that, Jesus stood against such culturally legitimized sins. All these allegations were contrasted by the Jesus movement. The herdsmen (shepherds), who were religiously sinners, were the first who received the good news of the birth of Jesus (Lk. 2:8-18). Jesus was the friend of the sinners, the publicans and the tax collectors. They were culturally and religiously estranged. But Jesus, in contrast to the existing culture, loved and kept accompany with them. True religion must never depend on assumption.

Like Jesus, religious leaders of today must not have prejudice over against anyone irrespective of trade, socio-economic status, gender etc.

iii) Children were Neglected

Despite the special esteem for children (Ex. 13:8, 14; Deut. 4:9; 6:7; Gen. 27, 48, 49), they were the powerless ones on the bottom stair of Hebrew and other ancient societies. Tradition and custom allotted the most important place to older people (Prov. 16:31; Job 12:12). Parents had almost absolute authority over children, who were educated through strict obedience often enforced by severe physical punishment (Prov. 13:24; 19:18; 22:15; 23:13).[31] Spitaler's summary of Mark Gospel clearly depicts the life setting of children. In his view, reports about children in Mark's Gospel indicate that its author views childhood as a untrustworthy stage of life, ranking a child's social status among the marginalized, poor, sick, powerless, dominated and exploited.[32] Thus, to 'become like children' means being society's 'last' (Mk. 9.35).

In contrast to that, Jesus taught that the Kingdom of God was to be received "as a child" (Mk. 10:15 par. Mt. 18:3 and Lk. 18:17). Who is the greatest according to Jesus' teaching? The lowly, the humble, those who, even adults, accept for themselves the low status of children are the greatest of all. In fact, adult are striving for power and position and aspire. In contrast to this, Jesus' teaching is that those who are humble like children will participate in the Kingdom of God. Caroll's interpretation of these passages is very true when he says,

> Jesus instructs the community of disciples, and especially those who exercise leadership within it. Genuine leadership in the Christian community is marked by humility, with the young child as model. Moreover, community leaders will not exercise power over helpless children but act in humility toward them, knowing that hospitality shown to a young child is shown to Jesus as well.[33]

Thus, welcoming the low and insignificant people 'such as children' reveals the theological agenda of the disciples and of Jesus. 'Whoever' acts like the disciples in the story rejects a kingdom serving the marginalized. 'Whoever' acts like Jesus shares his vision of God's Kingdom.[34] Service to the down trodden, marginalized and the oppressed means accepting God the creator. In the true *ekklesia* of Jesus, the weak and the powerless do have privileges.

iv) Jesus Took the side of the Aged People

Jesus rebuked those who went against Moses' law regarding honouring parents. Though the Jews were the strict followers of Mosaic Law, they wanted to exclude themselves from serving their parents by a vow called 'Corban.' Corban means 'an offering to God' (Mk. 7:11). This is their indirect way of dishonouring their parents, that is, the old age people. In fact, 'corban' literally means 'an offering to God.' But it was misused by the younger people against their older parents by saying, "Whatever you might be benefited from me is *an offering to God!* or *Corban* is whatever you might be benefited from me!" meaning, "You shall have no benefit from what is mine!"[35] It can mean insult or offense to aged people.

But Jesus takes the side of them and rebuked those who tried to twist their religious tradition. He also accepted the service of an old woman, Peter's mother-in-law (Mt. 814-17).

v) Jesus embraces the Impure Ones

One of the most terrible and abhorrent diseases during those days is leprosy. The OT often attributes the appearance of leprosy to God's punishment for sinful behaviour. Therefore, people abhorred and alienated them. In one way, such attitude was not taken as cruelty as they were the accursed ones.

Leviticus 13 is a detail examination of leprosy. It was taught that it was an unclean disease that could contaminate others and the atmosphere as well. They had to wear torn clothes and should cover his/her upper lips and cry out, "Unclean, unclean." They were excluded from the area of human habitation or be otherwise destroyed (Lev. 13:45, 46).

In Lk. 17, the lepers stand "outside," the village and at a distance from Jesus, in accordance with Leviticus 13:46. In the first case, (Mk. 1:40-45), Jesus' action in touching the sufferer is best understood as one of compassion. This touch also means he is symbolically welcomed back into the community.[36]

This attitude of Jesus is not only interesting but also the model of the true *ekklesia* of God. God's *ekklesia* is the inclusive community where everyone is welcomed, everyone is acknowledged, and everyone is clean. Leprosy here can be taken as a metaphorical leprosy today. In the true *ekklesia* of God, the upper caste, class, rich and intellectual people cannot act as the sound people who alienated the lepers in the olden days. Just like the head of the church, Jesus, embraced the lepers, the lepers of today, that is, Dalits, Adivasi, Tribals, women, children, aged people, materially poor, homeless, street beggars, slum dwellers, ignorant people, physically challenged people etc., any culture that alienates these disadvantaged ones must be confronted.

3) Jesus Conflicted Against the Political Authority

Some scholars have seen Jesus as revolutionary because he strongly challenged the existing politics of his own time. In the meantime, Jesus cannot be understood as blindly opposing the government. Jesus, although he is the son of God, he did pay the temple tax (Mt. 17:24-26). The two-drachma piece, that was paid by Jesus and Peter was approximately equal in value to the half-shekel collected annually from every Jew to support the temple (i.e., from males over twenty years of age; cf. Ex. 30:13–16; cf. 38:26; Neh. 10:32–33).[37] Matthew presented Jesus as a loyal Jew who pays the temple tax. Some scholars argued that this pericope concerns not the temple tax but Roman taxation. However, we can accept that this concerns not the paying of taxes to the state, i.e., the secular authorities, but a specifically religious tax for the maintenance of the temple and its ritual.[38] He acknowledged the temple government by collecting the tax.

Jesus clearly said that the tax has to be paid to the government (Mk. 12:17-Give to the emperor the things that are the emperor's, and to God the things that are God's). Jesus was not a revolutionary who tried to overthrow the Roman government. But neither did he put priority upon loyalty to secular government. He is a good citizen of a good government.

In the meantime, when he was warned to flee from Herod because he wanted to kill him, Jesus, who agreed to pay the tax, called Herod 'the fox' (Lk. 13:31-33). Jesus, when he addressed King Herod as 'fox', intends to mean few things:

1) A low cunning fox. In rabbinic literature the fox was typical of low cunning animal.[39] So, Herod, though he was a king, was compared to a fox due to his perverted life. To Jesus, political or social high status is nothing. In our world today, we write, teach and preach about political justice and the unjust politicians, IN THEIR ABSENCE, and that too if these big shots would not come to know that we are against them. But in their presence, our mouths are paralysed and our hands are tied up to proclaim justice against them.

2) An insignificant creature in comparison to the lion. This is more messianic since Jesus is the messianic lion of the house of David. However, this is not our intention here.

3) Jesus is righteous that he has no fear for the authorities. He outwardly spoke against him and decided to carry on his mission because Jesus did not have sin to fear the authorities. He

did the right thing and wanted to save the sinners. Herod, because he was unjust, wanted to get rid of the righteous prophets who revealed his guilt.

4) He humiliated the unjust king. It was nearly impossible for the courtiers to correct and inform the kings about their guilt. Jesus, knowing that his words would be brought back to Herod, put a mirror in front of him that the citizens deserve good rulers. Jesus, though a good citizen, boldly fought against the evil of the political authority because it was his mission to counteract and correct the politics that was defiled by the devil.

He also condemned the hierarchical and authoritarian form of government. Rather, he establish a government in which the leader is the slave of all (Mk. 10:42-44). The hardcore message of the true *ekklesia* of God is to proclaim the humble and just government. In this government, there is no tyranny. Rather it is a government of service to others.

In the true Ekklesia of God, the specially called out ones, the true church members must be prepared to follow the footsteps of Jesus, confronting all the evils within the church and the society.

Endnotes:

[1] Robert Henry Charles, *Pseudepigrapha of the Old Testament* (Bellingham: Logos Research Systems, Inc., 2004), 14.

[2] Eduard Lohse, "σαββατον, σαββατισμος, παρασκευς," in *Theological Dictionary of the New Testament*, vol. 7, ed. by Gerhard Kittel (Grand Rapids: William B. Eerdmans Publishing Company, [1971] 2006), 11.

[3] Ibid., 14.

[4] Robert A. Guelich, *Mark 1-8:26: Word Biblical Commentary*, vol. 34a (Dallas: Word Book Publisher, 2002), 139.

[5] Sabbath 15:2 in Jacob Neusner, *The Mishnah: A New Translation* (New Haven: Yale University Press, 1988), 198.

[6] John C. B. Webster, *The Dalit Christians: A History* (Delhi: ISPCK, 2009), 222f.

[7] Fred B. Craddock, *Luke: Interpretation, a Bible Commentary for Teaching and Preaching* (Louisville: John Knox Press, 1990), 159

[8] William Hendriksen, Simon J. Kistemaker, *Exposition of the Gospel According to Luke: Baker New Testament Commentary* (Grand Rapids: Baker Book House, 1953-2001), 638.

[9] Albrecht Oepke, "γυνη," *Theological Dictionary of the New Testament*, vol. 1, ed. Gerhard Kittel (Grand Rapids: William B. Eerdmans Publishing Company, [1964] 2006), 781.

[10] Ibid., 781.

[11] Sotah 3:4.

[12] Sotah 3:8E.

[13] Sotah 3:8F.

[14] Oepke, "γυνη," 782.

[15] *Flaccus* 89, Cf. Charles Duke Yonge, *The Works of Philo: Complete and Unabridged* (Peabody: Hendrickson Publishers, 1996), 732.

[16] H. Vorliinder, "Woman," in *New International Dictionary of the New Testament Theology*, ed. Colin Brown, vol. 3 (Grand Rapids: Zondervan Publishing House, 1981), 1055.

[17] Oepke, "γυνη," 781.

[18] Vasundhara Mohan, "Status of Women in India: Problems and concerns," Centre for Study of Society and Secularism, 20 in http://www.csss-isla.com/Status%20of%20Women%20in%20India%20Internees%20report[1].pdf (accessed December 10, 2013).

[19] Ibid., 24.

[20] Ibid., 25-27.

[21] "Education," http://www.unicef.org/india/education.html (accessed December 11, 2013).

[22] Mr. Simhachalam killed his two daughters, K. Swati (4 years of age) and K. Sravya (2 years) and wife Lavanya (31) on 9th November, 2012 at Ajjada village, Vizianagaram dist., AP because his wife did not give birth a baby boy. He was a drunkard and killed his daughters first, thinking that they were burden and then strangled his wife to death. Cf. "Man kills wife, two daughters," *Deccan Chronicles* (Visakhapatnam), November 11, 2012, 4.

[23] Mopada Vijayalakshmi married her distant relative Nanaji, a farmer of the same village, in 2009. The parents of the girl gave Rs. 1.5 lakh in cash and half acre farm land as dowry at the time of marriage. Vijayalakshmi gave birth to a son after which Nanaji and his family members reportedly started harassing her to get additional dowry form her parental home. Nanaji was said to have been quarrelling with his wife on the additional dowry issue for the past few weeks. Unable to bear the harassment, Jijayalakshmi jumped into a well, located in the village, along with her son and committed suicide. Cf. "Woman jumps into well along with son," *The Hindu* (Visakhapatnam), 31st August, 2012, 5.

[24] Dharmapuri CI Mahender said that T. Jyothi (22), a graduate, was married to Tirupathi (25), an autorickshaw driver. During the time of marriage on June 13 2012, Jyoti's parents handed over Rs. 1.8 lakh as dowry. However, Jyoti's husband and in-laws were demanding an additional dowry of Rs. 50,000. She informed the same to her parents, who expressed their helplessness to pay the amount. Unable to bear the mental agony, she committed suicide. Cf. "Dowry 'Harassment' Leads to Suicide," *The Hindu* (Visakhapatnam), 31 August, 2012, 11.

[25] http://timesofindia.indiatimes.com/city/thane/In-laws-booked-for-dowry-harassment/articleshow/23664542.cms, (accessed December 10, 2013).

[26] Qiddushin 4:14 (Mishnah).

[27] Joachim Jeremias, *Jerusalem in the Time of Jesus* (London: SCM Press Ltd., 1969), 303.

[28] Qiddushin 4:14 (Mishnah).

[29] Jeremias, *Jerusalem in the Time of Jesus*, 305f.

[30] Ibid., 306.

[31] Joseph A. Grassi, "Child, children," *The Anchor Bible Dictionary*, vol. 1, ed. David Noel Freedman (New York: Doubleday & Company Inc., 1996), 905.

[32] Peter Spitaler, "Welcoming a Child as a Metaphor for Welcoming God's Kingdom: A Close Reading of Mark 10.13-16," *Journal for the Study of the New Testament* 31 no. 4 (2009): 424.

[33] John T. Carroll, "Children in the Bible," *Interpretation* 55, no. 2 (April 2001): 130.

[34] Spitaler, "Welcoming a Child as a Metaphor for Welcoming God's Kingdom: A Close Reading of Mark 10.13-16," 440.

[35] Robert A. Guelich, *Word Biblical Commentary: Mark 1-8:26*, vol. 34a (Dallas: Word Books Publisher, 1998), 369.

[36] P. Ellingworth, "Leprosy," in *Dictionary of Jesus and the Gospels*, ed. Joel B. Green, Scot McKnight, and I. Howard Marshall (Downers Grove: InterVarsity Press, 1992), 463.

[37] Donald A. Hagner, *Matthew 14-28: Word Biblical Commentary*, vol. 33B (Dallas: Word Book Publishers, 2002), 511.

[38] Ibid., 513.

[39] I. Howard Marshall, *The Gospel of Luke: A Commentary on the Greek Text;* The New International Greek Testament Commentary (Exeter: Paternoster Press, 1978), 571.

Chapter 6
Paul's Vision for the *Ekklesia* of God

Roji T. George

Introduction

Paul, the apostle, went around the Roman Empire from the region of Syria in the east to Spain in the west of Rome preaching the message of Jesus, the Messiah, who transformed his life and commissioned him into His mission. The natural outcome of this was a sudden mushrooming of communities in the Roman cities which confessed Jesus as the King-Saviour.

The newly founded communes were composed of members from multiple ethnic, religious, and cultural backgrounds. He constantly moulded their theological thinking, resolved conflicts, controlled behaviours based on the ethical norms which he thought right/acceptable within the church, (re)structured their organizational make-up adapting to the socio-cultural environment, and worked relentlessly to create unity, mutual support and a sense of belongingness among the members beyond local communities, based on the gospel of Christ that he propagated. In fact, it would not be an exaggeration to state that he had a vision of the *ekklesia* of God which he passionately imparted to the members of his community. Hence, the entire Pauline corpus supplies us pertinent insights to developing a probable portrait of the church which Paul drew (and also later his followers drawing from him). It requires a couple of clarifications, I believe, at the outset:

(i) Disputed letters of Paul are included here to develop his vision of *ekklesia* because, even if Paul's authorship may be rejected as some would argue, it is broadly agreed that they were written by those who belonged to Paul's circle. To put it in plain words, these writings, then, reflect ideas which the later members of the Pauline circle found coherent and non-contradictory with the actual thought of Paul, the apostle; hence, they considered them authentic to attribute to him.

(ii) In line with this, the use of the term 'Pauline' does not imply that the seeming traces of later development of thought, like the developed ecclesial structure in the Pastoral letters, are purely innovative or forged in the name of the apostle for the sake of authenticity. Instead, to me, the term signifies those individuals/ communities who continued Paul's legacy in the later decades by adapting them to their own specific contexts. It implies openness to admit that some of these writings of Paul *may* have later undergone some editorial works. However, in no sense they speak things totally alien or contradictory to the teachings of the historical man, Paul. If so, the term 'Pauline' is an umbrella term which includes both the disputed and the undisputed letters of Paul.

In the remainder, at first the etymology of *ekklesia,* its origin and development in the early Christianity shall be discussed. It would underline the fact that the concept of *ekklesia* in the Pauline writings is not a new and innovative socio-religious institution, unique to the early Christian movement, but an adaptation of the then contemporary social institutions. However, Paul's writings reflect his vision of the nature and character of the *ekklesiai* of God he founded in the urban Roman centres. Hence, an overview of Paul's understanding of the *ekklesia* shall be briefly undertaken which will be followed by an elaborate discussion on the fourfold character of the church that Paul envisioned.

1. *Ekklesiai* in the Greco-Roman and Jewish World

1.1. The Etymology of *Ekklesia*

The etymological root of the term '*ekklesia*' translated as "Church" is contentious. In recent discussions, scholars consider the term 'Church' as the derivation of the Greek adjective *kuriakon.* According to Ward, from the third century it was used to refer to the *place of worship* in a substantive sense from which it later entered into the Gothic language as *kirika,* the root word for the English term 'church,' and *Kirche* in German.[1] The term signifies "belonging to someone" or "someone's possession" ("that which is Lord's") like "the Lord's table" (1Cor. 10:21) which later without any qualifying term came to "assume the total meaning" when used with the article.[2]

Customarily, it is maintained that *ekklesia* derives its meaning from the combination of the Greek proposition *ek* ("out of") and *kaleo* ("I call") meaning "the called out." Scholars reject the meaning of the term based on the etymological derivation because

> [H]istorically the idea of a 'calling out' or a summonsing was not a significant part of the use of the term among the Greeks. Though some lexicons define the word as 'a duly summonsed assembly,' the summonsed assembly was the *sugketikos ekklesia* whereas the regularly constituted assembly among the Greek city states was the *kuriae ekklesiae* 'the principal or sovereign assemblies.' The 'calling out' was not a part of the word itself but had to be expressed by a qualifying adjective.[3]

In other words, "[i]n usage *ek-kaleo* meant only, 'to call forth,' and not, as this interpretation would require, 'to call out from a larger group.' *Ekklesia,* in turn, meant only 'that which is called forth, an assembly.'"[4]

The term *ekklesia* has been used for various social-political entities in the Greco-Roman world while it bore religious meaning attached to it in the Jewish world. In the classical Hellenistic usage, maintains Ward, the term was used as a political term referring to a democratic institution i.e. "an assembly of citizens" which held "the ultimate power in the constitutional government of the Greek city-state." Of these, the most references are made to the *ekklesiai* of Athens where every Athenian citizen was free to assemble but not women, the disenfranchised people (*atimoi*), and the strangers.[5] In the Greco-Roman context, it referred to the political assembly, the Greek cultic societies or unions, and Greek fellowships.[6] In the first century CE context, *ekklesia* apart from Church referred to an assembly "as a regularly summoned political body."[7] The later quasi-technical usage of the term during the Roman times is evident in the direct adoption of the term into Latin because of "certain dignity...attached...to this word due to its political context."[8] Thus, Roberts maintains that "[t]he most natural supposition would be that the concrete meaning of the local community either as a whole or in assembly was borrowed to designate the local Christian group after the Christian movement had moved out onto Greek soil and then the universal concept developed as an abstract idea from this. Even if this process is the correct one, it is not agreed as to what the analogy was which furnished the basis of this adoption."[9] However, Tidball opines that the ability of Christianity to present itself as an ideal form of the prevalent social structure exemplifies her genius.[10] The early Christians also used terms apart from "assembly" (ἐκκλησια) such as 'overseer' (ἐπισκοπος) and 'elder' (πρεσβυτερος) to represent herself amidst other social institutions because these terms were also used to refer to the clubs and officers of a club.[11] Notably, the term πρεσβυτερος was used as a technical term among the nations "to designate civic as well as religious officials."[12] In other words, the church used the terms employed in the Greco-Roman world for various social institutions in order to define herself.

In LXX, both *'edah* and *qahal* are used to translate 'an assembly.' While the former is used for Israelite society, the latter refers to the actual assembly. Interestingly, *qahal* is normally translated as *ekklesia* whereas *'edah* is never done so. In fact, *'edah* is usually rendered as *synagoge,* though 35 times it is rendered to translate *qahal.*

More importantly, it is used 19 times in the first four books where the term *ekklesia* is never used.[13] However, this does not override the fact that *ekklesia* is the usual translation of *qahal* which, unlike in Hellenistic context, adds a new contour of meaning to *ekklesia* i.e. the People of God with religious connotation. Ward maintains that in the Jewish sources both canonical and non-canonical *qahal* or *ekklesia* has no religious connotation but it simply stands for an assembly.[14] However, in contrast, Roberts contends that within the theocratic worldview of the Old Testament, unlike in the secular Hellenistic milieu, *qahal* or *ekklesia* does not refer merely to a local, political, or democratic gathering but to an assembly assembling together for performing cultic rites in the name of the Lord. Particularly, "what is most important are those gatherings which are viewed as constituting or renewing the congregation as the people of God."[15] If so, as also contended by Roberts, the Jewish and the non-Jewish Christian auditors of Paul, familiar with the Old Testament theological insight attached with the term *ekklesia,* would have heard an additional meaning in his theological assertions.

1.2. The Origin and Development of Christian *Ekklesia* amidst the then Social Formations

Dunn maintains that the original root of the church lies in relation to Paul's mission which originated in some synagogue(s) in which the apostle entered. However, out of the several synagogue buildings discovered in various excavations, "[a]rchaeology has uncovered no structure which can be both identified as a 'church' and confidently dated earlier than a century or more later than Paul. So we have to assume that these meetings took place either in private homes or in larger premises rented for the occasion."[16] In the light of lack of concrete evidences in favour of larger premises rented for assembling, he argues, "[t]he only obvious conclusion is that the first believers met as 'church' in each other's house, with the wealthiest member and the largest house providing a regular venue for 'the whole church' in different centres."[17] This conclusion has been earlier well-affirmed by Meeks in his influential work, *The First Urban Christians: The Social World of the Apostle Paul*. He maintains that the early Christian church bore "at least a family resemblance" with other social formations within the then social world.[18] Meeks surveys the four significant analogies – the household, the voluntary association, the synagogue, and the philosophical or rhetorical schools – available within the then social environment.[19] He concludes leaning towards the household model as the most suitable, though not identical, to understand the Pauline churches in the Greco-Roman cities. He states:

> [t]he fact is that none of the four models we have now surveyed captures the whole of the Pauline *ekklesia*, although all offer significant analogies. At the least, the household remains the basic context within which most if not all the local Pauline groups established themselves, and the manifold life of voluntary associations, the special adaptation of the synagogue to urban life, and the organization of instruction and exhortation in the philosophical schools all provide examples of groups solving certain problems that the Christians, too, had to face.[20]

Treading cautiously towards drawing conclusion, he states that although it might "turn out that none of these categories quite fits," it is worth knowing: (1) how "a curious contemporary observer might have tried to identify and understand the Christians," while on the other hand (2) how the Christians viewed themselves in relation to the other analogical social formations or models within the Greco-Roman world.[21] A précis of Meeks' landmark discussion on the topic (chapter 4 of *The First Urban Christians*) stated here will serve suitable to the following discussion on Paul and his communities' stated vision of *ekklesia* in the letters. It would enable us to identify the essential traits of *ekklesia* that marked her different from other social formations with family resemblances. In fact, in a much informative survey of scholarly proposals building upon the lead provided by Meeks, Adams shows that though Meeks' proposal in several respect requires modifications, his study remains the standard reference for any discussion on the formation of Pauline *ekklesia*.[22]

Meeks states that analogical to the Greco-Roman household, the Pauline groups too met in private houses (e.g., 1 Cor. 1:11, 16; Rom. 16:10-11,14-15; Phil. 4:22). Such a social adaptation for a new group had larger implication(s) upon its internal and external network of relationships. While the internal relation was, at times, marred by inter-personal conflict, the church largely adopted the hierarchical structure of the *oikos*. However, in pure social terms household does not explain the existence of the apostolic/ charismatic power over the householder and the trans-local sense of unity and the anti-hierarchical tendencies occasionally visible within the church. Similarly, the early Christian *ekklesia* demonstrates several striking similarities with other associations, Jewish synagogue and the schools but her differences with them points to the unique form of adaptation made by the new group. Meeks enumerates several points of similarities between the voluntary association and the Pauline churches:

(1) Both promoted personal interaction between the members whose membership was not regulated by any fixed standards like race, rank, and so on.

(2) Both gave importance to the cultic rituals.

(3) Both were to a great extent patronized by the rich members. Nevertheless, Meeks maintains that the Pauline churches were exclusivistic "supplanting all other loyalties"[23] but were quite inclusive in terms of including peoples of vast difference in social status. The story remains the same with regard to the Jewish synagogues and the schools (Philosophical and Rhetorical).

Although, the former reflects certain similarities with the church – like, a sense of belonging to a larger group i.e. Israel; meeting in private houses though by the time of Paul's mission in Greek cities Jews already possessed buildings for corporate gatherings and functions; and the system of internal adjudication of internal disputes which Paul appears to have encouraged to be practised within the church in Corinth – it differed in the use of terms defining the functions and criteria used for granting membership (e.g. circumcision). Moreover, women had a greater role within the church compared to that in synagogues. Hence, Meeks concludes that "[t]he vehemence with which Paul and the other leaders of his circle closest to him combat that position suggests that for them some other conception of the community was operative, one not directly derivable from the experience of the synagogues."[24] The importance of the latter proposal, the school, is argued to be based on the tactical representation of the church posturing as a community of the intellectuals in order to evade Roman suspicion and reprisal.[25]

Hence, in the light of such a complex state of *ekklesia* as a nascent social entity, Meeks states, in the private homes "[it] is not easy to define it or to specify its newness. It was all the old things that observers in the first century might have seen in it...[y]et it was more than the sum of those things, and different from the mere synthesis of their contradictory tendencies."[26] In this line, Adams concludes surveying the post-seminal study by Meeks with a warning that the data relating to the social institution of the Greco-Roman world presented by the scholars are "not value free" and are conditioned by the shifting sand of modern archaeological discoveries and new knowledge flooding the intellectual discussions.[27] To add, he maintains that "[s]cholarly discussion of analogies to Paul's churches has often been based on a generalized view of 'Pauline Christianity'" and continues saying "it seems to me that more careful distinctions need to be made when handling the Pauline evidence."[28] In the light of the prevailing complexities, he proposes the future course of studies in the field must pay attention to the difference between "the *ekklesiai* as Paul would like them to be and the *ekklesiai* as they really were…and also between the *ekklesiai* as their members viewed and understood them and the *ekklesiai* as they were perceived and categorized by outside observers."[29]

Thus, in the remainder, an attempt shall be made only to study the characteristic features of the *ekklesia* in the vision of Paul and not to portray the actual picture of the Christian *ekklesia* as it was during the time of Paul. It is neither to investigate how the early Christians perceived themselves because the window to the required data for us is primarily Paul's own letters. In addition, to know how the outsiders must have perceived the early Christian *ekklesia* would be beyond the scope of the present study.

2. *Ekklesia* in the Pauline Corpus: An Overview

Within the Pauline corpus, the term ἐκκλησια is used in two important ways: (i) referring to the one universal Church of God (e.g., Gal. 1:13; 1 Cor. 10:23, 12:28, 15:9; Phil. 3:6; Eph. 1:23, 5:23 cf. Mt. 16;18) and (ii) referring to local Christian communities (e.g., Rom. 16:1, 23; 1 Cor. 1:2, 16:19; 2 Cor. 1:1; 1 Thess. 1:1; 2 Thess. 1:1; Col. 4:15-16; Gal. 1:1, 22). Interestingly, for Paul, the local church is as authentic body of Christ as the universal Church. Dunn maintains that "Paul's usage was drawn directly from Israel's self-identity. *Ekklesia* occurs about 100 times in the LXX where the underlying Hebrew is principally *qahal*, 'assembly.' Most notable are the phrases *qahal Yahweh* or *qahal Israel*."[30] Substantiating his position Dunn enumerates three arguments: (i) he often talks of the 'assembly of the Lord' (i.e. Christ); (ii) the use of *ekklesia* does not suggest a "polemical antithesis against the synagogue; and (iii) the direct use of 'the church(es) of God' without any qualification or scriptural evidences attests its non-polemical use in his writings.[31] However, L. T. Johnson maintains that probably to Paul it also meant a discontinuity with the past Jewish understanding. For him, the three elements from Paul's personal experience add an element of discontinuity from its Jewish background to it: (i) as an ex-persecutor of the Church of God on the basis of Deut. 21:23, he now recognizes that God is capable to act apart from dictates of the Torah, (ii) Paul now understands resurrection of Jesus as an eschatological event of 'new creation,' and (iii) the Jewish opposition to his mission to the gentiles, like he did earlier, proves then that "there is some real rupture within

God's people that must be reconciled. For Paul, then, the relationship between the church and Israel is not simply a matter of continuity or of discontinuity; it must rather be seen in terms of a dialectic within history."[32] Interestingly, it is this dialectic within history – not limited to the Jewish past in a narrow sense but also to include the larger Greco-Roman socio-cultural, economic-political context – that will prove to be vital in developing the vision of Paul for the *ekklesia* of God.

Paul employs several images and metaphors for "the assembly of God" which shed light on his vision for the church. Basically, for him, church is the family of God. In Gal. 1:1, Paul addresses God 'Father' of whom Jesus is the firstborn (Rom. 8:29). He is "the firstborn among many brethren" implying the status of God's children extended to all the believers in the church. In fact, it is extended to the believers by their adoption through "the Spirit of adoption" (Rom. 8:15). Interestingly, the composition of 'the family' is not ethnically defined as Jews would rather understand it based on one's biological connection with Abraham. Paul draws the family bond among the believers in the *ekklesia* based on their faith in Christ (Gal. 3:7). It is this fact that makes the church of God a multi-ethnic, multi-lingual, multicultural, and multi-national. The membership into the community is opened to all, who now share in the rich blessings promised by God to Abraham (Rom. 11:17). Moreover, God puts his seal to it by pouring out His Spirit upon *all* equally (cf. Gal. 3:1-5).

The theme of mutual belonging, unity, growth, and participation, are further elaborated by the metaphor "the body of Christ" (Rom. 12:4-5; Col. 1:18; Eph. 4:12). "Although it derives from Greco-Roman politics rather than Torah, Paul's use of it is distinctive. In this metaphor, the church is the body of the Messiah. The metaphor of the body combines the sense of a living organism and an articulate, many-membered structure."[33] Paul says that each member has important function(s) to fulfil in the body of Christ (Rom. 12:6). In 1 Cor. 12:12-27, Paul underlines the fact that the body is one though members are diverse, a unity in diversity. The expression "so also is Christ" in 1 Cor. 12:12, maintains Schreiner, signifies that "Christ, not the church, has priority. The fundamental reality in the people of God is Christ, not the diversity of gifts. Paul wants the Corinthians to take their eyes off their so-called dazzling gifts and focus on Christ."[34] In the later writings, Christ is the head (*kephale*) of the body (Eph. 1:22-23; 4:15-16; Col. 1:18; 2:19) which emphasizes the lordship of Christ over the church and the source of imparting growth to the body (Col. 2:19). He is said to rule over the church (Eph. 1:19-23). Similar theme embedded in the idea of the church as "the body of Christ" is communicated by the metaphor of the church as a building "built upon the foundation of the apostles and prophets with Christ Jesus Himself being the corner stone" (Eph. 2:20).

Another important metaphor employed by Paul for the church is "the temple of God" (1 Cor. 3:16-17) which in gospel traditions (Mt. 26:61 and Lk. 1:9) refers to the Jerusalem temple. In contrast to the Jewish temple, Paul does limit God's dwelling to any particular physical structure but considers the individuals and the collection of individuals in the church as the new dwelling place of God. In the Greco-Roman world such an innovation must have been frowned at but "[t]he newness of the gospel emerges at this very point."[35] Now "[a]ccess to God is available not through some cultic process but through faith in Christ (Rom. 5:2). ... In God's new temple Jews and Gentiles are no longer alienated from one another but are equal members of the same house."[36]

With these preliminary remarks about Paul's understanding of the church, we shall make an attempt in the remainder to critically explore the important features of Paul's vision of the *ekklesia* of God. How does Paul understand the interrelationship between the believers in the church? Does his understanding, as may be read from his writings, imply a radical vision of a community practising equality, justice, and holiness? Is the church in Paul's thought adaptable to the environment while ushering God's rule among the nations?

3. The Vision for *Ekklesia* in the Pauline Corpus: *The Question of Adaptability with a Difference*

Richard Horsley in his article "1 Corinthians: A Case Study of Paul's Assembly as an Alternative Society" proposes that Paul envisioned the assembly of God he founded in the then Greco-Roman world, as an alternative society to the dominant world. He enumerates four ways in which Paul appears to do so: (i) The structure of the mission and the nascent household communities gathering as sub-assemblies of the larger body in the Roman Corinth and in the Province of Achaia reflects "a nascent social movement comprised of a network of cells." (ii) The communities are desired to be autonomous and diametrically opposite to the dominant Greco-Roman society practising ethical purity and social-legal justice independent of the established courts. (iii) The assemblies in Corinth were to cut-off "from participation in the fundamental forms of social (and economic) relations in the dominant society" (parenthesis added) like eating of food offered to idols in order to ensure their integrity and survival. (iv) The assemblies must practice economic relations dramatically different from the Greco-Roman exploitative power relations which were vertically structured patronage system. (v) The political-economic dimension of the emerging trans-local assemblies is based on the rationalization of reciprocity towards Israel which contrasts with the tributary political system practiced in the Roman political system.[37]

Horsley's reading of Paul's ecclesiology is very helpful but he does not discuss several other important features of his vision. For example, the equality of all, celebration of diversity in the assembly of God, the Christocentric economic mutualism and *koinônia,* and the *diakonia* are not sufficiently developed. He primarily focuses to elucidate how Paul imagined an overthrow of the existing order of dominant socio-political systems. In the remainder, four important aspects of Paul and his communities' vision are discussed.

3.1. 'Christ Model' Economic Mutualism

Evidences to adjudge an exact state of the economy of the early Pauline communities is difficult because of the scanty nature of the available data both within Paul's letter and from the archaeological evidences. However, the available pointers to the early Christian economic relationships within the letters of Paul, though their interpretation is disputed,[38] enable us to understand the internal ecclesial economy envisioned, its theological roots and the economic sharing practised by Paul and his communities. The dawn of the twentieth century witnessed an unprecedented proposal in the study of the early Christianity initiated by Deissmann. Thereafter, the economic status of the Pauline community received the centre stage of discussion which in recent decades have been broadly divided into two main groups: the Old and the New Consensus. While the former view represented by Adolf Deissmann, John Gager, Justin J. Meggitt, Steven J. Freisen, et al. maintains that the early Christians who joined the new religious movement were from the lower class (however, the poverty or economic status may be defined and analysed),[39] the latter group represented by Wayne A. Meeks, Gerd Theissen, E. A. Judge, et al. maintains that the early Christians were, generally, the high class urbanites. In recent years, the representatives of the Old Consensus group, Meggitt and Freisen, have questioned the complex evidences laid down by Meeks and others of the New Consensus camp with fresh evidences which cannot be brushed aside unnoticed. It is these studies that enable us to recognize better the rational, significance, and relevance, of the robust economic mutualism practised within the Pauline community.

A critical re-evaluation of the New Consensus prevalent among the New Testament scholars by Justin Meggitt proves the sacrificial economic practises of the Pauline communities. Insistently arguing against those who argue in favour of individuals and groups within the Pauline communities from elite/noble social segment, Meggitt maintains that "[t]he Pauline Christians *en masse* shared fully the bleak material existence which was the lot of more than 99% of the inhabitants of the Empire."[40] He argues that they have either over-simplified or overlooked complex social facts in interpreting the so-called 'explicit' and 'implicit' literary evidences within the letters of Paul such as 1 Cor. 1:26, 4:10; 1 Cor. 8 and 10 in order to explain the social location (affluent and poor) of the warring groups/individuals.[41] More of our interest from his study is his proposal that "[a] number of different economic relationships were practised amongst the members of the apostle's churches within this subsistence context...(which were) αὐτάρχεια, almsgiving, hospitality, and 'mutualism'."[42] Of these all, mutualism is "by far the most prominent in the letters of the apostle and seem most clearly related to the specific conditions that his communities faced."[43] He defines 'mutualism' as "the implicit or explicit belief that *individual and collective well-being is attainable above all by mutual interdependence.*"[44]

To him, this Christian economic mutualism is most explicitly visible in Paul's collection of monetary assistance to the impoverished Jerusalem believers, the collection project of Paul because: (1) "it was aimed at promoting *material well being*" and (2) "it was thoroughly *mutual* in its character."[45] In fact, he argues, it was not merely their socio-economic practice but for the Christians occupying the subsistence level of social location "it performed the valuable function of a *survival strategy*…(which) *is a coping mechanism whereby a person living close to subsistence attempts to ensure adequate access to the necessities of existence*. It may take the form of a conscious and calculated action directly and clearly related to need…. It provided a means whereby individuals in precarious economic circumstances could attain some measure of material stability."[46] Such an economic interdependence is unique to Paul's communities and has no exact parallel among the then Greco-Roman *collegia*.[47] In other words, such a survival strategy of Christians reflects their social responsibility practised consciously within the community. It was an in-house economic mechanism of supplying material needs of the less fortunate members.

Now, such a conclusion might seem to some standing at odd with Paul's use of terms reflecting Greco-Roman patronage system. In Gal. 6:9-10, Paul exhorts his audience to undertake their 'in-house' social responsibilities enthusiastically. Paul states, "Let us not lose heart in doing good…. So then, while we have opportunity, let us do good to all people, and especially to those who are of the household of the faith." The significance of Paul's words are greater if read in line with Meggitt's conclusion. Paul's vision of a growing community of believers, although at the lower end of the economic pyramid, is that they are called to share not from their plenty but from their scanty resources. Unlike the rich patrons in the Greco-Roman world who ceased opportunities of benefaction to further their social status/honour by increasing the number of clients, the Galatian Christians are called to take-up the role of benefactors to all, especially to the fellow believers, for they will be divinely rewarded in the eschatological time. The principle of Christian socio-economic ethics taught by Paul here is best exemplified by the churches in Macedonia, who having known the poverty of the saints in Jerusalem acted of "their own accord" (2 Cor. 8:3). Paul says, they begged "with much urging for the favour of participation in the support of the saints" (2 Cor. 8:4).

Interestingly, this Christian economic mutualism was shown beyond the expectation of the apostle (2 Cor. 8:5). They gladly seeking the opportunity to do good to those of the household of faith, being indifferent to their own affliction and acute poverty, participated liberally in Paul's collection project (2 Cor. 8:2). Paul encourages the Corinthians that such act of liberality is truly mutual as "at this present time your abundance being a supply for their need, so that their abundance also may become a supply for your need, that there may be equality" (2 Cor. 8:13). In the Pauline tradition when the principle of 'Christ model' economic mutuality was found violated, stern dictate was given saying: "if anyone is not willing to work, then he is not to eat, either. ...some among you...doing no work at all...such persons we command...to work in quite fashion and eat their own bread. *But as for you, brethren, do not grow weary of doing good*" (2 Thess. 3:10-13 emphasis added). Evidently, even if these words did not originate personally from the pen of Paul, the veracity of such teachings was not doubted. At least, the author of the letter felt it not at odd with the earlier teachings and practice of Paul (2 Thess. 3:8-9).

If, in general, Meggitt's conclusion that Paul and his communities occupied the lower strata of the poverty scale is acceptable, then the question is: does there exists a correlation between their belief and a vibrant economic practice of mutualism within Paul's communities? Meggitt observes:

> [T]he enmeshment of the theme of economic mutuality in the theological, and in particular Christological, language of the community, also gave substantial weight to this form of exchange relationship. The theme of mutualism was inseparably bound up with Paul's participationist, corporate, Christology. ... A similar notion is found in the recurring Pauline theme of koinwni>a – the believer's fellowship with Christ also presumes fellowship with others.[48]

While Miggett's observation is coherent with the larger Pauline Christological teachings, it overlooks the idea of grace pre-eminently embodied in Christ. In other words, the economic mutualism envisioned by Paul draws on his Christological understanding i.e. the 'Christ Model' economic mutualism. To him, it lies very intimate to the practice of Christian mutualism taught and exhorted by Paul. He exhorts the Corinthians to abound in this gracious work (2 Cor. 8:7) which is succinctly modelled by Christ in his incarnation. Reminding it, Paul says in 2Cor. 8:9: "the grace of our Lord Jesus Christ, that though He was rich, yet for your sake He became poor, so that you through His poverty might become rich."

The significance of the gracious act, here, is not merely drawn from the image of Christ emptying himself i.e. He being rich/divine becoming poor/human for their sake (Phil. 2:6-7), but His readiness to make us rich (2 Cor. 8:9). It is such readiness on the part of the Macedonian churches in participating to contribute to the well-being of the saints in Jerusalem that Paul appreciates. He terms it as the grace of God given to them (2 Cor. 8:1).[49] In fact, it is not the size of the amount contributed rather the readiness to share from the frugal resources at hand. Paul categorically affirms it to the Corinthians saying that the readiness shown one year back (2 Cor. 8:1) in contributing towards the Jerusalem fund has to be completed "by your ability" (2 Cor. 8:11) because "it is acceptable according to what a person has, not according to what he does not have" (2 Cor. 8:12 cf. Mk. 12:41-44; Lk. 21:1-4).

3.2. Pneumatic Community of Equals

The role of the Holy Spirit in the formation of the community in Christ is central to Paul. He assumes the existence of a believer by faith in Christ as a life lived and walked "by the Spirit" (Gal. 5:25 cf. Rom. 8:13). For him, the Christian communities founded trans-geographically across the regions he traversed, both founded by him or by other gospel preachers, share equally in the life in the Spirit. More importantly, in Rom. 8:9, Paul claims that "if anyone does not have the Spirit of Christ, he does not belong to Him." In fact, the indwelling of the Spirit within a believer as the evidence of his/her belonging to Christ is parallel to Christ in us as the proof of the Spirit alive in us (Rom. 8:9-10). This close association between the two exemplifies the significance of being possessed by the Holy Spirit in defining the identity of a Christian community/individual "as one who has the Spirit of Christ."[50] What is "implied is that possession of the Spirit is the common denominator of all who belong to Christ, not the special prerogative of some over against the rest."[51]

This commonly shared life and the entire activity of every individual or community, as one belonging to Christ, take place in the sphere of the Holy Spirit which characterizes the life and existence of the community. According to Andrew Chester, "Just as the individual receives the Spirit at baptism, so also the community is correspondingly characterized by possession of the Spirit. Paul simply assumes this to be the case (e.g. Gal. 3.27), and sees it as a wholly positive phenomenon (e.g. 1 Thess. 4.8; 5.19; 2 Thess. 2.13), a sign and anticipation of the new age that has already begun."[52] This Paul explicitly states rhetorically in Gal. 3. Pointing out to the actual agent involved in their conversion from the present evil age (Gal. 1:4), Paul questions the non-Jewish Galatian believers seeking salvation by the works of the Law in Gal. 3:4: "Having begun by the Spirit, are you now being perfected by the flesh?" Paul reaffirms the undeniable fact of the non-Jewish Galatians receiving the Holy Spirit at the beginning of their conversion, the evidence of their justification by faith, in Gal. 3:5 as the Jewish Christians who are not saved by their works of the law. This elementary fact about Christian life Paul also teaches his Roman auditors in Rom. 8:9. Paul exhorts his Roman auditors reminding them that they are "in the Spirit, if indeed the Spirit of God dwells" in them. Easley maintains that it is not "something only for mature or advanced Christians. Rather, 'being in the Spirit' is as elementary as to be synonymous with being a Christian."[53]

There are two important theological truths concerning the basic reality of Christian life connected with it which explain the role of the Spirit in forming equality of all within the community of God. They are: (i) the Holy Spirit residing within every individual/community grants intimacy with God to the latter (Gal. 4:6 cf. Rom. 8:14-17). Paul writes to the Galatian believers that

"God has sent forth the Spirit of His Son into our hearts, crying, 'Abba! Father!'" (Gal. 4:6 cf. Rom. 8:15). The fact now the Holy Spirit indwells the Galatian believers, for Paul, proves the change in their status as the children of God. Paul says, "Therefore you are no longer a slave, but a son; and if a son, then an heir through God" (Gal. 4:7 cf. Rom. 8:16-17). Their intimate relationship is based on their unique status as God's children (lit. "sons") and their rights as "heirs" of God's promises. Further, it is aptly evidenced in the cry of the Holy Spirit from within their heart, "Abba! Father!"

In the Jewish usage, '*Abba*' suggests intimacy with God because it "is the Aramaic diminutive for 'Father,' perhaps suggesting the overtones of the English word 'Daddy'. It was the word Jesus habitually used in his prayers to the Father and which he passed on to those who through him became God's children."[54] Kittel states that "[i]t is almost never used, however, in relation to God" but only in "the formula: 'My father, who is in heaven'" underlining the distance maintained between God and human.[55]

Jesus by using the term to address God (Mk. 14:36) "applies to God a term which must have sounded familiar and disrespectful to His contemporaries because used in the everyday life of the family. In other words, He uses the simple 'speech of the child to its father'."[56] Its significance to the non-Jewish Galatian Christians is that as members of pneumatic community, whose life and activity is characterized by the Holy Spirit, they have an intimate relationship/access to God the Father like the Jewish Christians.

Second, while the Spirit establishes an intimate relationship between God and humans, reciprocally every individual/ community of God becomes the bearer of God through the indwelling presence of the Holy Spirit (1 Cor. 3:16-17, 6:19 cf. Eph. 2:22). Paul reminds the Corinthian believers twice repeatedly asking, "Do you not know that you are a temple of God and that the Spirit of God dwells in you?" (1 Cor. 3:16 cf. 6:19).

Interestingly, Paul employs the term naov at two levels – at a macro level, the whole community, church, and at a micro level, an individual Christian – without any differentiation. At first, on the one hand, naov in 1 Cor. 3:16-17 refers to the Corinthian church, the congregation of persons. It is the community of God among whom God finds his new residence as a holy place.... Secondly, on the other hand, 1 Cor. 6:19 specifies the physical body of a spirit-filled Christian as the dwelling place of the Spirit.[57]

Paul by terming the body of a Christian and the local community of God in Christ "temple" not only underlines the indwelling presence of God but also displaces the temple/tabernacle in the Old Testament as the locale of God's Holy presence. It, in fact, renders the Jerusalem temple redundant as a place of meeting God. Such a subversive act of God is sustained throughout the history, from the first century CE to the present, by the constant presence of the Holy Spirit within every believer/local church. In other words, the pneumatic community of God trans-historically and trans-geographically bears God's presence to all beyond every form of polarity that divide human race based on class, gender, ethnicity, race, etc. It is the community of all bearing divine presence daily, united in Christ, and nurtured by His care as the Abba! Father!

It is these who are brought into intimate relationship with God the Father and are made into the dwelling place of God's presence by the Holy Spirit, Paul says, are given "the gifts of the Spirit" (the spiritual gifts) and "the fruit of the Spirit." Concerning the former, in 1 Cor. 12:4, Paul speaks about the variety of gifts by the same Spirit as parallel to variety of ministries but the same Lord in v.5. The list of spiritual gifts enumerated in 1 Cor. 12:8-10 are given to all the members of the body of Christ by the one Spirit (1 Cor. 12:12-13).

The diversity of gifts is united in the one Spirit who gives them all to the church. Paul maintains that it is with the purpose of the common good (1 Cor. 12:7) that it is given to the pneumatic community of God. Highlighting this unity beyond functional diversity of gifts within a community as the challenge of diversity, Skaggs in her Presidential address at the *Society for Pentecostal Studies* in 1999, entitled "The Challenge of Diversity: Chaos or Community," observes that the unity beyond diversity in the Spirit is not "unanimity," "uniformity," or "union." Instead, the pneumatic community of equals empowered by the spiritual gifts must become "a rich tapestry of colours, a mosaic of images, a community of each part contributing to the whole."[58] Succinctly put in Andrew Chester's words,

> [f]or Paul, the community should exhibit gifts of the Spirit in abundance, as a clear correlative of possessing the Spirit. Paul's vision is in no sense narrow here: there is a wide variety of gifts, and all are potentially valuable. ... Paul's vision if the community sees spiritual gifts being used to the full, both for the mutual benefit of the community internally and also for the propagating of the Gospel and allowing the community to extend itself and its message to the world around.[59]

While the gifts of the Spirit form the external manifestations of the indwelling presence of the Holy Spirit, "the fruit of the Spirit" (Gal. 5:22-23) "epitomizes Paul's vision of what the Christian community and its true character should be."[60] Guthrie maintains that the term *karpos* in singular form reflects that all the virtues together form a corporate whole, not independent of each other, implying "an organic relationship" which requires "the fertilizing activity of the Spirit to bring out its full development."[61] In other words, "[t]he Spirit, in short, dictates what attitudes are desirable in the kingdom in its present form."[62] In Paul's words, it is "walk by the Spirit" (Gal. 5:16). Paul's exhortation is apt to the conflicting Galatian believers[63] who are exhorted to bear the fruit of the Spirit. Paul maintains that the Galatians' life in the Spirit (cf. Gal. 3:1-5) requires them to "walk by the Spirit" without which they are deemed to prove that they do not belong to the pneumatic community of equals in Christ.

3.3. Koinônia in Christ by Celebrating Differences

Another important aspect of Paul's vision of the *ekklesia* is encapsulated in a difficult word to translate, *koinônia*. The noun *koinônia* and its cognates are derived from the verb κοινωνεω of which the root stem is κοιν-. It is always used in a situation where something is shared commonly among two or more people. According to Schattenmann, "[i]n the Gk. and Hel. world *koinônia* was a term which meant the evident, unbroken fellowship between the gods and men. Even Philo spoke of 'the sublime fellowship [of Moses] with the father and creator of the universe (*Vit. Mos.*,

1,158)."[64] It was also a business term in the secular Greek which was used for business partners.[65] However, in New Testament, it is not "equated with *societas*, companionship or community. It is not a parallel to *ekklesia* and has nothing to do with the local congregation. Nor does it correspond with the Jewish *ḥᵃḇûrâh* (fellowship, union). It is not, as in the Stoa, a group of individuals united by a common idea. Hence, *koinônia* is to be sharply distinguished from both Gk. idea and Judaism."[66] According to Betty Jane Lillie, this common participation "is well adapted to express inner relationship."[67] J. Y. Campbell in his important study observes that "the primary idea expressed by κοινωνος and its cognates is not that of association with another person or other persons, but that of participation in something in which others also participate."[68] Campbell argues citing large number of evidences from the non-Christian writings that it appears generally with a genitive of the thing shared, though in some occasions it also appears with a dative of the person. He states that "[t]his marked infrequency of the dative of the person as compared with the genitive of the thing is further proof that the idea of 'participation in something' is the primary case."[69]

What is the meaning of *koinônia* in the New Testament? In the New Testament, it is Paul's typical style of writing and mostly appears in the Pauline writings in phrases expressing ones relation to Christ through faith. Jeffery Kloha's suggestion is helpful in this regard. He maintains that *koinônia* in the New Testament is used "to describe *the entire event, the totality of all* the elements" i.e., the thing shared in common, the co-participants, and the act of participation together creating a situation and relationship. In other words, "it is the manifestation of the relationship that exists between people who share together in a common thing."[70] It has both vertical (i.e. with Christ) and horizontal (i.e. with other humans) dimensions in which the former is primary and the latter is derived "from the vertical relationship, and can be understood in connection with it."[71] This is evident in Paul's use of the term with an allusion to the Eucharistic table.

In 1 Cor. 10:16, Paul uses *koinônia* with a strong Eucharistic language with twin purposes: (i) in order to refrain them from idolatry, and (ii) to remind them of their testimony of unity in the blood and body of Christ with one another shared by participating in the Eucharistic table. The *koinônia* taught by Paul is their participation 'in Christ' which is the commonly shared thing/space by all. It is this reality that is Paul counts paramount for a Christian *koinônia*. For him, it is initiated by God who calls the Corinthian believers "into fellowship with His Son, Jesus Christ our Lord" (1 Cor. 1:9). Paul sees no other common thing among the Christian believers that can replace her/his life 'in Christ.' Even in expressions like "participation in the gospel" (Phil. 1:5) or "fellowship of your faith" (Philm. 6), the centrality of the Christ event and the resultant communion of believers in Him by faith are retained. Anybody who partners in any other sacrifice other than that of Christ upon the cross is partnering with demons (1 Cor. 10:21). To put it in explicit terms, for Paul *koinônia* practised within the church is firmly Christological in nature. It is founded in Christ and assumes the character of Christ in every respect.

What does *koinônia* in Christ entail? The *koinônia* in Christ entails sharing of burden with others like poor saints in Jerusalem (2 Cor. 8-9), sharing spiritual and economic things[72] with those who teach God's word (Gal. 6:6), etc. Further, following the trail of passages where the term *koinônia* appears, one comes across the words of Paul to Philemon regarding his future course of behaviour towards his Christian brother and Paul's "begotten in imprisonment" (Philm. 10). The prayer of Paul for Philemon is that his "fellowship of faith," i.e. his love and faith about which Paul has heard, "may be effective through the knowledge of every good thing" in him for Christ's sake (Philm. 6). However, later Paul exhorts Philemon concerning another "proper" thing (Philm. 8) which he desires the latter to do out of his own goodwill (Philm. 14) and partnership with Paul (Philm. 17) towards Onesimus. Paul desires Philemon to accept Onesimus, his ex-slave, "no longer as a slave, but more than a slave, a beloved brother" (Philm. 16). This is important for Philemon to make his fellowship of faith effective. However, such a fellowship of faith entails a radical subversion of social status, a breaking down of walls (social, economic, ethnic, etc.) that undergird social domination and naturalize hierarchic relationship. Philemon ought to accept Onesimus as "a beloved brother," "both in the flesh and in the Lord" (Philm. 16) as now his slave too participates with him in the eating of the body and drinking of the blood of Christ Jesus. Such a radicalization of relationship by participation in Christ Paul succinctly states in Gal. 3:28: "There is neither Jew nor Greek, there is neither slave nor free man, there is neither male nor female; *for you are all one in Christ Jesus*" (emphasis added).

Does it imply that the socio-economic, cultural-ethnic differences are redundant and non-existent? Paul's position is ambivalent. On the one hand, 'yes' for it does not define ones' being in Christ except that he or she is a brother or sister in Christ. But on the other hand, 'no' because Paul honours Philemon's right over his (ex-)slave, now a Christian, and hopes Onesimus to serve his master forever (Philm. 15). To put it straight, now differences are celebrated 'in Christ,' not as earlier done without one 'being in Christ' but with due cognizance that both master and slave, Jew and Greek, male and female, the *varnas* and the *avarnas*, have equal *koinônia* 'in Christ.' They *all* in an unrestricted and unreserved manner participate in the rite of eucharist testifying unity and common share 'in Christ,' the fellowship of faith. It is truly a "fellowship of His suffering" (Phil. 3:10) that Paul experienced by denying his privileges for the sake of Christ apart from the physical and mental suffering he bore to build a community of *koinônia* 'in Christ' beyond geographical, ethnic, political boundaries. Similar was the suffering that Christ Jesus bore upon the colonial cross under the forces of this world that naturalized an unjust order of oppression and exploitation (politically by Romans) and denied 'other' their status as the bearers of the image of God (religiously by Jewish elites). Paul envisioned of the *ekklesia* as a community of those who participated (*koinônia*) in Christ without valorising relationships.

3.4. Modelling Diakonia in the Early Ekklesial Structure in the Pastoral Letters

The call to the followers of Jesus to serve others, *diakonia*, is not unique to any section of the New Testament or group of people mentioned within the Bible. "It is the favourite way of referring inclusively to the church's fundamental activities."[73] However, in the later centuries and the ecclesial writings, it came to be used as an official nomenclature to an office within the Church. This is, especially, true in the case of the Pastoral letters where it appears along with the term *episcopos* referring to an office within the church (1 Tim. 3:1 cf. 3:8, 12). It is unclear that to what extent the two 'offices' were mutually exclusive and what type of precise function(s) these ecclesiastical officials performed. To add, it is difficult to have an unqualified acceptance of the existence of such well-recognized offices within the church in Ephesus as early as 65 CE, though 1 Tim. 3 seems to mention the *episcopos* and *diakonoi* as two established offices. In the ecclesiastical tradition, the "deacons" were/are thought to be subordinate to the "overseer" which is a subjective deduction from the context.

The author of *the First Letter to Timothy* himself does not make any such direct injunction regarding it. In fact, if Timothy was the pastor of the church in Ephesus, then *episcopos* (1 Tim. 3:1), a singular form, should not be read against the plural form of *diakonoi* (1 Tim. 3:8) to argue the hierarchical structure - one overseer assisted by many deacons - because Acts 20:28 speaks of "overseers" (plural) in the church of Ephesus. Similar is the case even in the church at Philippi where there were "overseers" and "deacons" (both in plural form, Phil. 1:1 emphasis added). Therefore, it is also probable that the *episkopos* and *diakonos* in 1 Tim. 3:1 and 8, respectively, represent a division of labour among the equals within the church than a hierarchy of "offices."

Remember, the term "office" is added by the Bible translators/ interpreters but not present in the Greek text itself (cf. 1 Tim. 3:1). Such a gross imposition of the later evidences from the history of the Church upon 1 Tim. 3 has lead to a narrow understanding of *diakonos* as an ecclesial office. Ironically, the term came to be used devoid of its real meaning 'servant' but as a synonym to an office of power and authority within the church tradition/ administration. If so, why, then, does the author of *the First Letter to Timothy* use the term *diakonos* to refer to the ministry of 'some'[74] within the church? Does the ecclesial nomenclature, *diakonos*, refer to an attempt to enmesh the ministry of "service" of the Church in her very organizational framework? What did the term *diakonia/ diakonos* refer to? What was its significance within the early Pauline community/communities?

The term *diakoneô* meaning 'to serve' is the verbal form of its noun derivative *diakonia* which is found thirty four times in the New Testament. The person who performs the act of *diakonia* is *diakonos*, "the one who serves at table."[75] Hence, the ministry of *diakonia* may be understood in relation to *diakonos*. Hess states that *diakoneô* in secular Greek could refer to three forms of services: "(a) to wait at table; this is expanded to (b) care for household needs, and from this to the general meaning (c) to serve generally."[76] However, these concentric circles of meanings contradicted with the fundamental Greek desire for individual's freedom or independence. While in the third sense it is fitting for a free man to serve the community for a cause, in the first sense of the term it was not considered to be worthy and honourable for a free man because it involved personal subjection. In fact, such a "voluntary giving of oneself in the service of one's fellow man" was "alien to Gk. thought."[77]

It is in this context that though the author does not employ a term suggesting greater servitude like *doulos* or *pais*, he still finds appropriate to use *diakonia*, a cognate of *diakonos*, a term related to 'servant theme' to refer to the activity of the ecclesial 'officials.' According to Edmond Hiebert, *diakonos* refers to "a servant in relationship to his activity." It refers to "the thought of voluntary service" with a "nearest approximation to the concept of a love-prompted service. Thus basically the word "deacon" denotes one who voluntarily serves others, prompted by a loving desire to benefit those served."[78] It is further substantiated, as Heibert maintains, that if the term *diakonos* is derived from another Greek term *diêkô*, then "the root idea is one who reaches out with diligence and persistence to render a service on behalf of others. This would imply that the deacon reaches out to render love-prompted service to others energetically and persistently."[79]

Does the conscious use of such a nomenclature in order to refer to an 'office' within the ecclesia imply a deeper understanding of it? The choice of the word in the New Testament writings is vital in several respects including its use as a probable pointer to the original intention of the then existing ecclesial office.[80] I consider it a reasonable assumption because, as mentioned earlier, even if these writings (including Ephesians and Colossians, the other disputed letters) bear the marks of hand(s) other than of Paul but accepts them as Pauline in composition, then a study of Paul's use of the term (and its cognates) in his letter, probably, would shed more light on the topic. Paul exceptionally uses the term *diakonos* apparently referring to an office in Phil. 1:1 but generally he uses it in a non-official sense. Paul used *diakonia* to refer to his own ministry to the non-Jews (Rom. 11:13) and calls himself a *diakonos* of the new covenant in 2 Cor. 3:6 (cf. 1 Cor. 3:5). In 1Tim. 1:12, Paul is thankful to Jesus Christ "because He considered me faithful, putting me into service (*diakonia*)" (Parenthesis added). In fact, he defines his entire preaching ministry as the '*diakonia* of reconciliation' (2 Cor. 5:18) and the collection of financial help to the saints in Jerusalem as a *diakonia* (cf. 2 Cor. 8-9). Paul does not restrict the use of it for himself and his own ministry. Instead, he uses it for his co-workers including Phoebe (Rom. 16:1; Col. 1:7; 4:7; Eph. 6:21). One must remember that it is this inclusive term that later came to be used for a particular office within the ecclesiatical tradition. Hence, it is reasonable to assume that, in the then context, it must have carried its basic meaning drawn from its use within the writings of Paul and his communities.

Bartling points out that in Eph. 4:11-13 *diakonia* is ambiguously used but "the three phrases in v.12 are to be regarded as parallel." For him, they explain the reasons for which Christ has given His servants to the church. They are: 'for the equipment of the saints,' and 'for the work of the ministry (*diakonia*),' and 'for building up the body of Christ.'[81] However, to him, if the *diakonia* refers to all believers, which he argues it is, then, "it refers to the mutual ministration of saints through deeds of love."[82] Thus, far Bartling's argument is acceptable. However, his later argument that since it is referring to the ministry of all the saints "it must be some secondary ministry that is meant"[83] is not convincing. Instead, in the Pastoral letter the basic understanding of the church as the community of saints serving mutually is concretized within the ecclesial structure. For example, Hiebert points out,

> "Paul sent Archippus a special message" 'Take heed to the ministry...which you have received in the Lord, that you may fufill it' (Col. 4:17)" implies that *"[t]he ministry Archippus was to*

perform was pastoral in function, but as a voluntary service for the spiritual benefit of the church it had the character of deacon service."[84]

It is the act which is important than the office, unlike as it was understood in the later ecclesia tradition. It is exactly this that Jesus desired to teach his disciples in the Upper Room in Jn. 13:1-17 by washing their feet. The Gospel traditions preserve Jesus' self-consciousness about his mission in the language of servitude: "For even the Son of Man did not come to be served but to serve, and to give His life as ransom for many" (Mk. 10:45). Elsewhere, Jesus taught his disciples desiring the place of prominence in the Kingdom of God saying, "whoever wishes to become great among you shall be your servant" (Mt. 20:26). Blinded to this underlining truth about the concretization of the basic idea of "service" as the purpose of the church in the world, quite mistakenly from the post-Pauline era to the present the term is/was predominantly used as referring to an ecclesial office.

Conclusion

In conclusion, the church that Paul envisioned was adaptable to the environment of the first century CE. Paul founded the commune of new converts throughout the Roman cities as they belonged to God and gathered together for performing cultic rite in the name of the Lord. It is evident from the sociological studies that the *ekklesia* of God adapted herself according to the then varied voluntary associations, synagogues, and philosophical and rhetorical schools. But the Christian *ekklesia* continued to exist with a difference in an ambivalent way. Paul envisioned the new found communes of God maintaining unity trans-geographically, trans-ethnically, and trans-culturally. He employed varied metaphors like the body of Christ, the temple of God, a building built on the foundation of the prophets and the apostles, to drive his point(s) home.

In fact, these theologically loaded metaphors extend basis for Paul's radical vision for the church. The church as an alternative society in the Greco-Roman world, Paul desired to be practising economic mutualism based on the model of Christ. It was the need of the nascent communities to support each other in the name of Christ as they belonged to the one body of Christ. The church as the pneumatic community of God, Paul envisioned, was to be a community of equals. Unlike the hierarchical order of the Greco-Roman society, the church was to practise equality of all as evident in the out pouring of the Holy Spirit by God. Hence, they ought to celebrate differences without valorising relationships based on unchristian polarizing practises of the world outside the church. It is to be visible in the *koinônia* in Christ. Finally, the *ekklesia* of God, coherent with the teachings of Jesus, has to be a community of servants and not office bearers with power and authority. Paul using the term *diakonos* for himself and his co-workers expressed the basic intent of it. However, the term was later used for specific office in the very structure of the early church which caused the narrowing down of its meaning in favour of a designate office. These are the ideals that Paul approved among his converts inspired by the Spirit of God which are authoritative even today for us to be practised.

Endnotes:

[1] Roy Bowen Ward, "Ekklesia: A Word Study," *Restoration Quarterly* 2, no. 4 (1958): 175.

[2] J. W. Roberts, "The Meaning of *Ekklesia* in the New Testament," *Restoration Quarterly* 15, no. 1 (1972): 28.

[3] Ibid., 29. See also, Ward, "Ekklesia: A Word Study," 165.

[4] Ward, "Ekklesia: A Word Study," 165.

[5] Ibid., 164.

[6] Roberts, "The Meaning of *Ekklesia* in the New Testament," 30f.

[7] W. Bauer, W. F. Arndt and F.W. Gingrich, *A Greek-English Lexicon of the New Testament and Other Early Christian Literature,* 2nd rev. ed. (Chicago: University of Chicago Press, 1957), 240.

[8] Ward, "Ekklesia: A Word Study," 166.

[9] Roberts, " The Meaning of *Ekklesia* in the New Testament," 29f.

[10] Derek Tidball, *An Introduction to the Sociology of the New Testament* (Exeter: Paternoster Press, 1983), 88.

[11] E. E. Ellis, *Pauline Theology: Ministry and Society* (Grand Rapids: William B. Eerdmans Publishing Company, 1989), 136.

[12] Bauer, Arndt and Gingrich, *A Greek-English Lexicon of the New Testament,* 700.

[13] Roberts, "The Meaning of *Ekklesia* in the New Testament," 31f; Ward, "Ekklesia: A Word Study," 166.

[14] Ward, "Ekklesia: A Word Study," 166-168.

[15] Roberts, "The Meaning of *Ekklesia* in the New Testament," 32.

[16] James D. G. Dunn, *Jesus, Paul, and the Gospels* (Grand Rapids: William B. Eerdmans Publishing Company, 2011), 168.

[17] Ibid.

[18] Wayne A. Meeks, *The First Urban Christians: The Social World of the Apostle Paul* (New Haven: Yale University Press, 1983), 74.

[19] Ibid., 74-84.

[20] Ibid., 84.

[21] Ibid., 74.

[22] Edward Adams, "First-Century Models for Paul's Churches: Selected Scholarly Developments since Meeks," in *After the First Urban Christians: The Social-Scientific Study of Pauline Christianity Twenty-Five Years Later*, eds. Todd D. Still and David G. Horrell (Edinburgh: T&T Clark, 2009), 60-78.

[23] Meeks, *The First Urban Christians*, 78.

[24] Ibid., 81.

[25] Ibid., 75-84.

[26] Wayne A. Meeks, *The Moral World of the First Christians* (Philadelphia: The Westminster Press, 1986), 119f.

[27] Adams, "First Century Models for Paul's Churches: Selected Scholarly Developments since Meeks," 77.

[28] Ibid.

[29] Ibid.

[30] James D. G. Dunn, *The Theology of Paul the Apostle* (Grand Rapids: William B. Eerdmans Publishing Company, 1998), 537.

[31] Ibid., 538.

[32] Luke Timothy Johnson, "Paul's Ecclesiology," in *The Cambridge Companion to St. Paul*, ed. J. D. G. Dunn (Cambridge: Cambridge University Press, 2003), 202.

[33] Ibid., 206.

[34] Thomas R. Schreiner, *Paul Apostle of God's Glory in Christ: A Pauline Theology* (Secunderabad: OM Books, 2001), 336.

[35] Ibid., 342.

[36] Ibid., 343.

[37] Richard A. Horsley, "1 Corinthians: A Case Study of Paul's Assembly as an Alternative Society," in *Paul and Empire: Religion and Power in Roman Imperial Society*, ed. Richard A. Horsley (Harrisburg, Pennsylvania: Trinity Press International, 1997), 245, 247.

[38] The interpretive complexities involved in the reading of socio-economic data traceable in the Pauline letters are discussed by many. For example, Bruce W. Longenecker, "Socio-Economic Profiling of the First Urban Christians," in *After the First Urban Christians: The Social-Scientific Study of Pauline Christianity Twenty-Five Years Later*, eds. Todd D. Still and David G. Horrell (Bloomsbury: T&T Clark, 2009), 36-59.

[39] Justin Meggitt is critiqued by Steven J. Friesen for his binary economic division of the Roman society. But as also critiqued by Bruce Longenecker Friesen too falls in the same trap even after attempting to present a very nuanced analysis of the early Christians economic status based on seven levels of the Poverty Scale. See, Justin J. Meggitt, *Paul, Poverty and Survival*, The Studies of the New Testament and its World (Edinburgh: T&T Clark, 1998); Steven J. Friesen, "Poverty in Pauline Studies: Beyond the So-called New Consensus," *Journal for the Study of the New Testament* 26, no. 3 (2004): 323-361; Bruce Longenecker, "Socio-Economic Profiling of the First Urban Christians," 44. John Barclay refuses to accept Friesen's claim to present a revolutionary study and terms it as standing "on Meggitt's shoulders." John M. G. Barclay, "Poverty in Pauline Studies: A Response to Steven Friesen," *Journal for the*

Study of the New Testament 26, no. 3 (2004): 363. However, Friesen received a broadly favourable response from Peter Oakes, "Constructing Poverty Scales for Graeco-Roman Society: A Response to Steven Friesen's 'Poverty in Pauline Studies," *Journal for the Study of the New Testament* 26, no. 3 (2004): 367-371.

[40] Meggitt, *Paul, Poverty and Survival*, 99.

[41] Ibid., 97-154.

[42] Ibid., 155 (Parenthesis added).

[43] Ibid., 157.

[44] Ibid., 158 (emphasis original).

[45] Ibid., 159.

[46] Ibid., 163-164 (emphasis original), see also 173-175.

[47] Ibid., 164-173.

[48] Ibid., 174. Based on such observations, Dale B. Martin maintains that "even though Meggitt does not use the language of 'correlation,' his work falls within the basic interests of other scholars, following Meeks, who proposes a correlation between patterns of life and patterns of belief." Dale B. Martin, "Patterns of Belief and Patterns of Life: Correlations in *The First Urban Christians* and Since," in *After the First Urban Christians: The Social-Scientific Study of Pauline Christianity Twenty-Five Years Later*, eds. Todd D. Still and David G. Horrell (Bloomsbury: T&T Clark, 2009), 127.

[49] Roji T. George, "Divine Grace in the Making of Paul, the *Yesu Bhakta*: Reclaiming the Role of Grace in the Self-Consciousness of Paul as a *Bhakta* in the Light of St. Tukaram's *Bhakti* Thought," *Bangalore Theological Forum* 45, no. 1 (2013): 86.

[50] James D. G. Dunn, *Word Biblical Commentary: Romans 1-8*, vol. 38A (Dallas: Word Book Publisher. 1988), 444.

[51] Ibid.

[52] Andrew Chester, "The Pauline Communities," in *A Vision for the Church: Studies in Early Christian Ecclesiology*, eds. Markus Bockmuehl and Michael B. Thompson (Edinburgh: T&T Clark, 1997), 107 (Parenthesis added).

[53] Kendell H. Easley, "The Pauline Usage of PNEUMATI as a Reference to the Spirit of God," *Journal of the Evangelical Theological Society* 27, no. 3 (September 1984): 305.

[54] James Montgomery Boice, *Expositor's Bible Commentary: Galatians*, vol. 10 (Grand Rapids: Zondervan Publishing House, 1976), 473, 474 n. 6. See also Thomas R. Schreiner, *Baker Exegetical Commentary on the New Testament: Romans* (Grand Rapids: Baker Books, 1998), 426.

[55] Gerhard Kittel, "ἀββα," in *Theological Dictionary of the New Testament Theology*, ed. Gerhard Kittel, trans. Geoffrey W. Bromiley, vol. 1 (Grand Rapids: William B. Eerdmans Publishing Company, 1964), 5.

[56] Ibid., 6.

[57] Roji T. George, "'Body Politics of Paul' in Corinth: Temple and the Rules of Purity in Constructing Identity in 1Cor. 5:9-13," *Bible Bhashyam* 37, no. 1 (2011): 83.

[58] Rebecca Skaggs, "The Challenge of Diversity: Chaos or Community," *Pneuma: The Journal of the Society for Pentecostal Studies* 21, no. 2 (Fall 1999): 174.

[59] Chester, "The Pauline Communities," 107.

[60] Ibid.

[61] Donald Guthrie, *New Testament Theology*, (Secunderabad: OM Books, 1992), 561.

[62] Ibid., 562.

[63] Notice the list of the vices mentioned under "the deeds of the flesh" includes terms of conflict like enmities, strife, jealousy, outburst of anger, disputes, dissensions, factions, envying, etc. (Gal. 5:19-21, 26).

[64] Johannes Schattenmann, "Fellowship," in *New International Dictionary of the New Testament Theology*, ed. Colin Brown, vol. 1 (Grand Rapids: Zondervan Publishing House, 1975), 639f.

[65] Betty Jane Lillie, "*Koinonia* in the New Testament: Integral Dynamic of the Christian Life," *Proceedings- Eastern Great Lakes and Midwest Biblical Societies* 28 (2008): 55.

[66] Schattenmann, "Fellowship," 643.

[67] Lillie, "*Koinonia* in the New Testament," 55.

[68] J. Y. Campbell, "KOINΩNIA and its Cognates in the New Testament," *Journal of Biblical Literature* 51, no. 4 (1932): 353.

[69] Ibid., 357.

[70] Jeffrey Kloha, "Koinonia and Life Together in the New Testament," *Concordia Journal* 38, no. 1 (2012): 26 (emphasis added).

[71] Lillie, "*Koinonia* in the New Testament," 56.

[72] cf. Campbell, "KOINΩNIA and its Cognates," 27.

[73] Walter J. Bartling, "A Ministry to Ministers: An Examination of the New Testament *Diakonia*," *Concordia Theological Monthly* 33, no. 6 (1962): 326.

[74] It does not refer to those who held the so-called church "office," but to all those who involved actively in the conducting of the church who were qualified according to the prescribed social and moral standards in 1 Timothy 3.

[75] K. Hess, "Serve," *New International Dictionary of the New Testament Theology*, ed. Colin Brown, vol. 3 (Grand Rapids: Zondervan Publishing House, 1978), 546.

[76] Ibid., 545. Cf. Hiebert points out that *diakonos* is used in both official and non-official sense within the New Testament. D. Edmond Hiebert, "Behind the Word 'Deacon': A New Testament Study," *Bibliotheca Sacra* 140, no. 558 (1983): 151-162.

[77] Hess, "Serve," 545.

[78] Hiebert, "Behind the Word 'Deacon'," 153.

[79] Ibid. Hiebert states that "[t]he derivation of this word διακονος is not certain. It has been held that the term is a compound of the preposition δια, meaning "through, " and the noun κονις, "dust, " so that the term denotes one who hurries through the dust to carry out his service. But this suggested derivation is not generally accepted today. More probably the verbal root was διηκω, "to reach from one place to another," akin to the verb διωκω, "to hasten after, to pursue."

[80] To me, it is improbable that in such a short duration of time a hierarchical order emerged within the church with a clear recognition of an office as in the modern times. However, quite ambiguously, *diakonia* was recognized as a legitimate expression of special call of God upon some in the church without limiting it to a few who belonged to the class of clergy in the early church.

[81] Bartling, "A Ministry to Ministers," 328.

[82] Ibid.

[83] Ibid.

[84] Hiebert, "Behind the Word 'Deacon'," 159 (emphasis added).

Chapter 7
Paul's Understanding of *Ekklesia* as a "Community of Believers": A Christian Ethical Perspective

Ajungla Jamir

In the highly religio-pluralistic context of India, the characteristic perversion of *ekklesia* in our time is growing to be more Christian individualism than corporate institutionalism. Especially, from the vague notion that Christian faith consists essentially in private piety and morality, not every Indian believers feels comfortable to join a visible Christian community and, indeed, remain isolated from it. Consequently, it is only natural that the search for relevant perception of Indian ecclesiology should come under greater scrutiny. It is in a context as this that we need to obtain a fresh understanding of what constitutes *community* and to argue that *ekklesia* is inherently communal in structure.

In order to do so, particular attention will be drawn to the interpretation of Paul's understanding of *ekklesia* as a community of believers in the light of the Christian ethical perspective.

1. Paul's Understanding of *Ekklesia* as a *Community*

The word *ekklesia* was not uncommon to Paul. In his letters, we find that Paul has specifically addressed to "the church of God in Corinth (1 Cor. 1:2; 1 Thess. 1:1), "the churches in Galatia" (Gal. 1:2), "the church of the Thessalonians" (1 Thess. 1:1). So also we find that Paul had made references to churches meeting in individual homes. In Romans 16:5, Paul greets "the church that meets at their house" (cf. 1 Cor. 16:19). In the Colossians, Paul writes, "Give my greetings to the brothers at Laodicea, and Nympha and the church in her house" (Col. 4:15). It is maintained that the letters of Paul has 46 occurrences of it while the term occurs elsewhere in the New Testament as well.[1]

According to Ridderbos, for Paul, there are three primary viewpoints for the understanding of *ekklesia* –

i. as the "whole church"(an eschatological reality that transcends space and time) as found in many instances in Ephesians and Colossians (cf. Eph. 1:22; 3:10, 21; 5:23-32; Col. 1:18, 24),

ii. the "local congregations" as pointed out in Corinthians and Galatians (cf. 1 Cor. 1:2; 2 Cor. 1:1; Gal. 1:22),

iii. the "religious gathering" (of the called out ones at individual houses) that is apparent in many of the letters of Paul (cf. 1 Cor. 11:18; 14:19, 28, 34, 35; Rom. 16:5).[2]

To be sure, Ridderbos explains,

> [I]t is in our view incontrovertible that from the beginning Paul in his epistles ascribes more than one meaning to the title *ekklesia*: next to that of the local (house-) church and church meeting also that of the church in general, the church in totality. The passages in Ephesians and Colossians (and 1 Tim. 3:15) are therefore not in conflict with the general usage of Paul, though it remains true that in Ephesians and Colossians *ekklesia* has the meaning almost exclusively of the church-in-general while elsewhere the majority of Paul's pronouncements concerning the *ekklesia* have reference to the local church or church gathering.[3]

The idea of the 'local church' or 'religious gathering' describes Paul's emphasis of the word *ekklesia* as a community of believers. According to Robert Banks, Paul's strong thematic emphasis on community is developed as a "fundamental theological theme in his proclamation of the gospel."[4] For Richard B. Hays,

> [T]he focus on community is a part of the gospel itself. How so? If we ask, "What is God doing in the world in the interval between resurrection and *parousia*?" the answer must be given, for Paul, primarily in ecclesial terms: God is at work through the Spirit to create communities that prefigure and embody the reconciliation and healing of the world. The fruit of God's love is the formation of communities that confess, worship, and pray together in a way that glorifies God (see, e.g., Rom. 15:7-13). Such communities are palpable signs of God's reconciliation of the world.[5]

In regard to Paul's vision of community, Hays further maintains that,

> It should not be forgotten that the community whose unity Paul passionately seeks is not the human community as a whole, nor is it a pluralistic community within the polis. Rather, it is always the particular community of the church. To be sure, Paul hopes for the ultimate triumph of God's grace over all human unbelief and disobedience (Rom. 11:32; Phil. 2:9-11). Consequently, he

> hopes for the final reconciliation of all humanity to God. Until that eschatological consummation, however, Paul speaks only to the community of faith. He articulates no basis for a general ethic applicable to those outside the church.[6]

There is no doubt that Paul was greatly concerned for believers to continue their gathering of themselves together. "[T]he community whose unity Paul passionately seeks is not the human community as a whole, nor is it a pluralistic community within the polis. Rather, it is always the particular community of the church."[7] Christian community thus can be defined as – a people called-out by God, who are as close to God, who belong to and with God, who are members of Christ and of each other, who assemble and are present to God through Christ – whose Eucharistic gathering is communion with Christ and with one another. The notion that *ekklesia* is inherently communal in nature is furthermore reflected in Bonhoeffer's word that "there is in fact only one religion from which the concept of community is essentially inseparable, and that is the Christian religion."[8]

Underlying the ethical factor in understanding the church as a community, Marshall Horton has contended that "Christian ethics are ethics of the church, for the church, by the church – the discipline *of* the Christian community, prescribed *for* it by its Lord, practiced *by* it under his guidance and inspiration."[9] To this, Hays adds,

> The community is the primary addressee of God's imperatives. If the biblical story focuses on God's design for forming a covenant people-as Paul believes it does, then the primary sphere of moral concern is not the character of the individual, but the corporate obedience of the church. Paul's formulation in Rom. 12:1-2 encapsulates the vision: ["Present your bodies (*somata*, plural) as a living sacrifice (*thysian*, singular), holy and acceptable to God, which is your spiritual worship. Do not be conformed to this world, but be transformed by the renewing of your minds, so that you may discern what is the will of God – what is good and acceptable and perfect]. The community, in its corporate life, is called to embody an alternative order that stands as a sign of God's redemptive purposes in the world. This is the concrete social manifestation of the righteousness of God. The coherence of Paul's ethical teaching comes into focus only when we understand that he is consistently formulating the ethical mandate in ecclesial terms, seeking God's will not by asking

> first, "What should I do?" but "What should we, as God's people, do?"[10]

In other words, the first act of *ekklesia* is the "gathering" or "assembling" of the church in Christ and the key questions for Pauline ethics must be formulated in ecclesial terms. *Ekklesia* of believers, then, is to carry out the ethical notion of community – for fellowship, worship, teaching, instruction and edification in a way that glorifies God. They ought not to be fragmented, isolated as individual components but assembling together in common faith and effort to carry out the great commission and to strengthen one another.

2. Paul's Images of *Ekklesia*

Out of the many images in the Pauline corpus, three in particular is taken into consideration which inherently relates the communal nature of *ekklesia*. For Paul, *ekklesia* is described as the "people of God", the "body of Christ", and the "temple of the Holy Spirit".

2.1. The People of God

The earliest and most inclusive image "people of God" is captured by two Hebrew words – *edah* and *qahal*. Both are translated variously as *assembly, congregation, meeting* or *synagogue*. While *edah* referred simply to a congregation itself, *qahal* emphasized the origins of a community, stressing a cause behind its assembling. For instance, we find *qahal* indicating "all the people of the community of Israel" "the whole assembled congregation of Israel" (Ex. 12:6 *NIV*) or "the assembly of the people of God" (Judg. 20:2 *NRSV*). Of particular significance are thirteen instances in the Old Testament of the phrase meaning the "congregation or community of the Lord" (for example, Num. 16:3, 20:4; Deut. 23:2-4, Micah 2:5, and 1 Chro. 28:8). The root from which *qahal* comes means "to summon." According to William Barclay, "[i]n the Hebrew sense it (*qahal*), therefore, means God's people called together by God, in order to listen to or to act for God."[11] *Qahal* is the word most consistently translated as *ekklesia* in the Septuagint. Both the Greek and Hebrew terms stressed the divine nature of the assembly, in contrast to the notion of people merely congregating on their own initiative. Indeed, Thomas Torrance says, "[w]hen the Christian Church came to refer to itself as the *ecclesia* it was claiming continuity with the *qahal* or the People of God under the old covenant."[12]

The concept "people of God" marks "Christianity's consciousness of being a new Israel related to, yet distinct from, the *qahal Yahweh*."[13] In fact, if Schnelle is right, "showing the unity of God's acts in history and the continuity of the people of God composed in salvation history is a central theme of Pauline ecclesiology."[14] It is thus especially important for Paul that *ekklesia* is seen to share the same faith as Abraham (Rom. 4:1-16; Gal. 3:6-18). The church has been chosen or called to be the people of God, just as God called Israel in the past. For Paul, the people of God is the *community* belonging to God. Hodgson and Williams contends that,

> The image [people of God] carries with it national, ethnic, and political connotations that are never entirely lost but are profoundly modified. Paul broadens it to universal dimensions without losing sight of the fact that it specifies a temporal, historical reality. The ecclesia is a people without national boundaries or a common language and ethnic identity.[15]

Paul's understanding of *ekklesia* as the "people of God" was to provide a *koinonia* (fellowship), a sense of community that transcends that which people can find in any other place. The image furthermore implies certain ethical characteristics. For instance, read some of Paul's admonitions: "pursue love and strive for the spiritual gifts" (1 Cor. 14:1), "live in love, as Christ loved us" (Eph. 5:2); "let each of you look not to your own interests, but to the interests of others" (Phil. 2:4); "as God's chosen ones, holy and beloved, clothe yourselves with compassion, kindness, humility, meekness, and patience. Bear with one another and, if anyone has a complaint against another, forgive each other; just as the Lord has forgiven you, so you also must forgive" (Col. 3:12-14); "bear one another's burdens, and in this way you will fulfill the law of Christ" (Gal. 6:2). God expected His people to be pure and sanctified. The holiness code in Leviticus potently expresses this expectation: "Speak to the entire assembly of Israel and say to them: 'Be holy because I, the Lord your God, am holy'" (Lev. 19:2; cf. 11:44-45 and 20: 7-8). The character of God establishes a radical standard for His people's identity. As Paul indicates, conformity to God's holiness is the believers' "spiritual act of worship" (Rom. 12:1). Such ethical principles relates the church to being a worshipping community.

2.2. The Body of Christ

It is likely possible that Paul might have coined the term "body of Christ".[16] He predominantly used it as an integral theological metaphor in his understanding of ecclesiology. Common understanding is that Paul used this image to signify both the church universal (Eph. 1:22-23) and of individual local congregations (1 Cor. 12:27).[17] However, critical speculations[18] on the metaphor shed new light to some pertinent questions: Where did Paul derived it from? Why did he used this term? What was his understanding of it?

For Dunn, Paul used the *body* as "a vital expression of the unity of a community despite the diversity of its members."[19] According to him,

> The image of the city or state as a body (the body politic) was already familiar in political philosophy – the famous fable of Menenius Agrippa being the best-known example. And Paul's exposition in 1 Cor. 12. 14-26 in particular closely echoes the concerns of the fable: that the unity of the state depended on the mutual interdependence of its diverse members being fully recognized. This suggested origin does not explain the qualifying Christ reference ("body in Christ," "body of Christ," "so is Christ"). But that is most obviously explained precisely as Paul's adaption of the more familiar and widely used secular metaphor. The Christian assembly is a body, like the secular body politic, but it is different precisely because of its distinctive and identifying feature is that it is the body *of Christ*.[20]

Goppelt also suggested similar view. According to him, Paul's concept of the church as a body goes beyond those uses of "body" as a social, corporate expression in Greco-Roman traditions, in which persons constitute a body through residence in a common *polis*. For Paul, the church is "the body of Christ."[21] Adding to this is the contention put forward by Hodgson and Williams that the body is an ethical and social metaphor for Paul and not an organic one. To them,

> The literal reference to the physical body of the crucified Jesus is already transfigured into a symbol of self-sacrifice and self-divestment rather than of self-fulfillment, which is the customary association of the term. To this is added a second level of meaning when the community of faith itself is described by Paul as the "body of Christ." It is so not in the literal sense of being an organic extension of the incarnation, but rather in the sense that the self-giving love of Christ (his "body," given for us) now defines and constitutes its unique communal structure; he lives on in it and is corporately embodied by it to the extent that it actualizes the sacrificial quality of his life.[22]

Dunn offers two plausible explanations for Paul's usage on the metaphor of the body of Christ – the sacramental usage indicated in 1 Corinthians 10 and 11 wherein the body character of the community seems to be already assumed. And the more elaborated body imagery of 1 Corinthians 12 (as also Rom. 12 and Eph. 4) seems to have in view the interactive relations of the worshiping community in general, and not simply a community focused on the sacrament. It is noteworthy that Paul here offers an 'alternative corporate imagery' for the people of God. Dunn explains,

> Paul shifts the corporate image of the Christian community from that of nation state (historic Israel) to that of body politic that is, from a community identified by ethnic and traditional boundary markers to one whose members are drawn from different nationalities and social strata and whose prosperity depends on their mutual cooperation and their working harmoniously together. The identity of the *Christian* assembly as "body," however, is given not by geographical location or political allegiance but by their common allegiance to *Christ* (visibly expressed not least in baptism and the sacramental sharing in his body). The implication is clear that only when that common allegiance is given primacy in mutual relations can the potential factional differences be transformed into the necessary mutual cooperation for the common good. This shift in identity factors and boundary markers, therefore, gives a different dynamic to the understanding of community, where the key distinguishing factor is a sense of mutual interdependence in Christ, expressed in a mutual responsibility one for another which manifests the grace of Christ.[23]

In distinguishing Paul's usage of *the body of Christ* from *Christ*, William Barclay expanded his concept as follows:

> If we take the phrase, the body of Christ, in its mystical sense, if we regard the Church as the extension of the Incarnation, then it does mean in some sense Jesus Christ is identified with the Church. With Paul that is not so; there is always a clear and definite distinction between Christ and the Church. Christ is the Saviour of the body (*Ephesians 5:23*). The Church is subject unto Christ (*Ephesians 5:24*). The body is the instrument through which the decisions and purposes of the head are carried out; the body is the agent of the head...The Church is the instrument, the agent, the weapon, the organism through which the purposes and the plans of Jesus Christ must be carried out...Herein is the glory of the Church, that the Church is the necessary instrument in the hands of Christ.[24]

The image of the body of Christ correspondingly accentuates the ethical interconnectedness between all the persons by their allegiance to *Christ* who make up the church (1 Cor.12). Each believer encourages and builds up the others. "We will in all things grow up into him who is the Head, that is, Christ. From him the whole body, joined and held together by every supporting ligament, grows and builds itself up in love, as each part does its work" (Eph. 4:15-16). Christian community is to be identified by genuine fellowship. This goes beyond merely social interrelatedness; it means an intimate understanding of one another. "If one part suffers, every part suffers with it; if one part is honored, every part rejoices with it" (1 Cor. 12:26). The early church shows this by sharing even material possessions among the members. Thus, a new kind of togetherness was felt by the people who joined the Christian community. Jews and Gentiles, men and women, were recipients of God's grace and sharers in the life and work of Christ. Slaves and freemen/women were joined together in a new way as equals in Christ. The accidents of race and nationality were transcended; in Christ, all these differences were overcome by the new man/woman in Christ.[25] It is in such understanding that Paul's usage of the metaphor "body of Christ" called for inclusiveness in the midst of diversity.

2.3. The Temple of the Holy Spirit

In the Pauline corpus, *ekklesia* as the true community of believers is further affirmed by the metaphor of the Christian community as a temple (*naos*),[26] seen as the "creative work of the Spirit".[27] In the New Testament sense, the church as the temple of the Holy Spirit refers to the Holy Spirit dwelling in the members of the church individually and as a community. Underlying the metaphor of the church as the temple of the Holy Spirit, Springett elaborates,

> The early Christians, following Christ's example, took a twofold attitude toward the Jerusalem Temple. They affirmed it on the one hand as the divinely appointed way to worship God, but they also believed in the superiority of Christ over the temple cultus. This transcending of the cultus by Christ is not viewed by His followers as an act of irreligion but as the intended culmination and fulfillment of divine history. Jewish eschatology pointed forward to a time when God would erect a new and glorious temple in which He would dwell (Isa. 28: 16). Primitive Christianity considers the prophecy as already fulfilled. The prophecy is spiritualized to the extent that the community itself is the promised temple of the last times, of the messianic age (1 Pet. 2:4-5).[28]

It is likely possible that on such basis and against such a background that Paul appeals to the Corinthians, "Do you [plural] not know that you are God's temple and that God's Spirit dwells in you [plural]? If anyone destroys God's temple, God will destroy that person. For God's temple is holy, and you [plural] are that temple" (1 Cor. 3: 16-17).[29] That the temple here refers to the Christian community rather than an individual is asserted by the use of the pronoun "you" and the verb "you are", both in the plural in this text.[30]

For Hays, "[t]o read this last sentence as though it spoke of the Spirit dwelling in the body of the individual Christian would be to miss the force of Paul's audacious metaphor: the apostolically founded community takes the place of the Jerusalem temple as the place where the glory of God resides."[31]

Paul referred to the Christian community by means of temple imagery to bring to light what the early Christians saw as a major understanding of the temple. According to Springett,

> In an important sense the temple represented a community filled with the Spirit of God and offering a true spiritual worship to God. Other allusions to temple in the NT bring this to view. The Christian is the temple, the priest and the sacrifice in the metaphorical language of the NT, "I appeal to you therefore,

> brethren, by the mercies of God, to present your bodies a living sacrifice, holy and acceptable to God, which is your spiritual worship" (Rom. 12: 1). This sacrifice and worship... is essentially one of ethical and moral considerations in the daily life of the Christian.[32]

Indeed, for Paul, the community (as the temple of the Holy Spirit) is the place where God dwells. "For we are the temple of the living God; as God said, 'I will live in them and walk among them, and I will be their God, and they shall be my people.'" (2 Cor. 6:16). When the community suffers division, the temple of God is dishonored. But the presence of the Spirit in the community produce unity rather than conflict. This unity is not uniformity, but a oneness in aim and action. The early church is described as being "one in heart and mind" (Acts 4:32). The Spirit created in them a strong ethical consciousness of membership in the community. So they viewed their possessions not as "mine" but as "ours." This understanding of the temple of the Holy Spirit as the communal context of the believers' life is of greatest importance for Paul's understanding of how the Christian is able to know what he/she ought to and ought not to do. The believer's life and action are always in, with, and for the fellow believers in Christ. For the Christian believers, moral action is a matter of choosing and doing what is good for one another and what will strengthen the bond of the whole community of believers.

3. Community of Believers: A Radical Democratic Assembly of Equals

The above understanding of Paul's ecclesiology connects with the in-born need of human being for sharing and intimacy, for fellowship, worship, teaching, instruction and edification which can take place only in a community. It tends to revive the ultimate basis of rich interpersonal relationships of love within warm, caring human communities. Paul's community-based *ekklesia* stress the activity and gifts of the Spirit in all the members, and the dependence of all on the contributions of each. It is democratic, since it accentuates the biblical-participatory images of the body of Christ, the people of God, and the temple of the Holy Spirit, all of which harmonize that the church is essentially a fellowship of believers, a shared communion (*koinonia*) of grace in Christ. The logic of democracy in this *ekklesia* is determined by the notion of equal opportunity (inclusiveness, oneness) among the diverse members of the Christian community. Such a logic of democracy requires a radical redistribution as well as the elimination of social and political hierarchies.

Ekklesia is not simply a community; it is fellowship in God and with God. Paul's understanding of the church is simply another way of expressing the depth of this fellowship: the people of God, the body of Christ, the temple of the Holy Spirit, etc. Christianity from the very beginning existed as a corporate reality, as a community. To be Christian meant to belong together with the community of believers in a 'togetherness' and 'fellowship' with one another.

This understanding is not to suggest that the above is all that there is to the *ekklesia* of Christ. It is to be taken as a good starting point for a biblical understanding of the church as a people called together to a kind of assembly – a community of believers for fellowship, worship, teaching, instruction and edification in a way that glorifies God. They ought not to be fragmented, isolated as individual components but assembling together in common faith and effort to carry out the great commission and to strengthen one another. Such vision seems to be a correction of much of the misrepresentation of *ekklesia* as Christian individualism. It is, therefore, a noble task for all the Indian believers to give a sober reflection to the kind of *ecclesiology* they understand today.

If Christian individualism only matters, there is little need of concern about the understanding of church as the people of God, the body of Christ, and the temple of the Holy Spirit, all of which emphasize that every believer becomes an integral part of a community of believers and makes a firm commitment to it. Christian individualism will never take the place of the gathered community of people who meet in the church and who strive for a visible and concrete alternative of building and strengthening the kind of community that gives substance to the claims of Christian faith that is rooted in Christ. *Ekklesia* is a corporate matter and the Christian life can be fully realized only in relationship to one another – a community of believers.

Endnotes:

[1] J. Roloff, "ἐκκλησια," in *Exegetical Dictionary of the New Testament*, vol. 1, ed. Horst Balz and Gerhard Schneider (Grand Rapids: William B. Eerdmans Publishing Company, 1990), 411.

[2] Herman Ridderbos, *Paul: An Outline of His Theology* (Grand Rapids: William B. Eerdmans Publishing Company, 1992), 328.

[3] Ibid., 330.

[4] Cited by Richard B. Hays, "Ecclesiology and Ethics: In 1 Corinthians," http://cpcnewhaven.org/documents/Ecclesiology%20and%20ethics.pdf (accessed January 16, 2014).

[5] Ibid.

[6] Ibid.

[7] Ibid.

[8] Cited by Julio R. Sabanes, "Biblical Understanding of Community," in *Man in Community: Christian Concern for the Human in Changing Society*, ed. Egbert de Vries (New York: Association Press, 1966), 169.

[9] Walter Marshall Horton, "The Christian Community: Its Lord and Its Fellowship; The Biblical Basis for Christian Ethics," *Interpretation* 4 (October, 1950): 387.

[10] *Ibid.*

[11] William Barclay, *New Testament Words* (London: SCM Press Ltd., 1964), 68.

[12] Thomas F. Torrance, "Foundation of the Church," in *Theological Foundations for Ministry: Selected Readings for a Theology of the Church in Ministry*, ed. Ray S. Anderson (Edinburgh: T. & T. Clark, Ltd., 1979), 202.

[13] Peter C. Hodgson and Robert C. Williams, "The Church," in *Christian Theology: An Introduction to Its Traditions and Tasks*, ed. Peter C. Hodgson and Robert H. King (Philadelphia: Fortress Press, 1982), 225.

[14] Udo Schnelle, *Apostle Paul: His Life and Theology*, trans. M. Eugene Boring (Grand Rapids: Baker Academic, 2003), 564.

[15] Hodgson and Williams, "The Church," 225. Emphasis added.

[16] It is in Paul's writings that we find the term used for the first time, and it is specifically in the Pauline corpus that the term is used in the New Testament. That the term was coined by Paul is also asserted by Rudolf Schnackenburg, *The Church in the New Testament* (New York: Herder & Herder, 1965), 77, and Hans Conzelmann, *An Outline of The Theology of the New Testament* (New York: Harper & Row, 1969), 263.

[17] The universal church: "God placed all things under his feet and appointed him to be head over everything for the church, which is his body" (Eph. 1:22-23). The individual local church: "Now you are the body of Christ, and each one of you is a part of it" (1 Cor. 12:27).

[18] Several speculations have been offered over the years, most of them too little to the point. Attempts have been made to derive the imagery from other aspects of Paul's thought such as from his Adam Christology, or in the 'in Christ' of Paul's mysticism, or the related but contrived concept of 'corporate personality,' or as an extension of Paul's concept of the Messiah and of the people of God, all of which were unsatisfactory in their explanation of how and why the imagery was chosen by Paul. Equally unsatisfactory is the suggestion that Paul derived it from the words of the heavenly revelation on the Damascus road, as given in the Acts accounts. In the

middle decades of the twentieth century a popular and much promoted view was that Paul derived the concept of the body of Christ from the Gnostic primal man [*sic*] myth (individuals as pieces of the body of the original heavenly man). But the quest for a pre-Christian Gnostic primal man [*sic*] has now almost entirely been abandoned on the ground that the earlier ideas were not really "Gnostic" (in the sense intended), and to describe them as "pre-Gnostic" is as helpful and as unhelpful as describing the medieval church as pre-Reformation. See James D. G. Dunn, *The Theology of Paul The Apostle* (Grand Rapids: William B. Eerdmans Publishing Company, 2006), 548-552.

[19] Ibid., 550.

[20] Ibid., 550f.

[21] Leonhard Goppelt, *Theology of the New Testament*, vol. 1 (Grand Rapids: William B. Eerdmans Publishing Company, 1981), 146f.

[22] Hodgson and Williams, "The Church," 225.

[23] Dunn, *The Theology of Paul The Apostle*, 551-552.

[24] William Barclay, *The Mind of St. Paul* (New York: Harper and Row, 1958), 247-248.

[25] Elmer G. Homrighausen, *I Believe in the Church* (Nashville: Abingdon Press, 1954), 83.

[26] The original meaning of the word "temple" *(hieron* or *naos)* indicated a place of sacrifice, or a building, or in the case of *naos,* a place where the god lived. The NT has spiritualized the terms to refer either to the individual Christian or to the Christian community as a whole. The spiritualization of cult places was not new in the Greek world of Paul's time. As far back as the sixth and fifth centuries BCE, Xenophon and Heraclitus had spoken out against sacrifices and images. Later writers of the Stoic persuasion such as Zeno, Cleanthes, and Aratus of Soli, reinterpret and spiritualize the cultus of Greek religion. For these writers, however, the world is the temple of God or the individual soul, but not the community as in Paul. See Ron Springett, "The Spirit and the Church," available from https://adventistbiblicalresearch.org/sites/default/files/pdf/Springett-Spirit_and_the_church_0.pdf (accessed January 18, 2014).

[27] Hodgson and Williams, "The Church," 226.

[28] Springett, "The Spirit and the Church," 12.

[29] Emphasis added.

[30] Ibid.

[31] Hays, "Ecclesiology and Ethics: In 1 Corinthians."

[32] Springett, "The Spirit and the Church," 13.

Chapter 8
Kalisiya – ek Bharatiya Sânskârika Samudâya (*Ekklesia* - an Indian Sacramental Community)

Samuel George

Introduction

Church, today, is divided not only on the basis of its theological positions but also on its practice of sacraments. Some would say there are none; others claim there is one; most Protestants say there are two; Roman Catholics would insist on seven. The differences are not only on the number of sacraments but also on the nature of these elements. Catholics consider them a *cause* of grace in one's life; Anglicans and Lutherans believe they are a *means* of grace; Congregationalist, Baptist, and most of the Independent churches believe the ordinances are a *symbol* of grace.[1]

Such is the stark reality in the church and it is no different in the Indian context too. The purpose of this chapter is to understand sacraments from a contextual perspective and its implication for the Indian *Ekklesia*. It should also be noted here that our effort is not to delineate either the numbers or the modes of practice of the various sacraments.

Sacraments

It can refer to a sacred pledge of sincerity or fidelity, publicly symbolized by a visible sign of such a deposit of money or an oath of allegiance.[2] It comes from the Latin word *sacramentum* which is a loose translation of the Greek *mysterion*. The word *sacramentum* was used with a distinctively Christian meaning for the first time in the Old Latin Bible and in Tertullian (second century). In the Old Latin and in the Vulgate it was employed to translate *mysterion* (e.g., Eph. 5:32; 1 Tim. 3:16; Rev. 1:20; 17:7).[3] It should be noted that this term was not only used for religious rites but also for doctrines.

Jenson calls sacraments as "visible words."[4] They are embodiments of grace, enacted testimonies to the love of God in

Christ Jesus. Probably it was Augustine who first formulated the definition of sacraments, who called them "visible signs of an invisible grace." Another definition states them as "a holy ordinance instituted by Christ wherein by visible signs of Christ and the benefits of the new covenant are represented, sealed and applied to believers."[5]

Sacramentals

It was only in the Middle Ages that scholastic theologians made a differentiation between sacraments and sacramentals. Sacramentals are those religious actions and objects (e.g., blessings, holy water) which mediated grace in less specific ways.[6] They are sacred signs, resembling the sacraments; they signify certain effects, particularly spiritual ones, which are obtained through the intercession of the Church. By them people are prepared to receive the chief effect of the sacraments, and the various circumstances of life are sanctified.[7] They are visible signs, like sacraments, having certain effects when received worthily. However, unlike the sacraments, which engage the redeeming action of Christ, sacramentals have their effect through the intercession of the church.[8]

Sacramentals can be divided into two: (a) those closely related with the sacraments (e.g., the blessing of water in baptism, the blessing of ring in marriage); (b) those connected with various human activities (e.g., the priestly ordination, the prayers for harvest and the blessing of fields).

A Historical Review

First millennium did not see any systematization of the sacraments. However, this should not mean that the church did not celebrate the sacraments. It was more a celebration of the Christian mystery than a systematic liturgical expression.

During the Patristic period the emphasis was on the symbolic dimension of the sacrament: the sacraments were seen as effective *signs* of grace.[9] It is in the twelfth century that the church began to emphasize on the sacramental aspect of church life in a definite form. The scholastic theologians played a major role in this.

Scholastic period saw the instrumental dimension: the sacraments were seen as effective *instruments* of grace. The emphasis was laid on the effectiveness, and on their causality, not on the holiness of the minister but on the merits of the passion of Christ.[10]

In reality, traditional sacramentology never developed the personal, let alone the ecclesial dimensions of the sacraments. The sacraments were seen as instruments of the humanity of Jesus, distributing to each person the grace that Christ obtained for us with his passion.[11]

Medieval church with its emphasis on regulation and systematization of the sacraments, lost the very connection of the sacraments with the Paschal mystery. This form of sacramentology led to triumphalism, juridicism, and clericalism in the church.[12]

After the Vatican II there is a clarion call to return back to the richness of the sacramentology of the patristic period.

Sacraments are such a thorny issue among the Christian communities that it continue to divide churches. Ironically, it is one of the principal topics on which the efforts towards ecumenical consensus and the reunion of the churches repeatedly stall.

Interestingly, the Bible does not contain the term sacrament, nor does it specify their numbers. It is the Greek word *mysterion* (mystery) which was later translated into Latin *sacramentum*, which refers to the presence and purpose of God made known in Christ Jesus (not necessarily only through rites like the baptism or the Eucharist).

It was only after the thirteenth century that the number of the sacraments were 'fixed' at seven in the Roman Catholic and Eastern Churches: Baptism, Confirmation, Eucharist, Penance, Ordination, Marriage, and Anointing of the Sick.

The Reformation dealt a 'body-blow' to the systematization of theological formulations among the Roman Catholic Church. It reduced the number of sacraments to two, namely: Baptism and Lord's Supper. The argument being that these are to be limited to those practices clearly instituted by Christ and the Apostles.

Over the years one can find two important tendencies in interpreting sacraments:

• Objective reality of God's grace in and through the sacraments. For those who hold this view see the sacraments as divinely appointed rites, that if properly administered, would bring grace and salvation. In this sense the sacraments are effective in themselves.[13]

• Importance of our faith response. For those who emphasize this view see them as dramatic signs of the grace of God and are effective not in themselves but only as they are received by faith. Their purpose is to give people the chance to bear public witness to their faith.

These tendencies have been the 'thorn of contention' between the theological position of the Roman Catholic and Protestant churches as well as among themselves too. There is an urgent need to get pass the impasse created due to these and related tendencies.

Principal Sacraments

As noted above, there are serious disagreements among the churches on the numbers and practices of the sacraments. It is not our intention here either to support or reject these. The choice of principal sacraments are made not on the basis of any denominational purview, but are purely done from a theological locus.

Baptism

Baptism is the sacrament of *initiation* into the Christian life. In a believer's life, it marks the beginning of the journey of faith and discipleship. Water is the principal ingredient in this sacrament. The authorization of this sacrament comes from the Lord himself: "Go therefore and make disciples of all nations, baptizing them in the name of the Father and of the Son and of the Holy Spirit, and teaching them to obey everything that I have commanded you. And remember, I am with you always, to the end of the age."[14] "Baptism is based not only on the *command* of Jesus but on the *act* of Jesus in freely submitting himself to baptism."[15] The event of baptism also marks the beginning of the Christian's participation in the life, death, and resurrection of Christ.[16] It signals one's death to an old life-style and one's new birth in Christ.[17] It signals his/her 'entry' into the community of grace – the *Ekklesia*.

Unfortunately, baptism is marred by so much controversies especially in its mode or practice. Parekh's[18] objection to baptism is a stark reminder that how much baptism can be a 'thorny' issue in the Indian context. Many 'followers' of Christ refrain from baptism because of its social implications: social and familial ostracization. Baptism in the Indian context is not just a 'religious' act but also a 'social' act. A baptized person not only enters a Christian Church but also a Christian community, which in many cases is a complete 'severance' from their caste, and social structure. A formal, public, and outward ritual such as baptism puts lot of emotional and social pressure on the new believer. 'Change of religion' (*dharm parivarthan*) is still a big taboo in the Indian context, and baptism plays a very crucial role in this aspect of 'change.'

In the light of the ongoing discussions about baptism in India, Sebastian raises the following important questions:[19]

- Whether baptism belongs to the essential, the less-essential, or the nonessential element of Christian faith and church life;
- Whether baptism plays any role in the evolution of new, noncommunal forms of fellowship in Christ;
- Whether baptism has contributed to the communal baggage which burdens the witness of the churches today;
- Whether baptism has any relevance in the search for secular forms of community; and
- Whether baptism is a stumbling block in the religious and ideological pluralism of the Indian nation.

These are questions that need contextual reflections in every generations. The question of baptism cannot be 'fixed' once-for-all as we would notice in the following lines. And these should not be attempted too, as that would rob the sacrament of its vitality and sharpness to speak to the given context. The writer of the editorial of an important piece on the discussion of baptism in India has rightly pointed out:

> If the baptism is to be retained in Indian Christianity, the churches that retain it should be constrained to find in it (or for it) a meaning that is strongly supportive of Christian life and faith. Otherwise its liability to the Gospel in India can hardly justify its continued practice.[20]

In the light of the above discussions, Sebastian further raises the following questions that are crucial for any debate on the issue of baptism in India:[21]

- Whether baptism, as practiced in the Indian churches today, has become a liability because of its social function and understanding, and if so, whether its relevance and meaning, if any, could be recaptured and reinterpreted;
- Whether baptism has been understood as a ritual or ceremony (e.g., a name-giving ceremony); and
- Whether baptism in its relationship to the gospel has indeed become a liability.

Now these questions like the earlier ones cannot be either ignored or explained casually. There are no ready-made answers. However, these are to be contextually addressed. Addressing such an issue in the Indian context, Singh writes:

> ... [T]he Christian baptism has often been presented as a total repudiation of one's socio-cultural heritage and accepting a name, a style of life alien to one's own. This sort of idea and practice of baptism has kept many from accepting baptism. For many, baptism, particularly as presented in our churches, does not seem to be essential for the faith, response and commitment to Christ. In the light of the cultural and social demands that baptism has wrongly demanded from many, it may be important to ask the question whether the rite of the baptism could be the necessary condition for the entry into the fellowship of the Church.[22]

In the Indian context because of the sensitivity of the issue of conversion, the act of baptism becomes very 'tricky'. Often, after the baptism the "converted" person has not only changed his/her religion but also social milieu, habits, customs, and manners, in addition to forfeiting several legal rights, especially with regard to the inheritance of property.[23]

Another issue that needs serious reflection in the Indian context, is of the unbaptized believers in Christ. In a research carried out in 1976 in Madras, it was found out that there were more non-baptized believers in Christ in the city than there were baptized Christians.[24] Some of the pertinent reasons given for the refusal of baptism by these members include caste customs like marriage alliances, funeral customs, loss of status; financial concerns like loss of privileges from the government or jobs; and problems with the organized church like the persistence of caste feelings within the church.[25]

Another very important aspect of related to baptism in India is the growing emergence of charismatic preachers or healers. These would proclaim good news offered in Christ Jesus, but would vehemently deny the efficacy or the necessity of baptism. K. Subba Rao (1912-81) probably best portrays this tendency in the Indian context.[26] For him, the faith in Christ Jesus should not be entangled with the doctrinal and ritual practices of Christianity.[27] He was particularly peeved by the cheapening of the gospel by padres to a show, a religion, a jugglery, a business, and a baptism.[28] For him, the ritual of baptism has been used by many to legitimize unjust and unnecessary structures within the church and wants to have nothing to do with it. Interestingly, he called it the "madness of baptism," which for him is not a necessary qualification for admission into the school of Christ; rather, it is the conversion of the heart which is the true baptism.[29]

Water is the necessary ingredient in the sacrament of baptism. Water symbolizes the passage from death to life, from life marked by sin (personal, historical, social, and structural) to life. Just because there is a 'controversy' associated with the sacrament of baptism, should we then "throw the baby with the bathwater?" Baptism is the quintessential sacrament of the Christian tradition. There can be discussions on various theological differences and practices of it, but the Church cannot do away with the sacrament itself. Sr. Vandana,[30] an Indian theologian has pointed out the various facets of water both for the baptism and its implication for our lives.

Water in the Bible, as in the Indian traditions, is a symbol of God's life-giving, purifying, thirst-slaking, sanctifying activity.[31] Gospel of John, offers glimpses of how water has become the means, the occasion or the instrument of His grace outpoured on human beings.

Jesus' baptism at the hands of the Baptist introduces his Messianic office. The waters of Jordan become a means of making known the Saviour.[32] Even for the Baptist, it is only in the act of baptizing the Messiah *in the waters of Jordan,* that he recognized him. The waters were thus the first 'Witness' of the first recognition of Jesus.[33]

Water is also the symbol of the Spirit. In the Messianic age, water is symbolized as the life given by God. The picture of 'living water' is a well-known concept in the Bible. It is the Spirit of God that gives life to creation (both as water and Spirit) Jn. 7:37-9; Rev. 7:17; 22:17.

Water is also the symbol of **purification**. The Baptist proclaimed "a baptism of repentance for the forgiveness of sins" (Mk. 1:4; Lk. 3:3). Paul too writes, "God saved us ... by means of the cleansing waters of rebirth and by renewing us with the Holy Spirit" (Titus. 3:5).

Water is also the symbol of **regeneration**. God made the Church clean, and holy by washing her in water. It is a bath of regeneration. Vandana writes,

> The symbolism of water finds its complete meaning in Christian baptism. John used the waters of Jordan which had formerly cleansed Naaman the Leper (2 Kings. 5:10-14). But baptism is here seen to bring about primarily not the cleansing of the body but 'of the conscience (1 Pet. 3:21). It is a bath that cleanses us from our sin through the outpouring of the Spirit who is 'the remission of sin.'[34]

In the baptismal waters, by the power of the Spirit – all sins, no matter how heinous, are wiped away, and individuals are brought to a participation in the new life – the life of the Triune God.[35]

Christ standing in the Jordan waters might be taken as a sign and fulfilment of all the washings, bathings, purifications – for the sins of all people, of all times. His baptism becomes the prototype of all the baptisms. However, it should be noted here that no amount of bathing, washings, and immersions in the purest waters can cleanse people unless s/he is reborn of the Spirit.

Water is also the symbol of **awakening**. At his baptism, Jesus awoke to his true Self. The act of baptism raises an individual too to that awakening of self-realization of one's vocation and mission in adhering God's ways in Christ Jesus.

Eucharist (Lord's Table; Lord's Supper)

Like the baptism, Eucharist too is both a command of the Lord as well as a practice that he initiated.[36] If baptism is the sacrament of the foundation of Christian life in God's grace, the Lord's Supper is the sacrament of the *sustaining* of Christian life by that same grace.[37] It is the sacrament of *growth* and nourishment in Christian life. It marks God's continued *sharing* of life and love that gives strength to the new community and motivates it for service in the world.[38] It is a reminder of Christ's salvific death and resurrection.

The classical understanding of Eucharist is about real presence, sacrifice, and sacramental communion. H. de Lubac has described the importance of Eucharist to the church in a famous statement: "Eucharist makes the church, the church makes the Eucharist." It is the sharing of the meal and the cup. Communion is the paramount importance here.

It is the commemoration of the Christ-Event. Through the sharing of the meal and the cup, Jesus makes himself present here and now, and those who partake of this meal are made one community in him. It is not just a 'memorial service' but a perpetual celebration ("until He comes" 1 Cor. 11:26). Therefore, it has a prophetic dimension too. A prophetic sacrament will remove, reject any kind of discriminating and dividing frontiers. Rather it will help build communities of *koinonia* and *diakonia*.

Eucharist as the 'Act of remembrance' challenges every generation to take part in the Christ event and participate in the Kingdom mission. C. S. Song explains the Eucharistic memorial in these words, "the remembrance of the past that ushers the future into the past. It is also remembrance that anticipates the future which in turn redeems the past in the present."[39]

An Indian *Ekklesia* should focus more on the meaning than the ritualistic form or systematization of the Eucharist. Appasamy have attempted some meaningful contextual explanation of

Eucharist in the Indian context. These are helpful pointers but 'more' is needed. And this "can be done only within the context of a deeper relationship with the Church than some of our theologians have had,"[40] says Boyd.

Appasamy points out that in the Fourth Gospel Jesus teaches that he is the Bread of Life and exhorts his followers to feed on him. It raises the question especially in the Indian context that Christians are forced to eat meat ("How can this man give us his flesh to eat?" John 6:52), an abomination to orthodox Hindus. Turning to *Taittiriya Upanisad* 3: 2: "Food is Brahman: for from food creatures are born; by food the creatures thus born live; and into food they enter and perish," Appasamy points out that food becomes a vehicle or effective symbol of divine power and grace.

In the Fourth Gospel, the Logos has become flesh and so the body, matter, food are appropriate media for revealing God's grace. Appasamy writes,

> Behold, the living Christ enters into us and forms a part of our inmost self in the same organic way in which food and drink become a part of our being... Christ Himself comes into our souls through the elements and abiding in us endows us with His spiritual energy.[41]

In that sense, through the chosen physical elements of bread and wine Christ comes to us, not corporeally but to faith. When Christ said, "this is my body," Appasamy says it means that all created beings are "the body of God." Therefore, Jesus takes the created elements of bread and wine as the instruments for fulfilling his purpose. Appasamy writes,

> They were to reveal to men [*sic*] His utter love for them leading to the complete sacrifice of Himself on the Cross.... The bread and wine were to become a new body of our Lord. In tasting them we taste His live.... Truly the bread and wine become the body and blood of our Lord because through them He fulfils His end of making known His love to men [*sic*] and gathering them into intimacy and closeness of fellowship with Him.[42]

Boyd opines that it is an impressive interpretation, because God chooses and uses *this* 'body,' of bread and wine, and in receiving it we receive the 'Spirit' behind it, Christ himself.[43]

Sacraments – an Indian Perspective

There has been lot of negative voices raised against the ritualistic aspect of sacraments in the Indian context.[44] Part of the reason is that the Indian church is not yet being enough 'Indian' in its outlook and worship. The 'foreign' tag continues to prop up whenever church is spoken in the Indian context.

Over the years there has been many attempts towards 'Indianization' of the church both in its outlook and worship life.[45] However, even after almost seven decades of being an independent nation, the Church in India hasn't done 'enough' to be called a truly Indigenized/Local/Contextual Church. One of the main reasons of its failure to be truly indigenized is its failure to address the sacraments in a more contextual manner.

Indian *Ekklesia* is to be a 'transforming community'[46] as Devanandan has rightly pointed out. The *Ekklesia* in India should not be rejected or even ignored because of its obvious 'defects' (it is a gathering of sinful humanity for salvation). She owes her existence to Christ Jesus ("I will build my Church" Mat. 16:18) and the Holy Spirit. She can still be transformed, and used as a transforming agent of the society and the world where we live. Unfortunately, the case has been quite different until now. Boyd puts this scenario quite succinctly, "... the pace of change must [seem] unbearably slow. The western Church in India must die, in order that the Indian Church may arise. But it is uncommonly long in dying."[47]

Negativity towards the sacraments by many Indians point to the fact of their resentment against the Church's 'control' over the 'means of Grace' i.e., the sacraments. This so-called 'authority' and 'control' discourages the followers to have direct access to the Divine.

What is needed is re-formulation and re-definition of sacrament in a contextual manner. This has to be done in the light of a Christocentric paradigm.[48] Such a theology of the sacraments is also adequately Trinitarian.[49] Jesus Christ is the primordial sacrament: in him the decisive redemptive activity between God and human takes place. A Christocentric approach underscores the free, personal presence of God's grace in concrete, worldly form while also insisting that grace, as personal presence, calls for free personal response. The argument here is that if Christ is the primary sacrament, then all sacraments will correspond to their prototype. The sacraments are celebrated in Christ and re-present Christ.[50] God's presence is mediated to humanity by the power of the Holy Spirit in the concrete, worldly media of spoken word and enacted sacrament.

Emphasizing this Boyd writes, "The priority of the *Sruti*, of conscious confrontation with the living Christ through the hearing of the Word, must be maintained or Indian Christianity can easily relapse into idolatry."[51]

Sanskâr

Sacrament in Hindi can also be translated as *prasâda* (a religious offering (eatables) that has the blessing of the deity and consumed religiously by the devotees). In this sense it is a ritual/ rite that has both religious sanction as well as significance. There is a flowing of divine grace through these rites.

Sacrament is also translated as *Sanskâr*. It is a difficult word to translate. However, an attempt can be made to explain it. It is a process, which transforms a person into an ideal and outstanding personality by eradicating/controlling the negative mental tendencies existing in her/him and by inculcating human values and qualities to make her/him more dynamic, discreet, duty conscious and responsible towards herself/himself as well as family and the society.[52] It is about 'value enrichment.' It is the ingestion of ideals/values/divine grace. This can be done through various means including rites/rituals (*prasâda*).

For an Indian *ekklesial* context, sacraments is to be understood more as *Sanskâr* than as *prasâda*. More as ingestion/distribution of grace than rites/rituals. Indian *Ekklesia* is to be a community (*Samudâya*) of grace, where the values/ideals of Christ is the hallmark of its existence and praxis. The rites/rituals important ingredients of this community. To say that we do not need the sacraments because we have the Word is the distortion of the Christian gospel. This point is succinctly explained by Pannenberg,

> One must raise the counter question whether the development of any Christian church is conceivable without baptism and the Lord's Supper. As the breaking of bread was central at gatherings of the disciples and adherents of Jesus, so from the very first baptism has been fundamental for the expanding of this group by the winning of new members.[53]

Ekklesia as a community of grace is not an end in itself. It is to be a community of grace for others. Inviting, dialoguing with the Other is what this community should exuberate. A community that herself has not experienced the grace cannot spread the grace to others. That is where the importance of sacraments as rites/ rituals come.

Samudâya

How the *ekklesia* would become a sacramental community? As a *Samudâya* – a community it offers the 'means of grace' to the believing community. It is a community that belongs to Christ and it is community that serves 'grace' both through its life and praxis. "The law indeed was given through Moses; grace and truth came through Jesus Christ" (Jn. 1:17). Jesus becomes the harbinger of grace to this community and she in turn becomes the community of grace to others.

***Ekklesia* as the Universal Sacrament of Salvation**

Can the Church be sacramental? Well, if the sacraments are rites, through which created things become vehicles of God's blessings, Church then too can be defined as a sacramental community. Sacrament is an effectual sign of grace performed at Christ's behest. As noted earlier, Christ is the fundamental sacrament: his humanity is the sign of contact between God and humanity. Yarnold writes,

> Under Christ the church is also the fundamental sacrament: man [*sic*] has saving contact with Christ and therefore with God through Christ's body the church in its visible, sociological, hierarchical reality.in this sense the church can be described as the 'continuation' of the incarnation. The church fulfils this function by word and sacrament.[54]

Church is the sacramental community which through its life and ministry of the Word and sacraments disseminate the grace of God to all. It is the community of grace. It is the sacrament of communion (fellowship). As sacrament of communion, the Church becomes the 'very continuation' of Christ.[55] The Church permeates in history as a tangible sign of God-ever-with-us in Christ, for redemption of every people of every age, race, and condition.[56] Pannenberg points out,

> In fact, it is only from Jesus Christ and in distinction from him that we can appropriately establish and understand the sacramental nature of the church as a sign, the place of special mysteries of salvation in its life, and the significance of these for the sharing of believers in Jesus Christ as the one divine mystery of salvation.[57]

Ekklesia as a sacramental community in the Indian context depicts three unique characteristics:

Kenotic

By the self-emptying and self-giving act of Christ Jesus for the cosmos, he has put down the condition to be part of this sacramental community. His self-emptying is a clarion protest against all despotic, evil, and dehumanizing powers that be. Discrimination and dominion cannot be part of the sacramental community. Indian *Ekklesia* – the sacramental community, cannot be prophetic both in her outlook and ministry unless she commits herself to a self-giving ministry. She as the *Sânskârika Samudâya* – the sacramental community should emulate her Lord and Master in this selfless giving.

Participatory

"A participatory Church retrieves the democratic tradition of *Ekklesia* of the early centuries."[58] Dignity of every member, restoration of equal discipleship, performance of their vocational and missional roles are the marks of a participatory *Ekklesia*. "Relationships become less vertically mandated, and there is more interdependency, consultation, collaboration and mutual trust among the People of God,"[59] says Monteiro.

Every member is included in its formation and action, including the marginalized, and people with disability. They become co-workers, and co-leaders of the community where everyone works towards the edification of each other. For this every effort towards strengthening of gender, racial, caste, class, disability relations is to be made by the Church – the sacramental community – the *sânskârika samudâya.*

Dialogical

Intra and inter dialogue is essential for the *Ekklesia* to become the sacramental community – the *sânskârika samudâya.*

Church in India 'survives' in the context of various cultural, ethnic, and religious traditions both inside and outside. Contact, dialogue, and cooperation with these varied groups of people is both a duty and challenge for the Church.

Dialogue is vital for the survival of the *Ekklesia.* It is not just a tool for peaceful co-existence but *Ekklesia* in India should become agents of reconciliation and liberation for healing of the wounds of divisions, discord, and discrimination both in and outside the boundaries of the faith community. The challenge to the sacramental community – the *sânskârika samudâya* is to celebrate harmony in pluralism without destroying distinctiveness and difference.

Conclusion

An attempt was made in this chapter to understand sacraments from an Indian perspective. The goal was to define the Church, the *ekklesia* as the sacramental community - the *sânskârika samudâya.* As noted above, that to be an *ekklesial* community in India she has to be a sacramental community - a *sânskârika samudâya* – a community that spreads grace to others.

Endnotes:

[1] Norman Geisler, *Systematic Theology (Church, Last Things)*, vol. 4 (Bloomington, Minnesota: Bethany House, 2005), 146.

[2] J. Martos, "Sacrament," in *The Westminster Dictionary of Christian Theology*, ed. Alan Richardson and John Bowden (Philadelphia: The Westminster Press, 1983), 514.

[3] Steven Barabas, "Sacrament," in *New International Bible Dictionary*, ed. J. D. Douglas and Merrill C. Tenney (Grand Rapids: Zondervan Publishing House, 1987), 878.

[4] Robert W. Jenson, *Visible Words: The Interpretation and Practice of Christian Sacraments* (Philadelphia: Fortress Press, 1978).

[5] *Westminster Shorter Catechism*, quoted in Daniel L. Migliore, *Faith Seeking Understanding: An Introduction to Christian Theology* (Grand Rapids: William B. Eerdmans Publishing Company, 1993), 212.

[6] Martos, "Sacrament," 515.

[7] J. D. Crichton, "Sacramental Theology," in *The Westminster Dictionary of Christian Theology*, ed. Alan Richardson and John Bowden (Philadelphia: The Westminster Press, 1983), 515.

[8] Ibid.

[9] Victor Codina, "Sacraments," in *Systematic Theology: Perspectives from Liberation Theology*, ed. Jon Sobrino and Ignacio Ellacuría (Maryknoll: Orbis Books, 1996), 216.

[10] Ibid., 216f.

[11] Ibid., 217.

[12] Ibid.

[13] Patristic Father Ignatius called the Lord's Supper as the "medicine of immorality."

[14] Mat. 28:19-20 (*NRSV*).

[15] Migliore, *Faith Seeking Understanding: An Introduction to Christian Theology*, 214.

[16] But Jesus said to them, "You do not know what you are asking. Are you able to drink the cup that I drink, or be baptized with the baptism that I am baptized with?" (Mk. 10:38 *NRSV*).

[17] Migliore points out some important images of baptism in the New Testament: it describes a *dying and rising* with Christ (Rom. 6:3-4); it is pictured as the *washing* of a sin-stained life (1 Cor. 6:11); it is portrayed as a *rebirth* by the Holy Spirit (Jn. 3:5; Acts 2:38); it signals the *incorporation* of a believer into Christ (Eph. 2:9); it is also a *sign of God's coming reign* (Rom. 8:23). Migliore, *Faith Seeking Understanding: An Introduction to Christian Theology*, 215.

[18] Manilal C. Parekh (1885-1967) was a Gujarati Christian from the Jain tradition. Through Brahmoism he accepted Christ and baptism (February 06, 1918). Writing in 1924 ("The Spiritual Significance and Value of Baptism," *NCC Review*, September 1924) about baptism, he opines that it should be an expression of the spiritual discipleship of Jesus Christ and the public testimony to the salvation given in Christ Jesus and appropriated through faith. It should in no way severe one from his/her family, caste, and religious community. He was of the opinion that Christian community (*probably of his time and perhaps even today too*) denationalizes politically, and opposes indigenous cultural traditions like vegetarianism. Baptism for him should not become merely an ecclesiastical rite/ceremony or an instrument of proselytization. It has to be an instrument of *moksha dharma* (the destiny of spiritual salvation) rather than *samaj dharma* (the discipline of communal life). Cf. M. M. Thomas, "Manilal C. Parekh," in *Towards an Indian Christian Theology: Life and Thought of Some Pioneers*, ed. M. M. Thomas and P. T. Thomas (Tiruvalla: Christava Sahitya Samithi, 1998), 161.

[19] J. Jayakiran Sebastian, "Baptism and the Unity of the Church in India Today," in *Baptism and the Unity of the Church*, ed. Michael Root and Risto Saarinen (Grand Rapids: William B. Eerdmans Publishing Company, 1998), 197.

[20] "Editorial," *Religion and Society* 19, no. 1 (March 1972): 4.

[21] Sebastian, "Baptism and the Unity of the Church in India Today," 198.

[22] Godwin R. Singh, ed. *A Call to Discipleship: Baptism and Conversion* (Delhi: ISPCK, 1985), 2.

[23] Cf. Gauri Viswanathan, "Coping with (Civil) Death: The Christian Convert's Right of Passage in Colonial India," in *After Colonialism: Imperial Histories and Postcolonial Displacements*, ed. Gyan Prakash (Princeton: Princeton University Press, 1995), 183-210. Quoted in Sebastian, "Baptism and the Unity of the Church in India Today," 199.

[24] Singh, ed. *A Call to Discipleship: Baptism and Conversion*, 206-11.

[25] Ibid., 210.

[26] For a good study on Subba Rao refer to Kaj Baago, *The Movement Around Subba Rao: A Study of the Hindu-Christian Movement around K. Subba Rao in Andhra Pradesh* (Madras: CLS, 1968); Richard Leroy Hivner Jr., "Exploring the Depths of the Mystery of Christ: The Life and Work of K. Subba Rao of Andhra Pradesh, South India, with Special Reference to His Songs" (masters thesis, University of South Africa, 2004).

[27] He writes, "By religion and baptism you became a Christian. Don't you know that you too must become Christ by living like Jesus?" Kalagara Subba Rao, *Translations of the New Songs* (Vijayawada: n. p., n. d.), 20.

[28] Kalagara Subba Rao, *Retreat Padre*, Second ed. (Machilipatnam: n. p., 1972). Quoted in K. P. Aleaz, "The Theology of K. Subba Rao," *Bangalore Theological Forum* 23, no. 4 (December 1991): 48f.

[29] Cf. Aleaz, "The Theology of K. Subba Rao," 41-63.

[30] Sister Vandana [Hindus affectionately called her Vandana *Mataji* (mother)] was a Catholic nun of the order of Sisters of the Sacred Heart. She was hailed as an ardent promoter of Indian culture and spirituality in the Church. She pioneered the Christian Ashram movement in India. She was born a Zoroastrian and became a Catholic at the age of 20 while studying at Sophia College, Mumbai, run by the Society of the Sacred Heart of Jesus congregation. She later became the congregation's provincial in India.

Inspired by the Second Vatican Council, she lived and worked in the Hindu temple town of Rishikesh in Uttarakhand for many years as an example of evangelization envisaged by the Council. Until 2004, she was working at the Jeveen Dhara Ashram or life flowing monastery that she founded in the late 1970s in the foothills of the Himalayas. She was closely associated with the Sivananda Ashram of Swami Chitananda whose mission too is commitment towards Christian-Hindu dialogue and co-existence.

She has written many hymns and also few books including: *Waters of Fire* (1988); *Find Your Roots and Take Wing: Spiritual Formation for the East and the West: Three Essays* (1991); *Nâma Japa* (1995). In 2013, she died at the age of 92.

[31] Vandana, "Water Symbolism in the Gospel of St. John in the Light of Indian Spirituality," in *Readings in Indian Christian Theology*, ed. R. S. Sugirtharajah and Cecil Hargreaves (Delhi: ISPCK, [1993] 2004), 200.

[32] Ibid., 204.

[33] Ibid.

[34] Ibid., 206.

[35] Ibid., 208.

[36] The Lord Jesus on the night when he was betrayed took a loaf of bread, and when he had given thanks, he broke it and said, "This is my body that is for you. Do this in remembrance of me." In the same way he took the cup also, after supper, saying, "This cup is the new covenant in my blood. Do this, as often as you drink it, in remembrance of me." For as often as you eat this bread and drink the cup, you proclaim the LORD's death until he comes 1 Cor. 11:23-6.

[37] Migliore, *Faith Seeking Understanding: An Introduction to Christian Theology*, 220.

[38] Ibid.

[39] C. S. Song, *Third-Eye Theology: Theology in Formations in Asian Settings* (Maryknoll: Orbis Books, 1990), 149.

[40] Robin H. S. Boyd, *An Introduction to Indian Christian Theology* (New Delhi: ISPCK, 1994), 249.

[41] A. J. Appasamy, *Christianity as Bhakti Marga: A Study of the Johannine Doctrine of Love* (Madras: CLS, 1928), 132.

[42] A. J. Appasamy, *The Gospel and India's Heritage* (London: SPCK, 1942), 206.

[43] Boyd, *An Introduction to Indian Christian Theology*, 140.

[44] Sadhu Sundar Singh, P. Chenchiah, Subba Rao to name some.

[45] Robert Di Nobili, Bartholomäus Ziegenbalg and the various *Ashram* movements in India have enormously contributed towards indigenization.

[46] Paul D. Devanandan, *Christian Concern in Hinduism* (Bangalore: CISRS, 1961), 101f.

[47] Boyd, *An Introduction to Indian Christian Theology*, 249.

[48] There may be disagreements to this proposal due to the location of Indian *Ekklesia* – a religiously and culturally plural location. Is not a Trinitarian centric Sacramentology viable for the Indian context? The author is aware of the discussions pertaining to this very important discussions.

[49] Migliore, *Faith Seeking Understanding: An Introduction to Christian Theology*, 213.

[50] Ibid.

[51] Boyd, *An Introduction to Indian Christian Theology*, 249.

[52] http://sanskaramvatika.com/why.html (accessed February 12, 2014).

[53] Wolfhart Panneberg, *Systematic Theology*, vol. 3 (Grand Rapids: William B. Eerdmans Publishing Company, 1998), 343.

[54] E. J. Yarnold, "Sacramental Theology," in *The Westminster Dictionary of Christian Theology*, ed. Alan Richardson and John Bowden (Philadelphia: The Westminster Press, 1983), 516.

[55] De Lubac, *Catholicism* (London: Burns, Oates & Washbourne, 1950), 29.

[56] Evelyn Monteiro, *Church and Culture: Communion in Pluralism* (Delhi: ISPCK, 2004), 190.

[57] Panneberg, *Systematic Theology*, 342.

[58] Monteiro, *Church and Culture: Communion in Pluralism*, 201.

[59] Ibid.

Chapter 9
Ekklesia - The Body of Christ Defiled in the Church: A Christian Counselling Perspective

R. Lalruata

Introduction

Today, the word 'Church' has a wide variety of meanings referring to a church building or somewhat church structure in performing a religious service. Although, the understanding of the biblical concept of the word 'church' and its contemporary significance is becoming crucial when it comes to dealing with ecclesiological functioning of the present church where there is shift in intellectual and moral diversity, which resulted disunity, conflict and disagreement between ideas and beliefs. Therefore, it is very much essential to look at the basic concept of the church with regards to the original meaning as it was used in the New Testament time.

When dealing with the ecclesiological implication for the present church's structure, something needs to be dealt with in accordance to Pauline concept of church, taking 'the body of Christ' as inclusive community in the context where individual rights and freedom are in threat and disturbed. However, Paul's metaphor of the word 'church' as the 'body of Christ' seems to have significant relevance as the present church relationship are disturbed, divided, devalued and deprived for some interest. Therefore, highlighting *Ekklesia* in the context of inclusive community is much necessary. Particularly, focusing on the need for change in ecclesiological attitudes, approaches and ministerial function within the church structure is becoming a challenge for the Indian churches. Thus, this chapter focuses on the ecclesiological nature and functions of the church with an emphasis on Paul's conception of the church as body of Christ from Christian counselling perspective.

The Church

It is clear from the New Testament that there is only one church, only one people of God. The word for church as a gathering of people (*ekklesia*) is used in many different forms, including: a local congregation (1 Thess. 1:1), the universal church (Gal. 1:13), small house fellowship (Rom. 16:5), Hebrew congregation in Jerusalem and Gentile congregation in Antioch, a number of separate communities in distinct localities (Acts 15:41). Church therefore takes many different forms and wherever there is a gathering of God's people there is the church.[1] The church is therefore the visible sign of the outworking of the Kingdom of God here on earth. It brings the 'good news' to all people. It is therefore, responsible for bringing the good news in all of its fullness – reconciliation between human and God, restored communities, social justice, redeemed institutions, peace and reconciliation between human and creation.[2]

Church in the New Testament

The earliest New Testament meaning of the word *ekklesia* refers to a gathering or assembly of those who believe in Jesus Christ. This assembly may be a local body of believers or the entire church, the *Qahal* Yahweh. It describes the congregations of Christians united in Jesus Christ for the purpose of worship and prayer (1 Cor. 11:18; 14:19) and for instruction or deliberation (Acts 11:26; 12:5; 1 Cor. 14:4-5, 28, 34-35).

However, the core of the New Testament ecclesiology can be drawn out of two key terms, *ekklesia* and *kyrios*. In all languages the equivalent term for the church is derived from either of these two terms. *Ekklesia* means the assembly, gathering, community, and *kyrios* refers to the glorified Lord Jesus Christ. The church is therefore, the community of those who believe in and proclaim the Lord Jesus. Therefore, it is understood that both the *Ekklesia* and *kyrios* dimensions belong to the essence of the church.[3]

***Ekklesia*: the Body of Christ**

The most typical description of the church in Paul is that of the body of Christ. The most common use of *ekklesia*, however, is to describe a local church or assembly or congregation or body of believers in Christ. Paul refers to "one body" four times to emphasize Body unity (1 Cor. 12:12-13). Christians are one; salvation is the initial point of unity. They are all united because they are all baptized by one spirit into one body.[4] There are two ways in which *ekklesia* describes the people of God in the New Testament. One is the universal church which is quite different from the usual meaning of the church as assembled group of people, which is composed of all believers in the Lord Jesus Christ from the day of Pentecost to the Rapture. However, the most common use of *ekklesia* is to describe a local church or assembly or congregation or body of believers in Jesus Christ.[5] Paul often presents the truth of *ekklesia* through its analogy with the human body, a symbolism which can easily apprehended.

In the New Testament, the Church *Koinonia* (sharing, community, participation) was the meaning of church membership. Thus, this means two things: i) church membership is highly important and necessary for believer; ii) church membership should be understood primarily as participation and community in the body of Christ, rather than as joining an organisation or having one's name on a membership list.[6] Moreover, the New Testament does give a threefold meaning to the 'Body of Christ': Jesus' physical body, the church and the bread of the Lord's Supper. The close identification between the church and Jesus' physical body is seen especially in Eph. 2:13-16.[7]

The body is the church's unique position in Christ. The church is not a physical building, but a group of believers, not a denomination, but a spiritual body. The church is not an organization, but a *koinonia*-a communion, a fellowship that includes all believers.[8] It is therefore, certainly evident that the body of Christ is the concept of unity. "For just as the body is one and has many members, and all the members of the body, though many are one body, so it is with Christ" (1 Cor. 12:12). Thus, a body is made up of members functioning together.

Body of Christ: An Inclusive Dimension

The unity of Christ's church is a reality which transcends all of the barriers and division caused by human beings. We have seen indication when one becomes part of the church, or the body of Christ, it becomes one with all other believers and shares the unity and bears the responsibility to preserve the unity of the spirit in the bond of peace (Eph. 4:3).[9] In fact, the body's unity holds great importance for the churches today. Disunity, division and conflict in a congregation are a direct denial of the work of the spirit, and this is against the identity of the body of Christ.

One of the important facts which identify the body of Christ is diversity. While believers are one in the spirit, they are not all the same. Christ, is the head of the church, has given each believer a distinctive gifts, having distinct varieties which exists in an assembly is intended for the common good.[10] Therefore, the body of Christ represents distinct nature, talents and gifts for each individual member in the church. Recognition of this diverse gift will give us a proper understanding of the whole functioning of the body. It has to remember that, just as every part of the physical body is essential to its functioning, so also every gift and members of each individual is vital and necessary.

Another dimension of the body of Christ is the living experience of fellowship. The New Testament word for fellowship is *koinonia,* and its basic idea is that of close relationship. Fellowship of this kind brings believers together with a sense of common need, as a family. It is a sense of bearing one another's burden and experience a shared life.[11] In another sense, fellowship is a part of the wholeness. We belong together. It is in the caring fellowship where we have finest experiences of healing. However, the quality of fellowship does not just happen. It is developed by positive teaching and example. It is fostered by openness to one another, by listening lovingly, by sharing burdens, by expressing confidence and appreciation. It is renewed by the removal of unseen barriers like prejudice, suspicion, grudges, and unresolved guilt.[12]

Pastoral Care and Counselling in relation to the Body of Christ

When dealing about the church as the body of Christ, it has some significance in relation to the aspects of pastoral care and counselling. Let us look at some of the aspects of pastoral care and counselling as function of community's healing of growth and development within the Church.

Pastoral care is a broad term that refers to all that a pastor does, including organising, shepherding the people and communicating the gospel to them.[13] According to Alastair V. Campbell, "Pastoral care is that aspect of the ministry of the church which is concern with the well-being of individuals and of community. Pastoral care seeks to help people to know love, both as something to receive and as something to give."[14]

Moreover, Pastoral care has one fundamental aim, to help people to know love, both as something to be received and as something to give.[15] Thus, Campbell reveals the scope of pastoral care beyond individual and the congregation and extends it on to include the community. He wants to rediscover the human potentiality from the shepherding concept of feckless sheep. The ministry of pastoral care is wider and more closely related with the social forces of the community.

It has been certain that pastoral care is mostly carried out in or on behalf of Christian community. The context always refers to faith-based community. It should not be limited to the church, but also to the whole world. In other word, pastoral caring communities not only relate to the congregations but also offer care in secular settings. It renders service to individuals or groups, who are in need of support and care, in whatever settings, in response to the needs of human being.

However, Pastoral counselling is a specialised type of pastoral care offered in response to individuals, couples, or families who are experiencing and able to articulate the pain in their lives and willing to seek pastoral help in order to deal with it.[16] Thus, in a simplest term pastoral counselling is to help people who are in need of help and support within the religious community to a person or group of community. Moreover, pastoral counsellor is a person with commitment to and education for religious ministry who is functioning in an appropriate setting for ministry and accountable to a recognized religious community.[17] We can find that pastoral counselling or a pastoral counsellor is grounded on religious setting where it belongs to the well being of a religious community with person having a faith in their commitment.

In spite of different views and concept, the main concept of pastoral counselling lies in religious setting with specific order.

Moreover, it can also be asserted that, Pastoral counselling is a type of care offered by the religious community. However, pastoral counselling is a specific sub-type of the larger ministerial function of pastoral care. The biblical image most often used for this function is the shepherd's seeking the one sheep that is lost, while maintaining administrative responsibility for the ninety-nine who are not.[18] Thus, the pastoral role or identity in forming relationship and a sense of his or her responsibility is very central in achieving the ministerial functioning of pastoral care and counselling.

When it comes to the senses of community of the body of Christ, the most significant identity of the pastoral counselling and the body of Christ relationship lies within the framework on the community identity. The church as the body of Christ has a distinctive character of unity and diversity which in turn for the pastoral counselling, has to establish in forming relationship within the religious community, which is one of the basic functions of the church. The pastoral care and counselling dimension of spiritual based-community becomes so central when it comes to healing, whether spiritual or physical. The growth dimension is rested within the community relationship and caring responsibility of each individuals in the church.

Ekklesia: the Body of Christ Defiled in the Church

The emergence of new ecclesiological structures of the present day church has led to the need of having a kind of new ecclesiastical movement towards the irrelevant practices which is against humanity within the church structures. There have been witnesses of poverty, ignorance, domination and oppression which become as a threat to the institutional churches. However, when we look at the functioning of the body of Christ, the concept of "body life" has several important applications in the present day churches. It must be clearly stated that the body life involves the participation of every believer irrespective of their caste, gender, denomination, and status in the society. It is important for the local church to discover and exercise the spiritual gift which can be attained by every believer. There is no room for misguided concepts of humility or for exaggerated ideas of self importance. Therefore, the truth is that the body of Christ is designed to teach us that we need one another and that we must care for one another.

However, the present day church tradition is something a kind of building structures of human interaction. As it was therefore, the need of liberating the churches. For Snyder, liberating the church means freeing Christians to be a community of believers that serves as an agent of the Kingdom of God. It is able to create community and to enhance existing community not only among Christians but in society at large.[19] When we are talking about defiled church, it can be of the community which is against unity, domination and oppression within the church structures. Let's look some of the discriminative, dominative and corruption in the churches today.

Women's Identity in the Church

The situation with regard to the identity and role of women in the Church is not in any way different from what we find in the society due to the fact that the culture from which Christianity originated was patriarchal.[20] The identity and role of women in the church in India is also very much conditioned by the Indian culture as well as by the biblical tradition. Women in the Church did receive a certain amount of freedom and enlightenment due to the initiative taken by the missionaries to provide education to the women but did not affect the role that a woman was expected today in the church.

As the nature and emphasis of the church's mission changed, the role of those women became invisible. The women's fellowship was formed and the women took leadership positions in the women's fellowship. But they were always under the control of men. The emphasis of the women's fellowship was also on the role of women as married women and mothers.[21]

Though there were number of women involved in the ministry of the church, the role they were assigned with did not change. They were involved in social work concentrating on women, children and in the areas of financial management and management of property but excluded from the administration and management of the Church affairs. Due to the growing consciousness and untiring efforts of women leaders and other enlightened men, later the ordination of women was accepted by major church, and a number of women in various committees and decision making bodies increased. Theological Colleges opened their doors to women students and a number of women theologians emerged. Women's participation in the Churches' worship service and ministry became visible.[22]

Church Politics and Corruption

According to William Temple, as cited by John Stott, 'the church is the only cooperative society that exists for the benefit of non members.'[23] Sunil Kumar Singh states, "Church is a multi-national large organization. It is an enormous task to manage people, time, talents, resources, money, organizations with tremendous scope to shape the world and extend the Kingdom of God."[24] For him, "The church is basically the organization of the people by the people and for the people."[25]

As mentioned earlier politics is an art of management, dealing with people to live together. 'Church Politics' can be understood in a wider and fuller sense as the dynamic organization of the church.[26] It should be used in a good manner for the edification of the Church. But now, the concept of Church politics is corrupted. It may happen probably because of the way, objectives and behaviours' of the administrators of the Church. Also, people may look Church politics as the same way which has been misused like secular administration. So, the concept of the Church politics which was in early church is now corrupted and misused in several ways and for various intentions.

The Poor and Marginalised

In today's church, the church has a vital role to play in responding to social injustice. The nature of the body of Christ has to express caring for individuals where in the context of protecting the weak and the defenceless. The most essential needs are to engage in open confrontation so as to attain justice, dignity and unity. However, in looking at the present day context of institutionalised churches in India, our response is should people-oriented and of inclusive nature.

For M. M. Thomas, "The church's witness in the world of politics requires radical renewal in the spirituality and theology of the church."[27] This renewal should serve the people to raise voice against injustice and helps to liberate them from self-righteousness.[28] But the present church ecclesiologies are not being motivated to raise voice for the rights of underprivileged classes. Moreover, today's church has fail to handle the issues of the people who are struggling of poverty, rehabilitation, political exploitation and marginalised in all aspects of social life. Thus, the pastoral care and counselling dimension of spiritual based-community becomes so central when it comes to healing, reconciliation and liberation. The growth dimension is rested within the community relationship and caring responsibility of each individual, in considering the people who are deprived of their rights and responsibilities.

Reflection and Comment

We are in a context where an evident shift towards self-dependency among the youths are visible. This creates a feeling of inadequacy, ultimately self-pity and denial. Its outcome is also acknowledged by the society. Inferiority or low esteem due to selfishness and insecurity is experienced among the youths. The thing is that the present youth developments have changed our social settings, and have great impacts on the church as well. Various reports in newspapers, both national and local show that suicidal attempts are increasing among the youths. Teenagers drinking and declining of church attendance are challenges faced by the present churches. So, in order to face these issues, the church needs to draws every 'genuine believer' in Christ into His body and address the same in a relevant manner. The church as the body of Christ must share the unity and bears the responsibility in the midst of those people who are under bondage. The emphasis of Divine self giving love and human unworthiness enables ones' capacity to love one another.

Secondly, we are challenged by certain issues like HIV/AIDS and homosexuality, where victims face isolation and discrimination. Felling of insecurity and guilt consciousness is quite prevalent among them. These are God's people whom God saved and sustain hope for the future. As we have already noted, Jesus gravitated to the unlovely, the sick, the rejected, the lost, and the lonely. We have to build a trusted relationship, a fellowship of love and care.

It is our conviction that, the passion of faith is transformed into the suffering of unconquered doubt. As body of Christ, the church cannot ignore the suffering of its members as a result of HIV/AIDS but rather should be compassionate. Thus, the Pauline notion of solidarity in the body of Christ is very much relevant to those who are in pain, suffering and in need of hope and restoration.

Lastly, the present world is losing its confidence due to advancement of human reason and rising influence from worldly pleasures. The increasing scene of human despair, frustration, hostility and anxiety created much havoc in our society. So, for the church, it is our response to bring out the truth of sound theological solution for the community. The connection of Christ's resurrection with our hope of eternal life is understood when we see that it is Jesus the human who gave his life trusting the divine love. It is his disclosure of God's love, standing through all tragedy and despair. Thus, the church as the body of Christ should engage in praxis, in which stigma, shame and judgment are replaced by mutual care and compassion.

Conclusion

As discussed above about the dimension of the body of Christ, the very inclusive understanding of the nature and function of the body of Christ is pertinent. However, the church as an inclusive community should be both an expression of theological relevance as well as a sociological reality. Thus, it is necessary to search for constant reformation within the church and the society as a whole. When we look at the aspects of the body of Christ in the above narration, it is evident that the church in its physical reality is expressed in terms of community- the community of people with collective experiences. It is important to note that the church with its foundational structure is to be recognized as people-oriented. Therefore, the church is not an organisation or an institution but people with their distinct identities and experiences; in fact, that is what constitute the church. In the light of the study of the church as the body of Christ, Paul's inference is to uphold values that are inclusive and participatory. The church should avoid, caste, region, language, denomination, and oppressive structures. An authentic ecclesiology is where an inclusive, and corporate church community of diverse background, tradition, class, caste, gender are included.

Endnotes:

[1] Graham G. B. Evans, *"The Mission of the Church,"* http://chesterrep.openrepository.com/cdr/bitstream/10034/97541/4.htm, (accessed January 27, 2014).

[2] Ibid.

[3] Kuncheria Pathil, *Theology of the Church New Horizons* (Bangalore: Dharmaram Publications, 2006), 13.

[4] John MacArthur, Jr, *Body Dynamics* (Wheaton: Victor Books, 1982), 12.

[5] Gary Inrig, *Life in His Body* (Wheaton: Harold Shaw Publishers, 1975), 32.

[6] Howard A. Snyder, *Liberating the Church* (Downers Grove: Inter-Varsity Press, 1983), 107.

[7] Ibid., 108.

[8] MacArthur, *Body Dynamics*, 11.

[9] Inrig, *Life in His Body*, 33.

[10] Ibid.

[11] Ibid.

[12] R. Eugene Sterner, *Healing and Wholeness* (Indiana: Warner Press, 1978), 105.

[13] Ezamo Murry, *An Introduction to Pastoral Care and Counseling* (Delhi: ISPCK, 2005), 132.

[14] Alastair V. Campbell, *Paid to Care?: Limits of Professionalism in Pastoral Care* (London: SPCK, 1985), 1

[15] Ibid.

[16] J. Patton, "Pastoral Counselling," in *Dictionary of Pastoral Care and Counselling*, ed., Rodney J. Hunter (Nashville: Abingdon Press, 2005), 849.

[17] Ibid.

[18] Ibid., 850.

[19] Snyder, *Liberating the Church*, 131.

[20] Joan Chittister, *Women, Ministry and the Church* (New York: Paulist Press, 1983), 25.

[21] Emily C. Hewitt, *Women Priests: Yes or No?* (New York: The Seabury Press, 1995), 35.

[22] Ibid.

[23] John Stott, *Issues Facing Christians Today* (Bombay: Gospel Literature Service, 1986), 24.

[24] Sunil Kumar Singh, *Church Management in the Indian Context* (Delhi: ISPCK, 1998), 74.

[25] Ibid., 41.

[26] Teodora C. Bacani, *The Church and Politics* (Philippines: Claretian Publications, 1987), 43.

[27] Viju Wilson, *Ecclesiology of Prophetic Participation* (Delhi: ISPCK, 2012), 86.

[28] Ibid., 87.

Chapter 10
Ekklesia Model or *Kyriarchal* Model: Hermeneutical Choice and the Future of *Ekklesia*

Rosy Baroi

Introduction

From the very beginning, there has been a trace of the tensions and struggles between emancipatory movements in Early Christianity inspired by the democratic logic of equality on the one hand and the *kyriarchal* structures of imperial Roman society and religion on the other.[1] Thus, there has been a constant tension between *ekklesia* model and *kyriarchal* model, and it can be said that the preference of one model over the other has, over the years, shaped the present state of our churches. This article will, therefore, examine the various aspects of the *ekklesia* and *kyriarchal* models and its implications in the shaping of the present church.

I. Definition

i. *Ekklesia*

Ekklesia is a compound word, derived from two Greek words *ek* and *kaleô*. The first word *ek* is a preposition which means "out of," "out from," or "from." The second word *kaleô*, from which *klçsia* is derivative, is a verb which means "to call." In its most basic form, *ekklesia* means "those called out from." It refers to people called out from or out of something.

Ekklesia was the most general word for principal assembly of citizens of the democratic city-state in the old Roman State and of ancient Athens during its "Golden Age" (480-404 BCE). In ancient Greece, *ekklesia* came to be used for the people who were summoned from or called out of the community to the assembly. Its roots lay in the Homeric agora, the meeting of the people. The Athenian *Ekklesia*, for which exists the most detailed record, was already functioning in Draco's day (c. 621 BCE). In the course of Solon's[2] codification of the law (c. 594 BCE), *ekklesia* became coterminous with the body of male citizens 18 years and above, who had final control over policy, including the right to hear appeals in the *hçliaia* (public court), take part in the election of *archons* (chief magistrates), and confer special privileges on individuals. In Athens during the 5th and 4th centuries BCE, the committee of the council summoned the *ekklesia* both for regular meetings held at least four times in each 10th of the year, and for special sessions. Assemblies of this sort which existed in most Greek city-states, continued to function throughout the Hellenistic and Roman periods, though under the Roman Empire their powers gradually diminished.[3]

Christian usage of *ekklesia* as "church" was probably derived from the Septuagint, where it renders the Hebrew *qahal* (gathering). The New Testament writers used it also in both ways, namely to refer to democratic state and Christian gatherings and the Christian community as a whole.[4]

ii. *Kyriarchy*

Kyriarchy is a neologism coined by Elisabeth Schüssler Fiorenza[5] and derived from the Greek words *kyrios* 'lord, master, father, husband, elite propertied educated man' and *archein* 'to rule, dominate,'[6] to describe power's exploitative effects. "*Kyriarchy* means the domination of the emperor, lord, slave master, husband, the elite freeborn educated and propertied male colonizer who has power over all women and subaltern men."[7] It is an intersectional extension of the idea of patriarchy beyond gender which seeks to redefine the analytic category of patriarchy in terms of multiplicative intersecting structures of domination.[8] *Kyriarchy* operates not only along the axis of gender but also along race, class, culture and religion. These axes of power structures the system of domination in a matrix of interlocking system of oppression in which the subordination of one person or group to another is internalised and institutionalised. *Kyriarchy* is best theorized as a complex pyramidal system of intersecting multiplicative social structures of super-ordination and subordination, of ruling and oppression.[9]

In classical antiquity, the rule of the emperor, lord, slave, master, husband, or the elite freeborn, propertied, educated gentleman to whom disenfranchised men and all women were subordinated is best characterized as *kyriarchy*. In antiquity, the social system of *kyriarchy* was institutionalized either in empire or as a democratic political form of ruling. *Kyriarchal* relations of domination are built on elite male property rights as well as on the exploitation, dependency, inferiority, and obedience of women and men who signify all those subordinated. Such *kyriarchal* relations, according to Fiorenza, are still today at work "in the multiplicative intersectionality of class, race, gender, ethnicity, empire, and other structures of discrimination."[10]

The functional form of *kyriarchy* can be referred back to the Mediterranean societies of antiquity. Mediterranean societies, in fact, were dominated by a *kyriarchal* socio-political system that gave control to the emperor/lord/master/father/husband over male or female subordinates and subjugated peoples. *Kyriocentric* symbols of male superiority and dominance permeated cities and households. Such *kyriocentrism* makes distinctions between male and female to legitimize and sustain male ascendancy. As such, *kyrocentric* cultures grant power and privilege to those born as male.[11] Ancient Mediterranean households reflected the city's *kyriarchal* patterns and social life on a microcosmic scale in the same way that the city mirrored the cosmos. Just as rulers found religion a reliable ally for administering the empires political and economic agendas, fathers likewise had divine sanctions for sustaining their households.[12]

II. Theological basis of *Ekklesia* and *Kyriarchal* model as found in the New Testament

i. *Ekklesial* elements in the New Testament

The first place in the New Testament that we find the word *ekklesia* is in Mt. 16:18, where Jesus says, "And I tell you, you are Peter, and on this rock I will build my Church (*ekklesia*)..."[13] *Ekklesia* is basically a Pauline term. Paul never considered *ekklesia* as a physical structure but as a dedicated group of disciples of Jesus Christ.[14] He sees *ekklesia* as a new race, which he lists it alongside Jews and Greeks,[15] it is sufficiently equipped to fulfill God's purpose on earth, and it is the avenue through which the wisdom of God is made known.[16] In the Pauline literature the expression "*ekklesia*" is the very name for the Christian community. *Ekklesia* is the word that Paul employs when speaking of the Christian communities that gathered at various places throughout the Empire. This word carries multiple connotations within its context.

The most common reference for *ekklesia* in the Greco-Roman world was the civic gathering of the citizens of the city. This *ekklesia* was convened in order to make official economic, legal, and political decisions. Thus, to the non-Judean recipients of Paul's letters, the word *ekklesia* conveys the idea of this political assembly. This term also resonates with the language of the Septuagint, which employs the term *ekklesia* in order to refer to "the assembly of God." Thus, what makes the *ekklesia* of the early community distinct from the *ekklesia* of the civic assembly is that the early community, like Israel, is gathered together by God or Christ. Some, appeal to this observation in order to mitigate the potential political implications of Paul's use of this term.[17] However, within the Jewish Scriptures, the assembly of God was always understood as a theo-political entity. Israel was never simply a spiritual community; it was always an assembly with laws and values that governed all the concrete and material spheres of life. Paul employs the word *ekklesia* in order to connect the *ekklesia* of the early Christian community to both of the closely related Greco-Roman and Jewish definitions. Thus, the *ekklesia* of Christ has both a political and theological entity. Those who joined the *ekklesia* of Christ entered into a new ambiguous relationship to the Empire. On the other hand, those outside the assembly of Christ, particularly the ruling Powers look on these *ekklesia* with hostility. Rome did not look kindly on anything that came close to resembling an alternative order or political body.[18]

The new community of Christians broke with the Greek usage when it identifies itself as an *ekklesia*. It also broke with its Jewish usage by rejecting the term *Synagogue*. *Ekklesia* then was used in the New Testament in a way that infuses the word with new, distinctly Christian meaning.[19] The writers of the New Testament when they talked about the *ekklesia* meant a body of Christians called out of the Roman and Judean system to come together into a separate spiritual civil community. It meant a politically autonomous body of Christians under no king but Jesus. In the Christian *ekklesia* there was no hierarchy. No singular person ruled them.[20]

ii. *Kyriarchal* elements in the New Testament

Most of the New Testament literature was written in the last third of the first century and addressed Christian communities of that time. These communities seem to have experienced tensions, troubles, and even persecutions from their Jewish as well as their gentile environment. Although the post-Pauline literature seeks to lessen these tensions between the Christian community and Greco-Roman society by adapting the alternative Christian missionary movement to the patriarchal structures of their Greco-Roman society and culture, the primary Gospel writers insist that such suffering and persecutions cannot be avoided. Whereas the authors of the Epistles appeal to the authority of Paul or Peter to legitimize their injunctions for submission and adaptation to Greco-Roman patriarchal structures, the writers of the Gospels appeal to Jesus himself to support their alternative stress on altruistic love and service, which is demanded not from the least and the slaves but from the leaders and the masters, not only from the women but also from the men. While Mark and John highlighted the alternative character of the Christian community, and therefore accord women apostolic and ministerial leadership, the post-Pauline and post-Petrine writers seek to limit women's leadership roles in the Christian community to roles which are culturally and religiously acceptable.[21]

Thus, we see that although the early Christian community had its basis on the democratic equality, yet in the course of time, the *kyriarchal* elements penetrated into their *ekklesia.* The reason could be because of the socio-political, cultural context of their time. Hence, we find a series of the New Testament texts, namely the household code, which demands submission to the *kyrios*, the emperor, and the head of the household, i.e., the lord, slave-master and father. In these texts, three sets of relationships are mentioned: wife and husband, slave and master, children and father, and in each cases it is the *kyrios*/father to whom the members of the household owe submission. The purpose of these texts consists in reinforcing the authority of the *kyrios*/father by demanding submission and obedience from the socially weaker groups- wives, slaves and children and the whole community.

Family in the Roman Empire encompasses all those who are under the authority of the father including wife, children, slaves, clients, day-workers and even visitors. The household in the Roman

Empire was an economic production centre, education centre, trade and craft training centre, guarantor of social services and the locus of religious life. Politically, the household was the microcosm of the empire and the nursery of the state. According to Greco-Roman political ideology, a male citizen's authority rested in his dominance over his extended household. Thus, those who could not control their household risks losing control of the state. An emperor, therefore, had to maintain a firm patriarchal image and control his household so as to show that he is capable of ruling the empire. Thus, according to *Kyriarchal* ideology, the order of subordination of the empire was reflected in the submission of the *kyriarchal* household. To question this *kyriarchal* order and to destabilize the *kyriarchal* household was a threat to the order of the state.[22]

III. Hermeneutical Choice

The history of the church and its appeal to the authority of Scripture shows that Biblical traditions are not only life-giving but also death-dealing.[23] In short, the Bible and its subsequent interpretations are not only sources for liberation but also resources for oppression. It can be a resource not only for solving moral problems and generating moral challenges, but also for legitimizing dehumanization and violence.[24] This is true to the nature of *ekklesia,* when the church emphasizes the *kyriarchal* elements in the Bible and its socio-political and cultural context and neglected the *ekklesial* elements in the Bible.

1. Differences in Emphasis

i. *Ekklesia* model emphasize on radical democratic[25] elements

Ekklesia is not primarily a Christian, or even religious, term. It is a political entity, as this term originates from the democratic traditions of the Greco-Roman political order. Thus, *ekklesia* connects the matrix of Greek democratic concerns, with the issues of how citizenship and decision-making power express a radical equality and inclusivity.[26] As such, *ekklesia* has been translated as assembly, gathering or congress of full citizens, and it must be understood in terms of the political notions of "democratic congress of full decision-making citizens."[27] According to Fiorenza, *ekklesia* is a communal site of struggle where interests converge on the shaping of a radically democratic and inclusive community. To belong to *ekklesia* is to belong to a radically inclusive realm, a "cosmopolis," a "radical democratic assembly among many, in the cosmopolis of God's very different peoples." Although the ancient Greek polis still had patterns of exclusion, of women and others, but the notion of *ekklesia* marks a political space, a collective space of assembly, where radical democratic ethos is sought and forged through struggle.[28]

The very self-description of the early Christian communities gathered in the name of Jesus, as *ekklesia,* was a democratic one and one that seek to articulate a radical democratic ethos. Thus, when the Church adopted *ekklesia* as its name, it was a theological statement on the self-identity of the Church as a democratic community of equals and disciples. [29] The name *ekklesia* was self-description, to present the faith community not only as a new creation which practices equality and inclusiveness, but according to George Zachariah, it was also as a "pluriversal community" that converges different voices.[30]

In the *ekklesia,* both women and men have equal status, dignity and rights as images of the divine, an equal access to the varied gifts of the Spirit. Each and everyone enrich the democratic community of equals with their different experiences, vocations and talents. [31] In fact, the concept of radical democracy has been initiated by Jesus. Throughout the Gospels, we see that Jesus' attitude toward women was revolutionary. Contrary to Jewish custom, he freely socialized with women. Mark 15:40-41 states that at the cross were "Mary Magdalene, and Mary the mother of James the younger and of Joses, and Salome" who when he was in Galilee, followed him and ministered to him. In the home of Mary and Martha,[32] Jesus related to Mary as a teacher to a disciple and defended her right to a role which was commonly denied to Jewish women. In the Samaritan woman's story,[33] Jesus broke away from the Jewish principles by talking to this woman whom he would have scorned had he followed the tradition of his day. However, it is not only his actions which were positive toward women; his teachings also were revolutionary. By declaring that a man commits adultery in his heart when he looks at a woman for the purpose of lusting after her,[34] he affirmed that women have rights of their own and are not "things" to be "used."[35]

The evidence for an active, vital role of women in ministry in the apostolic age is stronger than is often acknowledged. Junia was considered an apostle prior to Paul.[36] When we look into the earliest days of the church, we find that women were involved in the Christian missionary movement at every stage of its expansion. Churches are identified as meeting in the homes of women[37] and there is no reason not to assume that these women gave leadership to these house churches.[38]

Women played an important role in the founding, sustaining, and promoting of these house churches. Women were also among the prophetic leaders of the communities. Luke characterizes Mary and Elizabeth, as well as Anna, as prophets. He mentions the four prophetic daughters of Philip[39] whose fame, according to Eusebius, was so great that the provinces of Asia derive their apostolic origin from them. Asia Minor continued to recognize women prophets even into the second and third centuries.[40] It should also be noted that Paul uses the same terms[41] that he uses for his male colleagues, when he refers to women in his letters.[42] These accounts from the bible represent the fundamental radical democratic spirit of the early Christian community. This emancipatory and democratic paradigm has been emphasized by the adherent of *ekklesia* model in biblical interpretation.[43]

Ekklesia is an alternative discursive site for exploration. *Ekklesia* constitutes itself wherever responsible people gather both to articulate, discuss, and celebrate their problems, visions, and goals and together decide on strategies and ways to political and religious self-determination.[44] To understand *ekklesia* as a radical democracy means to articulate a vision of radical equality for creating a world of justice and well-being. It means to make real the vision of justice and salvation which Jesus has proclaimed.[45] Radical democracy envisions equal opportunities for all to take part in decision making. It encourages people to take control over the course of their lives and supports structural arrangements that encourage citizens to exercise self-determination, to respect the rights of others, and to create opportunity for a truly participatory and egalitarian space.[46] Describing the *ekklesia* as of women and men, Fiorenza writes,

> This struggle for a radical democratic church is the struggle for freedom of thought, intellectual independence and personal integrity, for the free and uncensored speech of citizens, it is the struggle for church as *ekklesia*, as the congress of the people of God, as a fully decision making assembly.[47]

ii. *Kyriarchal* Model Emphasize on Authoritative and Dominating Elements

The studies of the social world of early Christianity, recognizing the significant role of the house-church for the early Christian mission suggested that the patriarchal ethics of the household expresses the ethos of the early Christian mission and that the Household codes was uniquely Christian because it addressed the subordinate group as moral agents.[48]

The early Christian vision of the discipleship of equals practiced in the house-church attracted especially slaves and women to Christianity but also caused tensions and conflicts with the dominant cultural ethos of the patriarchal household. What comes to the fore in the household code of the New Testament is the option for "an ethically softened or humanized notion of domination and rule." The writers of the New Testament conceive of the household code as a form of apologia for the Christian faith. However, unlike Josephus or Philo who write such defences for the attackers of the Jews, the writers of the New Testament addresses Christians, who are powerless and without legal recourse, urging them to adapt to the politics of Rome and its ancestral customs. In this way, the writers do not lessen the tension between the Christian community and the patriarchal society, since this tension is created precisely by the abandonment of the religion of the *pater familias*. The writers want to strengthen their rejection of the "old religion," but they do so by relinquishing the new freedom of those slaves and women who became members of the new priestly people. The accusation of second-century pagan writers that Christianity destroys the household by attracting especially women, slaves, and young people can thus not just be pushed aside as unfounded slander but must be taken seriously.[49]

The patriarchal-family was the nucleus of the state. Conversion of the subordinate members of the house who were supposed to share in the religion of the *pater familias* constituted a revolutionary subversive threat. Whenever slaves or wives converted to Judaism, to the Isis cult, or to Christianity, the order of the household was endangered and with it, therefore, the political order of the state. That Christians were suspected of political subversion and of threatening the societal order and institutions of the patriarchal house comes repeatedly to the fore in pagan attacks against Christianity in the second and third century. Christian slaves and wives, by being submissive and obedient to their "lords," can prove that the slanders against Christians are unjustified. Christians are not enemies of the Roman political order, but they support it. Naturally this "defense" could not establish that Christians did not disrupt the Greco-Roman order of the patriarchal house and state, since, by abandoning the religion of their masters and husbands, they in fact did so. However, this strategy for survival gradually introduced the patriarchal-societal ethos of the time into the church. As a result, in the long run it replaced the genuine Christian vision of equality, by which women and slaves had been attracted to become Christians.[50]

Key texts for the moral-theological justification of the patriarchal legitimation and repression of women's leadership and roles include e.g., Gen. 2-3 and especially the New Testament texts that demands the submission and silence of women in church. The texts which are classified as household code[51] enforces the submission and obedience of the socially weaker group, wives, slaves, and children on the one hand, and in the authority of the head of the household, the *pater familias*, on the other hand. The household dimension which characterizes the pattern of submissiveness includes obedience to the political powers of the state or address the governance of the Christian community. Thus, it pertained not only of individual families but also of church and state in terms of the patriarchal household. The Christian community soon comes to be called "the household of God" and from the time of Augustus the Roman emperor is himself understood as the *pater patriae*. The church has been shaped by this Biblical element of the household codes and their faithful remembrance and reinterpretation. The church's dominant structures and articulations are patriarchal and until very recently its moral and theological leadership has been exclusively male. The interpretation of these Biblical texts has led to the silencing and marginalization of women in the church and legitimized their societal and ecclesial exploitation by patriarchal family and church structures.[52]

2. Differences in Implementation

i. *Ekklesia* Model focus on Egalitarian Structures

Ekklesia comes from the understanding of the egalitarian social relations of the followers of Jesus, namely, a "discipleship of equals." To embrace the gospel means to enter into a community. The gospel calls into being the church as the discipleship of equals that is continually recreated in the power of the Spirit. The social implication of religious conversion was realized in the *ekklesia* as the discipleship of equals. Independently of their fathers and husbands women had membership and leadership in the Christian missionary movement. Paul's letter to Philemon mentions a woman among the leadership of the church in Philemon's house. In this letter Paul insists Philemon, a slave-master, with all the means of ancient rhetoric to accept Onesimus, his runaway slave, into the house-church not as an unfaithful slave but as a "beloved sibling," both as a Christian and as a human being. [53]

Ekklesia which is understood as the discipleship of equals in Mark's gospel is the community of sisters and brothers who do not have allegiances to "father" but has entered in a new relationship. It is the "new family" which has replaced all the natural-social kinship ties of the patriarchal family. It does not consist of rulers and subjects, of relationships of super-ordination and subordination. According to Paul, it is the assembly of the saints who have equal access to God in the Spirit and are therefore co-equal members in the body of Christ. Social roles in this *ekklesia* are not based on natural-social difference but on charismatic giftedness.[54]

According to sociologist R. Nisbet, conflict was the very essence of Christianity's relation to its age.[55] This conflict was a conflict of values and allegiances between the Christian community and the Roman patriarchal family. The Christian missionary movement conflicted with the existing order of the patriarchal household because it converted individuals independently of their social status and function in the patriarchal household. Christian mission caused social unrest because it admitted wives and slaves as well as daughters and sons into the house-church, even when the *pater familias* was still pagan and had not converted to Christianity. Thus when individual members of the household accept the message of the gospel and enter into the fellowship of *ekklesia,* they in a sense break away from the historic and deeply rooted kinship tie and embraces the community of Christians itself as the only real and true form of kinship. By offering the *ekklesia* as the new family kinship structure, the Christian movement disengaged women from their traditional patriarchal family roles and limitations.[56] As such, *ekklesia* is a communal sight that produces a radical democratic space where all members have equal rights, values, status and opportunities.[57]

In contrast to today's church, the early church viewed all its members as called and elected, gifted with the manifold talents of the Spirit. The New Testament writings do not know of a fixed and exclusive catalogue of ministry. Instead, a great number of *ekklesial* leadership functions are mentioned. Theologically and practically, the distinction between the sexes is insignificant in such a multiform exercise of ministry. The apostolic and prophetic ministry has always been exercised in the church by both women and men.[58]

Ekklesia presents an assembly where contradictory values and shared interests are equally embraced.[59] The discipleship of equals is thus best understood as a movement whose members like John the Baptizer and Jesus can be quite different in their strategies for change but they have in common their work to make present and experientially available God's different world of justice and well-being. According to Fiorenza, "such an egalitarian re-constructive historical model is able to place the beginnings of the Galilean prophetic *basileia* movement within a broader historical frame of reference."[60] Such historical model of emancipatory struggle sees the Jesus of history and the movement that has kept alive his memory not over and against Judaism but over and against structures of domination in antiquity and today. The *ekklesia* of the Jesus movement paved the way in the emancipatory struggles for a world of justice, liberation and freedom from *kyriarchal* oppression.[61] The concept of "*ekklesia*" is an expression of the unique libratory message of the Christian gospel.

ii. *Kyriarchal* Model Focuses on Imperial Structures

Those who opts for an institutionalized Church, uses the household code to justify the *kyriarchal* element in the Church from its very beginning. The sociological-historical justification for the household code maintains that the survival of the church in a patriarchal culture required an adaptation of its ethos and structures to the patriarchy of Greco-Roman society.[62] Besides, the household code also strengthened the unity of the Christian group and provided institutional patterns which enabled the church to survive.

Since conversion of the subordinated members of the house was posing a threat to the order of the patriarchal family which ultimately has its impact on the state, the household code attempted to soften this threat by asserting the resemblance of the Christian ethics with that of patriarchal house and state. However, it did not continue the ethos of the house-church, with its voluntary and collegial structures, but sought to modify it and bring it into line with the structures of patriarchal family and society. In doing so it Christianizes not only patriarchal ethics of inequality but also humanizes and modifies it, in such a way that it obliges the *pater familias* to love, consideration, and responsibility.[63]

By adapting the Christian community to its patriarchal society, the household ethos opens up the community to political co-optation by the Roman Empire. Submission and obedience, but not equality and justice, became institutionalized by the patriarchal ethos. Unfortunately, this ethos was not restricted to the household but was also adopted by the house-church. As such, Christian faith and praxis no longer provided a structural-political alternative to the dominant patriarchal culture.[64] The church as a Spirit filled community of equals was gradually Romanized and Christianity became an imperial religion. The state promoted ecclesiastical interests, church ministries became part of the imperial bureaucratic offices, the clergy became a privileged class, and the church adopted Roman imperial structures and measures.[65]

Like the Roman emperor, the Pope is called *pater patrum* and *pontifex maximus*. Like that of the Roman Empire, the church constituted of a combination of monarchic and aristocratic government with a facade of democracy in the election of the Pope. Like the Roman Empire, the Roman hierarchy has become an expansionist universal religious power that has exploited the resources and culture of the "subjugated provinces" i.e. the local churches. Like that of Roman imperialism, the hierarchy's universal mission has in the past used force, supported colonialism, and promulgated Euro-centrism, and still goes on to eliminate or appropriate the cultural and religious resources of its "subordinates." Military and mission, the gun and the bible, the sword and the cross went, and still go often, hand in hand.[66] As a result of the influence of the Roman imperial structure in the institutionalization of the Church, even up till now, many of the churches insists that the church can be represented by elite men only, draws its boundaries of identity in and through the exclusion of women from the sacred through the non-ordination of women. Its ethos is control, obedience and authoritarian exclusion.[67]

The very process of the transformation of the name of the early Christian community from *ekklesia* into "Church" which is derived from the Greek word *kyriakon*, i.e. belonging to the lord/ master/father, not from the Greek term *ekklesia*, indicates a historical development that has privileged the monarchic form of church.[68] This Church is characterized by hierarchical structures, represented by men, and divided into a sacred two-class system, the ordained and the laity. Hence, Fiorenza stresses that the expression laity/lay is not derived from the Greek *laos* - the people, but from *laikos*, which characterizes someone as subordinate to the clergy. It refers to those who are uneducated and belong to the secular realm, those who have no power and status in the church, those who are not religious. Because of their gender women are always laity. This division connotes not only second class citizenship for those who are not clergy men but also metaphysical difference.[69] Thus, *ekklesia* has been usurped to mean the church whose leaders rule the spiritual lives of their congregants through a clergy-laity system. Originally this was done to preserve the establishment of the Roman papal system. Later it was carried over to Protestantism at the time of the reformation.[70]

By breaking away from the Christian self-understanding as *Ekklesia,* the church became Roman when the church adopted the administrative organizational structures of the Roman Empire which were monarchical and hierarchical.[71] Since the *kyriakon/* ecclesia is a theological system which operates on a professional level, it emphasizes on the separation between the clergy and the laity, with much importance and prominence attributed to the clergy. Their rank-and-file are distinguished from the laity, as they function as priests-the self-proclaimed oracles of God. Unfortunately, this separation of the clergy from the community privileged the clergy over laity, leading to the entry of the hierarchical system in the church. The clergy then monopolize sacramental action, education and teaching, administration and leadership in mission, turning the laity into passive dependents who are to receive these services from the clergy and carry out their orders, but not participate in shaping, defining and embodying these activities themselves. Ministry becomes the special preserve of the ordained, rather than based in the community and articulated within and by it.[72]

Moreover, those who prefer *kyriarchal* model of the institutionalized church emphasizes that people cannot be bound together for any concrete action without some kind of organization. For them the essential thing about the church is its organization, an organization established by Christ when he gave authority to his disciples, who in turn delegates their power to others who succeeded them. Thus, for practical reasons, this makes the church principally clergy, for it is they who are given the power and authority necessary to maintain the organization.[73]

3. Differences in Preferences

i. *Ekklesia* Model Prefers Messianic Gospel of Radical Equality

The radical equality of the *ekklesia* is theologically grounded in the conviction that all are created in the image of the God and precious to God and all are blessed with the multifaceted gifts.[74] As a richly gifted people, *ekklesia* envisions and works for a community in which religious, racial and class no longer signify and legitimate status differences and relations of *kyriarchal* domination and subordination.

The principal and horizon of *ekklesia* is a radical democratic vision and movement that created community in diversity, commonality in solidarity, equality in freedom and love, a world community that appreciates the "other" precisely as the other. This theological conceptualization of the *ekklesia* seeks not only fullness of being, all-encompassing inclusivity, but also dynamic multiplicity and the convergence of many voices. It is for-shadowed in the image of Pentecost where people from different cultures could understand the spirit in their own languages. This image invites Christian women and men in the power of the spirit to struggle together with those from other religions and persuasions for the realization of the *ekklesia*.[75]

The church as an *ekklesial* community can be realized only when all women and men without exception have the opportunity to participate in the decision making process and power of church. The recognition of all people, both women and men, as full *ekklesial* citizens with all rights, privileges and duties demands a new self-understanding of theology and church. It requires the articulation of our identity not as sameness but as diversity and giftedness in the power of God. At the heart of the struggle for equality must remain the struggle for a radical democratic church, for equal authority, full citizenship and creative leadership.[76]

At this point it is important to explain the notion of equality. Equality is often understood as sameness rather than as equal standing or equal citizenship.[77] However, one does not have to understand equality as sameness and uniformity. Rather equality signifies a "correspondence" between groups of different persons/things that have the same quality in at least one respect but not in all respects i.e. they differ in many respects. Thus, equality means status equivalence, equitability and parity on grounds of having diverse gifts and experiences. Diversity and difference do not diminish equality, but enhance it. In this understanding equality is closely aligned with justice. In a radical democratic vision equality means equal access, equal respect, equal rights, and equal well-being. It must be realized as political, economic, social, cultural, religious, *ekklesial* equality. It does not mean sameness but difference and heterogeneity, inclusivity and partnership, self-determination and alternating leadership rooted in different gifts of the Spirit. This is evident from the fact that all members of the *ekklesia* in the early Christian community received the gifts of Spirit but not all are the same. They are all equal and at the same time different because of their manifold gifts. For Fiorenza, this *ekklesial* ethos of equality should be a motivation to resist the forces of domination, to continue our commitment to bring about not only a different church but also a different truly cosmopolitan society. A radical democratic spirituality requires a political-religious commitment not only to the struggle against sexism in church and society but also to those against racism, poverty, ageism, and capitalist colonialism, because they are structures of oppression.[78]

Christian ministry encompasses all believers who must gather together as a discipleship community which embraces the values of the reign of God. Such a vision of Christian ministry as the "discipleship of equals" is characterized by commitment, accountability, and solidarity in the *ekklesia*. The understanding of Christian ministry as a "discipleship of equals" is a central embodiment of the vision of a "new church" which is in solidarity with the oppressed and the "least" of this world.[79] This is also the vision of the *basileia*[80] of God. It is an alternative world of justice and well-being intended by the life-giving power of God as reality and vision in the midst of ongoing patriarchal oppression and human degradation. Thus, the discipleship of equals is based on the commission of Jesus that all disciples through the power of the Holy Spirit should share the good news of the gospel in a way which envisions an alternative world liberated from hunger, poverty, sexism, racism, discrimination and domination.[81]

Fiorenza argues that the vision of the *basileia* cannot be realized within a community which is patriarchal, hierarchal and exclusive. "God's *basileia* is realized in Jesus' table community with the poor, the sinners, the tax collectors, and prostitutes with all those who 'do not belong' to the 'holy people', who are somehow deficient in the eyes of the righteous." In other words, women are just as much included in the vision of the *basileia* as are men, in that this is essentially what God intended through His son, Jesus Christ.[82] *Ekklesia* is, thus, best conceptualized as an alternative space - not as a counter or anti-space - but as an alternative space to domination and *empire* because it is constituted not by super- and subordination but by egalitarian relationships. It is a *utopian* space that promotes an alternative vision of social and individual existence.[83] *Ekklesia* should continue to struggle to live in fullness and to realize its calling to be the radical democratic society.[84]

ii. *Kyriarchal* Model Prefers Gospel of Subordination

The gospel of domination and subordination has been the rule of the *kyriarchal* model since from antiquity. In the classical Greek *Kyriarchy,* the democratic state is structured and sustained by the pyramidal form of the patriarchal household in which the propertied male head, the father of the household, had legal power over his wife, children, relatives, slaves and other dependants. The structuring dividing lines run between men who owned property and those women and men who were owned, between rulers and those who were ruled, between those who as superiors commanded and those who as subordinates had to obey, between those who free from manual labour had leisure for philosophy and politics, and those who are economically dependent and whose labour was exploited.[85]

The *kyriarchal* model that was prevalent during the early centuries of the beginning of Christianity is that of the Roman Empire which exemplified a monarchical pyramid of intersecting structures of domination that incorporates elements of traditional democratic practices. At the apex of this *Roman kyriarchal imperialism* stood the emperor, who is called *pater patrum* or the "father of all fathers," and who is divinized and acclaimed as "God of Gods and Lord of Lords." Roman imperial power was seen as *Pax Romana,* a beneficial system of peace for all conquered peoples. Its harsh and exploitative rule is symbolically indicated in the Book of Revelation.[86] Neo-Aristotelian philosophy legitimated this Roman *kyriarchal* model of imperial power and entered into the Christian Scriptures in the form of *kyriarchal* injunctions to submission. The First Epistle of Peter, for instance, admonishes Christian servants to be submissive even to harsh and brutal masters (2:18–25) and instructs freeborn wives to subordinate themselves to their husbands, even those who are not Christians (3:1–6). Simultaneously, it entreats Christians to be subject to and honour the emperor as supreme (2:13–17).[87]

The *Kyriarchal* model which ascribes to the hierarchical pyramid of the institutionalizes church views the process of ecclesial patriarchalisation as the historically necessary development from *charism* to office, from Paulinism to early Catholicism, from a millenarian radical ethos to a privileged Christian establishment, from the egalitarian structures of the beginnings to the hierarchical order of the Constantinian church. This view maintains that the patriarchalisation of the early Christian movement was necessary if Christian communities were to grow, develop and become historically viable. The institutionalization of the egalitarian community could not, but be a part of the patriarchal institutional structures. [88]

Those who advocate the *kyriarchal* model appeal to the maleness of Christ, to essential gender differences, and to the Scriptural texts of subordination in order to legitimate church practices and structures that exclude all women and laity from sacramental, doctrinal, and governing power. The church understood as clerical-patriarchal hierarchy not only is exclusive of women in leadership, but also requires a Lord/Master/Father-centred symbol system and language for legitimization. As a result, the struggle of the feminist/womanist for the vision of the discipleship of equals has generally been met with outright rejection or subtle co-optation. Those who advocate patriarchal restoration of church and theology continue to insist either on women's exclusion from decision-making powers in the church or on obedience to patriarchal teachings.[89]

The implications of this for Christian ministry is that - the vision of the kingdom seems to be largely absent in our churches today. In preaching, reading and teaching from pulpits, as well as in academic discussions, this kind of vision is often either misconstrued, misinterpreted or, in some instances, just not mentioned. This understanding is acknowledged with particular reference to the way in which patriarchal and hierarchical structures continue to dominate the day-to-day operations of the church and society. In many instances, the church is still a *kyriarchal* institution which is dominated by the clergy and male members in which male-dominated interpretations of texts and teaching are encountered on a large scale.[90] Thus, the ethos of domination and exploitation has found its way into Christian Scriptures and Theology.

IV. Hermeneutical Choice and the Future of *Ekklesia*: Hopeful or Hopeless

At stake are two different visions of faith: the church of Caesar, powerful and rich, and the church of Christ, loving, poor, and spiritually rich,[91] a competition between radically different church structures and self-understanding of *ekklesia*, over and against the authority of hierarchal church organization.[92] Both models of church, that of submission and subordination characteristic of Roman imperialism and that of the discipleship of equals richly gifted in the power of God, are inscribed in Scripture and embedded in tradition. Thus, there is a constant struggle over the future of the church: either as an *ekklesia* or as an ecclesia.

If an *ekklesial* model of the church is to be envisaged we must continue to exercise our responsibility as the people of God by calling the 'malestream' church to conversion. Like the early Christians we must continue to model and build *ekklesial* communities that are not governed by control, subordination and obedience but realize the freedom of the children of God. We must celebrate and appreciate all the gifts of the Spirit that are given to us for the building up of the community. If our diverse struggles for equality, dignity, and well-being in society and church continue, this radical democratic tradition can become an ever-expanding reality. We are not alone in our struggles for a radical democratic church and world, says Fiorenza, because a "great cloud of witnesses" surrounds us and have preceded us throughout the centuries in the discipleship of equals. This radical egalitarian spiritual vision and hope for a different society and church of justice, equality, and well-being does not turn us into idealistic dreamers, but gathers the members of the *ekklesia* as a discipleship of equals.[93]

The belief that all are created equal and the notion of *ekklesia* as the discipleship of equals, are both incongruent with the reality of the contemporary church. According to Fiorenza, *ekklesia* is an alternative to the vision of *kyriarchy,* because of its notion of "radical democracy." If one analyses the present church, one could ask whether the church is democratic or not and, furthermore, should the church be democratic or not? However, a "radical democratic" vision is realized and personified repeatedly in the transformative liberation and freedom struggles of all marginalized and exploited creatures.[94] A radical democratic spirituality of struggle that is articulated and lived everyday by women and men is able to sustain hope in our varied struggles for a different, radical democratic future.[95]

Ekklesia as the discipleship of equals is perhaps one way in which Christian ministry could be viewed as a creative means which stimulates new ways of critical reflection and communication. A discipleship of equals also allows people at the margins to create for themselves a unique space within which to collaborate on issues such as identity, self-empowerment, spirituality and many other ethical and societal concerns. Only on these premises can all humanity be completely "healed", nurtured and strengthened to live their lives to the fullest measure of that which God intended for all of creation.[96]

The recognition of all women and men as full *ekklesial* citizens with equal rights and duties is central to the vision of a radical democratic church. It demands a new theological articulation and self-understanding of ministry and church. It insists that "ministry as a gift of the Spirit is more fundamental and comprehensive than order." It requires an articulation of identity not as sameness but as rich diversity and varied giftedness in the power of God.[97] If the Church as a called out community-*ekklesia* is to remain faithful to its calling as a discipleship of equals, the church should combat against all forms of exclusion as well as dominating and oppressing elements that is characteristics of an institutionalized *kyriarchy.*

In and through the struggles for change and liberation, the vision of the *ekklesia* of God's life-giving and transforming power should become an experiential reality in the midst of structural sin, in the midst of the death-dealing powers of oppression and dehumanization. The discipleship of equals calls us to proclaim the good news of God's alternative world of justice and love, through the gathering around the Eucharistic table, and by inviting everyone without exception to it. The *ekklesia* as the discipleship of equals realizes this vision of God's renewed creation by feeding the hungry, welcoming the stranger, healing the sick, liberating the oppressed,[98] cherishing the earth, and being in solidarity with those who are wronged by racism, nationalism, poverty, neo-colonialism, and hetero-sexism. In this way, the members of *ekklesia* can live as a discipleship of equals,[99] and thereby redeem the Biblical understanding of the "discipleship of Christ" as an "*ekklesia*"- "a discipleship of equals." This hermeneutical choice can give hope to the future of *ekklesia*.

Endnotes:

[1] Yet, it must not be overlooked that ancient movements of emancipatory struggles against exploitation and domination do not begin with the movement around Jesus. Rather they have a long history in Greek, Roman, Asian, and Jewish cultures. The emancipatory struggles of biblical wo/men must be seen within the wider context of cultural-political-religious struggles for freedom from oppression. Elisabeth Schüssler Fiorenza, "Wo/men of the Word: Reclaiming Our Power of Memory," http://www.futurechurch.org/watw/btg/schusslerfiorenza.htm (accessed August 06, 2013).

[2] Solon (c. 638-558 BCE) was an Athenian statesman, lawmaker and poet. He is remembered particularly for his efforts to legislate against political, economic, and moral decline in archaic Athens. His reforms failed in the short term, yet he is often credited with having laid the foundations for Athenian democracy.

[3] http://www.britannica.com/EBchecked/topic/177746/Ecclesia (accessed August 08, 2013).

[4] http://christadelphians.wordpress.com/what-and-why-ecclesia/ (accessed July 14, 2013).

[5] Elisabeth Schüssler Fiorenza, *But She Said: Feminist Practices of Biblical Interpretation* (Boston: Beacon Press, 1992), 8.

[6] Elisabeth Schüssler Fiorenza, "Introduction: Exploring the Intersections of Race, Gender, Status, and Ethnicity in Early Christian Studies," in *Prejudice and Christian Beginnings: Investigating Race, Gender, and Ethnicity in Early Christianity*, ed. Laura Nasrallah and Elisabeth Schüssler Fiorenza (Minneapolis: Augsburg Fortress Press, 2009), 9.

[7] Elisabeth Schüssler Fiorenza, *The Power of the Word: Scripture and the Rhetoric of Empire* (Minneapolis: Augsburg Fortress Press, 2007), 158.

[8] http://feministphilosophers.wordpress.com/2008/05/01/word-of-the-day-kyriarchy/ (accessed August 08, 2013).

[9] Fiorenza, *But She Said: Feminist Practices of Biblical Interpretation*, 123.

[10] Elisabeth Schüssler Fiorenza, *Wisdom Ways: Introducing Feminist Biblical Interpretation* (Maryknoll: Orbis Books, 2001), 118.

[11] Beginning with the household, the head of the household, i.e. the father, performed different rituals to determined kinship and encode gender distinctions. Thus, the father in ancient Greek households performed the rite, in which he carried his child around the hearth, as part of his decision to accept the child as a legitimate heir. The Roman father inherited the responsibility for all religious rituals in his household; thus, he held a priestly status. Jewish fathers circumcised their infant sons under obligation of the Law of Moses, following the example of Abraham (Gen. 21:4).

[12] Rick Talbott, "Imagining the Matthean Eunuch Community: *Kyriarchy* on the Chopping Block," *Journal of Feminist Studies in Religion* 22, no. 1 (2006): 23-25.

[13] Peter Ditzel, "Ekklesia or Church, Does It Matter?" http://www.wordofhisgrace.org/ekklesia.pdf (accessed January 20, 2014).

[14] Philm. 2; Col. 4:15.

[15] 1 Cor. 10:32.

[16] "Church," in *Mounce's Complete Expository Dictionary of the Old and New Testament Words*, eds. William D. Mounce, D. Matthew Smith and Miles V. Van Pelt (Grand Rapids: Zondervan Publishing House, 2006), 110.

[17] Johannes Weiss argues that the assemblies of those in Christ are multinational but not political entities, and James Dunn argues that Paul's Jewish talk in this regard is more theological than political.

[18] "Reading Paul in the Context of Empire: Roman Imperialism, Pauline Resistance, and Contemporary Implications," http://miketodd.typepad.com/files/paul-the-politics-of-empire.pdf (accessed January 21, 2014).

[19] Lawrence O. Richards, *Expository Dictionary of Bible Words* (Grand Rapids: Zondervan Publishing House, 1985), 164f.

[20] Roger Gaikwad, "Towards a New Ecclesia: Re-Reading the Concept of 'Ecclesia' in the Bible: A few Pointers," *Religion and* Society 56, no. 2 (June 2011): 14 (12-20).

[21] Elisabeth Schüssler Fiorenza, *In Memory of Her: A Feminist Theological Reconstruction of Christian Origins* (New York: Crossroad, 1983), 334.

[22] Fiorenza, *The Power of the Word*, 151-153.

[23] For example, the appeal to Scripture has authorized persecution of Jews, burning of witches, torture of heretics, national wars of Europe, the subhuman conditions of American slavery, and the anti-social politics of the Moral Majority.

[24] Elisabeth Schüssler Fiorenza, "Discipleship and Patriarchy: Early Christian Ethos and Christian Ethics in a Feminist Theological Perspective," *Annual of the Society of Christian Ethics* (1982): 133.

[25] Democracy is determined by the notion of equal power among members of a society. It, therefore, requires a radical redistribution of wealth as well as the elimination of social and political hierarchies. Elisabeth Schüssler Fiorenza, *Rhetoric and Ethics: The Politics of Biblical Studies* (Minneapolis: Augsburg Fortress Press, 1999), 192.

[26] Mark Lewis Taylor, "Challenging Theological Studies: Critical Feminism and Liberating Interpretation," *Theology Today* 66, no. 2 (July 2009): 236.

[27] Elisabeth Schüssler Fiorenza, "Equality: A Radical Democratic Ekklesial Vision," http://www.cta usa.org/reprint11-98/fiorenza.html (accessed August 06, 2013).

[28] Taylor, "Challenging Theological Studies: Critical Feminism and Liberating Interpretation," 236.

[29] Elisabeth Schüssler Fiorenza, "Equality: A Radical Democratic Ekklesial Vision," http://www.cta-usa.org/reprint11-98/fiorenza.html (accessed August 06, 2013).

[30] George Zachariah, "Church without Walls: Church Happening in the Street," *Masihi Sevak: Journal of Christian Ministry* 38, no. 3 (April 2013): 18-19.

[31] Lutasha Ann-Louise Abrahams, "A critical comparison of Elizabeth Schüssler Fiorenza's notion of Christian ministry as a 'Discipleship of Equals' and Mercy Amba Oduyoye's notion as a 'Partnership of both men and women'" http://etd.uwc.ac.za/usrfiles/modules/etd/docs/etd_gen8Srv25Nme4_7804_1181886366.pdf (accessed August 26, 2013).

[32] Lk. 10:38-42.

[33] Jn. 4:1-42.

[34] Mt. 5:28.

[35] Roger L. Omanson, "The Role of Women in the New Testament Church," *Review & Expositor* 83, no. 1 (Winter 1986): 16-19.

[36] Rom. 16:7.

[37] Mary, Acts 12:12; Lydia, Acts 16:40; Priscilla, Rom. 16:3-5; 1 Cor. 16:19; Chloe, 1 Cor. 1:11; Nympha, Col. 4:15.

[38] The house church was the beginning of the church in a city or district. It provided space for the preaching of the word, for worship, as well as for social and Eucharistic table sharing.

[39] Acts 21: 9.

[40] Elizabeth Steele, "The Role of Women in the Church," *Currents in Theology and Mission* 13, no. 1 (1986): 15.

[41] Priscilla was a "fellow-worker in Christ Jesus" (Rom. 16:3); Mary "worked hard" among the Roman Christians (Rom. 16:6); Junia was a person "of note among the apostles" (Rom. 16:7); Tryphaena and Tryphosa were "workers in the Lord" (Rom. 16:12); Euodia and Syntyche "labored side by side" with Paul in the gospel (Phil. 4:3); and Phoebe was a "deacon in the church at Cenchreae," who had helped many (Rom. 16:1-2).

[42] Omanson, "The Role of Women in the New Testament Church," 15-25.

[43] Daniel Darko, "a book review on, *Transforming Vision: Explorations in Feminist The*logy*, by Elisabeth Schüssler Fiorenza," http://www.bookreviews.org/pdf/8348_9131.pdf (accessed February 28, 2014).

[44] Ibid.

[45] Fiorenza, "Equality: A Radical Democratic Ekklesial Vision."

[46] Elisabeth Schüssler Fiorenza, "A Critical Feminist Spirituality of Struggle," http://www.womenutc.com/elisabeth.htm (accessed August 06, 2013).

[47] Elisabeth Schüssler Fiorenza, "We Are Church-A Kindom of Priests," *WOW* (July 22, 05)http://women-churchconvergence.org/WOW%20anniversary%20addresses/WE%20ARE%20CHURCH%20%20A%20KINDOM%20OF%20PRIESTS%20by%20Elisabeth%20Schussler%20Fiorenza.pdf (accessed August 26, 2013).

[48] Fiorenza, "Discipleship and Patriarchy: Early Christian Ethos and Christian Ethics in a Feminist Theological Perspective," 141.

[49] Fiorenza, *In Memory of Her*, 251-262.

[50] Ibid., 264f.

[51] Col. 3:18-4:1 and Eph. 5:22-6-9; 1 Pet. 2:18-3:7; 1 Tim. 2:11-15; 5:3-8; 6:1-2; Tit. 2:2-10; 3:1-2; 1 Clem. 21:6-8; Ign. Pol. 4:1 - 6:2; Pol. 4:2 - 6:1; Did. 4:9-11; Barn. 19:5-7.

52 Fiorenza, "Discipleship and Patriarchy: Early Christian Ethos and Christian Ethics in a Feminist Theological Perspective," 135f.

53 Ibid., 143f.

54 Elisabeth Schüssler Fiorenza, *Bread not Stone: The Challenge of Feminist Biblical Interpretation* (Boston: Beacon Press, 1995), 75.

55 Quoted by Fiorenza, "Discipleship and Patriarchy," 144f.

56 Ibid.

57 Fiorenza, *In Memory of Her*, 344.

58 Fiorenza, "We Are Church-A Kindom of Priests."

59 Darko, "a book review on *Transforming Vision: Explorations in Feminist The*logy*, by Elisabeth Schüssler Fiorenza."

60 Yet, it must not be overlooked that ancient movements of emancipatory struggles against exploitation and domination do not begin with the movement around Jesus. Rather they have a long history in Greek, Roman, Asian, and Jewish cultures. The emancipatory struggles of biblical wo/men must be seen within the wider context of cultural-political-religious struggles for freedom from oppression.

61 Elisabeth Schüssler Fiorenza, "Wo/men of the Word: Reclaiming Our Power of Memory" http://www.futurechurch.org/watw/btg/schusslerfiorenza.htm (accessed August 06, 2013).

62 Fiorenza, *Bread not Stone*, 79.

63 Fiorenza, "Discipleship and Patriarchy: Early Christian Ethos and Christian Ethics in a Feminist Theological Perspective," 149f.

64 Fiorenza, *Bread not Stone*, 78f.

65 Fiorenza, "We Are Church-A Kindom of Priests."

66 Elisabeth Schüssler Fiorenza, "Wo/men, Mission and the Catholicity of Theology," in *The Church in Mission: Universal Mandate and Local Concerns*, ed. Thomas Malipurathu and L. Stainslaus (Gujarat: Gujarat Sahitya Prakashan, 2002), 158.

67 Fiorenza, "We Are Church-A Kindom of Priests."

68 Fiorenza, *The Power of the Word: Scripture and the Rhetoric of Empire*, 78.

69 Fiorenza, "Equality: A Radical Democratic Ekklesial Vision."

70 Albert James Dager, "What is 'the Church'?: With whom did God make His New Covenant?" *Media Spotlight: A Biblical Analysis of Religious and Secular Media* https://www.yumpu.com/en/document/view/10258417/what-is-the-church-media-spotlight (accessed January 07, 2014).

71 Elisabeth Schüssler Fiorenza, *Discipleship of Equals: A Critical Feminist Ekklesiology of Liberation* (New York: Crossroad, 1993), 2.

72 Rosemary Radford Ruether, "The Church as Liberation Community from Patriarchy: The Praxis of Ministry as Discipleship of Equals," http://womenchurchconvergence.org/WOW%20anniversary%20addresses/The%20Church%20as%20Liberation%20Community%20by%20Rosemary%20RR.pdf (accessed January 27, 2014).

73 Paul Hessert, *Introduction to Christianity* (New Jersey: Prentice-Hall, 1958), 290f.

74 Fiorenza, "Wo/men, Mission and the Catholicity of Theology," 168.

75 Fiorenza, *The Power of the Word: Scripture and the Rhetoric of Empire*, 78f.

76 Fiorenza, "We Are Church-A Kindom of Priests."

77 According to the common usage of equality, for women to become equal means that they have to become like men. Just as for blacks to become equal means

they have to become like whites, or for the laity to become equal means that they have to become like clergymen. In this vision maleness, whiteness and clergy status are the standards of being human and Christian. As long as structures of domination and subordination exist, equality is only possible for those who are in the dominant position. The vision of the *ekklesia* understood as a radical discipleship of equals compels us to question and change such structures of domination and to define equality differently.

[78] Fiorenza, "Equality: A Radical Democratic Ekklesial Vision."

[79] Lutasha Ann-Louise Abrahams, "A critical comparison of Elizabeth Schüssler Fiorenza's notion of Christian ministry as a 'Discipleship of Equals' and Mercy Amba Oduyoye's notion as a 'Partnership of both Men And Women'" (masters thesis, University of the West Cape, 2005), 23.

[80] The term *basileia* is normally translated as "kingdom" or "rule"

[81] Fiorenza , Fiorenza, *Discipleship of Equals: A Critical Feminist Ekklesia-logy of Liberation*, 12.

[82] Ibid., 121.

[83] Fiorenza, "Wo/men of the Word."

[84] Fiorenza, *The Power of the Word: Scripture and the Rhetoric of Empire*, 79.

[85] Fiorenza, *But She Said: Feminist Practices of Biblical Interpretation*, 115-117.

[86] Fiorenza, "Introduction: Exploring the Intersections of Race, Gender, Status," 11f.

[87] Fiorenza, *But She Said: Feminist Practices of Biblical Interpretation*, 115-117.

[88] Fiorenza, "Discipleship and Patriarchy," 149f.

[89] Fiorenza, "Equality: A Radical Democratic Ekklesial Vision."

[90] Abrahams, "A Critical Comparison of Elizabeth Schüssler Fiorenza's Notion," 28.

[91] Fiorenza, "Equality: A Radical Democratic Ekklesial Vision."

[92] Fiorenza, *In Memory of Her: A Feminist Theological Reconstruction of Christian Origins*, 302-303.

[93] Fiorenza, "Equality: A Radical Democratic Ekklesial Vision."

[94] Abrahams, "A Critical Comparison of Elizabeth Schüssler Fiorenza's Notion," 26.

[95] Fiorenza, "A Critical Feminist Spirituality of Struggle."

[96] Abrahams, "A Critical Comparison of Elizabeth Schüssler Fiorenza's Notion," 29.

[97] Fiorenza, "We Are Church-A Kindom of Priests."

[98] Fiorenza, *Discipleship of Equals: A Critical Feminist Ekklesia-logy of Liberation*, 12.

[99] Fiorenza, "Equality: A Radical Democratic Ekklesial Vision."

Chapter 11
Ekklesia in the midst of Religious and Cultural Pluralism

John Basy Paul

Introduction

Indian church exists in a pluralistic context surrounded by different cultural and faith traditions. It is not a single entity but a reflection of various faith traditions. Although the Indian church is Christian in its nature, it is influenced by other religion and their architectural styles. Besides, Church is never static but dynamic. It always tries to revive itself time to time in order to become relevant and contextual. To have a broader understanding about the role of church in a multi religious and cultural context like India, this article is divided into three sections. Firstly, we try to understand the role of church as a 'temple' and devotion as '*Bhakti*' in Indian context. Moreover, it also deals with the aspect about the Indian way of meditation and worship. Secondly, a church structure is analyzed which was constructed with a pluralistic message, where the structure itself stands and starts dialoguing by its architectural style and presence. Further, it states how a structure itself can speak and initiate a dialogue to have interreligious harmony. Thirdly, an attempt is made to critically analyze the present ecclesial conditions to make a radical shift, so as to make church relevant and more contextual in the midst of religious and cultural pluralism.

1. Understanding the Role of 'Temple' and 'Worship' in Indian context

1.1. Temple

1.1.1. Temple – A Place of Worship

The two Greek words *Hieron* and *Naos* are translated as 'temple.' *Hieron* refers to the collection of buildings which comprised the temple of Jerusalem.[1] *Naos* refers most specifically to the sanctuary. On the other hand, *Hehkal* and *Hayith* denote 'temple' in Hebrew, referring to the complex buildings in Jerusalem which is the centre for the sacrificial cult of Hebrews.[2]

It indicates that temples are the earliest structures built by human beings to worship the god in their house. The Tower of Babel is the first structure mentioned in the Bible which gives an example for existence of temple in the early times (Gen. 11:4). It stood as an attempt made by human beings to climb to heaven, symbolizing their confidence to meet god.[3] Furthermore, the central place in the religious life of ancient Israel is 'temple' which is reflected throughout the Bible. This clearly emphasizes that 'temple' is the object of religious aspiration. There were three temples that stood successively on the mount Moriah (2 Chr. 3:1) in Jerusalem. In the present times it is known as Haram-al-Sherif, which is considered as the holy place of Muslims. The first one was built by King Solomon; the second by Zerubabbel and Jews, after returning from the exile; and the third which was in use and began during the time of Jesus, largely built by Herod the Great.[4] Thus, it is evident that ancient temples served as state treasures empties to pay tribute, or filled or decorate with booty according to the power of the land.

But, in the New Testament the term 'temple' is used figuratively in numerous ways. Jesus spoke of the temple of his body (Jn. 2:19, 21). In Corinthians, an individual believer is the temple of God (1 Cor. 6:19). But, in the book of Hebrews, Christ as the fulfillment of the typology of the temple rituals is elaborated. On the other hand, the English word 'Church' is derived from the Greek adjective *Kyriakos* and also used in some phrases as *Kyriakon doma* or *Kyriake oikia* which means 'the Lord's house'. It symbolizes a Christian place of worship. However, in the New Testament the Greek term *'Ekkelesia'* is used in reference with the local congregation of Christians and never referred to a building.[5]

Further, in the Indian context, starting from the pre-*vedic* times, worship and worshiping place have a pivotal role to play in life and the living of the people. Worship places are the spaces where people can easily get connected and contemplate about God. Temples were geographically situated at the high altitudes like mountains and hills as a symbolism of divine highness. In Hinduism, temple is a sanctuary of a god or a goddess and not a place of public worship. There is no liturgy or sacraments, devotees do not flock into the shrine. The priest performs all the rituals and ceremonies with and participation of laity.[6] Thus 'temple' is considered as a place of worship.

1.1.2. Temple – A Place of Identity

Worship is the prime focus of any religion. And the worshiping place whether it is a Temple, Mosque, Church or Gurudwara are not just a place of worship but also an icon of identity. The scenic beauty and the style of the architecture in the old royal temple are an art of honor. These provide an evidence of how rulers of a kingdom made attempts to identify themselves with the world of Gods.[7] In the past through temple structures, kings identify themselves with God, but in the present times, people identify themselves with their religious worship places.

Worship places are also one of the prime reasons for conflict. It plays a major role not just in spiritual wellbeing of the people but also in socio-political, economic fronts. In Indian context there are several examples where worship places have become a hub for conflicts with political significance. The demolition of *Babri Masjid* in Ayodhya, claiming it as the holy birth place of Lord Rama and the later violence that erupted in India which continues even today is the best example, to understand how people are sensitive more towards worship places than worship in India. In the present context the worshiping places are not just places of worship but it's a place of identity too. Furthermore, in the Indian context, temple is not only a place of worship and identity but also a place where people express their faith in the form of *Bhakti* (devotion) through meditation. Though these concepts are from Hindu tradition they crept into the Christian church and are relevant in church worship as an expression of people's devotion through their *Bhakti* to the ultimate divine.

1.2 *Bhakti*

According to Ramanuja,

> The radical awareness of our dependence on God and firm conviction that, left to ourselves, we are unable to live, act and work out our salvation, prompts us to take refuge in him, to have recourse in his divine help. This is the starting point of *Bhakti,* which should ultimately lead the seeker to the highest form of knowledge namely, the direct, intuitive experimental knowledge of the divine form in liberation.[8]

On the other hand God as a person has many attributes and qualities and the relationship between God and soul varies according to the individual's personal relationship with God. This personal relationship can be expressed in different ways and forms like singing, praising, adoring God, offering gifts and committing oneself to God.[9] These ways of expression in Hindu tradition is known as *Bhakti*. It is one of the important paths to attain the ultimate revelation of God.

1.2.1. *Bhakti* – Devotion

Bhakti can be simply defined as the spontaneous out pour of the heart's love towards an object of its desire. Continues meditation on God with great love is also called as *Bhakti.*[10] However, a broader understanding on Hindu concept of *Bhakti* will open the horizons wide to understand about the devotion in Indian church. Because, in the Indian church devotion is influenced by Hindu concept of *Bhakti*.

Bhagavata-Purana divides devotion or *Bhakti* into two categories. Firstly, *Santa-Bhakti,* wherein the devotee expresses his/her feeling towards God as, 'I am His', and the devotion ends with the merger of the devotee into divine. Secondly, *Prema-Bhakti,* the devotee expresses his/her feelings towards God as, 'He is mine', and there is an intense affection and passion towards God through love and devotion which provokes a devotee to serve God as a servant, child, friend, spouse or lover.[11] In addition, there is an attitude with which a devotee expresses his/her devotion to God.

There are seven ways or attitudes with which a devotee expresses his/her devotion to God. Firstly, *Sisu-Bhava* here the attitude of the devotee towards God is like a child to his/her parents.[12] God is seen as a father or mother wherein devotee expresses his/her love and devotion with healthy fear and reverence.

Secondly, *Vatsalya-Bhava,* which points toward the attitude of the devotee towards God is like a Mother towards his/her child. God is considered as a helpless and dependent child. Thereby, devotee through his/her attitude is in love with Child-God. The devotee sings lullabies to God, putting him to sleep and explains his innocent acts of child. We can also find several Christian hymns in the regional languages which express such devotion.

Thirdly, *Dasya-Bhava,* where it represents the attitude of the devotee towards God is like a servant towards his/her master. Fear, admiration and attention are the important sentiments between God and devotee. God has a total will to use his devotee, and the devotee will be submissive to that will.

Fourthly, *Sakhya-Bhava,* which suggests the attitude between devotee and God will be as a friend to friend. There is more openness and spontaneity where devotee shares all his/her secrets to God. The devotee maintains an informal relationship with God through his/her informal talks.

Fifthly, *Sisya-Bhava,* indicates the attitude between devotees towards God is like a disciple towards Guru (teacher). God as a Guru removes all ignorance and darkness out off his disciples/ devotee.[13] The disciple takes refuge in God to liberate him/herself from darkness and ignorance.

Sixthly, *Kanta-Bhava,* which means the devotee, considers him/herself as a bride and God as a bridegroom. There is an intense love, passion yearning for God. The thoughts, imagination and mental activities of the devotee are preoccupied with God.

Seventhly, *Kamuki Bhava,* it signifies the attitude between devotee and God will be as between two lovers. There is a blind love for the loved one and a kind of intoxication. There is also an agony of separation. A mystical erotic language is used to explain the relationship between a longing soul of a devotee and God.[14]

However, the grace of God plays a major role in *bhakti*. It is *bhakti* movement which introduced the dynamic grace of God in the ritual and spiritual scenario of Hinduism. The early school like *Samkya, Nyaya, Vaisesika* and *Mimamasa* did not consider God's grace. But, they gave importance to the efforts of devotee to control his/her mind, deeds and passion. The devotee him/herself decides their destination through their deeds.[15] But *bhakti* advocated the importance and the involvement of God for spiritual perfection.

Similarly, when we closely try to understand the lyrics of the Christian hymnal it clearly identifies these expressions of *bhakti* in Christian worship too. Several Christian hymn writers are converted from Hinduism to Christianity. They had brought expression of *bhakti* in their ways. And now it became a part of Christian worship. So the above mentioned attitudes between devotee and God are even part of Christian church in India basically expressed through singing. Apart from *bhakti,* meditation also plays a major role as an expression of *bhakti* which is common in both Hindu and Christian traditions.

1.2.2. Meditation

Meditation is an attribute connected to 'yoga' which means 'union.' '*Yuj*' means unite, a sort of integration. It is the union of soul/self with the Supreme Being, the ultimate goal of a devotee in his/her spiritual life. It is an effort to attain liberation through the culmination of both physical and spiritual energies. Meditation is a prolong exercise of concentration where the devotee hold his/her mind on a particular object with an unbroken flow of thought.

In addition to that, time, place, seating and posture are important for meditation. A clear, serene environment is important for meditation. Sacred places usually help the one who meditates to concentrate and helps him/her to enter into a state of reverence with God. Apart from this, there are several ways and means through which people meditate and get united with God. Among them object meditation, picture meditation, music meditation are important. Apart from that there is also awareness meditation – a process of self emptying all thoughts from the mind and become intensely aware that presence of God can fill our emptiness.

Furthermore, in Christian tradition we meditate on the word of God. Yet, in some of the indigenous churches, an environment is created wherein a devotee experiences the presence of God not only through *bhakti* but also through meditation. Leonardo Mercado write, "'People are the best contextualizers' and the role of a theologian is to function as a mid wife as they give birth to a theology that is truly rooted in the culture and moment of history."[16] In the same way there are several theologians in the history of the Indian church who acted as midwives and gave birth to a new theology and a new style by adopting and adapting architectural changes in church structures through dialogue, with the existing culture and religious system of the land. They believed in the constant dialogue between the theology and the faithful, who are the subjects of culture. One product of such dialogue is the Epiphany Cathedral of Dornakal in Warangal District, Telangana, India.

2. Dornakal Cathedral – an Epitome of Pluralistic Structure

2.1. Historicity

In protestant denominations the Anglicans have a well-established hierarchical system and the church buildings are in European traditions. With its Episcopal tradition the church in England constructed beautiful cathedrals of European style in India. During the 20th century the European style was replaced by Indian art and architecture with the raise in nationalism and Indology. In 1915 Bishop V. S. Azariah wanted to build a church to the people who did not know Christ – a cathedral of Indian experience, Indian ways and Indian design.[17] The foundation was laid on January 14th 1915.

Nevertheless the work did not begin till 1919, because Bishop insisted it to be constructed with 'Indian money, Indian men [*sic*] and Indian method.'[18] There were several hardships because of war and famine. As well as it took twenty four long years for the completion of the cathedral. The Epiphany Cathedral was consecrated on January 6th 1939, which stands as great image of pluralism with its high theological significance as a structure.

2.2. A Model for Dialogue through Structure – 'Talking' Structure

The words 'indigenization' and 'dialogue' are commonly used terms in present times but the Dornakal 'Epiphany Cathedral' started a dialogue from the very moment of its inception with its presence as a structure, through its multi -religious architecture. It was named as 'Epiphany' Cathedral, as epiphany is the festival to commemorate the manifestation of Christ to gentiles. The cathedral blue print was designed by Bishop V. S. Azariah along with Sri. Muthaiah, an engineer from Madras. The architectural style chosen was both Saracen and Arabian and modern-Dravidian temple architecture. Saracen style is opted since Nizam were ruling the Deccan region during that period. Besides, Dravidian temple architecture symbolizes the people in the Dornakal region in those times.

This structure speaks through its presence, from a far distance. The two high and mighty white domes give an impression of a Mosque. The exteriors and the massive main door with brass-studs, the sculpture of the pillars and porch gives an appearance of a Hindu Temple.[19] Nonetheless, the cross over the two white domes and a big cross fixed over the vertex of triangular elevation between two domes gives the symbolism of unity of whole humanity in Cross and Christ. Unless and until a person reach near the Cathedral this symbolic unification is hard to identify. [20]

Moreover, every pillar has a neatly carved 'cross' and 'lotus'. The Cross and Lotus signifies the savior's 'Godliness' in South India. Cross indicates Christ's sacrifice to the whole humankind while, Lotus is the national flower of India which signifies the plurality and purity of church in India.[21] Lotus has a high reverence in Hindu mythology for its beauty and purity. On the other hand, the inner court pillars are carved with a plantain fruit growing and blossom from a deadly **datura** (thorn apple-symbolizes lifelessness). The plantain is an emblem of life immortal and the hanging **datura** indicates lifelessness. They together symbolize 'life out of Death.'[22] Several such symbolisms are engraved into the Cathedral architecture which portray high theological significance and reflects the pluralistic nature of the church.

The cathedral functions like a pilgrim center wherein people from different faiths come, not just to see the exterior structure but to participate in the worship which is very much indigenous in its nature. The cathedral, as a structure stands amidst the community with its pluralistic architectural style. The architectural style itself sends a message. The structure speaks with its architectural style which is more audible and acceptable than hundreds of sermons on pluralism and religious harmony. People in the past had a heart to open their space for 'others'. They invited 'others' by making the structure with a style that is acceptable to them and make them comfortable. Here 'others' refers to the people of other faiths. Christian leaders were open in their approach and Dornakal Epiphany Cathedral is the product of that openness and acceptance of 'others' into our space and structural style.

3. Indian *Ekklesia*: A Change in Dynamics

Further, in the recent time the church architectures have stopped dialoguing with the people and their conditions. People started to build high tower pointing towards the heaven making no relevance in the lives and the living conditions of the people. But we have seen earlier that Hindu forms of worship, *bhakti* and meditation have made their way into church and people. They acknowledged and adopted these new forms with openness. They made liturgies and hymn lyrics in a more indigenous way, wherein Hindu terminologies are incorporated in the Church while adoring God. The Dornakal Cathedral stands as a prime example for dialoguing architecture. In the current time the Indian church is no more in the path as Christ envisioned. Now, it has turned into a social empire which concentrates more on structural elegancy.

3.1. Structural Elegancy

Church is a place where a community's faith reflects. It has a communitarian dimension which reflects the life and living conditions of the people. But in the present context, churches are situated on profound state where plurality is alienated. Local churches reflect with more bureaucratic and discriminative images. They are no more the genuine local community.[23] There is no sense of communitarian feelings, but just a sociological presentation of various units. The structural quality, height and style are given more priority than the scriptural teachings. Church is having the magnanimity but lacks the two magnetic poles; context and culture which keep people under intact.

3.2. Social Empire

Further, Church in India which was a 'talking' church, interacting church and a dialoguing church is now turned into a social empire. In the feudal regime (11-13 CE) the priestly organizations of some particular churches took on political character of the great feudal lords. A symbiosis between church and secular society emerged with firm roots and characterized as

Christendom. In the same way a lordship is emerged in the present church where hierarchy plays a role with a vertical axial. On the other hand, religious buildings have not been constructed primarily to provide facilities for large number of regular worshippers but to demonstrate the religious and secular ambitions and status of the builders.[24] Church as a social empire has buildings but they are not dialoguing ones.

4. Indian *Ekklesia*: A 'Grounded' Church rather than a Grandeur Structure

Moreover, churches in the past though maintained the Episcopal order they still made an attempt to reach out to the society at large without confining to the Christian community itself. But in the present time, church became an invisible institution with its creeds, rituals and organizational setup. In such a scenario the church can replicate only as 'one religious structure among many others.'

If the church is confined to a religious structure or symbol we can never attribute it to the uniqueness or universality that we ascribe to Christ. Churches' understanding of Christ are limited to the historical memory which it has received. Church just confesses Christ's truth but does not possess him or his truth. Church as a structure is much institutionalised with its grandeur structures which hardly reach or understand the ground realities. In a multi religious context like India, church will be more relevant to the people or society when it is grounded and relate itself with the living realities of the people.

4.1. Denying 'Towers'

In addition, the image of a church should have a servant image not an image of a prideful army conquering all before it. The main purpose of church is to promote humankind and unification of human community through dialogue and collaboration. The church should take its pride in life as a witness and not on the high towers and structural elegancy. The correct way in which the transformation and unification takes place is a mystery that only God reveals.[25] Church is called to play a pivotal role in the history. It is not an honour to feel superior and make others inferior. Church should uphold the universal equality of all individuals and religious identities, by denying the towers.

4.2. Deepening 'Foundations'

C. S. Song writes,

> People must explain who Jesus is, people are to reveal where Jesus is. Jesus does not tell people why they suffer; it is the people who tell Jesus why he has to suffer. And people must liberate Jesus before Jesus can 'burn again inside them as a flame'. The people who are determined to tell who Jesus is, to disclose where he is, and the people who struggle to liberate Jesus – Jesus calls them blessed.[26]

Similarly, to deepen the foundations of the church we need to liberate the church. So those churches through its liberative message liberate and become relevant to the community at large. Church must explain about Jesus as a suffering servant who suffers along with the people. It should discover Christ in the suffering humanity amidst of poverty and hunger. Church should replicate the suffering servant image and the Christ on the Cross, to deepen its foundation in the Indian context. Further, before the 'conversion' of an individual or a community, conversion of the church need to happen in order for proclaiming Christ on Cross as the 'co-sufferer.' It should be the corner stone for Christian Church foundation in a pluralistic context.

4.3. Relocating 'Boundaries'

Moreover, Indian Church though claim to be 'united', is scandalously divided in the name of caste, gender, creed, denomination and ethnicity. Among several disparities and divisions within the church, caste and gender discrimination are primary among them. Indian church is a 'dalit' church as majority of the people got converted with a hope, to attain social equality and human dignity. Soares-Prabhu writes, "There is surely something sick about a church which agitated by infractions of the liturgy, but tolerates without qualms the obscenity of untouchability. If dalits exists and suffer in the church in India this is surely a sign it is not yet 'Church.'"[27] This directly points out to the fact that church in India should relocate its boundaries to the peripheries of the society. Gospel was accepted by the people 'outside' the society – the dalits, before it reaches the insiders. However, still the one who are the first fruit of the gospel in India are still outside the church. On the other hand, dalit view their religion both as a vehicle of protest consciousness and of potential change.[28] Church in such a context should give a preferential option for the oppressed by sharing their plight and reviving their consciousness and making them potential by envisioning a change, through the liberative acts of God in Christ through the Holy Spirit.

5. Indian *Ekklesia*: An Inclusive Emblem - A Replica of Christ's Life in India

5.1. Church as Christ – Reinventing Self

Church as a presence of Christ has to reinvent itself. The temples those are established in the past provide a therapeutic environment that helps for a speedy recovery from mental and physical ill health.[29] The religious experience is multi-dimensional and more likely to occur when the mind is put at rest by the inclinations created by particular predefine environment. Church provides that predefined environment which is therapeutic in nature. Indian church should question herself how she lives out the life of Jesus to be a prophetic witness to all people.[30] The sacramental character of the church does not come out from her connection with a particular culture but the witness of Gospel in a different context and culture through word, deed and through the sign of salvation of Jesus Christ. The church has to reinvent herself by restoring herself by being sacramental in character and therapeutic in nature, as a hope for the suffering humanity amidst struggle and strife.

5.2. Church as Christ – Revolutionary in 'Reaching'

Moreover, the church as body of Christ in the New Testament is a connection of *Qahal Yahweh* as the whole Assembly of God. People in this new covenant are drawn from every region and culture to worship God in Christ. These new people of God become both continuity and discontinuity of Israel. And Israel will be no longer the original chosen race (1 Pet. 2:10, Rev. 21:3).[31] Furthermore, though the early church affirmed the esteemed universal dimension of one undivided *Ekklesia* of God but it is also understood *ekklesia* in local sense. The single word *ekklesia* is used to express the concepts of universal, local and Eucharistic Assembly of God which is identical in a local context. Every local church replicates and symbolizes the mystery of the body of Christ which embodies according to time and space.[32] These revolutionaries the system, the local church becomes a universal church in itself through Eucharistic fellowship. On the other hand, Christ was a revolutionist; he revolted against the existing structures of his times when it comes to the reaching of the people at the peripheries. On several occasions he brought the peripheries into the centre and he being centre reached the peripheries. Present church needs to get rid of its 'centralized' nature and move to the peripheries as the true image of Christ.

5.3. Church as Christ – Resisting Social Evils

In addition, Church is a part of the society and various social evils have crept into the church. One such thing is the discrimination of women. In ancient India an ideal woman is characterized in two ways, firstly, *brahmavadini*- an ascetic woman who strives for highest knowledge, living a life of spiritual wellbeing. Secondly, *sadyaovadhu*, a domestic type of woman who spends her time in the household duties of any kind.[33] Traditions and social structures have made women dependent on men and made them to appear intellectually inferior to men. Church has been less active in taking up women issues as church issues and it has responded inadequately to the social stigmatization of women because church also encourage it within church limits. The 'culture of silence' within the church structures need to be broken and a new structure need to evolve within the church where women have a right space to contribute to the mission of Christ in mutuality and reciprocating with men.[34] Jesus gave every space and opportunity to both men and women by resisting the existential traditional and social structures of his times. Church as God's community, need to resist the social evils like gender and caste discrimination.

5.4. Church in *Garbhagrha* – Recreating Religious and Cultural Harmony

Besides, the Hindu temple consists of a scared enclosure called as *Garbhagrha*. *Garbhagrha* is the most essential component of a

Hindu temple. Here the deity is in the womb-chamber. It's like a foetus and the temple is in its fullest manifestation. Entry into *Garbhagrha* symbolizes rebirth as there is no salvation without being born again.[35] This is something we can find a relation with our own Christian thought of rebirth and salvations. *Garbhagrha* represents a dark womb like cave as a dark chamber. Darkness is a necessary condition for transformation and recognition of God in his full potentiality. It also represents the darkness and chaos before the creation of cosmos, and how cosmos came into existence through chaos. According to Hindu traditional understanding, the saving knowledge and life giving light is hidden in darkness. Passing through darkness we wait to experience or come into light. When we unlearn what we have already learnt we experience the diving mystery.[36] Thus, *Garbhagrha* makes an individual to identify the life and light amidst the darkness where we empty ourselves to experience the divine mystery. If we imagine the whole cosmos as a *Garbhagrha,* church will exist as an image which helps people to relate with the divine mystery amidst darkness and confusion. Here church will not be an idol to worship or a deity where an individual relate as a personal deity but a channel that leads people from darkness to divine light.

On the other hand, *Garbhagrha* also has a social implication and relevance. Originally *Garbhagrha* represents a womb of a mother. Therefore doing violence to a helpless woman is greater crime than burning down Mosque or destroying a Temple. A society that tolerated violence against women is also society that is blind to ecological crises.[37] Cosmos is also considered as a womb where life generates in various forms and ways. Church is an image amidst a cosmic *Garbhagrha.* It is not only relevant to the Christian community but also to the whole Indian society at large. It is not a religious symbol but a mysterious image that leads us to the mysterious ultimate divine. The cosmos is a *Garbhagrha* of darkness where discrimination in the name of religion, culture and tradition prevails and also social evils like caste and gender discrimination exists. Church in its radical form becomes a light amidst this cosmic discriminative darkness creating cultural and religious harmony. Jyoti Sahi identifies culture as not just a vehicle that transport ideas but a way to see *Darshana.* And unless we see through culture we literally cannot understand the real gospel message.[38] Church should not be a transporter of European ideas and ideologies; it needs to explore its own 'new' gospel message in/for diverse cultural and religious belief systems in India to recreate religious and cultural harmony.

6. Conclusion

In summary, it can be said the ecclesial vision in Indian context demands the fundamental vision of church which should be in relation with the Kingdom of God and not related with any particular traditions of past history. The Kingdom of God is the ultimate revelations of God's unconditional love which in turn becomes a project for a new human community. The right proclamation of Jesus' message can bring healing to the individual and communities. Church should embody such vision by moving away from the traditional vision of 'saving souls.'[39] A new community should emerge where respect and mutual recognition can be experienced by all individuals. Jesus through his life and ministry challenged every structure that divides, discriminates and disintegrates that makes a genuine *Koinonia* impossible.[40] Church in Indian context need to be a place where multi-religious and cultural *Koinonia* emerge out of intellectual darkness and ignorance, establishing itself in the form a new humanity where there is no division in the name of religion or tradition and discrimination in the name of caste, gender, creed and colour.

To conclude, we have already seen that, in the past there are prominent people like Bishop V. S. Azariah in the history who made attempts to send out a strong message by incorporating various 'other' architectural styles into the traditional church buildings. They are not confined to one faith tradition but incorporated all the major religious belief and worship patterns and made church into more local and Indian in its nature. Some of the Christian hymns are also influenced by Hindu *bhakti*. Even the ways people meditate in the churches are also influenced by Hindu traditions. On the other hand, ideas like *Garbhagrha* helps to explore new avenues of understanding faith, liberated from darkness and ignorance. There is always a lot to learn from the 'others' out there. As in Lk. 9:50 – Jesus told him, "Do not stop him, whoever is not against you is for you." The 'others' out there are for us having a lot to offer to enrich our own understanding of the ultimate divine provided we do not feel insecure or consider them as inferior.

Endnotes:

[1] R. J. McKelvey, "Temple: Temple in the New Testament," in *The New Bible Dictionary*, ed. J. D. Douglas (Grand Rapids: William B. Eerdmans Publishing Company, 1970), 1247.

[2] John B. Graybill, "Temple," in *The New International Dictionary of the Bible*, ed. J. D. Douglas and Merrill C. Tenney (Grand Rapids: Zondervan Publishing House, 1994), 990.

[3] McKelvey, "Temple in the New Testament," 1243.

[4] Graybill, "Temple," 990.

[5] D. W. B. Robinson, "Church," in *The New Bible Dictionary*, ed. J. D. Douglas (Grand Rapids: William B. Eerdmans Publishing Company, 1970), 228.

[6] R. Antoine, "Rituals and Worship," in *Religious Hinduism*, ed. R. De Smet and J. Neuner (Mumbai: St. Pauls Press, 1996), 204.

[7] George Michell, *The Hindu Temple: An Introduction To Its Meaning And Forms* (Chicago: University of Chicago Press, 1977), 54.

[8] Augustine Thottakara, *Indian Spirituality: Hindu Spiritual Traditions, A Christian Interpretation* (Bangalore: Dharmaram Publications, 2010), 145.

[9] Ibid., 144.

[10] Ibid., 146.

[11] Ibid., 147.

[12] Ibid., 149.

[13] Ibid.

[14] Ibid., 151.

[15] Ibid., 154.

[16] Tony Neelankavil, "From Inculturation to Interculturality: A Methodological Move in Asian Churches' Encounters with Cultures," in *The Church and Culture in India, Inculturation: Theory and Praxis*, ed. Paul Pulikkan and Paul M. Collins (Delhi: ISPCK, 2010), 16.

[17] M. Edwin Rao, *The Glorious Fifty Years of The Epiphany Cathedral* (Hyderabad: Pragathi Printers and Publishers, 1988), 2.

[18] Ibid., 16.

[19] Ibid., 34.

[20] Ibid.

[21] Ibid., 36.

[22] Ibid.

[23] V. Devasahayam, "Doing Dalit Theology: Basic Assumptions," in *Frontiers of Dalit Theology*, ed. V. Devasahayam (Madras: Gurukul Lutheran Theological College, 1997), 279.

[24] R. E. S. Tanner, *Religious Experience and Culture: An Enduring Reciprocity* (Bangalore: Dharmaram Publications, 2012), 203.

[25] Devasahayam, "Doing Dalit Theology: Basic Assumptions," 279.

[26] C. S. Song, "Oh, Jesus Here With Us!," in *Asian Faces of Jesus*, ed. R. S. Sugirtharajah (Maryknoll: Orbis Books, 1993), 144.

[27] Anthony D'Cruz O. Praem, "Towards a New Humanity," in *Committed to the Church and the Country*, ed. Kuruvilla Pandikattu, James Ponniah, and Thomas Kuriacose (Pune: Jnana-Deepa Vidyapeeth, 2013), 6.

[28] M. E. Prabhakar, "Christology in Dalit Perspectives," in *Frontiers of Dalit Theology*, ed. V. Devasahayam (Madras: Gurukul Lutheran Theological College, 1996), 424.

[29] Tanner, *Religious Experience and Culture An Enduring Reciprocity*, 203.

[30] Praem, "Towards a New Humanity," 7.

[31] Evelyn Monteiro, *Church and Culture* (Delhi: ISPCK, 2004), 13.

[32] Ibid., 21.

[33] Bhavya, "Indian Women and the Experience of Inculturation," in *The Church and Culture in India, Inculturation: Theory and Praxis*, ed. Paul Pulikkan and Paul M. Collins (Delhi: ISPCK, 2010), 205.

[34] Ibid., 211.

[35] Subhash Anand, *Hindu Inspiration for Christian Reflection, Towards Hindu-Christian Theology* (Gujarat: Gujarat Sahitiya Prakashan, 2004), 110.

[36] Ibid., 122.

[37] Ibid., 130.

[38] Jyoti Sahi, "'Inculturation'" From the Perspective of an Artist," in *Renewed Efforts at Inculturation for and Indian Church*, ed. Erasto Fernandes and Joji Kunduru (Bangalore: Dharmaram Publications, 2002), 80.

[39] Praem, "Towards a New Humanity," 9.

[40] D. Manikaraj, "Mission, Evangelism and Conversion," in *Frontiers of Dalit Theology*, ed. V. Devasahayam (Madras: Gurukul Lutheran Theological College, 1997), 461.

Chapter 12
Ekklesia - The Radical Democratic Assembly of Equals; Towards an Indian Ecclesiology: A Pentecostal Perspective

V. V. Thomas

Introduction

Jesus, the founder and the corner stone of the Church made His famous utterance that He will build His Church and the gates of hell shall not prevail against it (Mt. 16:18). How do we define that which Jesus said He will build? Who belongs to that Church? What has been the presumed identity and the self-perception of the Church? How the identity of the Church has been perceived in the early Church and through the centuries until our present day context? These are questions that have not found any one single acceptable answer in the history of the Church so much so that there has not been one single or perfect model of the Church or the way it has been understood and interpreted through the centuries.

While it is true that there has not been one single and definite understanding of what constitute the Church or who constitute it, I like the way Miroslav Volf explains as to what constitute the Church. Volf says, "A Church is a community of people who congregate in order to call on, to testify and to confess Christ the liberator… They do not need to be characterized by a certain grade of personal or social holiness in order to be called the Church. The Church … lives solely on the sanctifying presence of Christ, who promised to be wherever people congregate in His name…. The Church is therefore not a club of the perfected but a community of people who confess to be sinners and pray: *debita dimitte* (forgive us our sins). Any group which gathers around the one Christ, around God in his salvific devotion to people, who celebrate in him their liberator and Lord, who is open to all people and where all people have the same dignity, such a group is a Church because Christ has promised to be present among them."[1] Although like many others Volf may not be perfect in his understanding of the Church, I believe his views shed light up on the fact that the 'Church is a democratic community of the equals' where one is not above the other but all stand on the same platform and seek for God's mercy and forgiveness. This understanding can take away so much of our arrogance and exclusive kind of attitude whereby we cast the other out from our spirituality and from our hearts.

The Nature and Identity of THE CHURCH: A Brief Overview

The primitive Church when it appeared in the first century had to find its identity in the Jewish world. The Christian Church was the 'new Israel' a reform movement within Judaism in contrast to the 'old Israel' and this attitude made them to see themselves not 'in relation to' but 'over-against' the Jews. However their self-definition/s that they were the 'new Israel' led to tensions not only with the Jews but within the Church itself. The early Christians felt that they were the Easter community of the exalted Messiah. The Church faced the same situation again when it left the fold of Palestinian Judaism and entered into the wider world of religion and cultures. The Church entered into the Graeco-Roman world with the understanding that "there is no longer Jew and Greek" (Eph. 2:13-16, Rom. 10:12, 1 Cor. 12:13, Gal. 3:28 etc). As far as the Church was concerned it was a fatal proclamation because it suddenly abolished its old identities as part of the chosen people, the old Israel. This was almost the end of toleration by the Jewish people within Israel of this new sect called Christians. It was the launching of the Church's mission to the larger world. It was a kind of relocation of Christianity from one world to another. It was the beginning of Church's world mission. Now the major question was with regard to the Church's identity and mission in a society of pagan religions and Greek philosophies. Where will the Christian teachings fit in the philosophical traditions of the Greeks? Here again there was no one single approach to face the issue. Many Christians held on to Paul's instruction "not to be yoked together with unbelievers". 'What has Athens to do with Jerusalem' was the attitude of many within the Church. At the same time there were others in the Church who saw Christianity and Greek philosophy not in terms of opposition but in terms of similarity. They held to the Johanine understanding that Jesus Christ is the 'light that lights every human being' coming into the world. Justin was very positive in his evaluation of Greek philosophy. He says "Christ is the Logos of whom every race of men partakes and those who live rationally are Christians even if thought to be atheists.... Whatever things have been rightly said by any one belongs to us Christians."[2] This approach was in a sense a positive way of defining Christianity in relation to Greek philosophies and cultures. For such people Christian identity was not 'over against' but it was relational.

Moving on from the early part of the Church into the period following the conversion of Constantine in the early part of the fourth century, the whole face of Christianity was changed from that of the lowly into an affluent people in the society. The Jesus that we encounter in the Gospels is one who came into the world as 'Good news' to the Poor. He Himself says that the Spirit of the Lord is upon Him because He has been anointed to preach the good news to the poor. We read that Jesus always lived His life in solidarity with the poor. He was accused by the Pharisees and the Sadducees that He was a friend of sinners, tax collectors, publicans and so on. This Jesus was spat upon, mocked, smitten, arrested, tortured, and finally crucified. Throughout His earthly life he demonstrated that He was a 'servant king' (Mk. 10:45), a suffering servant (Mt. 8:17), and a king with crown of thorns. Not only that Jesus was tortured and crucified, even His disciples had to face the same fate their master faced. According to tradition, except for one disciple all the other eleven disciples became martyrs for their master.

In fact the Church that was founded by Jesus Christ was persecuted severely until the early part of the fourth century. Starting with Nero in 64 CE, the persecution continued until the time of Constantine in 312. However, the situation radically changed when Constantine declared himself a Christian after his victory over Maxentius in 312 and at the age of twenty four, Constantine was the supreme leader of the West - the first Christian emperor. In the same year he published what is known as the Edict of Milan, which gave the Church freedom of worship and returned to the Church all her properties that had been confiscated. Constantine made Christianity the official religion of the Roman Empire. He aided the Church and the clergy with public grants. He sought the peace of the Church; The Church came under the umbrella of the state, a change that was to radically change the entire history of the Church from then on. The persecuted Church now became the protected Church; The Church that was hitherto insulted now became a powerful Church; it became rich with the blessing of the emperor himself. The Church had ceased to be regarded as an enemy of the state and was now in alliance with it. If being a member of a Church was dangerous, now it became advantageous. The Church had become an accepted and important part of the richest and most powerful empire in the ancient world. The Jesus of Nazareth who could not find a place to lay His head is now 'residing in massive Cathedrals'. The humble image of Christ the Good Shepherd is now replaced with Christ the King.

As far as my thinking goes, probably the single most issue that the Church struggled with for about one thousand years, almost till the reformation, was the Church-state relationship following the conversion of Constantine. Of course the Church state issue has always been there from the time the Romans crucified Christ, but more technically from the time of Constantine. In fact the Church must have been grateful that the persecution has now come to an end, but they were not aware of the dangers of the sate getting into the affairs of the Church.

The new situation into which the Church 'fell' began to deeply influence every part of its existence in the world. Although Christians remained as the people of God even after the conversion of Constantine, they lived, thought, worshipped, governed and conducted themselves very differently from those Christians who had to pass through the shadow and the fiery period of persecution. Three areas in which these changes appeared most notably were: a) The government of the Church; b) The Church's relationship with the state; c) The way in which the worship of the Church was changed.[3]

Before the Church came under the state, there was no empire-wide structure of government for the Church. The Church had more of a local character and its authority was also local. There were monarchial bishops in larger cities and they had significant influence on the Churches that came under their spiritual care. There was fellowship and interaction among the Churches in different places. However, there was no common government, no common Church law, no one 'head' of the Church other than the founder of the Church, the Lord Jesus Christ.

As the Church came under the state the above mentioned characteristics of the pre-Constantine Church changed drastically. Now with the emperor beginning to take control of the situation, he began to call for synods and councils to deal with different issues in the Church. From now on holding of major Church councils became common in the life of the Church.

These councils became important factors in creating common belief systems of the universal Church; it promoted unity of the Church and to some extend some order and regulations within the larger set up of the imperial Church. Another major factor during the post Constantine period was the development of a clear distinction between the laity and the clergy. The laity who were the majority in the Church had no office; the clergy were Church officials who were set apart from the laity by ordination. As time went by the entire function of the Church fell into the hands of the clergy, a situation that made their office more 'powerful' with lasing implications. There were now lower clergy, higher clergy, and the episcopate.

The lower clergy consisted of those who would help in the services of the worship and other areas in the Church. They were the sub-deacons who formed the secretarial staff of the bishop. The higher clergy were the deacons and presbyters. The care of the poor, originally entrusted to the deacons, was now discharged by the lower clergy. Deacons became the chief administrative assistants to the bishops. Presbyters conducted services and administered sacraments; they were the spiritual arm of the bishops. Later these presbyters were called as priests.

The episcopate consisted of the bishops of the Church. The lowest in rank was the country bishop. Next in order was the city bishop. Both the country and the city bishop were subject to the archbishop, called metropolitan in the east, who was the bishop of the capital city of province. The archbishops in turn were under the authority of the patriarchal bishops.[4] At the beginning of the 4th century there were three patriarchal bishops via the bishop of Rome, Antioch, and Alexandria. Later when Constantine made Constantinople as the capital of the eastern empire, the bishop of that city became a patriarch. At the council of Chalcedon in 451, the bishop of Jerusalem was similarly honored and became a patriarch. The patriarch of Rome from the beginning been called the Pope and has been called that way until the present day.[5] This has been the hierarchical order of the Church that was developed which turned into powerful offices that mostly became corrupt as the Church entered into the medieval period. The situation has remained the same even to this day wherein the institution called Church has become worse than some of our political parties fighting with muscle power and human power.

The Church after the conversion of Constantine (especially after the 6th century) gained not only spiritual but the actual responsibility to run the government especially in the western part of the Roman Empire. However, when the tribal chiefs in Europe captured power, they were now called kings. These kings were not happy that the Church was governing the state. They wanted to regain the power not only over the state but even over the Church which became wealthy. In fact by the time of Reformation, the Church owned more than half of the land in Europe. Power was based on the amount of land that was owned. By the time of the reformation, there was lot of corruption within the Church. There were people within the church who were convinced that the only way corruption could be removed from the Church was to remove the state from having power over the Church. In fact it was secular kings who appointed officials to the Church. The Church members argued that the lay people should not appoint the officials for the Church. They thought that this could be done by making the office of the Pope more powerful. The Pope then could have an army and in fact this was done by the Pope to develop an army and in fact they were used against Islam during the time of crusades. In the high Middle Ages an accommodation was reached by the state and the Church. It had two elements. First, the appointment of the Pope was no more made by the State. Hence forth there will be an electorate consisting of bishops, arch bishop etc., to appoint the Pope. The second element was that the bishop and high clergy could be elected by the clergy of the diocese without any involvement of the civil authorities. The church would appoint people who are in religious matters, and the state would simply approve them. The high Middle Age was an age of power for the church. However they did not lost. In the late middle ages everything began to change.

In the history of Europe, perhaps the most important periods are late 14, 15, 16 centuries, which are often referred as a period of renaissance. It was an anti-Christian movement. However within the renaissance movement there was a group of people known as humanists. Renaissance meant that one discovers a culture of the present standard by going back to the roots and that the present is measured by the past. The Christian humanists believed that the essence of Christianity must be determined by the apostolic Christianity and the New Testament must be the judging measuring rod. In that sense, the past serves as the authority over the present. The authority of anybody in the present was not absolutised. Two schools that made too much noise during this period were the Holy Roman Empire and the Holy Office of the Pope.

The arrangement of the church and the state was called Christendom. The renascence that took place in the late Middle Age was a connecting point or a catalyst to another movement called nationalism – a concept of nation states. In fact the chief opponents who are against the nationalism were the Holy Roman emperors or the kings and the Holy Roman Church. The Church's wealth had been in the possession of the land and they were not happy with the nation states who wanted to form their small kingdoms away from the Holy Roman Empire or the Holy Roman Church. This nation state people never wanted their money to go out of their country. During this period the Popes became desperate for money. This also led to lot of corruption. In fact, Popes began to collect money in any means including selling of the indulgences through his agents in different countries. The nation kings were happy with anybody who supported them. In fact, Luther was supported by some of those nation kings/princes. Luther on the other hand supported the local princes in their struggle for the freedom. Nationalism became an important issue during this period. All these issues put together made a re-evaluation of the church and state relationship. It is for this reason, that I believe the single most issue in the post-Constantine period was this Church-state issue.

In the same way during the post-Constantine period, there were a number of changes taking place in the very content of the Christian faith. The councils that were held one after another in the post Constantine period gave rise to a number of doctrinal definitions. There was of course the influence of the Greek philosophy. God began to be referred as 'Supreme Being', 'Substance' and so on. God's being became more important than God's deeds in history. The idea of the knowledge of God through experience was increasingly replaced by that of rational knowledge. The Ecumenical councils were more bothered about the nature of Christ than what He did during His earthly ministry. Unfortunate as it stands, such 'unproductive' situation has remained the same even to this day wherein the institution called Church has become worse than some of our political parties fighting with muscle power and human power.

It is so unfortunate that the Church, the body of Christ which was a fellowship of the believers passed through different stages and has now become so degraded. When it started in Jerusalem, it was as a fellowship of believers; We read in the book of Acts that they were together as one community as fellow believers; when they moved out of Jerusalem into Antioch we read in Acts 11:26 that the disciples of Jesus for the first time were 'called' as Christians; (It is interesting to note that they did not call themselves as Christians but they were called Christians by others). As it moved into Athens, the centre of philosophy, people tended to look at Christianity as a philosophy or tried to relate the Greek philosophy with Christianity. As it moved into Rome especially after the Church came under the umbrella of the state, the Church or Christianity began to become more institutional. When it moved to Europe during the medieval period and even later, Christianity became more of a culture of Europe - Europe is Christianity and Christianity is Europe. In the present day India, Christianity is more identified with 'projects and programs' than a ministry or a fellowship. Every leader of any Church or denomination has a project or programme as he or she goes out of the country in name of 'ministry' or even within the country. (The way some so-called Christian leaders in India do ministry or mission work look as though they have taken India or Asia on contract basis from God on a business kind of a deal not realizing the fact that Christian ministry is not a contract ministry, it is a ministry of commitment).

In North America today it is more like a business or commercialization of the Gospel!! In other words the precious body of Christ, the Church, is for 'sale' today, the most degenerated condition any institution can get into, a situation that has no parallel with the early Church or its message.

Having discussed a general understanding of the Christian Church in the history, let me now come to the Pentecostal understanding of the Church and its functions in the world. I will briefly discuss about the origin and development of the modern Pentecostal movement, the various aspects of the movement including some of its understanding of the mission of the Church in our contemporary world.

Modern Pentecostal Movement: An Overview

The Protestant Reformation in the 16th century that lasted for few decades was not end of an event but the beginning of a long process within the Church and society and its effect is seen even to this day. The reformation set a course of events in the direction of renewal and revival within the Church of which the 20th century Pentecostal movement has played a major role. According to Dyron Daughrity, "Christianity, the world over, is becoming Charismatic and Pentecostal today."[6]

The beginning of the modern Pentecostalism as a worldwide movement was started by a charismatic revival as early as 1901, in

Topeka, Kansas. However it gained momentum and worldwide acceptance only after April 1906, with the "outpouring of the Holy Spirit" at the Azusa Street in Los Angeles. There are two personalities around whom the Azusa Street revival evolved. They are Charles Fox Parham and William J. Seymour, a white and a black respectively. Charles F. Parham was a Methodist minister in the early part of the 20th century. He attended South Western, a Methodist Episcopal college at Winfield, Kansas. According to Steve Durasoff, Parham left the Methodist Church because of certain ideological differences and became an independent evangelical preacher and remained a preacher for about thirty-five years.

In 1898 he founded the Bethel Healing Home in Topeka, for lodging and faith training for individuals seeking a divine cure. In 1900, he opened an informal Bible school for Christian workers where about 40 students registered for the first batch. Ms. Agnes N. Ozman, one of the Bible school students, occupies a unique place in the modern Pentecostal movement. It is claimed by the Pentecostals that Ms. Agnes experienced the baptism in the Holy Spirit with evidence of speaking in other tongues. When one takes speaking in tongues as the major criterion for a Pentecostal experience, it can be said that Ms. Ozman is the first known Pentecostal of the modern Pentecostal movement with the initial physical evidence of speaking in tongues.

From Azusa Street Pentecostalism spread to other parts of the world by members who experienced the Pentecostal revival and formed Pentecostal Churches.[7] What is important here to note is that the very claim of the Pentecostals, namely the baptism in the Holy Spirit was first experienced by a woman is of extreme importance when one thinks of the contribution that women have given to the Pentecostal Church in particular and the Charismatic's and others in general.

Pentecostalism in India

The Pentecostal movement emerged in the 20th century out of the revivals that took place in the United States of America. In India it was no different. Therefore it will be difficult to say when exactly the Pentecostal movement started in India. As noted above this is because it is closely associated with the Protestant revival movements of the 19th century. If speaking in tongue which is the main symbol of the movement should be taken as the beginning of the Pentecostal movement then, it has already been seen in many of the revival movements that were taking in the various parts of the country in the early part of the 20th century. According to one of the leading Assemblies historians, Garry B. McGee the first Pentecostal experience was manifested among the Christian and Alliance mission's missionaries at Akola, Maharashtra in 1906 but this was not documented.[8]

Another incident of speaking in tongues was witnessed among the girls at the Mukthi mission run by Pandita Ramabai a Brahmin convert to Christianity. This was a result of the revival to which an eye witness, Minnie F. Abrams reported that "there was weeping, long prayer, confession of sins, and visions."[9] However, classical Pentecostalism in India appeared through the efforts of the Western Missionaries who were part of the Azusa Street revival in 1906 in United States. The first Pentecostal missionary to come to India with the Pentecostal message that represents the Azusa Street was A. G. Gar who came in the year 1907 to Calcutta. The others include Thomas Barrett (Norway), George Berg, Robert F. Cook, Mrs. Mary Chapman who was the first Assemblies Missionary to India who came to Madras (Chennai) in 1915.[10]

Different Types of Pentecostals

a. Classical Pentecostals:[11] What distinguishes this group is their acceptance of the "initial evidence" theory which holds that glossolalia (speaking in other tongues) is the necessary first evidence of receiving the "baptism in the Holy spirit". Classical Pentecostalism shares the main tenets of evangelicalism as far as the authority of the Bible, individual salvation, life after death, return of Christ, etc., are concerned. However, the main distinctive theological aspects of classical Pentecostalism were the doctrine of the baptism in the Holy Spirit and speaking in tongues as the initial physical evidence of the Holy Spirit baptism. The Assemblies of God, The Indian Pentecostal Church of God, The Sharon Fellowship Church of God, The Church of God (India), etc. fall under this category. Theological differences between these various denominations of classical Pentecostalism are minimal but they are more or less unanimous as far as the role of the Holy Spirit in the life of the individual and Church is concerned.

b. Mainline Protestant Charismatic/Pentecostals: They are members of their own Churches. They do not leave their Churches, but remain loyal within them. While they believe in the gift of speaking in tongues, they do not insist on the "initial evidence" theory.

c. Catholic Charismatic/Pentecostals: This group also does not leave their mother Church. They also do not insist on the "initial evidence" theory.

d. Independent Pentecostal Groups, which are mostly Person-Oriented: These Churches are sometimes known as "Faith Churches." Several Dalit Pentecostal Churches come under this category.

e. Third World Indigenous Groups:[12] This group is mainly found in house churches without having any codified doctrines or any major leadership. They are 'Pentecostal/ Charismatic' like movements.

Third Wave Revival Movements

This term third wave is used to designate a movement that is almost similar to the classical Pentecostal movement (first wave) and Charismatic movement (second wave), but with certain fairly important differences with the first wave and second wave movements. Third wave revival movement is composed largely of evangelical Christians who, while appreciating and supporting the work of the Holy Spirit among the classical Pentecostal churches and the charismatic movements, have decided not to be identified with either of the above two (first wave or second wave). The adherence of the third wave movement while experiencing the power of the Holy Spirit in the healing of the sick, casting out demons, exercising the gift of prophecies and participating in different charismatic kind of manifestation do not want at the same time disturbed the philosophy of ministry or the pattern of ministry in their own congregations and churches.[13] Following are some of the distinctive features of the third wave revival movements:

1. Baptism of the Holy Spirit occurs at the time of conversion (I Cor. 12:13) rather than as a second work of grace, subsequent to conversion.

2. Expectation of multiple fillings of the Holy Spirit subsequent to the new birth, some of which may closely resemble what others call "Baptism in the Holy Spirit."

3. They do not hold to the view that the initial physical evidence of the Baptism in the Holy Spirit is speaking in tongues, but rather speaking in tongues is seen as a gift used by some for ministry or prayer language.

4. They are of the opinion that the ministry under the power of the Holy Spirit should be the door way of entrance in to the third wave experience rather than a spiritual experience which is typical of the first two waves. For them the context of ministry is most commonly a body of believers rather than some specially gifted individuals or individual activities like a faith healer or a renowned speaker.[14]

The third wave became prominent in the 1980s and this very term was coined in 1983 by Peter Wagner. In the last few years it has become clear that the third wave could be viewed as part of a broader category "neo-charismatic" that includes the vast number of independent and indigenous churches and groups world-wide that cannot be classified either as Pentecostals (first wave) or as Charismatic (second wave). These third wave Christian bodies are people with Pentecostal-like experiences but at the same time do not have traditional or Charismatic denominational connections. According to David B. Barrett these new Charismatics actually outnumbered all Pentecostals and Charismatic combined.[15] The greatest concentrations of the third wave revival movements are in the prophetic African independent churches called by different names like "Banta separatist churches", "Aladura," "Spirit churches," and "Zionist churches". As far as Asia is concerned, we see them in the house church movements in China and also in India; in Latin America they are mostly seen in Brazil.

In a condensed form one can say that Pentecostalism is that segment of Christianity which believes that there is a unique aspect of the Spirit's manifestation, namely baptism in the Spirit and the initial physical evidence of the Spirit's baptism is speaking in tongues. They also believe that this baptism in the Spirit is normative for every Christian believer. They believe that the New Testament record of the event of Pentecost is not merely a "record of what happened in one generation, but a blue print of what should happen in every generation until Jesus returns again.[16]

Pentecostals claim that they are a community of Restoration movement as they claim to restore the Apostolic elements such as holiness, Baptism in the Holy Spirit, the gifts of the Holy Spirit and so on. They also say that they are a Protest movement because the other Churches according to the Pentecostals have left behind important elements from the apostolic teachings and added those things which were rather part of the tradition and not of the scripture such as historical episcopacy, infant baptism, papal authority etc.

It also claims to be a movement of Liberation since they try to break open the silence of the subaltern, the caste barriers and other oppressive structures in the society. It is interesting to note that most of the adherents of the Pentecostal faith all over the world are from the lowest strata of the society. People, who were economically and socially weak, have found identity in the Pentecostal movement although it has changed in the present situation.

Factors for the growth of Pentecostalism in India

Over the past one century, Pentecostalism in India has grown far and wide. Right from the beginning the movement has shown a great trend towards growth. One often hears people asking the question as to what was the secret behind the growth of the Pentecostal Churches in India and elsewhere! While we can come up with many reasons, let me highlight a few major factors.

Divine Factor

The first factor that I want to identify is what I call the "divine factor". The divine factor was the work of the Holy Spirit. It is for this reason that Pentecostals are often known as 'Evangelicals with a plus'. Evangelical Christianity has emphasized upon seven major ingredients as their theological basis. They are:

1. The authority of the written word of God for life and conduct of human lives.
2. The orthodoxy of Biblical doctrines.
3. The importance of personal faith.
4. Commitment to the Lord Jesus Christ.
5. The importance of Evangelism and Mission.
6. The place given to fellowship.
7. The importance of social concerns (Of course this has been a neglected area within the evangelical Christianity till the recent years).

The Pentecostals are fully in agreement with all the above evangelical doctrines. However they go one step further and give a lot emphasis to the role of the Holy Spirit in the lives of every Christian. It is for this reason that they are known as 'Evangelicals with a plus'.

The early Pentecostal leaders in Kerala and elsewhere were not people with a lot of secular education or 'head knowledge'. But the fact that the Lord used them to build his Church in many parts of the state and in several other places can only be attributed to the working of the Holy Spirit in their lives. God used those ordinary people of the early days to accomplish extra ordinary things and the secret was the power of the Holy Spirit.

Human Factor

The second factor I call it as "human factor" for the growth of the movement. This has to do with the kind of life the early Pentecostals lived in Kerala. There was so much of fellowship and solidarity among the early believers. They were tied together by many factors. They carried the burdens of one another. There were many tarrying meetings in the Churches and people had living testimonies to share. There were prophetic ministries in Churches. The prophets of those days were able to discern the right from wrong (although today that sought of Pentecostalism is waning out). Modern Pentecostalism has entered into their fourth generation. The fourth generation Pentecostals are unaware of the way Pentecostalism has travelled through. For the first generation Pentecostals, Pentecostalism was an experience of the infilling of the Holy Spirit. The second generation it was an experience with a kind of imitation of what their parents experienced. When it came to the third generation they began to loose the vitality because there were a number of changes that came into the movement. Today in the fourth generation, Pentecostals are trying to 'act' like the early Pentecostals but they are not really able to make an impact in their generation.

'Push' and 'Pull' Factor

A third factor is one might call the 'push' and 'pull' factors. The 'push' factor has mainly to do with the failures of other religious groups and denominations in meeting the spiritual needs of the people especially the Dalits. It has to do with certain real failures on the part of some of the mainline Churches in India. The 'pull' factor has to do with certain characteristics and particularities of Pentecostalism which in a real way respond to the spiritual/ emotional needs of the people. These pull factors include gifts of the spirit, convincing teachings of the Pentecostals, and meaningful worship to name only a few.

In major Indian cities like Mumbai, Bangalore, and Chennai the fastest growing Churches are the Pentecostal and Charismatic Churches. In fact the other Main Line Traditional Churches, such as the Roman Catholic, the Eastern Orthodox, and the Anglican, are threatened by the tremendous growth the Pentecostal Churches are showing. Many of their members are leaving these Churches and joining with the Pentecostal and Charismatic like Churches. For example the NEW LIFE FELLOWSHIP Churches which is very similar to any other classical Pentecostal Church is growing leaps and bounds in India. The fact is that the common people in these cities who long for God-experiences, hearing of God's word, close fellowship in community and true pastoral care are all fed up with dogmas and doctrines, formal worship services and rigid disciplines in their erstwhile Churches.

In fact the rigid institutional nature of some of these Main Line Churches frightens the poor and makes them uncomfortable.

It is because the poor feel excluded from these highly organized and elite institutional Churches where they have no role to play. The common people seek for a more emotional and indigenous forms of worship. Miracles, dance, drums and traditional songs continue to give meaning to their empty and broken lives. The believing communities around them stand in support. This kind of Pentecostalism is welcomed by large number of people in north Indian states such as Orissa, and Uttar Pradesh.

Two years ago, while on a ministry tour, I myself witnessed two consecutive worship services in the same Pentecostal Church, in the outskirt of New Delhi, attended by more than 6000 people, who were mostly from surrounding villages from the state of Uttar Pradesh. Some of them had to start their journey from homes as early as 3:00 AM to reach the Church by 10: 00 AM. Most of them were from the Dalit background from Uttar Pradesh and Delhi. I was thrilled to listen to their testimonies which narrate stories of their everyday life experiences. Stories like a child was bitten by a snake and the parents simply prayed for the child and the child was miraculously saved… and many other similar stories. In fact the pastor had a hard time in controlling people from sharing their weekly experiences due to the lack of time. These were all people from village background and some from towns.

So, the social location of the Pentecostal movement continues to be among the agrarian community who are mostly the Dalits and also among the urban middle class and lower middle class. To a question as to where we can locate the real Pentecostal Church the body of Christ in India today, I would say that it is outside the so called 'official Church', where she stands with the poor, the sick, the homeless, those suffering injustice and those looking for truth and justice. Therefore, I am of the strong opinion that the powerful expressions of Pentecostalism are found outside the four walls of the 'official Church' than within it.

A careful study of most of the newly formed Christian groups in India will reveal the fact that most of them adhere to the 'Pentecostal kind of faith' although they may not be known as a Classical Pentecostal Church as such in the strict sense of the term.

The above observation that many of these 'new generation' Churches may not be called purely as 'Classical Pentecostal Churches' sheds light on another reality and that is what I call as "Post Pentecostal movements." From a Christian perspective, if the 20th century could be termed as the century of the growth of Classical Pentecostalism, what I perceive of the 21st century is a "Post-Classical Pentecostal Century" or simply as "Post-Pentecostal Century" which will be characterized by the growth of several 'Pentecostal like movements'.

In fact those sociologists and theologians who predicted the collapse of traditional religion and the triumph of secularization have been proved wrong. As a matter of fact there is a resurgence of religiosity and what is happening in the Indian mission field is only a pointer to the reality that people still look for a way out of their everyday struggles not in a new political party or mere socially based organizations but to 'religion-based' forms of people groups where they meet with God in real life situations. I am excited by reports of what has been taking place in India in the mission field where most of the new converts to Christianity prefer to join a Pentecostal or Charismatic like fellowship where their spiritual needs are met. Pentecostalism as religion filled with both this-worldly and other-worldly concepts of spirituality appeals to the poor, specially the Dalits. The Dalits on the other hand, complements Pentecostal spirituality with their emotional nature of worship their longing for oneness and equality. The down trodden people in their search for dignity, freedom and recognition find the Pentecostal spirituality appealing to them. Of course it may seem like an assumption here and I do not deny the fact that it has to be verified and proved through empirical/field study. It is here that we need young scholars to do research and bring out facts into the open space so that people know who belongs where and for what reasons!

Of course there is another side to the whole story as to why there is a "Post-Pentecostal Movement". The answer to that question will open up another area of research into the already existing main line Pentecostal Churches in India such as the Assemblies of God, the Church of God, and the Indian Pentecostal Church. These

Churches seem to have fallen into the 'trap' of their predecessors who gave precedence to institutions and structures over simple believing Christians. What once Pentecostals used to protest has now become part of the Church. In other words there is no 'protestant classical Pentecostal Church' today.

What was considered once 'insignificant' has now become acceptable practice in some of these main line Pentecostal Churches. Pentecostal movement in India and of course elsewhere has gone through several changes in its 100 years of existence. From being a movement, Classical Pentecostalism has moved into a structured, institutionalized and established organization/s (while I do not want to deny the need for proper administration of the Church) so much so that today there is a tendency among the Pentecostals to promote their 'Church' than promoting the founder of the Church and His Gospel which gave importance to empowering the poor and the downtrodden. There is a false understanding of evangelism among many Pentecostals who promote the Church building or an organization over the people, without realizing the fact that the Church as a building or denomination has the poorest appeal of all to 'sinners'. Bishop F. D. Washington of the Church of God in Christ says "... most of the sinners do not go to Church. Yet the fantastic fact remains that the person of Jesus Christ-when he is presented right- has the greatest single appeal to the human heart in this world".[17]

I think this is the crux of the matter. The 'new generation' groups are not so much interested in building up denominations as they are in presenting Christ as the Lord to their listeners and bringing them into the saving knowledge of Jesus Christ, while the main line Pentecostal Church leaders are busy in "Pentecostalizing" and fully incorporating their existing members into their Churches than adding new ones – a contention that I know many Pentecostal leaders in India may not agree with.

Going by the history, modern Pentecostal movement has entered its second century and we are in a Post-Pentecostal period. There are several developments that have taken place which I call as Post-Pentecostal developments. The Charismatic movements, the third wave movements etc., are some reactions or post Pentecostal developments which need to be studied. There are also several other challenges faced by the Pentecostal movement today from both within and outside. At the same time there are several potentials and possibilities that Pentecostals can offer to the Church at large.

Potentials of Pentecostalism

Pentecostal Mission Praxis: A Model to the Mission of the Church in India

The Pentecostal movement in India has challenged the Indian Church in many practical ways as an authentic mission. I would like to identify few of them in the following section.

Pentecostalism as a Movement of the 'Empowered Poor'

One of the very interesting features of the Pentecostal movement from the very beginning was that Pentecostalism has been the religion of the lowly, including the poor, racial minorities, women, and "uneducated". The congregation of the Azusa Street Mission was composed of the lowly and "coloured people and sprinkling of whites."[18] In America where Pentecostalism was born, its first adherents were the Blacks and the marginalized whites who were working in the sugar cane fields and factories. The movement however shook the complacent and the optimistic mainline Christianity in America, which had sidelined the needs of the poor and the marginalized.

This aspect of Pentecostalism being the religion of the poor is true mainly of Dalit Pentecostalism. While it is true that mainline Pentecostal Churches are becoming ever more sophisticated in their understanding and use of the media and of popular cultural styles,[19] Pentecostalism is still mostly among the poor around the world including India.

The Dalit Pentecostals stand as equals when they participate in conventions and when they worship in Church. There is no class difference when they worship. Therefore, it can be said that Dalit Pentecostal worship is an expression of true democracy and equality which is not the case with many other Churches including some Syrian Pentecostal Churches.

It is precisely for this reason that Pentecostalism has appealed to many of these rather unlettered Dalits than to the 'learned' people in the society. Along with several other reasons it can said that many Dalits who were caught up in the struggle for upward mobility at the turn of the twentieth century responded to the Pentecostal movement because they claimed to have witnessed its capacity to transform individual lives in the here and now for the immediate better. Among others things, it offered two valuable things to the people. It offered hope and lived solutions to problems arising out of structural conditions which were beyond the power of the people as individuals. Thus, converting to Pentecostalism empowered people in ways that had tangible consequences for themselves and for society.

Cultural Adaptability and Pentecostalism

Pentecostals to a great extent have been successful in sensing the differences between 'religion' and culture and generally have been successful in creating indigenous Churches, which incorporate unique local forms. According to Synan, "Pentecostalism has appeared in cultural settings that range from high pontifical masses in St. Peters in Rome to African outdoor services that meet under trees where the faithful dance before the Lord, to the rhythmic throb of African drums."[20] Due to the belief that the Holy Spirit confers gifts and callings directly upon believers apart from their associations with the ecclesiastical institutions, Pentecostals have been able to contextualize their Church worship to a great extent.

Pentecostals promoted an indigenous kind of worship because they were more at home with such patterns. People did not experience much of a cultural dislocation when they joined the Pentecostal movement because they saw a cultural continuity in many Pentecostal aspects of worship pattern. Of the many examples that can be looked into, one can cite the example of beating the drums and singing in ecstasy in Pentecostal Churches in their worship. The noise of the drum brings in a kind of atmosphere in the congregation to worship. This phenomenon has its parallels in other communities as well. Beating the drum is part of major functions/festivals among many Dalits communities whether they are Christian or Hindu.

As someone who has been to many Pentecostal gatherings, I have personally witnessed some of these cultural realities within the Churches. I have witnessed how at the noise of the drum people can get into a mood of worship. I have even heard Pentecostal believers saying after the Church 'today the worship was not lively' because either the drum was under repair or the person who beats the drum had not turned up on that particular Sunday or even the sound of the drum was not sufficient. Therefore the drum plays an important role in the worship of Dalit Pentecostals.[21] One of the major reasons for many people mostly the Dalits to move into the Pentecostal movement was because they saw in Pentecostalism an ideal place to express some of their cultural systems along with their newfound faith. In other words they did not have to be totally detached from their cultural setting when they accepted Pentecostalism. The Dalits saw in Pentecostalism powerful continuities with those folk elements which were part of their past culture, although they would not explicitly say this. These included the Spirit-filled worship, which has strong emotional elements, the transmuted elements of Spirit-possession in worship centred on the third person of the Trinity, the whole aspect of faith healing and exorcism, which Pentecostalism offered.

Religious activities and concepts were an integral part of their social existence. To put it in a different way, Pentecostalism made it possible for people who embraced the Pentecostal faith to express their religious experiences in their spirit, language (language of the people) and culture which is basically the culture of the poor-in song, dance, shouts, laments etc.

Pentecostals and model Church Structure

Many Pentecostal Churches are built out of their own resources and efforts. Most of their pastors/evangelists are trained for the work in the field without attaining a degree at graduate level. The pastors/evangelists go through a short-term course, which does not last more than two or three years, although this trend is changing. This seeks to break down the barrier between the so-called "qualified" pastoral workers and ordinary Christians. All believers are equipped to preach and evangelize by their experience of the baptism of the Holy Spirit. One of the interesting features is that the gift of the Spirit can fall as easily on the illiterate as on the educated, and *glossolalia* can bless an ordinary member of the Church as effortlessly as the gifted singer in the Church. Such democratic character of the Pentecostal movement has given itself a definite edge over other Churches where Church offices are held by the 'learned and able men'. On the other hand we see in many Pentecostal Churches that individuals are brought into the community of the Church, rescued from a life of abandonment and with a new hope, recovering their dignity opening up before them. One can observe in Pentecostal Churches, to a large extent, an egalitarian experience in different aspects of their day to day life especially in the context of ministry.

Another aspect to be noticed is that the Pentecostals identify organized religions with modernism[22] as opposed to traditional ways of life and systems. According to them in the modern age dogmas and doctrines are carefully worked out for worship services. Many Pentecostals are not comfortable with this because they think the institutional nature of religion is always for the elite. The poor/Dalits cannot play a role in such an institutionalized religious setup. On the other hand they are more at home with primal forms of worship which are more emotional. Miracles, mysteries and myths still fill them with awe and wonder; dance, drums, and songs help them to give meaning to their empty and broken lives; and the community around them stands in support. Further there is a thirst for an experience of God among the Dalits, which is expressed in their own language. There is a longing among them for fellowship in community because they are still the underdogs in the society. This is one of the major reasons for the formation of many independent Pentecostal Churches in the recent years.

Pentecostalism and its way of life as a kind of 'puritan rules of life style' which rejects alcohol, drugs, and participation in the evil entertainment's of postmodern media and certain contemporary culture such as going to a theatre for movies etc., are considered as some other factors for the success of the movement. Many Pentecostals still insist on chastity and modesty for both sexes and are not influenced by the postmodern life styles. This does not mean Pentecostals are still 'primitive' in their life style but to say that they are not caught in the post modern life style. This is all the more true about the Dalits among the Pentecostal Churches. At the same time they contain elements familiar with both the pre-modern and postmodern. It brings forward enough of the pre-modern and the local to enable it also to carry the global and radical possibilities of the individualized, self-consciousness of the postmodern world. Dalit Pentecostalism is able to re-package some of the pre-modern religious awareness and to alter familiar elements of ethnic, familial and other habits of collective solidarity within a movement, which also induct new experiences of postmodern individualism, autonomy, mobility and self-determination. Pentecostalism has offered its converts a novel experience of spiritual autonomy.

The Orality of Pentecostal Worship and 'Liturgy'

Pentecostals do not have a written liturgy in their church worship. Their liturgy is more verbal. They are against an established and organized form of worship and prefer an oral form of liturgy because everyone can participate in it, both the educated and the uneducated. Within the oral form there is a lot of freedom that allows a person to worship God using his own understanding of a personal God. Although the liturgy is not written, everyone knows what he or she is supposed to do. One is allowed to express oneself because they are not bound by a hierarchical liturgy. It has facilitated many to be attracted to the movement.

The Narrative Nature of the Witness and Theology of Pentecostalism

Unlike the abstract theological elements that have dominated the worship and witness in other churches, Pentecostals prefer a narrative expression of their theology and witness. For Pentecostals God is more than a concept. God is an experience for them. There is a thirst among them for the God-experience. They experience God when their children are healed, when their financial needs are met, etc. They would like to narrate their experiences of God and that gives them a lot of satisfaction.

I have witnessed this in many Pentecostal Churches where one can observe people testifying, praying spontaneously, preaching without written manuscripts but with a lot of 'theology' that relates to the everyday lives of the people, their struggles, their agonies, their burdens. People find this kind of worship and preaching a satisfying experience. Pentecostals have been successful in creating indigenous Churches, which incorporate unique local cultural forms. The story telling form which is a popular Indian medium of communication and preservation of traditions is a common form through which Pentecostals have formulated their 'theology' and communicate it to others more clearly than through carefully written theology and dogmas.

Whole-hearted Participation by the People

There is a great emphasis upon group participation in prayer and singing. The sermons are generally simple with plenty of opportunities for men and women to respond not only verbally but with actions as well. The strength of the Pentecostal Churches is that they allow full participation of almost all the members. One's participation is not dependent on a gradation of their physical qualifications but depends largely on the function of the Spirit in one's life. Therefore they participate fully in all the activities of the church like prayer, reflection, and decision making. Through all these they form a community that is reconciliatory. Everyone has a part in the decision making process of the church. Again this is true mostly in the Dalit Pentecostal Churches.

The Place given to Dreams and Visions in Personal and Public Forms of Worship

Although the written Word of God is considered the fundamental revelation, this does not preclude God's direct communication through other means, such as visions, audible voices, dreams, tongues with interpretation, and other means. Dreams and visions form one of the most important part of Pentecostal worship. The experiences of God do not come from the theological books of great people but from the everyday experiences of the people. Their dreams and visions include a future where God is on their side and there will be no more injustice done to them.

Pentecostals experienced a re-visioning of their Christian life by embracing the Pentecostal faith. This re-visioning of Christian life found its place in the concept of community and its worship. Worship is at the heart of Pentecostal spirituality. In fact they function as a worshiping, witnessing, and reflecting community. They worship both verbally and non-verbally. The most important goal of the worship in a Pentecostal church is a personal encounter with the Spirit of God. They believe that God's personal presence is experienced among them when they worship. They claim to meet with God in their worship. They also emphasize an encounter with the Spirit of God in their worship and experience the transformational power of the Spirit of God. Singing in the Spirit is an important part of worship. Prayer is another important aspect of their worship. Through prayer they often 'unburden' themselves. It is quite often vocal and not silent prayer. Another part of the worship is sharing 'testimony'. It is telling one's story of how in the past the Lord led him/her through difficult times such as sickness, financial difficulties and other struggles of life. It is a kind of confession that they make before the congregation, of the ways God which brought them through. Often the community is shaped by the testimony of its members.

Another important part is the sermon. While testimonies express the stories of God's people, the sermon declares the story of God. Sermons are usually preached in a narrative or story-telling form. It is a kind of dialogue with the congregation.

Community and Pentecostal Formation

Pentecostal spirituality is not devoid of social relationship. They do not see spirituality and their social relationship as two different things. They believe that in the Spirit 'there is no longer Jew or Greek, there is no longer slave or free, there is no longer male and female but we all are one in Christ'. There is no place for hierarchy. Worship is the expression of real democracy and equality. There is a celebratory form of worship and communal life. This celebration and communal life is highly participatory.

Women play an equal role in Pentecostal worship. They stand as equals when they worship with their male counterpart. In fact in many Pentecostal churches women play a vital role in worship through their singing, prayer, and even pronouncing the word of God on certain occasions. Women play the role of prophetesses, inspired tongue speakers, healers and visionaries. In Pentecostalism salvation is essentially the same for men and women.

While the above are some positive observations of the results of Pentecostal praxis of mission, there are many negative aspects, which they need to rectify at the same time. Money and numbers play an important role in some 'powerful' Pentecostal miniseries today. For many Pentecostals without these there can be no divine favour or blessing. There seems to be a tendency towards 'successful' ministry but most of it are stage-managed ministries. According to Cheryl Bridges Jones,

> Pentecostalism is an ethos which has more than its share of arrogant evangelists who use the masses for material gain. We have scandals of great proportion and witnessed unholy marriages between military dictators and Pentecostal congregations. Such things tamper any attempts to presume to have arrived at any plateau of spirituality.[23]

There is very often a tendency among the Pentecostal leaders who are involved in what we call mission to enhance and build their own empire. Donald Gee, a Pentecostal theologian makes an eye-opening observation about modern day Pentecostalism. He says that 'Pentecostalism more often draws attention to the brilliance of the individual and glorifies one. However, true ministry on the line of 'spiritual gifts' leaves one in the background and glorifies God. Such was true apostolic ministry.'[24]

Challenges Facing the Movement in the Present Time

Pentecostal-Charismatic Tensions

There were some interesting developments taking place within the classical Pentecostal denominations in the post second world war period. From a separation that fed on rejection and its own early tendency toward isolation and intolerant exclusiveness, classical Pentecostalism has become interactive with Protestant evangelicalism and, in certain cases, even with the broader ecumenical Christian community. In many countries the result has been relatively higher level of acceptance and respectability-which Pentecostals now share with non-separatist charismatic who never suffered as high a level of rejection. Because many Pentecostals, fearing compromise of basic convictions that might lead to a loss of distinctiveness, are not yet entirely comfortable with the entrance into the mainstream of other Christian denominations. The result has been that the movement tends to be divided between those who identify with the past and those who value their newfound identification with the larger church world.[25]

Growing pains became evident with the emergence of the charismatic movement. Pentecostals, who by the middle of the 20th century were identifying closely with mainstream evangelicals, initially applauded the movement. But when many charismatic remained in their own churches rather than shifting to classical Pentecostalism, more dogmatic Pentecostals became frustrated with them. However, the Charismatic's aligned to their own church traditions and have tended to recognize the decline and flow of earnest spirituality in Christian history and have found their identity as part of the latest wave of renewal without moving out from their local affiliations.

Nevertheless, in the 1980s and 1990s many Pentecostals recognized that the Holy Spirit was accomplishing a new work and sensed an affinity with it. The charismatic renewal brought pressure on the Pentecostals to broaden their identification within the universal church to groups previously considered apostate. In this regard, the untiring efforts of the late David J. du Plessis (1905-87), one-time secretary of the Pentecostal World Conference, proved to be particularly instrumental in building bridges between Pentecostals and charismatic.[26] Through such efforts, the early ideal of ecumenism among the Spirit-baptized has extended beyond the Pentecostal World Conference, primarily made up of classical Pentecostals, so the recent North American Congresses on the Holy Spirit and World Evangelization (meeting annually since 1986), which have encompassed all stripes of classical Pentecostals, together with charismatic Baptists, Episcopalians Lutherans, Mennonites, Messianic Jews, Methodists, Presbyterians, Reformed, Greek Orthodox, and Roman Catholics. These events rank among the most important modern gatherings of Christians because of their size as well as their theological significance. Viewed with suspicion by both Pentecostals and charismatic as the new wave on the shore, neo-charismatic- by their very nature independent and resistant to ecclesiastical connection-have yet to be integrated in significant numbers into these ecumenical dialogues.

Let me make the following observations. I am of the opinion that there are some important aspects that unifies the Pentecostal movement probably not on the doctrinal levels. It is in the aspects of doing theology-experience related, oral form of expressions, its ecumenical nature (its world-wide forms ranging from classical Pentecostalism to third wave revivals in number of countries, mostly in the third world countries).

According to Hollenweger, the famous Pentecostal theologian and historian, genuine Pentecostalism is distinguished by faithfulness to its roots both in its theology and in its outward manifestation. It began with a black ecumenist, by the name William J. Seymour, in the black, oral Afro-American culture; it integrated important elements of Catholic spirituality; it was inspired by the social and political interpretation of holiness developed in the American Holiness Movement.[27]

The Tension between Ministry as a "call" and "Profession"

When Pentecostalism started in the early part of the 20th century, the movement was filled with people who had a sense of call from the Lord. However as the time went by the "call" began to dim and more of "professionalism" began to emerge. Today, the question must be asked: Is it the call or the profession-which is the driving force behind the Pentecostal Churches or Pentecostal ministry? It must be said here that ministry is basically a calling and in that sense it is not a career or a profession that we do. There is vast difference between a career and a calling. A career is something that I choose for myself where as a calling is something that I receive. A career is something that I do for myself but a calling is something that God does through me. A career promises status, power, money and positions and many other things whereas a calling involves difficulties, pain, suffering but at the same time it gives me an opportunity to be used by God. A career is all about upward mobility where as in calling you decrease and allow the *Guru* to increase in your life. Career is what you are trained for but calling is something that you receive from the Lord. Pentecostals should not look at ministry as something that they can perform but something that becomes part and parcel of their life, an extension of their life.

This phenomenon is very often seen among the younger generation of Pentecostal scholars. I fear that very often minor things have taken over our major concerns which are our life and relationship to God. The catch words in the movement today are 'faster, higher, and stronger,' words which we have borrowed from the contemporary society.

Pentecostal Movement has gone through several changes. From being a movement, Pentecostalism has moved into a structured, institutionalized and established organization/s. So much so today there is a tendency among the Pentecostals to promote their 'Church' than promoting the founder of the Church and His Gospel. There is a false understanding of evangelism because many Pentecostals today attempt to promote the Church building or an organization without realizing the fact that the Church as a building or denomination has the poorest appeal of all to 'sinners'. Bishop F. D. Washington of the Church of God in Christ, says that 'most of the sinners do not go to Church. Yet the fantastic fact remains that the person of Jesus Christ-when he is presented right-has the greatest single appeal to the human heart in this world.'[28]

The Danger of "Prosperity Theology"

Another serious concern is with regard to the prosperity theology that many 'So-called Pentecostal preachers' propagate today around the world. Prosperity theology emerged from some quarters of the Pentecostal and charismatic movements. At the same time a few highly responsible Pentecostal leaders have been very critical of such newer developments within Pentecostalism. Basically prosperity theology is a North American phenomenon. The socio-economic and political background of North America is the context of its development. Now it has been spread to different parts of the world especially among some Pentecostal and charismatic movements. It is basically a 'theology of success.' It asserts that material prosperity is God's will for every Christian. Unfortunately, the popular contemporary Pentecostal preachers are the proponents of such a theology. Many of these preachers advocate piety and prayer to be security against dangers and harms in life and criteria for material blessing. It is an insurance theology. But the question that has always been raised is how can success be at the centre and prosperity be the goal of the Christian faith and mission whose central symbol is the cross and the son of God hanging on it, forsaken even of God? They forget the fact that the distinguishable mark of the spirituality and ministry of the Church throughout the ages has been the crucifying Christ and His cross and not the success oriented Western theology and mind set.

In the present day context of our country where around 45% of the people are below the poverty line, where even after 57 years of independence the poor mass is still oppressed politically, economically, socially, and religiously, where the majority are deprived of drinking water, housing, health care, where in the name of development the poor tribals and the farmers are dislocated in mass, where caste system continue to hold the Dalits and other marginalized groups under darkness, where women and children are treated in dehumanizing ways, what is the mission and ministry of the Church? I believe the ministry of the Church must be one of incarnating into the lives of people and their situations. Incarnation is nothing but identity with the pains and sufferings of the people so that death is at work in us and life in the deprived ones of our country. It should be life and life abundant. Therefore there is an urgent need for Pentecostal missiology to go back to its root when it was known as a 'religion of the empowered poor' where there was no discrimination based on any kind whether wealth/class/ education etc.

The Tension between "Quantity Vs "Quality"

Another aspect that needs serious re-thinking in Pentecostal missiology is its concept of quantity or the craziness for adding more members to the Church. Today there is a 'mega Church' concept that is crept into the Pentecostal Churches and its mission thinking. Very often this craziness for the number game is at the cost of quality and compromising many vital values. There is a big 'hue and cry' about souls being lost without Christ. Buenos Aires, a former Associate General Secretary for the Latin America of the International Fellowship of Evangelical Students made the following significant statement, "There is no place for statistics on how many souls die without Christ every minute if they do not take into account how many of those who die, die victims of hunger." [29]

No doubt there is a lot of influence of globalization that is a major concern. Globalization projects an ideal culture that is mostly the culture of the West. The basic value of this culture is consumerism and profit. The idea is that you have to make your product appealing. This kind of culture has begun to influence the way Christians/Pentecostals do ministry. The Gospel is seen as a 'product' which the preacher must 'sell'. The more the preacher sells, the more he/she becomes famous. According to Gerloff, "When Reinhard Bonnke[30] makes ten thousand people speak in tongues in half a minute or when he stages miracle after miracle in his services, then religion is marketed like a new shampoo or a disco song. That is neither the renewal of the Church nor of society."[31] Unfortunately, some of the basic values of the Gospel like love, grace, mercy, relationship are now replaced under such marketing mentality with words like 'prosperity' and 'success'. In the urge to become famous some 'labourers' of the Gospel use whatever means are available at their disposal. For many, the end justifies the means, not knowing (or intentionally ignoring) that in God's Kingdom the means matters to the end. What we see here is a 'commodification' of the Gospel, human relationship and values. A lot of emphasis is laid on Church growth, not realizing the fact that all that grows is not the Church.

External Challenges

We are living in a historical moment, for it is a new millennium and a new age. We are faced with a number of challenges from the world around us and no responsible Christian and more so the Pentecostals can run away from the realities that they face. In the last three or four hundred years we have had several significant developments taking place in the world that affected human relationships and values.

Modernism

In the first place the whole concept of **Modernism** in the last few decades has challenged human thinking and values. (What I mean by modernism here is nothing but scientific rationality or reasoning.) At the same time modernism also brought a crisis along with the challenges.

As a result of modernism there began to emerge a critical spirit; this means people did not accept traditional thinking in its totality. They began to question the traditional way of thinking. Pentecostal tradition was not free from this challenge of modernism, which definitely influenced their concept of mission. There emerged a critical scholarship. It had both positive and negative impacts upon church and society.

Industrial Development

The second issue is the change in the social systems in our society. In the past century a lot of development has taken place in the industrial world. **Industrial development** has given way to a large extent to the agricultural way of life. Therefore we have a structural changes taking place around the world which posed a challenge to the mission of the Church. The market began to control our life in the society. Everything was affected through the market concept including the mission of the Church.

Globalization

Thirdly the whole issue of **globalization** that we have today is another development which posed a great challenge to the mission. It is primarily an economic process, and unfortunately this whole economic process is now being controlled by a few international/ multinational powers. There is a global market, which is controlling us. As I said in the above paragraph in the traditional society we controlled the market, but now the market is controlling us. The market decides what product we need. Globalization has become a reality today.

There are also other realities in the Indian society like **poverty, pluralism, castesism, political instability, environmental degradation**, which have become great challenges to the mission. No responsible Christian can ignore such realities and do mission.

The consequence of the above developments has its own impact and implications for the mission in India. There is an ever **widening gap between the rich and the poor**. The poor are becoming poorer and the rich becoming richer. There is an **ever-growing migration of people** for security and economic reasons to 'other' places. There are ever growing **internal conflicts and disintegration of communities**. There is **communalism**, which is also a great challenge for mission. As a result of **environmental degradation** all sorts of disasters are taking place. People are turning to be militants and terrorists because their raised hopes and expectations are not being fulfilled.

All these are great challenges to the mission of the Church in India today.

Reasons for 'Failure' in the Growth of Pentecostal Movement

What are some of the reasons for these above failures in Pentecostal movement or in the Churches? I would like to identify a few and welcome other friends to identify other reasons.

Prosperity

In the first place as I mentioned already the whole issue of prosperity that has saturated the movement today. There was a time when the movement was known as a 'religion of poor'. However that label is fast disappearing and there is a lot of emphasis laid on 'blessings' meaning mostly the material blessings. What has happened/happening to the many Pentecostals today is similar to what has happened to the Israelites when they entered into the land of Canaan. Once they entered the land of Canaan they almost forgot the warning that was given to them through Moses while they were in the wilderness that there were every chance to forget the Lord when they get into the land of Canaan flowing with milk and honey. In fact what was feared has come true in the lives of the Israelites. They were no more in 'need' of the Lord because unlike in the wilderness where they had to wait for the water from the rock, they now have wells to draw their water from; now they have their own defence while in the wilderness the Lord fought the battle for them; I feel this is almost what has happened to the Pentecostals in India and especially in Kerala! There was a time when they were very low in their economic status in the society. Like the Israelites in the wilderness, the Pentecostals had to depend fully on the Lord for their provision for each day. Now that situation is over and they are well paced in the society.

Proxies for God

The second problem I see among the Pentecostals today is that they have found many **proxies for God**. In the beginning of the movement they felt the immediacy of God. They felt the nearness of God but once they crossed certain hurdles on their journey, they began to distant themselves from God. For the third or fourth generation Pentecostals the concept of God, Church, revival etc., have become 'fussy'. There was a time when God was so near but where is that God today? Their so called "ministry" became their priority than the one who gave them the ministry. The approval of God is not the main aim in the lives of many Pentecostal leaders and members. I fear our 'busy work' for God took us away from reflecting his characteristics like his holiness, integrity, justice, selfless love etc.

Nominalism

The third reason I find for the failure of Pentecostals is the kind **Nominalism** that crept into the Church. In the early years Pentecostal movement they felt the clear guidance of the Lord. Like the Israelites saw the presence of God through the clouds that followed them, the Pentecostals literally experienced the presence of God in their lives. However now there is lot nominalism. The original vision seems to have dimmed. Worship, preaching, and other ministries of the Church have become very superficial.

Lot of 'Symbols'

Another dangerous situation is that we have a lot of **symbols**. Symbols are good but when it takes the place of the reality of God it is dangerous. Worshipping God from the heart should not take the place of making some noise or words like "Halleluiah". Such words should not become a symbol or it should not replace our love for God.

Compromising Attitude

Another reason for the failure can be our **compromising attitude** or going after the worldly pleasures. In the history of the Israelites, we see some of them seeking after the blessing of Baal. It is high time for the Pentecostals to see what are the areas that they have compromised with the world. Pentecostals must always remember that like Disciples of Christ, they are primarily called to be with Him and then send by Him for the ministry. We must always remember that unless we continue to abide in Him we cannot bear fruit for Him. What is the level of our consistency of being with Him? Sometimes we are so close to Him but at other times we are far away from Him. What is the level of our nearness to Him? Are we improving upon our level of knowledge of Him? Apostle Paul's writing to the Philippians says that "I want to know Him" (3:10). All that I have known about Him is only little. I want to know more of Him. The closer we get to Him, we know His demands better. However for many Pentecostals Christ is someone to follow at a distance because His demands are not in line with their agenda. Who is the real me or who is the real Pentecostal or more so who is real disciple or Christian is an urgent question that each of us need to answer.

Conclusion

I am well aware of the fact that this paper is not an evaluation of the Pentecostal Churches but I cannot write a paper on the importance of empowerment in the Pentecostal Churches apart from an evaluation of them. Therefore, it is important that the Pentecostal Church/Churches should focus its attention on the way to remedy the situation that we face in our mission practices today.

In the first place, I suggest to go back to the earlier emphasis on **purity of life and transparency in our relationship with God and with one another.** The life of the Apostolic Church was embodied by truth and purity. Secondly, we **move from the concept of human rationality to a Trinitarian community of discourse**; let us learn to look at truth not as power but as love; let us learn to look at God as a communion and not as a power monger. Let us learn to look at the creation relationally and not as something that we can use to achieve our purpose. Let us not try to fix our problems by our own strength but listen to God so that He may instruct us as to what to do and how to go about resolving our problems. The people of God in Babylon in captivity could not fix their problem but had to listen to God who fixed their problem. Prophet Isaiah had to tell them that it is only those who wait upon the Lord shall renew their strength and not those who think that they can do it by themselves.

Thirdly, I suggest that **instead of looking at people as commodities, let us learn to look at people through the perspective of God.** Today, we see everything as commodities. Let us learn the fact that if we want people to know the love of God, it can only be done through the love that God has shown to us through the cross of Christ.

Fourthly, I suggest that **we move from individualism to covenant practices, practicing hospitality whereby we welcome the stranger**. Today, there is this fear of others. However, let us learn the fact that welcoming the stranger is the biblical way. Hospitality is the practice of an established community. Let us learn that welcoming the stranger begins with our own conversion to the Gospel.

In the fifth, place and the most important one I suggest that **we take a journey from future to memory.** In Deuteronomy chapter 8 we see God reminding the people of Israel through Moses to go back to memory and see how the Lord led them through the wilderness through their forty years of journey. Israel only exists because of its memory. Without memory Israel becomes not my people. Only by living in the memory of God's mercy do we become his people. Erasing the memory is to forget God and become no people of God.

The sixth area that we need to develop is that we must become a Church that is patterned after the model of Christ. Jesus gave himself up for humanity.

The seventh area is that we must truly make every attempt to present an Indian Church that would reflect the Indian cultural values and heritage. It was in this context that the Indian Church History Association came out with a new approach to the very writing of Indian Church history. The Church History Association of India (CHAI), especially through its publication *Indian Church History Review*, encouraged Indian church historians to write their history from a nationalistic prospective. As a result many historians started reflecting in their writings a position and protest against the Euro-centred approach to the expansion and development of Christianity in India. Their emphasis was mainly on Indian contribution to the development of Christianity in India. They projected Christianity as part and parcel of the total history of India and brought about an authentic Indian identity for Christianity. It was said that "History of Christianity in India is viewed as an integral part of the socio-cultural history of the Indian people rather than as separate from it. The history will, therefore, focus attention upon the Christian people in India, upon who they were and how they understood themselves; upon their social, religious, cultural and political encounters, upon the changes which their encounters produced in them and in the appropriation of the Christian gospel, as well as in the Indian culture and society of which they themselves were a part."[32]

The last issue, which we saw as an internal challenge to the mission of the Church, was the issue of superiority complex. Here I suggest that we see ourselves not 'over against other religions, but in relation' to our friends from other faiths. The identity of the Church must be relational or else we can become like 'frogs in the well' whereby we do not see anything outside the 'well'.

Last but not the least, Pentecostal mission must also include a programme to promote human rights issues. No responsible Christian missionary can ignore the fact of human rights issues. Our mission in India today should also give emphasis to transforming human situations. Transformation of humanity and empowering the weak has to take priority over every other agenda because that was/is the main agenda of the Lord of mission during His earthly sojourn.

Endnotes:

[1] Miroslav Volf, "Kirche als Gemeinschaft. Ekklesiologische Ueberlegungen aus freikirchlicher Perspektive," *Evangelische Theologie* 49, no. 1 (1989): 64, 66, cited in Walter J. Hollenweger, *Pentecostalism: Origins and Developments Worldwide* (Peabody: Hendrickson Publishers, 1997), 264.

[2] Justin Martyr, *Apology* II, 3.

[3] Harry R. Boer, *A Short History of the Early Church* (Grand Rapids: William B. Eerdmans Publishing Company, 2001), 134.

[4] Ibid., 136.

[5] Ibid.

[6] Dyron B. Daughrity, *Changing World of Christianity: The Global History of a Borderless Religion* (Bern: Peter Lang, 2010), 151.

[7] Hollenweger, *Pentecostalism: Origins and Developments Worldwide*, 184.

[8] Garry B. McGee, *Selected Documents on the Early History of the Assemblies of God in India* (Springfield, Massachusetts: AGTS, 1991).

[9] Minnie F. Abrams, "How Pentecost came to India," *Pentecostal Evangel* (May 1945): 6.

[10] J. Edwin Orr, *Evangelical Awakening* (Madras: CLS, 1970), 96.

[11] The term 'Classical Pentecostal' first appeared in the work of Kilian McDonnell about 1970, and it distinguishes the Pentecostals who trace their origin to the beginning of the 20th century from those neo-Pentecostals or Charismatic who appeared during the second half of the 20th century within the mainline Protestant Churches, the Roman Catholics, and the various independent Churches.

[12] Vinson Synan, "Pentecostalism, Varieties and Contributions," *Pneuma: The Journal of the Society for Pentecostal Studies* 9, no. 1 (Spring 1987): 32-34.

[13] Stanley M. Burgess and Eduard M. van der Mass, eds., *The New International Dictionary of Pentecostal and Charismatic Movements* (Grand Rapids: Zondervan Publishing House, 2002), 1141.

[14] Ibid.

[15] David B. Barrett and Todd M. Johnson, "Annual Statistical Table on Global Mission: 1999," *International Bulletin of Missionary Research* 23, no. 1 (January 1999): 24f.

[16] David du Plessis, "Pentecost," *A Quarterly Review of World-wide Pentecostal Activity* 30 (Dec. 1954): 17.

[17] Bishop F. D Washington at the 62nd convocation of the Church of God in Christ 1969 (*Holy Convocation*, ed. J. O. Patterson, n. p. 1969) as cited in Hollenweger, *Pentecostalism: Origins and Developments Worldwide*, 28.

[18] "Weird Babel of Tongues," *Los Angeles Daily Times* (Los Angeles), 18 April 1906, 2, cited in Wonsuk Ma, "Toward an Asian Pentecostal Theology," *Asian Journal of Pentecostal Studies* 1, no. 1 (January 1998): 33.

[19] The Main Line Pentecostal Churches like Assemblies of God, Indian Pentecostal Church of God, Church of God in India, Sharon Fellowship etc., have changed to a large extent to modern ways of life. Their worship and Church structures are almost going back to the main line traditional Churches although these Pentecostal Churches do not have a written liturgy. They use all kinds of western musical instruments available in the market and pattern their worship after the Western model.

[20] Synan, "Pentecostalism, Varieties and contributions," 41.

[21] This was also true of Syrian Pentecostals in their earlier years, but now with all other modern musical instruments, many Syrian Pentecostals have ceased using the drum. The other factor is that as the Syrians went up on their economic status especially in the recent years, some of the old practices of using the drum and sharing testimony, etc., are giving way to a more 'programmed' kind of worship, where everything is controlled by the pastor. In other words what I see is a connection between one's economic status and spirituality. However that is another area that needs thorough research.

[22] With the rise of modernism there emerged a critical spirit. People began to question everything including religious faith. In this context people began to have more organized form of religion. Modernization is also a process whereby a society changes from a pre-modern, pre industrial economy to a modern industrial economy. It includes increased urbanization, workers shifting from agriculture to industry, increased literacy, and increased opportunity for political participation. However the Dalits who hold tradition very high identifies organized religions with some of this modern thinking. They still follow their earlier patterns of worship and communal structure.

[23] Cheryl Bridges Johns, "Pentecostal Formation-A Pedagogy among the Oppressed," *Journal of Pentecostal Theology* Supplement Series-2 (Sheffield: Sheffield Academic Press, 1993), 9.

[24] Donald Gee, *Concerning Spiritual Gifts* (Springfield: Gospel Publishing House, 1972), 52.

[25] Ibid

[26] Ibid

[27] Hollenweger, *Pentecostalism: Origins and Developments Worldwide*, 397.

[28] Bishop F. D Washington cited in Ibid., 28

[29] Ibdi., 305.

[30] Reinhard Bonnke is a popular itinerant German evangelist who attracts tens of thousands of people for his evangelistic crusades all around the world but mostly in African countries.

[31] Roswith I. H. Gerloff, "Afrikkanische Diaspora," as quoted by Hollenweger, *Pentecostalism: Origins and Developments Worldwide*, 364.

[32] A. Mathias Mundadan, *History of Christianity in India*, vol. 1 (Bangalore: Theological Publication of India, 1984), 7.

Chapter 13
Sociological Perspectives for Ecclesiology: Towards a Sociology of the Church Based on François Houtart's Thoughts[1]

Jerome Sahabandhu

In this article the researcher has engaged in an extensive research on ecclesiology of François Houtart, one of the important sociologists of religion in our times. This contributes to the debate of dialectical interaction of ecclesiology and society within a wider framework of religion and society debate.

François Houtart

François Houtart (born in 1925) is a Belgian social activist and a sociologist of religion who defends the position that religion, as a social reality, can be an agent of change in society. Houtart, whose ideas originate from Weber, Marx and Gramsci, believes that religion is a social construction. Throughout his career, Houtart has struggled for social justice, particularly in subaltern societies. This has been expressed in his forceful resistance to capitalist globalisation, his encouragement of the convergence of social movements and his emphasis on the importance of collective consciousness and praxis in the changing global situation.

In a Gramscian sense, Houtart is an *engaged intellectual*. This is the result of a gradual evolution and a process of becoming. His first sociological and ecclesiastical focus was the *Sitz im Leben* of the working class in mid-twentieth-century Europe. Houtart was then influenced by Cardinal Cardijn, echoing the method of *see, judge* and *act* in his own work, while exposure to Latin American liberation theology challenged Houtart to rethink the established notion of developmentalism. Houtart adopted liberation thought and reinterpreted the role of religion in this light, thus learning about the correlation between theory and praxis.

Houtart went on to study religion and society in India and Sri Lanka. He also studied Buddhism in Sri Lanka as a professional sociologist of religion. Today we meet Houtart as a social critic in the discourse on global justice.

Houtart is a Roman Catholic priest. He has made a significant and lasting impact on Christian social witness in Asia.

Religion and Society

François Houtart has undergone two main transitions in his social thought: 1) From religious sociology to sociology of religion; 2) From sociology of religion to the sociology of the Church. The first transition he made in two steps: First, from "religious" sociology to empirical sociology and, then, from empirical sociology to the specific field of his research and thinking, namely, the religious phenomenon. Houtart early realised that empirical sociology usually ended up in presenting accurate statistics, but he was always convinced that to understand the religious phenomenon one needed much more than statistics, however important statistics might be.

In the first period, he studied society with a religious interest; in the second period, he studied religion with a social interest. In this article we centre our focus on Houtart's directing his attention to the specific form of religion called the Roman Catholic Church, placing the RC Church within the wider "sacred canopy" (Peter Berger) of the whole field of religion and not outside or above the religious field. In this line, we have been engaged in a discussion on the dynamics of the relationship between religion and society. Now we shall do likewise studying the dynamics of the relationship between church and society. There are two major arguments that Houtart build up:

1. There is a dialectical relationship between religion and ideology.
2. Religions as institutions with social functions.

In the Houtartian sense this same framework is applicable to the Church as one of the many manifestations of religion vis-à-vis society. There is no reason, of course, to place the Christian religion outside the above framework and discourse. What distinguishes Houtart is that he goes a step beyond and reaches a site that we may call "Church and society," where he could not only explain the ecclesiastical structures as they exist (*to see*), but also make a critique of them (*to judge*) from the perspective of the social milieu in which they are set, and challenge them (*to act*) to change in order to be more relevant, significant, and meaningful in the social ensemble. We could even say that Houtart begins with the scientific and detached study of "Church and Society" as though he were an outsider and concludes with a prophetic appeal for the mission of "the Church at the service of society," as a fervent insider. To put it another way, Houtart wants the Church not simply to be functional (or less dysfunctional) but to affirm that it has a social function and to voice that the Church's social function should be carried out effectively and efficiently in a changing society. This process helps us to unlock and discover how Houtart has been developing the discourse on Church and Society, especially in the early phase of his social thought (1960s-1970s). Thus, the whole discussion bears not only a sociological relevance but a theological relevance as well.

Therefore, the task of Houtart as a rigorous sociologist of religion is *to see*—to describe and to explain—in a good scientific phenomenological approach. The second and third movements of the method Houtart learned in his youthful involvement with the YCW (*to judge* and *to act*) are the functions of the prophet-theologian and the pastor respectively. In short, the scientific sociologist should be descriptive and nor prescriptive. However, Houtart is also a believer and a priest, not alien and indifferent to the religious phenomenon under his scrutiny; he cannot be totally detached from reality as an outsider because he is existentially attached to it as an insider, as a believer and a pastor.

The question addressed in this section will be how Houtart looks at the Church, at "the Holy Mother Church," from a detached sociological point of view. Is it possible or desirable? The theologian and philosopher of religion Paul Tillich may provide the answer to this question with his well-known methodological postulate that, given the subject matter under study, a theologian, in order to have a scientific stance, should have one foot inside the subject of his study as a believer and the other foot outside as a scientist, in order to preserve his phenomenological distance and thus be impartial in his treatment (the method of co-relation). Though not a professional theologian, but a professional sociologist, Houtart cannot separate the Church from society, and we cannot separate Houtart from the Church!

Having this in mind, we consider Houtart's ecclesiological studies and limit our discussion to the following topics, which are some key areas in Houtart on the Church:

1. Vatican II.
2. Some questions Houtart has been raising for ecclesiology from the point of view of sociology.
3. The Church as an institution and how it changes.
4. Communications and the Church.
5. The social sciences and ecclesiology.

Houtart's ecclesiological insights must be understood in the context of the Second Vatican Council.[2] Being caught between the currents of the Vatican Council II as an attached believer and the professionalism of sociology of religion as a detached scientist, Houtart has raised a number of relevant questions for the Church by the inspiration of both disciplines: theology and sociology.[3] Not only has he raised them, but also he has tried his best to contribute by pointing to the way towards the right formulation and possible solution of some of them. He has brought some sociological insights to evaluate the Church as an institution among other institutions in the societies in which she has to carry on her mission. These questions are of utmost value for theologians and pastors alike.

Vatican Council II

Houtart's ecclesiology, as we have already noted, should be placed, understood, and interpreted in the spirit of the ecclesiology of Vatican II.[4] The Sri Lankan author D. R. S. Fernando writes in connection with Vatican II about a paradigm shift in ecclesiology:

> *Aggiornamento* was the key notion introduced by Pope John XXIII when he convoked the Ecumenical Council. It is a reformation that is self induced, a change in ecclesiastical life that tends to dislodge the old ways of life. It is a coming to terms with the modern world. Therefore, it is not a mere adjusting or retooling the machinery, but a radical change and reform.[5]

The majority of the former ecumenical councils were occupied with orthodoxy and heresy, but the focus of Vatican II was on the world and the exercise of faith and of the Church's mission in the world.[6] This has been a paradigm shift from a church-centred world to a world-centred church,[7] implying an attitudinal change in the church's relationship with the world. The Church is a witnessing community in the world and exists in a dialogical relationship with the world that involves communication with the world, including both speaking to the world and learning from the world.[8] As Karl Rahner insisted, the Church is not only the speaker of the Word but also and mainly "the hearer of the Word." However, most theologians tend to interpret the Vatican Council II as a renewal movement.[9]

The role that Houtart played at Vatican II is worth noting here. Houtart was one of the key facilitators in the group that drafted the introduction of *Gaudium et Spes*. In the process of preparation of the document there was a sub-commission called "The Signs of the Times" to work for the introduction of the *Gaudium et Spes,* for which Houtart acted as the secretary as confirmed by some historians of the Vatican Council II, such as Giuseppe Alberigo and Joseph A. Komonchak.[10] In a personal letter in response to my inquiries, Prof. C. Soetens of the University of Louvain la Neuve also confirms the role Houtart played at the Vaitican II; Soetens further writes in his résumé on the convergence and compilation of the Vatican II documents:

> Well-prepared by his studies on the links between the Church and the contemporary world, Canon Houtart actively participated in the work of the special commission on "Signs of the Times" and in the drafting of the preface and the preliminary outline of *Gaudium et Spes*. Professor Houtart, who was a pioneer in the study of religious sociology, also played a leading role within many initiatives, groups and meetings organised at the time of the Council, but independently of it. I believe that these manifold activities must be taken into account in order to understand the evolution of people's minds and the general atmosphere during the Council. One of these initiatives was the creation of the Centrum Orientationis et Coordinationis pastoralis (Centre of Pastoral Orientation and Coordination), which enjoyed a brief existence. Some documentation provided by Professor Houtart himself gives an insight into the *Centrum,* the congresses it held, the investigations it carried out into

> pastoral training in seminaries, and also the obstacles which led to its dissolution.[11]

For Houtart, as for many other students of the Vatican Council II, the Dogmatic Constitution on the Church (*Lumen Gentium*) and the Pastoral Constitution on the Church in the Modern World (*Gaudium et Spes*) are the two pillars of Vatican II.[12] The overwhelming stress of *Gaudium et Spes* was on understanding and assessing the role of the Church in the context of the wider world of today. It is not a sociological document but a pastoral document, as the title itself states. In order to operate in the world, the Church needs to understand the ways of the world, and this function of understanding corresponds to the task of sociologists, not of theologians. According to Houtart, a substantial part of *Gaudium et Spes* has been devoted to describing what the world is. The approach of the Pastoral Constitution on the Church in the Modern World has not been the traditional deductive, but an inductive approach.[13] The inductive approach starts with the world and then comes to the Word of God. The direction is not the verticalist coming down from above to below, but from below to above. What we are interested in the present article is getting an overview of his approach to ecclesiology.

Undoubtedly Houtart's ecclesiological approach represents the currents that paved the way to the Council, which, according to both Fernando and Chenu, was a Copernican revolution in ecclesiology.[14] Yet Houtart worries about how this revolution will take place in the life of the Church; and in the context of Vatican II, he writes:

> Almost all revolutions are provoked by a cultural lag between *new values and old institutions*. The Catholic Church, in this period of transition from the pre-conciliar to the post-conciliar church, is being described by many analysts as existing in a pre-revolutionary situation. The new values of participation, collegiality, freedom, and personal responsibility set forth in the documents of Vatican II are meeting with resistance from structures within the Church that have become rigid with age and tradition; and many are questioning whether these new values can become a part of the institutional Church in time to avoid a crisis of open revolution or of quiet defection.
>
> Adaptation is made more difficult within the institutional Church because of the rapid social change which is affecting all

of secular society and, since "the world" is the field of Christian activity, the Church as well.[15]

We are not interested here in debating whether the Vatican II has been a revolution or a reformation. Houtart's spirit, however, has been summarised by Pieris, in this regard taking Rahner's advice to the young theologians at the time of the council, "do not waste time on the Vatican II":

> It was not, therefore, Vatican II as the "end-product" of a process, but Vatican II as "the process itself," that Rahner invited us to master. For, the task of our generation was to proceed from where the Council would leave us. Vatican II, he insisted, was not a point of arrival, but "a point of departure" (*punctum a quo proficiendum est,* to quote his own words!). In other words, our mission was to complete its *unwritten agenda* by means of a theo-praxis that is commensurate with its new orientation.[16]

Response is an important word in understanding Houtart's ecclesiological interests. Houtart is interested in why the Church must respond and how it should respond to the various issues and to the different phenomena that emerge in the world. Response is a relational term, implying that Houtart expects the Church to communicate with the wider society and give a response in different forms, affirming the relevancy and significance of the Church in the world. Every meaningful response demands a change in structures, values, and attitudes. It was in this context that Houtart began to raise issues for the Church while being in the Church. He uses the sociology of religion as a tool in his endeavour, turning his professional specialty into a "sociology of the Church."

Some Questions and Issues

It is relevant to observe how the dialogue between sociology and theology bears fruit in Houtart's thinking on the Church. In what type of questions has Houtart been interested in relation to the Church? A sample of questions/issues would enable us to grasp Houtart's "ecclesiological psyche."

1. Why and how should the Church respond to such phenomena as industrialisation, the secularisation process,[17] globalisation,[18] and others?

2. What is the response of the Church to the social changes in the different geopolitical contexts in the world?[19]

3. How does the Church behave and interpret its mission in societies in transition, mainly from colonialism to new sovereign nations?[20]

4. What are the means of the encounter with the social movements in various cultural contexts, such as with Marxists, revolutionary movements, and Christian beliefs of different traditions?[21]

5. Does the Church have any contribution to make to the solution of the problems of poverty, underdevelopment, and economic and social injustice in the world? If so, how?

6. Why should and how can the Church employs the tools of the social sciences in her evaluations of self-understanding, pastoral planning, and mission in the world?

7. Can the Church dig into its own structures[22] of ministry using sociology? How do these approaches help the promotion of life and mission of the Church: for example, sociology of liturgy, sociology of pastoral ministry, sociology of Christian communications, sociology of theological education and reflection?

8. Why is social analysis a crucial element for social ethics?[23]

These are only a few among the many questions on ecclesiology that Houtart has been raising and struggling with throughout his career, parallel to his other areas of interests. They are not the theoretical questions of a theologian saturated with the knowledge of Sacred Scripture, ecclesiastical tradition, the study of the ancient Fathers, and so on. They are all practical questions on how the Church should carry on her ministry to the ever-changing world with fidelity to her own tradition, on the one hand, and in solidarity with the world to which her message is addressed, on the other. The quantity of material, which has addressed these questions and issues, witnesses to his tenacity in approaching these questions and perspectives over and over again.

The table given below outlines three columns: the correlated 1) questions or issues, 2) contexts, and 3) references, as a way of example. We will attempt to flesh out such an outline, but the limitations of space do not allow us to go into all of Houtart's insights on ecclesiology, which will be examined in a later work by the present author. At least one example of some of these questions or issues might be helpful in supporting our conviction that Houtart, among others, has initiated a debate that no student or researcher can ignore, whether in ecclesiological and missiological studies or in the study of the social aspects of religion.[24] In the given table, we offer some bibliographical items as samples; they are far from a complete list of Houtart's writings on the mentioned issues. The outline shown in the table should be considered and used only for an initial impression of Houtart's ecclesiological insights, and it is hoped that such an introduction will be of some hermeneutical value to the ecclesiologist as well as to the theologian.

What are some basic sociological concepts Houtart uses in his analysis of the Church? The outline of Houtart's ecclesiological interests leads us to uncover some of his preoccupations, in terms of the concept of the Church, from the perspective of a sociologist of religion. By placing the analysis in the light of the discussions that have been conducted in the preceding sections (religion as part of the symbolic representation and religion as an institution with social functions), it is possible to highlight some specific perspectives of Houtart on ecclesiology from the viewpoint of sociology.

Some Issues for Ecclesiology

Question/Issue	Particular Context	Reference
1. Secularisation	The Church's response to the secularisation and industrialisation in the Euro-American context: a sociological approach, written in the context of Vatican II.	*Challenge to Change: The Church Confronts the Future*, (New York: Sheed and Ward, 1964).
2. Social change	The Church amidst social changes in Latin America	"Roman Catholic Church and Social Change in Latin America" in *The Church and Social Change in Latin*

		America, ed. Henry A. Landsberger (Notre Dame: University of Notre Dame Press, 1970), 112-133.
3. New nations in transition	The developing countries and a response of theology: as a sociologist Houtart raises some issues for the theologian.	"Church and Developing Nations: Some Questions for the Theologians," in *Theology of Renewal,* vol. 2, *Renewal of Religious Structures* (Montreal: Palm, 1968), 358-383.
4. Secular movements	Christian faith and Marxism.	*Marxist Analysis and Christian Belief,* Faith and Ideology (n.p.: Socio-pastoral Institute, 1975).
5. Economic injustice	The case of South Africa: a response of the Catholic Church.	"Demand for Economic Justice: Southern Africa and Portuguese Colonies" in *Towards a Discipline of Social Ethics, Essays in honour of Walter G. Muelder,* ed. Paul Deats (Boston: n.p., 1972), 194-217.
6. The use of empirical social sciences in the work of the Church.	The response of Indian Catholicism towards transition: self-understanding.	*Size and Structures of the Catholic Church in India: The Indigenization of exogenous Religious Institution in a Society in Transition,* (Louvain-la-Neuve: CRSR, 1982).
7. Sociology of ministry	Pastoral care: how can we look at the pastoral ministry sociologically for better ministry?	*Sociology of Pastoral Care* (Chicago: Franciscan Herald Press, 1965).

8. Socio-ethical issues	Violence and religions	"The Cult of Violence in the Name of Religion: A Panorama," *Concilium* 4 (1997):1-9.

We will limit ourselves here only to two of those perspectives:

1. The Church as an institution.[25]
2. The Church as a sign.

The use of both theological and sociological concepts is helpful in such an approach. As an authentic insider of the Catholic tradition and as a sociologist of religion, Houtart uses both theological and sociological language in this task.

The Church as an Institution[26]

We begin with the concept of institution and the question of how an institution changes. Houtart argues, "The Church is an institution with its own values and norms, its own system of legitimation and its organisation."[27] Houtart, then, begins with the affirmation that the Church is an institution.[28] Like any other institution, the Church has her aims and an institutional framework to carry out her objectives. She has a leadership and a membership; that is, people are involved in it, people of flesh and blood, bracketing out all transcendent beings not subject to empirical analysis. Additionally, she has also a financial system, a communication system, a certain type of pedagogical pattern, and the like; all these systems or subsystems within the encompassing institution are definite parts in the organisation. Like any other social institution, the Church is subject to sociological investigation and evaluation and is not an exception. Of course, from a purely theological perspective, the Church should be considered as a living organism; from a purely sociological perspective, on the other hand, the Church must be considered as an organisation, alongside many other social, political, economic, and cultural organisations. Every living organism requires some kind or organisation, of course. Houtart is consistently a sociologist when describing the Church as an institution and the like.

The Church is situated as one among many in the web of human institutions. The Church is an institution in the religious domain that exists in relation to other social institutions, although this does not intend to deny the other dimensions of the Church (as "living organism"), such as mystical, doctrinal, and mythical. The Church's self-understanding is that she has a divine mission, but she still exists within the human community. Houtart justifies this methodological position stating that "Christ founded his *Church within humankind,* under the guidance of the Holy Spirit, but as an institution, subject to the normal laws of human growth and development."[29] This statement also implies that the institution should not be static but dynamic in relation to other spheres of the social life and in communication with the world around it. It is inevitable that, to be significant and functional in this relational social order, the institution must undergo changes in a changing world. These changes, which include crisis and tension, are healthy signs of growth if they are managed positively and creatively.

We mean by *positively* what Houtart called a "prospective" attitude. Houtart writes, "The prospective is a new word for a new science, a science of the future which, by assessing facts of the past and trends in the present, will try to predict future developments in human situation."[30] (Futurology, or the science of future planning, is a new branch of sociology that does not concern us directly here. A cursory mention of it is sufficient). The prospective attitude directs the institution to seek for wisdom and discernment in choosing the mechanisms for change because change is part of growth. This attitude enables her to see conflicts and tensions positively.

Houtart concedes that the Church, like any other institution with its organization, has a tendency to inertia, conservatism and even immobilism. If we move forward—the "immobilists" seem to say—we have to change, and if we change, we may lose our identity. But Houtart is not afraid of change. Even tension could be a healthy sign of change, and so of life. Harvey Cox, writing an introduction to *Challenge to Change* (1964), sums up the Houtartian attitude, which is even applicable for today's Church and her social thought and praxis:

> Perhaps the single most important insight Houtart offers is that tension in an organisation is not a curse to be avoided but a sign of health. Tension indicates that the organisation, in this case

> the Church, is undergoing the pain and distress, which are necessary by-products of genuine change. An institution in which there is no tension is dead or dying. An institution, which is able not only to funnel and accommodate tension but also even to generate it, is truly alive. For Houtart, who welcomes the tension we all notice in the church today, the question therefore is not just how to manage it but how to make it continue to appear.[31]

Thus, Houtart approaches crisis and tension not only positively but also and largely creatively. Institutions can generate crises proactively by making some decisions that will alter their direction and role when they become too sclerotic and fossilised, in order to make them dynamic and "evolutive," at the risk of strong dissension from the more traditionalist, conservative, and even "immobilist" segments of the institutions. He proposes the transformation (not only "reformation") of the Church herself to become another kind of institution: "This is why we must develop a new type of institution, an evolutive institution, one which is not defined once and for all but is capable of development, one within which we can "institutionalise" change."[32]

Houtart calls those decisions that can generate crises that lead to change "*crisigenic* decisions." Recollecting Houtart's words in a conference held in Colombo on the subject of institutional change in the Church, Aloysius Pieris writes,

> A *crisigenic* decision, without which no renewal is possible, cannot achieve its objective save by forcing the institution to pass through a dark corridor of dissension and confusion thanks to the efforts of renewalists to redefine the roles and functions of its members, even at the cost of departures...from its membership.[33]

Thus, for Houtart, to an ever-changing world should correspond an ever-changing Church, in correlation. For him the main question is not only "to interpret the signs of the times" (Mt. 16:3), but also to act according to what we have interpreted in those signs: there is no right action without a true interpretation, but the interpretation will not be true if it does not lead to a corresponding right action. The interpretation of the "signs of the times" is a socio analytic task, necessary for the Church to involve herself in the changing world; the practical involvement in a changing world cannot be effective without corresponding changes in the Church herself; and that is the reason Houtart proposes not only to introduce some changes into the institution but also to institutionalise change in the dynamics of the Church. Otherwise, the Church will be present and active in the world, but not in the world of today but in the world of yesterday, like "a *museum,* a relic of the past which could not attract the younger generation, the people living vital, developing society."[34]

Changing Institutions and Institutionalising Change

The Church as an institution undergoes change within the changing society, which is a challenge to be welcome, according to Houtart. He called this process *adaptation*[35] and defined it as the ability to change as well as the ability to institutionalise changes to meet new challenges. This process demands redefining aims and goals, re-visioning roles and positions, restructuring processes, and reinterpreting faith together with a proper interpretation of the signs of the times.[36] Houtart writes in *The Eleventh Hour,* "The old ways of doing things may not be easily adapted to the new interpretation. This means that they will have to be changed or abandoned completely and new ways will have to be developed to accomplish the redefined aims."[37]

It is extremely important to understand some social lags in this process; we mention only two, sufficiently all embracing:

1. The lag between the development of facts and the organisation.

2. The lag between the real-life situation and the level or stage of thinking.

The lag between the development of facts and of the organisation. The Church is running after the facts without being able to catch up to them.[38] This points to the structures that are not capable of catering to new situations any more. Houtart writes,

> There is great need for a bringing-up-to-date as Pope John[39] said, because the Church has become so set in its institutions, yet must find new ways to meet new problems. Thus the development of facts and the adaptation of the institution becomes one of the primary concerns. The Church as an institution will always be a little late with the facts but should not be too late.[40]

The Lag between the Social Reality and Ecclesiastical Thought

A lag occurs not only between the development of facts and organisations but also between the social reality and the ecclesiastical thought (level of reality and level of thinking). On occasions, old theories and old theologies are not only unable to explain the realities but also irrelevant for facing the challenges posed by the social reality.[41] Houtart's message is that the current information and up-to-date knowledge at all levels, plus a fresh thinking are crucial for change to happen.[42] It is this process that helps the Church to institutionalise changes. The leadership in an institution is of paramount importance for changes to take place.

What are the qualities of a leader? How Houtart grapples with this issue is central to the discussion of our understanding the Church as an institution in the world.

Leadership and Institution

According to Houtart, leadership at all levels is crucial in the institution to bring about changes. There is a shift in the concept of leadership. Houtart says,

> In order to meet the problems of our rapidly changing world we must come to a new type of organisation.... The role of a true leader is no longer administration, but rather one of *provision and of planning*. This is a great function of a leader: *to lead in a prospective type of attitude*. A leader in any kind of institution who is just administering the institution to secure that things are going well, that everyone is at his proper place, that the organisation is running smoothly is no leader in our present civilisation.[43]

Houtart coins a new term—*evolutive*—using his sociological knowledge. He continues,

> Leadership in our very changing world requires the ability to see what must be done today for tomorrow, what provisions we have to make now to be ready for the work that must be done tomorrow. And really we are now in a difficult stage of transition to a new type of institution, the *evolutive institution*.[44]

Evolutive Quality

What does Houtart mean by *evolutive* institution and *evolutive quality*? Houtart answers,

> Because we are living in a society where organisations are a necessity, we cannot function without them. But we are also very much aware of the inflexibility of many of our institutions and the organisational detail that often delays action past the point where it can be effective. This is why we must develop a new type of institution, an *evolutive institution* [italics added], one which is not defined once and for all, but is capable of development, one within which we can institutionalise change.[45]

Thus, the Church must have an evolutive leadership and should be an evolutive institution. In fact, Houtart relates this new concept to all aspects of the life of the Church.

The application of the evolutive quality in the life of the Church (as an institution) requires new roles, new relations, and new types of action, new organisations, new sub-structures within the structure, and new thought. Let us consider only two examples. The first example is specifically from a Roman Catholic context, though indirectly the idea is relevant to all churches, and the second is directly applicable in an ecumenical context.

Taking a pastoral context as the first example, Houtart suggests a change in the deaneries, developing from administrative jurisdictions to pastoral jurisdictions that create new roles. In this new attitude, a diocese not only would have ministers for their own parishes but would even have ministers separated and specialised for working on national and international issues.[46] These new roles and attitudes also should be subject to constant evaluation and appropriation before they become irrelevant.[47]

In the second example, on the intellectual level, Houtart suggests that the Church must have *engaged intellectuals* together with researchers. Engaged intellectuals[48] direct their thought to the actual progress of humanity, as the academy should be in touch with real-life situations.[49] Antonio Gramsci called them "organic intellectuals" refereeing to the importance of intellectuals being part of everyday life.[50] This is a very serious concern amidst the enormous social problems of our day.

Our next question will be on communication. In nurturing the evolutive quality in an institution, in this case the Church, she must consider the field of communication seriously. The Church communicates with the world in word and action/praxis and by being just herself in the world.

The Church as a Sign

We shall recall Houtart's use of the word *sign* here. *Lumen Gentium* declares, "The Church is by her relationship with Christ a kind of sacrament or *sign* of intimate union with God and of the unity of all humankind."[51] So *sign* is related to the field of communications.[52] Sociologically speaking, the question should be addressed from the point of view of the sociology of communication. Thus, Houtart develops this aspect. Every communication requires three elements:

1. The transmitter.
2. The receiver.
3. The sign (which serves as bearer of communication).

How does Houtart connect these three aspects?

> The sign is a sensible manifestation of a reality, which can only be grasped indirectly. When we speak of manifestation, we mean that the receiver should perceive what the transmitter wishes to transmit to him. If the sign is incomprehensible because the receiver does not understand the language of the transmitter, for example, there is no communication, and consequently no manifestation. But the manifestation can be expressed in a variety of ways—words, gestures, and symbols. And so there is a verbal and non-verbal communication. According to the reality to be grasped, communication can be of various kinds.[53]

Houtart applies this concept to ecclesiology in the following ways:

1. As a social being, as an institution within the wider society, the Church uses communications; in other words, the Church speaks as a social being.

2. The Church herself bears a communicative character by her own nature because she is a *sign*. The whole organisation is a medium of communication. This means the very institution itself speaks by the very fact of "being there."

3. The Church ought to be expressed in a way perceptible by the people of our time. Otherwise, she could become a non-significative sign or a non-sign.

4. This concept requires a degree of sensitisation to the wider world, with special reference to the modern values, attitudes, behaviour, culture, and context. To put it another way, it demands skill to read and interpret the signs of the times.[54]

Communication is not limited only to words, but requires action, that is, a praxis. For Houtart, action or praxis essentially is connected to the mission of the Church. In other words, the mission of the Church is the mission to the world and in the world. The challenge of *Gaudium et Spes* is for a mission in the wider community, and it calls for a ministry of social witness in the world.[55] The Church is a community of witness within the social order.

The social sciences, to a great extent, can enable the Church for a meaningful preparation in the process of her praxis. Thus, one of the major concerns of Houtart is to discover and explain how the social sciences are enabling and facilitative instruments in the fruitful exercise of the ministry and the mission of the Church in the world. We shall highlight a few areas of concern.

First, we begin with the inside story. Introducing Houtart's scheme of social analysis, Dietrich and Wielenga question why the social analysis should be necessary for the Church.[56] We must begin by granting that the Church is part of the existing social ensemble; then, it is of the utmost importance to look inside the Church as an institution for a positive self-critique and evaluation of the Church herself. This is applicable, of course, not only to the Church, but also to all religious institutions that function in society.[57]

The religious institutions are part of the economic structure and engage in a number of economic activities. They own land, have budgets, pay salaries, rent buildings, and run schools, hospitals, and projects. The Church is also part of the social system of caste, class, education, and income; these are some areas that help us to determine her internal social status.[58] The religious institutions are also part of the political system. Whether they support rulers or keep away from politics or support the opposition, in all cases the Church is taking a political position.

The Church is not free from the ideological realities, as her economic and political activity implies certain ideological choices. Any work of development run by the Church has its own ideological underpinnings.[59]

The social sciences could also enable the Church to evaluate her own pastoral and other ministerial structures and to integrate the results of surveys in her pastoral forecast and planning in order to create new structures. For example, the Church could test the attitudes of her members and substructures towards issues such as development.[60] Alternatively. the Church could conduct a survey on the orientation of the priests, seminarians, nuns, and the lay elite from the point of view of their social ideology[61] or make use of empirical-social research in new pastoral or frontier ministries. This survey could address uprooted peoples, underdevelopment, and even the areas of leisure and play.[62]

The use of the social analysis by the Church and by the theological disciplines on the issues involved helps to promote a creative theological reflection. Some examples of topics suitable for this type of reflection include the study of violence,[63] ethnic conflict, poverty, ecology, the population explosion, and so forth. This field would be very useful for the ethicist and will be considered further in our final section on application of some Houtartian concepts in social ethics.

However, the general reading of the *signs of the times* involves a skill in collaborating positively and critically with others who are also working in the same areas of development and progress of the world. The consideration whether these other people are Christians or not is not a question anymore in this qualitative attitude toward mission. Houtart calls this a participatory attitude and leadership.[64] However, when we talk about partnership and collaboration in praxis, it requires a use of language that is understandable and acceptable to the collaborators, irrespective of their creed or ideological affiliation, calling for the ability to use a kind of common socio-ethical language, which is a part of this problem of communication.

To sum up Houtart's contribution in this field, we start with the Vatican Council II and show a great awareness of the fact that the Church exists in the world, not in isolation but in connection with the social, economic, political, and cultural spheres of life. Houtart himself has contributed to this new understanding of the Church in the modern world by way of research on many of the important issues. Houtart challenges us to change the conceptions of the institutional organisation and of the leadership of the church, which will be conducive, if put into operation, to a change of the structures themselves. Both the institution and its leadership must nurture the *evolutive* character of the structures of the Church.

To this process, the social sciences have a great contribution to make, so that the thought, word, and action of the Church as a sign may be significative and significant. Arguably one may even interpret that Houtart has been engaged in a dialogue between sociology and ecclesiology while involved in the wider discourse of religion and society. Karl Rahner writes, "There are realities which we understand only when we love them. The church is one of these."[65] Undoubtedly, François Houtart is one who loves that reality, of course a social reality, called "The Church." In brief, Houtart's thesis has been that the social commitment is part of Christian commitment, and sociology and social analysis help as tools in her social commitment.

Variations on the Theme of Houtart's Ecclesiology

While His Holiness Pope John Paul II was in Cuba at Fidel Castro's invitation in January 1997, Monsignor François Houtart was also present in the Caribbean Island, at the invitation of the Central Committee of the Cuban Communist Party. He was certainly not in the Pope's entourage but in the capacity of a special guest from the other partner of the encounter. Later, he wrote a rather mild and benevolent article, tongue in cheek, on the outcome of the encounter: "The Pope in Cuba: A Visit Which Aimed at Being a Turning Point and May Have Been But a Parenthesis."[66]

This episode in Houtart's life is not only of anecdotal value but is also a significant symbolical event that illustrates Houtart's stand in the social and historical divide between the Church as an institution of power and the people down below, the virtual recipients of the Church's utterances.

The reader may have developed a growing awareness of two facts about the relationship of François Houtart with the institutional Roman Catholic Church, his own Church, and her hierarchical figures (whom he calls "leaders"). On the one hand, we detect in Houtart an unfailing fidelity and loyalty to the Church and corresponding respect for her hierarchies; on the other, we see a thorough and sometimes impatient criticism of their failure to exercise their authority to implement what they have so vigorously stated in their official documents. From some of Houtart's most vigorous and impatient criticisms of the Church for failing to put into effect her teachings in *Gaudium et Spes*, one even gets the impression that, for Houtart, there is an abysmal gap between her solemn declarations and her conspicuous inactivity; in other words, to borrow the witticism of some Latin American theologian, that the Church is "zealotist in words and Herodian in action."

We may wonder what kind of relationships with the power structures and decision making institutions of his own Church he developed or had to endure along his many years of research.

Since the beginning of his career François Houtart has been in the "bad" company of scholars like Chenu, Congar, and later, people like Schillebeeckx, Hans Küng, Tissa Balasuriya, and the Latin American liberation theologians, prominent among them Gustavo Gutierrez, Leonardo Boff, and his former fellow seminarian and good friend, Joseph Comblin. They all had two things in common: 1) their solidarity with the grass roots, and 2) at one point or other in their lives, each one of them has been warned of dangerous doctrines, ostracised, or openly censured and condemned. Houtart himself has consistently been looked upon with suspicion by the official Roman Catholic hierarchies and, on some occasions, openly prohibited from attending some important gatherings, such as CELAM's gathering in Medellin. His relationship with the hierarchy of the Catholic Church has been complex and ambiguous to say the least, and perhaps it was a love-hate relationship. From his writings, we do not get much information on his relationships with the official institutions of non-Roman churches that are equally Christian. Houtart is consistently discreet in this respect.

It is difficult to assess Houtart's contribution to the ecumenical dialogue because he is not a theologian by profession and his contacts with the World Council of Churches and other international, national, and local Christian organizations have been of a practical nature, of what is sometimes called "applied ecumenism."[67] Perhaps this is the reason for his seeming lack of ecumenical sensitivity when writing constantly about "the Church," meaning the Roman Catholic Church, and more specifically her decision-making structures and institutions. This usage baffles me sometimes. (In his later years of fervent militancy calling to churches, movements, and groups of all sorts to combat globalisation, Houtart is much more inclusive in his language).

Reading Houtart, I also perceive that his own stance is at odds with the official Roman Catholic positions on the social issues that he shares with most Latin American theologians of liberation. One of the main criticisms one perceives in reading Houtart's socio-religious studies calling the Church truly to understand the environing society and engage in social action to transform its unjust structures is his very frequent criticism of the Catholic Church's failure to respond effectively to the changing nature of contemporary society. On this issue, Houtart puts his voice at the disposal of the voiceless, and the professional sociologist in him turns into a prophet. With equal frequency and fervour, Houtart makes vibrant appeals to the Church (i.e., the Roman Catholic power structures) to listen to the voice of the victims of injustice and join in the process of their liberation. In such instances, we have "Father Houtart" the pastor in action. Again, we see in his professional and vocational life the threefold dimension of the method of analysis the critique and action of the Young Christian Workers movement: the sociologist who *sees,* the prophet who *judges,* and the pastor who *acts.*

In order to analyse different aspects of Houtart's opinions of the role of Church in society and in so doing illustrate the complexity of his analyses, it is necessary to look again at the events and people that influenced his adoption of a pluralistic dimensional approach in analysing the Church from theological and sociological perspectives.

Houtart himself recalls his engagement with the Young Christian Workers (YCW) in the late 1940s as a period that marked the origins of his preoccupation with the sociology of religion as a tool to analyse society and, thus, to serve the Church better. In other words, he wanted to understand the modern world and put his findings in this field at the service of the hierarchical Church. From the beginning, we perceive that his undeclared intention was thoroughly apostolic, though not in the least detached from the subject of his study. He deepened his theoretical knowledge of sociology during his postgraduate studies in Chicago, where he applied this knowledge in conducting a study into the relationship between the Church and the working class.

Houtart's ecclesiology also has to be understood and interpreted in the spirit of the vigorous and dynamic ecclesiology of the Vatican Council II.[68] His involvement and later disappointment with the rich theoretical outcome and the poor practical implementation of Vatican II, together with his connections with the most conspicuous theologians of liberation in Latin America, is of utmost importance in understanding his shift of attention and intention from the top of the pyramid to the bottom, from the centre to the periphery, from theoretical formulations to practical action and implementation.

In his youthful apostolic enthusiasm of his Chicago period, Houtart focused his attention on the de-Christianised working masses in the cities and looked up to the Church hierarchies to come down with the Church's effective message of salvation to bring those masses back to the Christian fold. In other words, while he is studying this world with its social structures of sin-oppression, he has in mind the ecclesial structures of salvation, but salvation in the motherly bosom of the Church. Following the current ideology of the Catholic Action at that time, salvation is to be found in the Church, and so people must enter the Church in order to be saved. Incidentally, we see the same sort of orientation in the known missionary appeal of The International Missionary Conference, meeting at Edinburgh in 1910 with its urgent call "to evangelise the whole world in our own generation."[69]

Later on, he discovered the character of the Church as a sacrament of salvation that is and needs to be a sign and an instrument[70] of the Gospel of salvation-liberation that she has been entrusted to hand over to the world. The Church must enter the world if she wants to be an effective sign and instrument of salvation. Salvation must be realised and found in the world, and the Church needs to be in the world. Soon, Houtart had to discover that the Church cannot be nor act from outside or from above the world, but only from below, inside the world, in solidarity with the world, with its "joys and hopes."

Houtart progresses beyond mere criticism of the Church and reaches a stage where he not only describes and explains the ecclesiastical structures as a sociologist but also challenges them to change so that they may become more relevant, significant, and meaningful to the contemporary social structures. In other words, Houtart does not simply want the Church to be functional (or to cease being dysfunctional), but he puts great emphasis on her social function and how this function can and has to be adapted to a changing society.[71] Thus, when Houtart refers to the relationship between the Church and the world, he means more specifically, the Church as an institution getting involved with the struggles and efforts of an increasingly technical society.

The heart of the Vatican Council II, as seen by Catholics themselves, was a deliberate attempt on the part of the Church to come to terms with the rapidly changing modern world. A never-changing Church in an ever-changing world could not achieve this. During the early stages of Vatican II, while the document "Dogmatic Constitution on the Church" was being elaborated, the Church was seen by many both inside and outside the Council as verticalist in her orientation, pyramidal in her structures, centralist in her administration, and immobilist in her general outlook. From this perspective arose the fourfold need and task of coming down to the horizontal reality of the world, flattening the pyramid to make it co-extensive with the world, de-centralising authority to introduce a system of collegiality, and unburdening her dogmatic, legalistic, and ritualistic baggage to make her a more agile and dynamic fellow traveller. All these needs, and much more, are implied in the programme of *aggiornamento.*

These tasks are precisely what the more conservative Catholics rejected in the programme of *aggiornamento*, regarding it as an abandonment of the essentials of the faith.[72] This reaction was made all the worse when the Church seemed to tolerate the concepts of the Theology of Liberation, which was put forward most charismatically and with the greatest effect in Latin America, with the consent of and even under the inspiration of the entire CELAM. The Theology of Liberation created an environment in which members of the Church and theologians alike advocated for a deep, committed, and sustained involvement in radical political movements, seeking earthly justice, and therefore entering into an acute opposition with the authorities of the State.[73]

When John Paul II came to the papacy, he sought to rectify what he believed to have been too great an abandonment of the traditional doctrine and practice of the Church.[74] He reemphasised the centrality of the Pope's authority, thus weakening the principle of collegiality of bishops. He reiterated, in the strongest possible way and with unfailing frequency in his many travels, the Church's traditional views on sexuality—condemning the use of artificial means of contraception to regulate the unmanageable demographic growth of society, opposing the ideas of married priests and of women entering into the ordained priesthood, denouncing abortion and all other kinds of "interference" with the natural exercise of the sexual functions.[75] In the political arena, he made some equivocal and ambiguous symbolic gestures that some have interpreted as an embracement of tyrannical persons and regimes, such as Reagan in the USA, Videla in Argentina, and Pinochet in Chile,[76] while openly and unambiguously condemning Sandinismo in Nicaragua.

The Church has always been associated with politics and the State and, at one time, reached almost an absolute power in doctrine and morals (ideological power) in the European Christian lands; however, the Protestant Reformation, the scientific discoveries of the Renaissance, and later the Enlightenment, the industrial revolution, the progress of secularization, and the democratic republican revolts with their insistence on the autonomy of the secular world and consequent separation of

Church and State, effectively diminished its monopoly on the doctrinal and moral guidance and also the political life in many western societies. Moreover, with the emergence of the ecumenical movement, a new self-understanding of the Church's role in society has been emerging. Houtart welcomes these movements and supports the reform that they entail and, consequently, advocates for a new role for the Church in society. He actively collaborates with those involved in the Theology of Liberation. Eventually, he co-founded the World Social Forum (WSF), a meeting place for those involved with the anti-capitalist movement, and passionately believes in social action on the part of the Church as the only means to spread the Gospel. As far as he is concerned, the main "task of the Church is to spread the Gospel, and this is the world's most basic need."[77] This task is best expressed through social action. Houtart considers that the social dynamism of the Christians, both priests and laity, can be the sign of the Gospel for humanity in a changing world, just as Christ's solicitude for the sick and the poor was the sign of his mission to the people in his earthly sojourn and of the presence of the Kingdom of Heaven in the kingdom of this world.

One crucial aspect of Houtart's conviction that social action is the most effective means of spreading the Gospel is his persuasion that men and women are convinced not by reasoning, but by acts.[78] Within this belief, the first sign of evangelisation is to approach people through their fundamental day-to-day occupations because humans accomplish their divine mission only by performing their daily tasks. This being the case, a principal task of the laity (the people of God) is to get involved in every part of human evolution, from scientific research to its technical applications, and especially the organisation of the world on bases that are functional to its present development.

As a direct consequence of his philosophy and praxis, Houtart invites all those who follow Christ to enter into direct conflict with capitalist governments, and this type of engagement by a priest is something that the Catholic Church usually opposes. As previously mentioned, Houtart's ecclesiological insights are more clearly understood in the context of the Vatican Council II[79] and of his professional study of the sociology of religion. Inspired by his experience with the working-class youth in Belgium and Latin America, Houtart embraced sociology as the most effective tool with which to study and gain a meaningful understanding of society.[80] From there, he turned to a corresponding understanding of the Church. During his direct involvement in the proceedings of the Vatican Council II, Houtart raised a number of pertinent and searching relevant questions for the Church and her changing place and role in society. Moreover, not only did he raise questions, he also added very valuable sociological insights to the evaluation of the Church as an institution among other institutions in society.

In the Houtartian paradigm, all the societal, technological, and political changes—in industrially developed as well as in the underdeveloped countries and regions of the world—are bringing about, for the Church, new ways of viewing many activities, which have existed since the beginning of the Church but now have to be seen in entirely new perspectives in the light of the present-day developments. Correspondingly, if the Church is to accompany the world in its pilgrimage (a *populus viatorum*)[81] and become a partner in dialogue and action, she has to undergo radical changes in orientation, structures, and language.

The Church also has to change her language to enter into a meaningful dialogue with the world. She has to make a thorough revision of her theological orientation and the formulation of its contents, of her liturgy, her catechesis, and her general teaching ministry. First of all, a liturgical renewal in an urban, mobile society has to take place on a much more practical approach and has to reflect the day-to-day needs of the Christian and of the wider communities. In addition, her catechetical work has to undergo a tremendous renewal.[82] The same could be said of her teaching ministry in the formation of priests and religious agents. Some advancement has been made in all these fields, it is true, but they must not be taken as a final goal but as stations in an ongoing journey of the Church as a community accompanying the world as a society. Thanks to these advancements, the Church has acquired a new dimension for the transmission of religious values in the technologically advanced and post-industrial societies. It goes without saying that the Church has always performed these activities, but with the new challenges to face and in view of the dramatic changes in culture, her catechetical work, priestly formation, and theological education have acquired even greater significance as the means for transmitting the faith.

Additionally, the development of ecumenism is also related to the growth of a technical society. Today we witness a much deeper contact with other Christian churches and religious groups, as well as other religions, and an increasing emphasis has to be placed on convergence and cooperation rather than on apologetics and confrontation.[83] In order to achieve all of this, a sound sociological research is necessary, not only research in the sociology of religion, but an accurate knowledge in the sociological field at large, to enable the Church to better understand all the changes taking place in society and the resulting consequences for the Church.[84]

In his insistence on the lay participation in the overall apostolate of the Church (and not only of the Church's hierarchies) Houtart is, no doubt, indebted to Yves Marie Congar in his seminal ideas of the "theology of the laity."[85] Both Congar and Houtart served as consulting experts (*periti*) at the Vatican Council II. However, Houtart mentions Congar only once in his *Challenge to Change* (p. 204), acknowledging Congar's influence on some aspects of his thought.

Houtart and the YCW Movement As a Starting Point

A retrospective look at Houtart's formative years may be appropriate in understanding his later development and understanding that, for him, the Church's involvement in the problems of the world, and especially the poor of the world, is of paramount importance for the Church to be faithful to her divine imperative and mission. During this study, we see that this is precisely the connecting thread that gives unity and coherence to Houtart's career.

As we have mentioned often—perhaps too often—Houtart situates his involvement with the Belgium YCW movement as the first important stage in his intellectual development and his first encounter with the institutional Church's role in the modern industrial society. He worked closely with Cardinal Josef Cardijn, the founder of the movement, and describes the situation faced by the European working class during and after the 1939-1945 conflict as extremely appalling and, therefore, challenging for the Church to do something about it.[86] After his ordination in 1949, Houtart conducted some research into the religious malaise in urban areas, aiming at determining why the working class had adopted an attitude that was very hostile not only to the Church but to religion in general. This negative reaction of the working class, according to Houtart, happened in contrast to the Gospel's teaching of social justice and identification with the poor. The reasons were as much practical as historical. Thus, contrasting view of the demands of the Gospel, on the one hand, and the absence of the institutional Church from the sphere of the poor, on the other, will never abandon Houtart's long career as a social scientist, as a prophetic voice and as an activist.

In societies marked by a secular approach to the social and political realities, as was the case throughout much of nineteenth century Europe, religion may no longer fulfil its direct ideological functions. Nevertheless, even though religion and the Church are for them no longer necessary as an explanation for and legitimatisation of the social relations and political power, it does not mean that they have no significance at all for the Church. When in the Europe of the nineteenth century, part of the bourgeoisie decided to renew its damaged ties with the Catholic Church, it did not do so for theological or altruistic reasons but as a political manoeuvre because the Church had previously acted as an ally against the so-called "radical" social disturbances and as a staunch defender of the status quo.[87] Thus, part of the reason for the hostility of the working class was an emerging class struggle that also caused the workers' opposition to the Church as a traditional ally of the bourgeoisie. Furthermore, in his study, Houtart identified more practical reasons for why, in Brussels in the late 1940s, the working-class areas had less than 10 percent regular church attendance or religious observance in contrast with the middle-class neighbourhoods, where it was more than 50 percent.[88]

During the high point of the nineteenth century industrialisation, the Church associated itself with the bourgeoisie and, throughout the entire nineteenth century, was literally absent from big cities in general and working-class neighbourhoods in particular. Even at the time when Houtart conducted his research, the pastoral services were much more readily available in the middle-class neighbourhoods than in the working-class urban districts. During his postgraduate studies in Chicago, Houtart conducted a similar study in the cities of the US and observed just the opposite situation. In the USA, he saw that large Catholic migrant groups had travelled from Europe accompanied by their local priests, who were meant to keep an eye on them.[89] The solicitous pastoral care of the Church was, thus, present among the immigrants, and in their respective parishes people had something familiar they could relate to. In the parish enclosure, the Catholic immigrants could have a feeling of "back home." The parishes created a strong affective link with their societies they had left behind in their emigration. This created a situation wherein people took advantage of the services offered by the Church and, in return, allowed priests to identify with their parishes and the cause of the working class. These studies were the basis for Houtart's belief that, for the Church to remain relevant, she cannot adopt a merely theoretical approach; she has to become actively involved in the challenges and problems faced by the working-class majority of her fellowship. This early conclusion of his early work will coincide with the final conclusion of his life, as we shall see later in this study.

The Sociology of Religion is Not a Theological Discipline

It is also relevant to observe how the dialogue between sociology and theology influences Houtart's thinking on the Church and the type of questions he asks in relation to her. Houtart's first formal encounter with sociology proper (and not only "sociology of religion") occurred during his postgraduate studies in urban sociology at the University of Chicago. His early sociological study was influenced by Jacques Leclercq, professor at the Catholic University in Louvain (CUL) and a leading figure both in sociology and in Natural Law; Houtart also fell under the influence of Emile Durkheim and Aron Gurwitch.[90] In those early years of his career, Houtart had to defend the autonomy of sociology of religion vis-à-vis the theological disciplines. Sociology of religion, he insisted, is not, in itself, an ancillary discipline of theology, though its findings can be and should be of the utmost help for theological formulations in the present times.

His decision to treat sociology of religion as a social rather than a theological discipline became a practical problem for Houtart after he founded the Centre for Socio-Religious Research (CSRR) and in the same year became the secretary general of the International Conference of Sociology of Religion. The CUL administration argued that the CSSR should be included in the Faculty of Theology, whereupon Houtart made it clear that sociology of religion is *not* an ecclesiastical, but a sociological discipline.[91] He granted that sociology of religion doubtlessly can and has to be used for pastoral purposes, but firmly stated that it is not the purpose of sociology as such. Sociology of religion is not part of theology, though it can be taken as an ancillary tool for theological education and priestly formation. As the Church recognises the autonomy of the political social realities, she has also to acknowledge the autonomy of social and political studies. The sociology of religion is a part of sociology and, thus, an autonomous social science; in order to be a useful tool for the Church, in its project of societal analysis, such study should be as independent as possible from any kind of institutional control.[92]

A further reason why the Church, and more specifically, the administration of CUL resisted Houtart's approach to sociology in general and sociology of religion in particular was his adoption of, first, Weberian and, subsequently, Marxist principles and methodologies. The three main themes of Weber's sociology of religion are the effect of religious ideas on economic activities, the relation between social stratification and religious ideas, and the distinguishable characteristics of Western civilization.[93] His goal was to find reasons for the differing paths of development taken by the Occidental and Oriental cultures, without judging or valuing them, as some of his contemporary thinkers following the social Darwinist paradigm were doing. Weber wanted to explain the distinctive elements of Western civilization and, in so doing, introduced the concept of culture to his sociological analysis; however, for Houtart, this scientific stand, on its own, did not go far enough.

Consequently, although, he started his Ph.D thesis on the sociology of Buddhism in Sri Lanka with a Weberian approach, Houtart arrived at the conclusion that the exclusively Weberian approach was not totally satisfactory to answer the main theoretical questions concerning the ways in which human groups organise their material life; hence, his coterminous engagement with Marxism led to his incorporating and increasingly making use of a Marxist methodological approach in his sociological research. Houtart has to insist, over and over again, that the Marxist analysis, however, has to be a tool for looking more deeply into the social phenomenon and not a dogmatic system, with fixed presuppositions.[94] This sociological approach, together with the fact that he was closely involved in developing a Marxist methodology of social analysis[95] in Asia, placed him once again outside the mainstream intellectual currents of the Catholic Church. Nevertheless, Houtart argues that this kind of analysis is the best instrument to help us understand the major social problems of capitalist societies and, therefore, is in no contradiction with Christian teachings.

Houtart and Latin America

This commitment to cultural analysis, together with the social struggle, deepened and developed when Houtart travelled to Latin America in the 1950s. His visit was necessitated by his work on an article about the situation of the Church in Latin America, dealing with many of the social issues that the countries in the region were confronted with at the time. The research concerned all Latin American countries from both sociological and religious perspectives and was published between 1958 and 1962 in the run up to the second Vatican Council.

It was during this highly influential period of his intellectual, vocational, and spiritual development that Houtart's thinking crystallised in the progressive formulation of his aforementioned philosophy of the Gospel as social action. Like Las Casas half a millennium before him, it was with the dispossessed peoples of the South that it became clear to Houtart that Christianity is best practiced through identification with and in the service of the discriminated, disadvantaged, and dispossessed. We could say of François Houtart what Archbishop Oscar Arnulfo Romero said of himself: "It is the poor that have taught me how to read the Gospel." Or to put it another way, preaching the Good News from a position of relative comfort, safety, and privilege to those facing discomfort, danger, and destitution was neither an indication of Christian love nor an efficient or effective means of evangelisation. Effective evangelisation is, in Houtart's opinion, achieved only by demonstrable actions, not pious rhetoric, no matter how well meaning.

Thus, from a Houtartian perspective, the Church has to discard the conservative, straight, and reductive outlook, which considers the problems of humanity from a strictly ecclesiastical point of view and, instead of attempting to mould the world into the Church's beliefs, organisations, and internal preoccupations, should proactively engage with and support the people in their daily lives. This attitude is reflected by Msgr. Helder Camara, Archbishop of Recife, who, pondering the number one problem of Latin America, concluded that it was not the number or lack of priests but the development and the involvement of the Church in improving social conditions.[96] The Church can be nowhere near the beginning of evangelisation until it ventures into the world and meets its fellow men and women in the context of their individual and collective preoccupations.

From Houtart's perspective, the Church is a community of faith, worship, and charity; however, to be perceived in the first two aspects, it must express itself in the third. Faith and hope, for Houtart, must be fecundated and made fruitful by love, and Christian love must be exercised in the social and political fields; otherwise, it is mere assistentialism. Furthermore, for Christian love to be a sign in and to the contemporary world, it must be directed to the true problems and with appropriate means, which are collective in nature. "It is no longer enough to build schools and hospitals, we must understand the new forms of human—

community development"[97] and actively plan future actions. According to Houtart, this is necessary to "break through our 'parochialism' and our congregationalism, work out unheard-of collaborations with Christians of other faiths or with non-Christians, and promote social transformations which can fearlessly be called revolutionary."[98] Houtart will heartily agree with the statement that,

> The most perceptible sign of the Church of Christ for the poor in Latin America and everywhere else will be her participation in the "social revolution," that is, in the profound transformation of the structures of a society that is unjust, because it does not assure the existence and well being of its members.[99]

For the first time in recorded Catholic historiography, a conciliar document, *Gaudium et Spes*, deals directly with the issue of culture, a topic that, as a sociologist, Houtart is particularly interested in. The chapter on culture had the most long-lasting consequences of all in *Gaudium et Spes*. Most important of all, for the first time, the Church used the word "culture"[100] instead of civilisation. Years later, Pope John Paul II established the Pontifical Commission of Culture in 1982, as a new department of the papal Curia. Of all Vatican II documents, *Gaudium et Spes* addresses the situation in the world most directly. The document made sustained attempts both to engage in dialogue with the "world"—namely with its own fellowship, with members of other religions and movements, as well as with communities outside its direct influence—so as to open up further opportunities for such dialogue in the future.

The implementation of the chapters on the socioeconomic life and the political community are much more in line with the social teaching brought forward from the time of Leo XIII onwards and have differing impacts in diverse regions around the world. In Africa for instance, the social, economic, and political circumstances have, in many respects, deteriorated rather than improved since the 1960s. Christianity plays a major role in Africa, especially south of the Sahara, where the Catholic Church is prominent in several countries; consequently, *Gaudium et Spes* has been particularly influential there. These two chapters of the conciliar document emphasise the interdependence of countries and continents; the importance of mutual help and cooperation; the recognition of imbalances in the world economy; the recognition too that the world's goods belong to all; "that the good things of creation should be available equally to all,"[101] the legitimate diversity of social and political structures; and the importance of loyalty to one's country. The latter is indicative of the Church's adherence to the maintenance of the political status quo.

The Second Vatican Council occurred in the middle of the era when the peoples of Africa were moving from being colonies of European countries towards titular independence. However, the Council in general and *Gaudium et Spes* more particularly had little to say about this change in the world order, save for a passing reference to "nations on the road to progress and recently becoming independent."[102] The Council seemed unwilling to take sides openly regarding the realities of the African struggles for national independence from European colonialism. The document tries hard to address the whole world, yet the model for much of what it says is clearly Europe, and the documents are redolent of Eurocentrism. In retrospect, there appears to be an almost simplistic assumption, either naïve optimism or Eurocentric arrogance, that the remedies for Europe can be exported to other continents, including Africa, and that all will be well.

One aspect that Houtart identified as affecting the global role of the Church is the new relations of the Catholic Church with Africa and Asia, the two continents where Christianity is not the religion of the majority. For Houtart, the Catholic Church cannot make significant progress in the nation-states born out of struggles for independence because not only is Catholicism too closely identified with the Western powers and culture, but also it has no connection with the cultural practises of the peoples of Africa and Asia. Therefore, Houtart posits that the Catholic Church has to adapt and adopt a cultural, rather than a "Roman Canon Law," approach to engaging and working with the peoples of the world's two most populous continents. This type of postcolonial Catholicism still identifies itself, more or less, with the cultures, customs, and traditions of the West. Houtart wholeheartedly supported the indigenisation (Houtart uses the term "indianisation") of the entire liturgy, not only rubrics, vestments, and adornments, but also of the language with all the symbolic richness of the liturgy: not as a translation from the Latin Mass, but as a true enculturation. Thus, writing on "The Indianization of Catholicism," Houtart presents the Indian bishops something like a programmatic shopping list:

> Consequently, Indianization has other aspects than those which we shall treat here—in the liturgy and ritual, for instance, in the introduction of local languages into religious acts, in a closer approach to the forms of oriental thought in the manner of elaborating theology, in a dialogue with representatives of other religious groups, not to speak of a Christian mode of thought relating to the concrete situations of the Indian people, their social and economic problems, their internal structures of injustice and their struggles for liberation.[103]

Houtart proposes for the Church not only an internal reformation of the ornamental exteriority but also and largely a greater emphasis on social action, a more hands-on approach to the daily concerns of the people, and a closer collaboration between different Christian churches and other religions, and a real solidarity with the aspirations of the victims of oppression in their struggles for liberation, a very concrete liberation!

The struggle against continuing colonialism, especially in the Portuguese colonies, was one issue that brought Houtart into conflict with the established Portuguese Catholic Church, which was fully allied with the Portuguese government in supporting colonialism under the guise of incorporating the African colonies into the nation of Portugal as "overseas provinces," and all as a part of the pretended struggle against communism in Africa.

Theology of Liberation

The most dramatic development in the few years after the Council was the emergence of the Theology of Liberation in Latin America that swept like a wildfire through the Church and society all over the subcontinent. Undoubtedly, *Gaudium et Spes* influenced the movement. Almost all the leading thinkers of the movement were Catholics, were cognisant of the proceedings of the Council, and were intimately familiar with *Gaudium et Spes*. This view of the relationship between the absolute future (God),[104] for which

Christians hope, and the human efforts to transform the world into one that is more socially just are echoed in the following statements from Vatican II's *Pastoral Constitution on the Church in the Modern World*.[105]

> Far from diminishing our concern to develop this earth, the expectation of a new earth should spur us on, for it is here that the body of a new human family grows, foreshadowing in some way the age that is to come. That is why, although we must be careful to distinguish earthly progress clearly from the increase of the kingdom of Christ, such progress is of vital concern to the kingdom of God, insofar as it can contribute to the better ordering of human society. When we have spread on earth the fruits of our nature and our enterprise—human dignity, sisterly and brotherly communion, and freedom—according to the command of the Lord and in His Spirit, we will find them once again, cleansed this time from the stain of sin, illuminated and transfigured, when Christ presents to his Father an eternal and universal kingdom "of truth and life, a kingdom of holiness and grace, a kingdom of justice, love and peace." Here on earth the kingdom is mysteriously present; when the Lord comes it will enter its perfection.[106]
>
> ...Furthermore, God is bringing about this transformed world now, far beyond the frontiers of the Church. Our task is to get in tune with what God is doing. We have to find out where the Kingdom is already present in an initial and germinal way. We have to discern and nourish such *seeds of the Kingdom* by putting our resources and energies there. In discerning and nourishing these seeds of the Kingdom, contemplative prayer and presence will have to balance active social and political involvement.[107]

This statement is supported by Karl Rahner's assertion that "the Reign of God for which Christians hope is the absolute future which is God himself. God himself ... wills to be the infinite future of humanity, infinitely transcending all that human beings could ever plan or fashion for themselves."[108] This hope in God as *the* absolute future challenges the Church to adopt a critical stance towards the historically given state of any society. As Rahner further observes,

> Such a critical stance can be radical, patient and courageous; it implies neither a conservative glorification of the present situation, underpinned by ideology, nor a destructive impatience which seeks violent means to force a new world into existence by sacrificing the men of today.[109]

On the contrary, so this Houtartian perspective, as articulated by Rahner, posits that the Christian affirmation of God as the absolute future, far from undermining the value of socio-political commitments throughout history to the present times, which seek to transform the world characterised by injustice and inequality, provides a perspective that can imbue these transformative efforts with enduring significance and true value. This it does in three ways: firstly, by offering a framework of meaning profound enough to do justice to the complexity of life and to support human efforts to transform the world; secondly, by functioning as a critical perspective which de-absolutises all human achievements of justice; and thirdly, by providing a positive incentive to humans in their efforts to transform human life in history.[110]

The link between *Gaudium et Spes* and the Theology of Liberation seems to have been that of an inspiration and a catalyst rather than of a simple literal application of the Pastoral Constitution to the situation in Latin America. The Theology of Liberation can be seen as a faithful reinterpretation of the outcomes of the Vatican Council II in the light of Latin America's own social, cultural, economic, political, and religious experience. Whereas the European Church, which had the greatest influence on the conceptualisation and formulation of *Gaudium et Spes*, may have felt that Christianity had drifted too far away from the modern world and so sought a reconciliation between the two, the Latin American Church, by contrast, felt that Christendom had become too identified with the modern world and its structural injustices and, therefore, sought rather to break away from it.[111]

However, many, especially in Rome, felt that Liberation Theology was a deviation from the Church's *magisterium*, a distortion of *Gaudium et Spes* rather than an application or faithful interpretation of the Pastoral Constitution. Most notably, under Pope John Paul II, the Congregation for the Doctrine of the Faith, headed by the "watchdog' of orthodoxy Cardinal Joseph Ratzinger, in its "Instruction on Certain Aspects of the Theology of Liberation" (1984), made a most severe criticism about 1) its many ambiguities, 2) the apparent reduction of the Gospel to mere activism, and 3) the danger of equating Christian liberation with the Marxist revolution.[112] There was an overwhelming sympathy and solidarity of the Roman Catholic theological centres with the Latin American theologians of liberation (though the "Instruction" did not mention any of them by name); perhaps this deluge of published letters of sympathy moved the Congregation for the Doctrine of the Faith to publish two years later a milder document with softer tones: "Instruction on Christian Freedom and Liberation."

We do not know if Houtart published any response to the two documents of the Congregation for the Doctrine of the Faith, but this instance of the publication of the two documents is a clear exponent of the dramatic extent of the ideological, theological, and methodological chasm between Houtart and the orthodoxy of the established Catholic Church; both present antagonistic positions on the issue: the total embracement of Liberation Theology on the one hand (Houtart's position) and an equally emphatic repudiation of the movement on the other (the official Vatican position). From Houtart's perspective, no fundamental theological objections exist to the complimentary and collaborative co-existence of the Christian social teachings with a Marxist social analysis approach and social action because the social reality, the social struggle, and the struggle for liberation are never totally pure and unambiguous. Houtart regards action as more important and beneficial for the role of the Church than any amount of theorising. To this effect, in a personal interview, Houtart told the author of this research,

> Christians agree in general with revolutions for social justice, but with one condition, that is that the angels make them! But angels make no revolution, and so we tend to object to revolution. Of course, there are always ambiguities. Can we wait for an unambiguous situation? No! The problem is whether to choose the ambiguities of the rich or the ambiguities of the poor. We have to choose, and the Gospel tells us to embrace the ambiguities of the poor. This means a critical commitment: critical in fruition of the values of the Gospel and commitment because we live in history, not beyond history.[113]

After Vatican II and the great social encyclicals from Pope John XIII to Paul VI, the Church now has a clear mandate to be involved in the promotion of justice in civil society. However, much ambivalence still exists. On the one hand, the Church's official teaching at the highest level calls for a restructuring of the international economic order;[114] it proclaims that working for justice and the transformation of society is "a constitutive dimension of the preaching of the Gospel."[115] On the other hand, there is a glaring gap between the official teaching and the actual practice of the Church as represented in the pronouncements and activities of its official leaders. What is done in practice tends to become the acceptable teaching, and the official teaching becomes more and more like rhetoric, honourable in theory, but unrealistic and idealistic in the absence of practical application. In the words of Michael McCabe, "To be loyal to the Church almost seems to demand an acceptance of the unjust *status quo*, keep your head down and don't rock the boat or cause too much disturbance."[116]

The official statements support McCabe's thesis. For example, there is the official document warning against the danger of reducing evangelisation to the economic, political, social, and cultural spheres, warning of the dangers of the excessive politicisation of the role of the Church.[117] Priests are admonished to leave politics to the politicians. Every so often, articles appear, in the secular and religious newspapers alike, with sensationalist headlines, such as "Pope warns Church to keep out of politics" and "Church condemns Liberation Theology" and "Priest/Bishop told to preach the Gospel and stay out of politics."[118] Pope Benedict XVI's first Encyclical Letter, *God is Love*, echoes this ambivalence. While insisting on the inseparability of love and justice, the encyclical nonetheless also insists that it is the task of the State to ensure justice and that the Church "cannot and must not take upon herself the political battle to bring about the most just society possible."[119] Pope Benedict XVI seems to be saying that, while the Church must educate and seek to appeal to the consciences of people about the demands of justice, the "action on behalf of justice and participation in the transformation of the world"[120] is not really part of the Church's mission.[121] The Church's policy of non-engagement means that Houtart, with his active involvement in the social struggles, especially in the global South, operates, at best, on the furthest extremities of the mainstream Catholic teaching and does not enjoy a high regard or reputation in the Catholic Church's European heartland.

However, in spite of his deep disappointment with the lack of a consistent implementation of *Gaudium et Spes* on the part of the official hierarchical Church, not forgetting the fundamental difference between his and the official Church's positions vis-à-vis the level and tone of engagement with society in general and with Liberation Theology in particular, Houtart chooses to remain within the Church. He observes that the structures can best be analysed and changed from within.[122] Houtart states vigorously and repeatedly that the social sciences are important for the Church and that a sound social analysis is a prerequisite for sound social ethics. For Houtart, the social commitment in the kingdom of this world is the way of expressing the values of the Kingdom of Heaven. Thus, social ethics is one of the main tasks of the religious institutions and has to be expressed through analysis of society because, without knowledge of how a society functions and where and how unequal relations are constructed, a merely passive and ineffectual condemnation of the effects of unjust structures is possible but barren, devoid of an accurate, scientific, and meaningful assessment of the causes, much less of a proactive strategy towards committed engagement in social action. To condemn the abuses of the structures is to deplore the effects without touching the causes, to trim the sick tree without touching its roots. That, according Houtart, is one of the main weaknesses of the social doctrines of Christianity and other religions, such as Hinduism and Buddhism.

For Houtart, the Theology of Liberation is precisely the theology and theological thinking that does not ask itself whether God exists, but where he is. The main questions are the following: In what kind of society do we live? What is the meaning of the love of God in a society which is so unequal and unjust and where so much injustice exists? The problems of the Theology of Liberation are to see precisely where social groups are struggling for justice, to determine the main values of the "Kingdom" as a mirror of the human society as willed by God, and to have a theological reading of those events. In that respect, the kind of ecclesiology Houtart subscribes to is very much related to the history of the Liberation Theology and Third World Theologies. Social ethics is one of the specific tasks of the religious institutions, but it cannot be expressed except through an accurate analysis of society. Houtart claims that,

> You cannot make a judgement on society if you do not know how the society is built and what the mechanisms are that build unequal relations. This would be just to condemn the effects, but never to understand the causes. In the Christian churches, the social doctrine is based on a hidden type of analysis. It is only recognised in terms of social stratification but not in terms of social classes.[123]

Making judgements without analysing the social structures, for Houtart, is the weakness of the Christian social teaching. In the main documents of the Holy See, for example the social Encyclicals, there is little analysis of the causes of the problem. The reason for that lack of analysis, Houtart concludes, is the Catholic Church's fear that if it deals with the causes it would have to mediate the social and political sciences and, thus, have to adopt a Marxist analysis herself.[124] Because of the amalgam between atheism and Marxism, the immediate reaction is to condemn those deploying a Marxist analysis, saying that it is linked with an atheist movement and if one uses those instruments, his methodological choice will invariably lead to atheism, from a "methodological atheism" to a real "ontological atheism." The Theology of Liberation has accepted the mediation of a class-oriented analysis, and ethics is a major aspect of this form of ecclesiology. Houtart regards this mediation as extremely important for the social teachings and definitions of ethics. The Theology of Liberation adopts a class analysis in the sense that society is seen not just as a superposition of social strata, but also as a structure itself with people at the top and people at the bottom.

For Houtart, the problem for a Christian or religious institution is how to avoid the institution becoming an end in itself rather than an instrument to bring certain values to humans and society. Houtart espouses the idea that theology in general needs more rationality and more institutionalisation and that the Church, as an institution, needs to be sensitive to the suffering of the masses in order to be able to achieve its primary objective of transmitting values in society. Despite his heavy involvement in *Gaudium et Spes*, the Vatican Council II and its implementation remain a disappointment for Houtart:

> I would say, during the time surrounding Vatican II we had such hope that a fundamental transformation [in the Church]

> would happen. We were thinking that the institutional Church, as a world institution, would be able to exercise a more moral power than it had in the past. We were thinking that with *Gaudium et Spes* and with the whole work of the Council we would have a more prophetic Church and in a sense more radical, not only speaking for justice in an abstract way.[125]

On the contrary, after the Council, a return to and a real work of restoration of the old Church was undertaken, partly out of fear of the consequences of the Vatican Council II. On the practical side, Houtart argues: "I felt we spent so much time and energy with the Vatican Council II to try to change the structure of the Church, in order to have another Church and we had to realise that the result was negative."[126]

He did not abandon the idea laid down by the Vatican Council II completely, for as he explains, he would have had to leave the Church. Moreover, as a Christian, rather than representing the Church as an institution in an official capacity, his approach was to act as "one of the people struggling in the field of international work, international issues or local issues and showing that it is possible for a Christian and a member of the Church to be there and that's all."[127]

Part of this commitment was CETRI, which Houtart founded in 1976 as an instrument with a sociological approach and the objective of realising solidarity with the Third World.[128] Working with numerous and heterogeneous societies, he nevertheless stuck to his approach in attempting to explain the role of religion in society and the extent to which it contributed to building cultures, thus orienting the general shape of societies.

Conclusion

In general, it can be argued that Houtart with his sociological analysis of the Catholic Church remains outside of the mainstream currents of the Church. He and his work remain almost unappreciated and sometimes unknown in Europe, even though he enjoys some popularity in the global South, especially among the Protestants and people of other faiths and ideologies. Though he has published an enormous number of papers and books discussing the Church's role in society, his sociological approach, though commendable, appears at times almost naïve, as though the Church would only have to take the class and social struggle into serious consideration for a wholehearted reform of the Church to be possible. For Houtart, it is exactly at this conjunction in the relations between the Church and the World wherein lie the fundamental hopes and tests for success or failure of the Council and, thus, of the reformation and transformation of the Church. If the Church loses its concern for the world, he seems to say, then the world will lose its concern for the Church, and the Vatican Council II will have failed conclusively, and the Church will be meaningless in and for the world.[129]

Today, there are several new challenges that the members of the Church, together with sociologists of religion, have to take into consideration. For instance, Houtart argues that, with the rapid spread of secularisation in western societies, the religious phenomenon of life has taken on a new dimension. Houtart is persuaded that, especially since 1968, a basic cultural crisis has appeared in western societies resulting in, among other things, a general disaffection with religious practises. Even among committed Christians and the middle classes traditionally allied to the Church, there are those who are separating themselves from the Church, and many churches are empty during Sunday religious services. This phenomenon, even if in a different form, is also apparent in other continents. In Latin America, as a case in point, many people consider themselves culturally and nationally Catholic and equate their Catholicism with their national belonging, not with the Church. Nevertheless, instead of adapting, instead of changing, the clergy appear to become increasingly conservative. These, according to Houtart, are two interconnected phenomena for sociologists of religion, as well as being the wrong approach if the Church does not want to become increasingly meaningless.[130]

According to Houtart, the growing Pentecostal communities, with their emphasis on an emotional expression of their religiousness, are havens that provide an answer to this dislocation of social links.[131] Here, he argues, the Church should learn because it remains remote from people within society, paying too much attention to protocol and not enough to pastoral care and social action.

Generally, an emphasis on and commitment to social action, a greater consideration of class issues, and a social science approach to the analysis of society are needed for the Church to become or remain relevant. Houtart himself has, after the disappointment of the Vatican Council II (during which and shortly after, he still believed in the possibility and feasibility of a complete reformation and transformation of the Church as an institution), turned his focus away from an ecclesiological approach and concentrated his thought and energies on an active involvement in the Church as an institution, in an action-led approach wherein he uses his sociological analytical skills for his involvement, as in the World Social Forum and the *alter* globalisation movements. He now considers himself, as a professional, involved in transnational *alter* globalisation movements: a professional who happens to be a priest.[132]

Endnotes:

[1] This article is a modified version of my Ph.D. thesis submitted to the University of Dublin in 2009.

[2] François Houtart, *Challenge to Change* (New York: Sheed and Ward, 1964). (Title has been written in the context of the Vatican II.)

[3] For an overview of the dialectical relationship of theology and sociology see Gregory Baum, "Sociology and Theology," *Concilium* 1 (1971): 22-31.

[4] Ibid., xii.

[5] D. R. S. Fernando, *Contextual Theology in Sri Lanka* (Leuven: Katholieke Universiteit Leuven, 1987), 85.

[6] Houtart, *Challenge to Change*, 7-8.

[7] Fernando, *Contextual Theology in Sri Lanka*, 86.

[8] Ibid., 100.

[9] Aloysius Pieris, *Crisigenic Council with Unwritten Agenda* (2005) http:// eapi.admu.edu.ph/eapr005/ pieris2.htm (accessed November 7, 2007).

[10] Giuseppe Alberigo and Joseph A. Komonchak, eds., *History of Vatican II*, 5 vols. (Maryknoll, New York: Orbis Books, [1995] 2006), 415.

[11] Cl. Soetens, "Les Archives Vatican Ii a Louvain-La-Neuve," in *Sources Locales De Vatican II*, eds. Cl. Soetens and J. Grootaers (Louvain-La-Neuve: Leuven, Bibliotheek van de Faculteit der Godgeleerdheid, 1990). Dr. Jose Luis Lana of the Theological College of Lanka, Kandy, Sri Lanka has translated this for the author. I have also personally inquired from Prof. Soetens of Louvain-la-Neuve University in June 2007 about this work and of the Lumen Gentium Center of the same university, which keeps some invaluable journal records and correspondence of Prof. Houtart in this regard.

[12] Jerome Sahabandhu, "Portraying the Person and Work of François Houtart," *Australian E-journal of Theology* (2006). Available from http://dlibrary.acu.edu.au/research/theology/ejournal/aejt_8/index.html.

[13] Marie-Dominique Chenu, "The Church's 'Social Doctrine,'" *Concilium* 10 (1980): 71-75.

[14] Fernando, *Contextual Theology in Sri Lanka*, 86.

[15] François Houtart, *The Eleventh Hour: The Explosion of a Church* (New York: Sheed and Ward, 1968), 15 (emphasis added).

[16] Pieris, *Crisigenic Council with Unwritten Agenda* (emphasis added).

[17] Houtart, *Challenge to Change*, 15.

[18] S. Amin, and François Houtart, eds., *Globalization and Alternatives* (Geneva: CETIM/AAJ/LIDLIP/WILPF, 2000), 3.

[19] François Houtart, "The Roman Catholic Church and Social Change in Latin America," in *The Church and Social Change in Latin America*, ed. Henry A. Landsberger (Notre Dame: University of Notre Dame Press, 1970), 113-133.

[20] François Houtart, "Religion and Development," *Religion and Development in Asia*, Baguio Feres Seminar Report, (n. p. 1976), 2-25.

[21] Houtart, *Challenge to Change*, 24f.

[22] François Houtart, "The Point of View of a Sociologist: The Crisis of Authority in the Church," *Convergence* 5 (1969): 7.

[23] Cf. François Houtart, "Traditional Christian Ethics and the Social Reality: A Critique," *Dialogue* 30 (2003): 93-103.

[24] Some issues that Houtart studied can serve as models for other religions as well, for example, how some specific popular Buddhist practices could be approached sociologically, how Hinduism faces secularization in India, how Buddhism faces Marxism. The point I wish to make is that some of Houtart's studies bear a kind of hermeneutical value for intercultural studies.

[25] In an interview with the author on June 27, 2005, at CETRI, Louvain-la-Neuve, one of Houtart's students Bruno Kervyn of Louvain, mentioned that the very presentation of the "Church as an Institution" was quite a revolutionary idea at that time.

[26] François Houtart, "The Church and the Developing Nations: Some Questions for Theologians," in *Theology of Renewal*, ed., L. K. Shook, vol. II (Toronto: Palm Publishers, 1968)," 382.

[27] François Houtart and André Rousseau, *The Church and Revolution: From the French Revolution of 1789 to the Paris riots of 1968, from Cuba to Southern Africa, from Vietnam to Latin America* (Maryknoll: Orbis Books, 1971), 325.

[28] Ibid.

[29] Houtart, *The Eleventh Hour: The Explosion of a Church*, 16 (emphasis added; inclusive language mine).

[30] Houtart, *Challenge To Change*, 6 (inclusive language mine).

[31] Houtart, *The Eleventh Hour: The Explosion of a Church*, 12.

[32] Houtart, *The Challenge to Change*, 82.

[33] Aloysius Pieris, "Vatican II: A *Crisigenic* Council with Unwritten Agenda," *East Asian Pastoral Review* 42, no. 1-2 (2005): 7-24. Also available at http://eapi.admu.edu.ph/content/crisigenic-council-unwritten-agenda (accessed January 25, 2014).

[34] Houtart, *Challenge to Change*, 25.

[35] Ibid., 24.

[36] Houtart, *The Eleventh Hour: The Explosion of a Church*, 30.

[37] Ibid., 148 (emphasis added).

[38] Houtart, *Challenge to Change*, 73.

[39] Houtart refers to Pope John XXIII.

[40] Houtart, *Challenge to Change*, 81.

[41] Ibid., 84.

[42] Ibid.

[43] Ibid., 81 (emphasis added).

[44] Ibid., 82 (emphasis added).

[45] Ibid.

[46] Ibid., 189. Houtart continues to argue that every diocese must have at least two clergy working on international issues. (Interview with the author on the July 27, 2006 in Louvain-la-Neuve.)

[47] Ibid.

[48] We find Gramscian undertones here in this concept.

[49] Houtart, *Challenge to Change*, 84f.

[50] B. Burke, *The Encyclopaedia of Informal Education*, s.v. "Antonio Gramsci, schooling and education," (1999, 2005) http://www.infed.org/thinkers/et-gram.htm (accessed December 27, 2007).

[51] Houtart, "The Church and the Developing Nations," 358f. (Emphasis added; inclusive language mine).

[52] Ibid., 359.

[53] Ibid.

[54] Ibid., 361.

[55] Denis Turner, "Christian Activity in the World," in *The Church in the World*, ed. Denis Turner (Dublin: Scepter Books, 1968), 56-71.

[56] Gabriele Dietrich and Bas Wielenga, *Towards Understanding Indian Society* (Tiruvalla, India: CSS, 1998), 9.

[57] Ibid.

[58] Ibid.

[59] Ibid.

[60] Cf. François Houtart, "Attitude toward Development among Catholics in Sri Lanka," *World Development* 8 (1980): 603-612.

[61] François Houtart et.al, *A Socio-Religious Analysis of the East Ramnad District, Tamilnadu* (Louvain: KUL, n.d.), 487-495.

[62] Houtart, *Challenge to Change*, 118.

[63] François Houtart, "The Cult of Violence in the name of Religion: A Panorama," *Dialogue* 29 (2002): 3-9.

[64] Houtart, *The Eleventh Hour*, 183.

[65] Richard Lennan, *The Ecclesiology of Karl Rahner* (Oxford: Clarendon Press, 1995), x.

[66] François Houtart, "The Pope in Cuba: A Visit Which Aimed at Being a Turning Point and May Have Been But a Parenthesis,"*COELI – Centre Oecumenique de Liaisons Internationales*, 82-83 (1997): 29-32.

[67] Houtart has specifically mentioned his collaboration on the WCC's programme to combat racism (telephonic conversation with the author on October 26, 2006).

[68] Jerome Sahabandhu, "Dialectical Interaction of Religion and Society: A Dialogue with François Houtart," *Australian E-Journal of Theology* no. 10 (Pentecost 2007); Sahabandhu, "Portraying the Person and Work of François Houtart."

[69] For the proceedings of this Conference, see the standard work: Ruth Rouse, Stephen Neill, and Harold E. Fey, eds., *A History of the Ecumenical Movement: 1517-1968*, 4th revised edition ed. (Geneva: WCC Publications, 1993).

[70] For a definition of the Church as a sacrament, see the Dogmatic Constitution on the Church, I, 1, in *Vatican Council II: The Conciliar and Post Conciliar Documents,* ed. Austin Flannery (1964; New York: Costello, 1996), 350. After this timorous attempt, the same definition appears in several other documents of Vat. II. See also Avery Cardinal Dulles, "The Church as Sacrament," in *Models of the Church* (New York: Image Books/Doubleday, 2002), 55-67.

[71] Houtart, *The Challenge to Change,* 24.

[72] Ibid.

[73] Immanuel Wallerstein, *The Catholic Church and the World* (2005). http://www.binghamton .edu/fbc/159en-corrected.htm (accessed May 27, 2007).

[74] Sahabandhu, "Portraying the Person and Work of François Houtart."

[75] Wallerstein, *Catholic Church and the World.*

[76] For a sketchy chronicle of John Paul II in Chile, see the carefully worded article by Roberto Suro, "John Paul Calls for Chileans to Move towards Democracy," *The New York Times*, April 3, 1987.

[77] François Houtart and Emile Pin, *The Church and the Latin American Revolution* (New York: Sheed and Ward, 1965), 206.

[78] Ibid., 208

[79] Houtart, *The Challenge to Change,* 7.

[80] Sahabandhu, "Portraying the Person and Work of François Houtart."

[81] For the concept of the "Pilgrim Church," officially sanctioned by Vat. II, see especially the *Dogmatic Constitution* (*Lumen Gentium)*, C. VII, ## 48-51, Austin Flannery, ed., 407-413.

[82] Houtart, *The Challenge to Change,* 186.

[83] Ibid.

[84] Ibid.

[85] Cf. Yves Marie Congar, *Lay People in the Church. A Study on the Theology of Laity* (Westminster: Newman Press, 1957).

[86] Sahabandhu, "Portraying the Person and Work of François Houtart."

[87] François Houtart, "Religious Identity," in *How to Conquer the Barriers to Intercultural Dialogue: Christianity, Islam and Judaism*, ed. Christiane Timmerman and Barbara Segaert (Bern: Peter Lang, 2007), 105-116.

[88] Sahabandhu, "Dialectical Interaction of Religion and Society: A Dialogue with François Houtart."

[89] Sahabandhu, "Portraying the Person and Work of François Houtart."

[90] Sahabandhu, "Dialectical Interaction of Religion and Society: A Dialogue with François Houtart."

[91] Ibid.

[92] Ibid.

[93] Ritzer and Goodman.

[94] Sahabandhu, "Dialectical Interaction of Religion and Society: A Dialogue with François Houtart."

[95] For security reasons, it was then called "structural analysis."

[96] Sahabandhu, "Portraying the Person and Work of François Houtart."

[97] Sahabandhu, "Dialectical Interaction of Religion and Society: A Dialogue with François Houtart."

[98] Houtart and Pin, *The Church and the Latin American Revolution*, 209.

[99] Michael McCabe, "The Role of the Church in Civil Society: Some Theological Orientations," http://www.africamission-mafr.org/mccabe_gb.doc (accessed May 12, 2007).

[100] Cf. Norman Tanner, *The Church and the World: Gaudium Et Spes, Inter Mirifica* (New York: Paulist Press, 2005).

[101] Cf. Austin Flannery, ed., *Vatican Council II: The Conciliar and Post Conciliar Documents* (New York: Costello, 1984).

[102] Tanner, *The Church and the World: Gaudium Et Spes, Inter Mirifica*, 39.

[103] François Houtart, *Size and Structures of the Catholic Church in India: The Indianization of an Exogeneous Religious Institution in a Society in Transition.* (Louvain la Neuve: C.R.S.R. Université Catholique de Louvain, 1982), 94.

[104] Dennis Edwards, *Resurrection of the Body and Transformation of the Universe in the Theology of Karl Rahner*, http://www.krs.stjohnsem.edu/Edwards Dennis 2005.pdf (accessed May 27, 2007).

[105] McCabe, "The Role of the Church in Civil Society."

[106] Flannery, *Vatican Council II: The Conciliar and Post Conciliar Documents.*

[107] McCabe, "The Role of the Church in Civil Society," (emphasis added).

[108] Edwards, *Resurrection of the Body and Transformation of the Universe in the Theology of Karl Rahner.*

[109] Ibid.

[110] Ibid.

[111] Sahabandhu, "Dialectical Interaction of Religion and Society: A Dialogue with François Houtart."

[112] John Bowden, ed., *Christianity: The Complete Guide* (London: Continuum, 2005), 703-5.

[113] Sahabandhu, "Dialectical Interaction of Religion and Society: A Dialogue with François Houtart."

[114] Vatican, *Populorum Progressio*, [Encyclical of Pope Paul VI on the development of people, March 26, 1967], 57-60. http://www.vatican.va/holy_father/paul_vi/encyclicals/documents/hf_p-vi_enc_ 26031967_populorum_en .html (accessed May 15, 2007).

[115] "Pontifical Council for Promoting Christian Unity, Peace in the World: Dialogue among Christians and Other Religions," 6. http://www.vatican.va/roman_curia/pontifical_councils/chrstuni/ documents/rc_pc_chrstuni _doc_20020107_peace-kasper_en.html (accessed May 12, 2007).

[116] McCabe, "The Role of the Church in Civil Society."

[117] Vatican, *Evangelii Nuntiandi*, 33 – 35. http://www.vatican.va/holy_father/paul_vi/apost_ exhortations/documents/hf_p-vi_exh_19751208 evangelii-nuntiandi_en.html (accessed May 12, 2007).

[118] McCabe, "The Role of the Church in Civil Society."

[119] Vatican, *Deus Caritas Est*, 28. http://www.vatican.va/holy_father/benedict_xvi/encyclicals/ documents/hf_ben-xvi_enc_20051225_deus-caritas-est_en.html (accessed May 12, 2007).

[120] McCabe, "The Role of the Church in Civil Society."

[121] Most Rev. Diarmuid Martin, Archbishop of Dublin, interprets this differently: "Many were surprised by a comment of Pope Benedict XVI in his Encyclical *Deus Caritas Est*, which affirms 'that the just ordering of society and the State is a primary

responsibility of politics' and adds later that 'the Church cannot and must not take upon herself the political battle to bring about the most just society possible.' Some have seen this as a recipe for the retreat of the Church from commenting on the public arena. I look on this as a remarkably strong emphasis on the importance of politics and on the real purpose of politics," see the article on "Companion to the Compendium of the Social Doctrine of the Church," http:// www.dublindiocese.ie/ index.php?option=com _content&task=view&id=745&Itemid=372.

[122] Sahabandhu, "Dialectical Interaction of Religion and Society: A Dialogue with François Houtart."

[123] Ibid.

[124] Ibid.

[125] Sahabandhu, "Dialectical Interaction of Religion and Society: A Dialogue with François Houtart."

[126] Ibid.

[127] Ibid.

[128] About the same time, Houtart began to be interested in Asia and the Asian religions, especially Buddhism, so much so that in 1974, he published his Ph.D dissertation on the sociology of Buddhism in Sri Lanka.

[129] Sahabandhu, "Portraying the Person and Work of François Houtart."

[130] Ibid.

[131] Ibid.

[132] Ibid.

Chapter 14
Ecclesiology in Context: Reflections from an Indian Perspective in the Light of Current Ecumenical Deliberations

O. V. Jathanna

I

The Church is an integral part of the Christian faith, and is woven into its very fabric. For the Christian faith has a strong historical and communitarian dimension. This is closely linked with the Christian understanding of revelation, which is historical-eschatological and communitarian-representative. The Church, therefore, is in some sense, constitutive to the Christian faith. It not only exists as a historical continuum, but also has a mission in history. This, however, does not mean that a particular concept, form, structure or pattern of administration of the Church is sacrosanct at all times and in all places. The Church as the Body of the Incarnate Lord has to incarnate itself time and again in every new situation, if it has to be the Church of Christ in a changing world. Hence the quest for the most adequate concept and form of the *ekklesia* in a given place and time should go on. It is precisely in striving to be authentically the church of Christ in mission in a particular context, that the Church becomes the embodiment of the Church universal, being one with its historical stretch and geographical expansion, preserving its dynamic identity in the midst of change. This means, the contextuality of the Church belongs to its very nature. Ecclesiology seeks to express the understanding of the nature and function of the Church in a coherent manner from biblical, historical-theological and systematic-contextual perspectives.

II

Though the ecclesiologies of various confessional families in India were basically borrowed from their respective "mother" churches, ecclesiological reflections were not entirely absent.

Especially since the late 19th century, several Christian thinkers have been grappling with the question of the nature, necessity and function of the Church in the Indian context. Brahmabandhab Upadhyaya (1861-1907) is a notable example of this.[1] The International Missionary Council meeting held in Tambaram in 1938 made the concept of the Church central to its deliberations.[2] It triggered off a lively discussion in India on Kingdom-centred theology and Church-centred theology. Several Indian Christian thinkers expressed their dissatisfaction with the ecclesiology of Tambaram 1938, while some others saw in it the much-awaited movement from missions to "local" churches, with the full recognition of the latter's identity.[3]

The church union movement in India may also be seen as an attempt to evolve an Indian ecclesiology at the level of a concrete ecclesial life situation. Two decades ago, an edited work was published by the National Christian Council of India, seeking to give expression to a new understanding of the Church. It bears the significant title, *The Church: A Peoples' Movement.*[4] This was the last of a series of three books: The first one, *The Indian Church: Identity and Fulfillment* was published in 1971 and the second, *Beyond Identity, On To Participation* came out in 1973.[5] The Indian Theological Association (Roman Catholic) has brought out a collection of essays on ecclesiology under the title, *Searching for an Indian Ecclesiology.*[6] Again, *Jeevadhara,* a well- known Catholic periodical, published a series of articles in two separate issues in 1989 and 1990 on ecclesiologies of all the major confessional families in India. Besides, a number of articles are brought out in various journals on different aspects of ecclesiology.

III

The importance of ecclesiology is increasingly felt in the present-day ecumenical movement. One important example of this is the ecclesiological concern of the Commission on Faith and Order that emerged particularly in the years of the BEM[7] process and responses, that is, 1982-1990: In the light of the unprecedented response of the world-wide churches to the BEM document, the commission came to see the need to take up the question of ecclesiology as a major theme, along with the issues of scripture and tradition as well as sacraments and sacramentality, if intra-church dialogue should continue fruitfully.[8] It was in this light that the Plenary Session of the Commission on Faith and Order that met in Budapest in 1989 decided to take up ecclesiology as a major study project.[9] In the light of the specific emphases by different ecclesial traditions, the following four basic understandings of the Church were identified: (1) The Church as the gift of the Word of God (*creatura verbi*); (2) The Church as the pilgrim people of God; (3) the Church as servant and prophetic sign of God's coming kingdom; and (4) The Church as mystery or sacrament of God's love for the world.[10] The WCC Central Committee in 1991 affirmed as a major project "a study and convergence document on ecumenical perspectives on ecclesiology," and this work was also supported by the Canberra Assembly in the same year. The Fifth World Conference on Faith and Order held at Santiago de Compostela in 1993 is said to have been "to a large degree an ecclesiological conference." The concept of *koinonia*, as affirmed by the World Conference (1993) is expected to provide all Faith and Order studies with a coherent theological orientation. In view of this, "The Church as *Koinonia*-An Ecumenical Study," would be a major study programme, which would be central for the new working period of Faith and Order after Santiago de Compostela Conference.[11] It also proposed, as further study on ecclesiology, a collaborative work with Unit III on ethics and ecclesiology.[12] The proposed study on ecumenical perspectives on ecclesiology is meant to clarify and formulate common or converging or different ecumenical perspectives on ecclesiology.[13]

The Central Committee of the WCC that met in January 1994 decided that the study on ecclesiology and ethics be continued and developed further, with the intention of evaluating how different Christian traditions understand the relationship between ecclesiology and ethics.[14] The joint meetings between the Faith and Order and Unit Ill discussed this matter first in Ronde (1993) and then in Tantur (1995). The Ronde meeting put forward the designation "moral community" for the Church, and the Tantur meeting explored the notion of "moral formation" as a description of the Church's engagement in ethical process.[15] It is in this context of a wider ecclesiological study that we are meeting here to discuss "Theological Issues for the Indian Church Today and Tomorrow," with a view to articulate a "Theology of Life" from an Indian perspective.

First of all, the collaboration between the Faith and Order (which belongs to Unit I of the WCC: Unity and Renewal) and Unit Ill of the WCC that is, the Unit on Justice, Peace and Creation, should be welcomed as a healthy sign of mutual interaction-theological and ethical reflections coming together in relation to ecclesiology. Without theological reflection Christian ethics loses its foundation as well as horizon; and without ethical reflection Christian theology forfeits its concrete life-orientation and societal relevance.[16] In the very fact that theological reflection is life-related, an ethical dimension permeates the whole of theology. And the recognition of the truth that value is value only in relation to a given world- view makes it clear that, without a theological undergirding, ethics cannot survive. In fact, even the Lima Document on *Baptism, Eucharist and Ministry* (1982) in its own way took the ethical implications seriously, especially in the section on Baptism.[17] The present collaboration can now further this concern greatly and enrich both theological and ethical reflections in relation to the life and work of the Church.

At the same time, the Justice, Peace and Creation Unit can benefit at a deeper level from the Faith and Order concern for the doctrinal, sacramental, ministerial and structural aspects of the Christian faith. This will help ethical reflection not to become one-dimensional, by just confining itself to the socio-economic and political realms of reality and thereby further contributing to the prevalent positivistic and reductionistic view of life. The designation of the Church as "moral community" and the understanding of the Church's involvement in the world of terms of "moral formation,"[18] however, does not seem to be theologically adequate or helpful. The Church alone cannot call itself moral, on the one hand, and the Church's reality cannot be confined to the moral dimension, on the other. We can hope that, in the course of further dialogue and deliberations, a more satisfactory concept would emerge.

IV

We can now turn to briefly consider some of the ecclesiological issues that are important for the self-understanding and the life-in-mission of the Indian Church in the present-day context. As I am a member and presbyter of the Church of South India, some of my comments will naturally reflect more the experience with this particular church. Mutatis mutandis, however, they can apply to the Indian church in general. These issues are: Christian identity; ecclesial unity; ministerial and ecclesiastical structure.[19]

a) Christian Identity

Christians all over the world today are conscious of the question of their identity more than ever before.[20] While it is, thus, an ecumenical issue, it has special acuteness in the Indian context. Due to historical, sociological and religio-cultural factors, Christianity and the Christian Church is still regarded in India as something foreign. Along with Islam, Christianity is also seen as a religion that has come from outside India. The concepts *swadeshi* and *swadharma* that emerged during the freedom movement are applied to the religious realm, especially by religious militants and communalists. By and large the mainline, Brahminic Hinduism is seen as the norm and content of Indian culture, and is used as the definition of being an Indian, especially by the communally politicised sections of the Hindu fraternity. "Hindutva" is the current short-hand term for this. Indian Christianity also has its share of responsibility in this regard for projecting a "foreign" self-image. This problem is now widely recognised, especially in theological circles, and conscious efforts are being made to surmount this problem, in so far as it is a false self-projection and does not belong to the core of self –understanding of the Church, based on the Gospel of Jesus Christ. However, it is yet to make a tangible impact at the level of congregational life, which, in fact, is most crucial. The question is, what does it mean to be an Indian and a Christian at the same time? At the inter-religious and inter-ideological dialogues this matter may be taken up as one of the themes, with a view to bring about a better understanding between communities.

In the context of India's pluralistic society, the question of identity is faced in a general way by all Indians at different levels and Indian Christians naturally share in this. Though India is one of the oldest civilizations, it is, on the other hand, still relatively a young nation. It is a nation of plurality of religions, cultures, languages, regions, and ethnicities. Every Indian having a multiplicity of identities is a reality. In the consciousness of the people, they are Indians precisely in belonging to, and having, this or that distinct identity. At different times, one or the other identity may be in the forefront. Yet, life needs a living axis, which acts as an integrating principle. No doubt, for Christians it is the faith that gives meaning and coherence in the midst of these multiplicity of identities. But then, the faith should be understood in such a way that it would truly be able to make room for all legitimate aspects of the multiple identities. At the conceptual level, "transcendence by inclusion" might be helpful. In this connection, one may explore further the meaning of being a Christian in terms of being radically human (Hans Küng)[21] or participating in the New Humanity in Christ (M. M. Thomas).[22]

With regard to the question of identity, the caste factor plays a dominant role in Indian society. Though the iron-hold of the caste system has been somewhat weakened, particularly due to the impact of modern humanistic and scientific education, especially in the cities, it still continues to be a powerful influence in India. The religious sanction adds to its strength and tenacity. Apart from the terrible discrimination that the caste system perpetuates, the danger that the Church faces is that, it stands in constant pressure to identify itself as a caste within the larger caste structure. In fact, in the popular Indian mind, Christianity is broadly identified as caste. Though the Syrian Christians identified themselves as a higher caste and enjoyed certain social privileges, the Christian community, by and large, is seen as a lower caste group after the mass movements.[23]

If Christians identify themselves as a caste within the caste hierarchy of the Indian society, their survival as a closed and self-perpetuating community may thereby be assured. But it will be at the cost of denying their fundamental vision and mission of being an open community of the New Humanity of Jesus Christ.[24] The prevalent minority complex among the Christians also makes them prone to this temptation. This also contributes to a Christian brand of communalism. Though in the Indian context Christianity did contribute substantially to the development of a critical awareness regarding the evils of caste system and helped-through preaching, teaching, community life centred around the Table of the Lord and social programmes-to usher in a more humane and egalitarian understanding of the "human family," the churches themselves, however, did not make an uncompromising break with the complex phenomenon of caste, viewing it just as a part of the social custom of the country.[25] As a result, Indian churches are not totally free from this malise.

In this connection, we have to take seriously the Dalit issue. In spite of the additional privileges granted to the Dalits in the Indian Constitution, few of these privileges really reach them. As a result, the majority of Dalits continue to live in abject poverty and oppression. In fact, the reservation is also meant to act as a means of keeping the Dalits away from joining the Church, as they lose their privileges if they do so. The subtle and tricky aspect of this is that in order to be entitled to these special privileges Dalits have to continue to remain within the caste structure and thereby acknowledge it. As Christian Dalits are discriminated against in this regard on the basis of religion, by being excluded from these additional privileges, it is said that in some places some Christians maintain a double identity-one in the church as Christians, and the other in the government records as Dalits, implying that they are "Hindu" Dalits, for the sake of reservation privileges. The situation will improve, if the government would decide to extend the privilege to Christian Dalits as well. This, however, is opposed by certain sections of the society, including some non-Christian Dalits. While the legitimacy of the demand of Christian Dalits should be recognised and wholeheartedly supported, the Church needs to reflect seriously, on the implications of this for the future life of the Church, since it would perpetuate the caste distinction within the Christian community. At the same time, the Church has to become self-critically aware of its own failure to adequately strive to bring justice to all Dalits, especially to those who are of the Dalit background within its own fold, particularly in the villages, and do all that it can to set things right.[26]

Even though after the Mass Movements, the Indian Church came to be identified largely as a poor, rural, less-literate, and downtrodden community, over the years, a sizeable chunk of the Christian community "progressed" quite well on the socio-economic scale. In the process, however, the Church is being caught up between identifying itself with the poor, on the one hand, and with those who are aspiring-to-be-rich, on the other. This situation needs to be taken seriously and realistically, if the Church wants to address this problem. In the light of the new economic policy and globalisation, this problem has become more serious and urgent than ever before.

While the caste factor is the most dominant one, religious communalism, linguism and regionalism also need to be taken seriously, when we consider the question of identity in the Indian context. While religious confession, ethnicity, language and region all legitimately belong to our historical identity, they should not be allowed to become divisive and destructive forces, either in the society-at-large or within the church.

The question of baptism needs some consideration in this connection. In India, baptism is seen as the cut-off point between a convert and his/her family. Without going into the various aspects of this complex issue in this paper, I wish to just point out the following: Due to the influence of the caste system, baptism is often seen simply as moving from one caste group to another, which in fact distorts the theological meaning of baptism. Further, in the Indian context, due to separate personal laws for the major religious communities, with implications for marriage, divorce and inheritance, one legally ceases to be a member of his/her own family and community after baptism. Hans Staffner has argued that a uniform civil code would be of help in this respect.[27] Kaj Baago and Raimon Panikkar responded to the issue by advocating the view that the Church should not understand itself as a religion among other religions, but must lose its 'identity by allowing itself dissolved in other religions to be an effective instrument of transformation and fulfillment.[28] Anto Karokaran, thus, speaks of "a mission without baptism."[29] In this connection, reference is also made to the non-baptised believers in Christ.[30] Gispert-Sauch suggested that we need to think of the Church less in terms of a sociological community and more in terms of a fellowship of believers in different communities.[31] This, however, would raise the following questions:

1) Would this not necessitate some form of fellowship among those who are touched and transformed by the Christian vision of reality for mutual support and enrichment, though they prefer to remain within the fold of their respective religious communities? What would be the nature of such fellowships within different communities? And would there be a fellowship of such fellowships?

2) Would such open-ended and open-minded fellowships, or even persons who can no longer be able to accept the caste system, be tolerated and accommodated by the caste-conscious communities of which these fellowships or persons seek to be a part?

3) Without denying the historical nature of the Christ-event would it really be possible not to take seriously the historical fellowship of Jesus Christ down the ages that we call the "Church"?

Dr. J. R. Chandran's efforts to redefine the meaning of baptism as a commitment to the transformation of all our relationships, which also includes national and inter-national communities is helpful, especially because of its corrective value and wider vision. In the light of Jesus' baptism, Chandran sees baptism as an act of solidarity with all, transcending all divisions.[32] We may also note that M. M. Thomas speaks of the need for a new pattern of combining Christian self-identity and secular solidarity with all human beings.[33]

Further, in the light of our deliberations on the issue of Christian identity, the following questions seem to be of crucial importance:

1) How to present Jesus Christ as the universal Liberator and Reconciler and not as a mere sectarian god?

2) How to give visible and meaningful expression to one's discipleship to Christ, and commitment to the truth and values of the Kingdom?

3) How to make the Church an open community, which would be an effective sign, a foretaste and an instrument of the

Kingdom of God? And what kind of a visible "form" it should take that would be helpful in fulfilling its mission.

According to M.M. Thomas, the Indian Church will realise its true identity only in so far as it engages itself in mission, in the service of the Kingdom of God by being faithful to the Good News of Jesus Christ, on the one hand, and by being sensitive to the contextual needs, on the other.[34]

b) Ecclesial Unity

The unity of the Church has been an important concern of the Indian Church, where the scandal of disunity has been keenly felt. What has been achieved in this realm is truly significant. The movement that officially began in 1919 bore its fruit in 1947 in the formation of the Church of South India, which included the congregational, presbyterial and the episcopal polities of the Church, that is Congregationalists, Presbyterians, English/ Wesleyan Methodists and Anglicans. The Continental component was represented by the Basel Mission churches. The Church of North was inaugurated in 1970 with the Anglicans, Baptists, Disciples, British and Australian Methodists, and the United Church of North India, comprising the Presbyterians and the Congregationalists. A further landmark in the history of church unity in India was reached when the CNI-CSI-Mar Thoma Joint Council was set up in 1978. At this point, the intention was to form eventually the *Bharath* Christian Church.[35]

I shall concentrate on the Church of South India (CSI) as regards the nature of church union and the question of its adequacy in the Indian context. The founding "fathers" wanted the CSI to be an indigenous, missionary and a pastoral church. It was envisaged that the unity of the church would greatly deepen and enhance the missional commitment of the church. The bishopric was seen in pastoral and not in administrative terms-bishop as the chief pastor and father-in-God, expected to set an example to the flock.[36]

Over the years, the old denominationalism has been to a considerable extent surmounted and the identity of the CSI has slowly established itself. In a majority of places *The Book of Common Worship* is used. A common Synod is functioning for the united Church. Yet, at present, there is a widespread feeling that all is not well with the CSI, and that for its own health and vitality the CSI needs radical reforms at the earliest. The Official Report of the CSI, *Church of South India After Thirty Years*, makes some important observations:

• That the unity is often marred by casteism and parochialism, regionalism and linguism.

• That lack of integration is reflected in the widespread tendency of the people to take to lawsuits and to agitational methods.

• That the structures give dominant position to the pastorate and the diocese, and that the local congregations are neglected; that the bishop at the diocesan level and the presbyter at the pastorate level have emerged as powerful functionaries.

• That unholy joy is displayed in electioneering and dubious methods of canvassing.

• That "there is too much decision-making at the top, too much apathy at the grass-roots and too much jockeying for positions in the middle."[37]

This is indeed a grim yet an honest evaluation of the situation. The sad thing is that the CSI administration has not done anything seriously to set things right. In fact, the situation has further deteriorated since then. Corruption is mounting. Groupism and cliques are on the increase. Huge sums of money are said to be spent at the time of elections, both at the diocesan and the synodical levels, especially for the episcopal elections. Now the fear is that corruption is being institutionalised. Episcopacy has become monarchical and authoritarian and has lost its credibility.[38] Service-oriented institutions, like schools, are used to exploit the public to make money for private gain. Interest in mission and ministry is generally diminishing at the official level. Whatever little money, energy and enthusiasm remain are spent on running the machinery of the church, which is increasingly becoming top heavy. With a single synod for the whole of South India, the administrative mode of operation is becoming more and more mechanical and impersonal. Democracy is threatened to be reduced to a numbers game, especially with money power. An enlarged meeting of the CSI Theological Commission that met in Bangalore in May 1995 in view of the forthcoming Golden Jubilee celebrations of the union, made several helpful proposals for the amendment of the CSI constitution. One of the recommendations was to make bishopric a term office. Another one was to establish an election commission to curb electoral malpractices. On the part of the administration, however, there does not seem to be any enthusiasm about this.

This does not mean that the CSI has just collapsed. Far from it! A lot of projects are on. There is a lot of activity around. Usually, every Sunday, most of the churches are full. There is hunger and thirst among people for the Word and Spirit. At the same time, the ecclesiastical atmosphere is vitiated with administrative and structural vices mentioned above. There are also signs that a good number of people are increasingly seeing spiritual nourishment outside the CSI, in sectarian, charismatic or other denominational groups.

In retrospect, we can see three motivatin g factors that contributed to the formation of the CSI: Firstly, the conviction that the unity of the Church is the will of God, which would further the mission of the Church. Secondly, there was the communal desire to come together as a minority community in the midst of a vast majority of non-Christians. And thirdly, there was pressure from the mission boards and "mother" churches to form the union. In all this: the decisions were taken by a few leaders, while the congregations, by and large, remained passive. Since 1978 very little, if any, progress has been made on the path of church union. Lutheran, Methodists ("American Methodists, that is, Methodist Church in India), and several other churches, including the Pentecostals, have not joined to form a wider united Church.[39]

It should be clearly pointed out that all the problems and malaise cannot simplistically be ascribed to the church union itself. In fact, many of these problems are also present in different degrees and forms in those churches which are staying outside the union. At the same time, it seems that the megalithic and monolithic nature of the united church and the structure that it developed for itself makes the united church more liable to the vices mentioned above.

At all events, the union did not help the united Church in any significant way to be more indigenous, missional, democratic, transparent and effective than those churches which did not join the union.

In view of this, the question should be raised, to what extent the concept of unity and the model of union that was opted by the CSI was really helpful. It may be called the organisational-organic model of church union. The CSI indeed was a pioneer in this regard and it had to tread an uncharted path. This has historical significance, which inspired several other churches world-wide to take up the unity of the churches seriously. However, in the light of the present-day situation, the model of union that the CSI adopted does not seem to be helpful:

Firstly, this model favours unity in terms of uniformity, with the goal of having a monolithic church. Unity is achieved by turning all into Episcopalians. In the process, the congregational element is increasingly eroded.

Secondly, despite the name "organic," it turns out to be primarily an administrative union, which does not leave much room for the freedom of the Spirit. This does not facilitate unity-in-freedom.

Thirdly, the model is primarily past-oriented as it is concerned to reconcile the past differences and preserve the inherited structures. This has resulted in inheriting a heavy machinery, which is not flexible enough to carry out the mission of the Church with the changing times and needs.

Fourthly, this model has turned the united Church into another numerically powerful denomination over against other denominational churches, which, due to its numerical strength, tends to be arrogant in relation to smaller denominations.

Any model that we adopt should be future-oriented, while we continue to learn from the past and respect the past. It should enable the churches to grow in the grace of God and fellowship with one another, and help the church to fulfil its mission both faithfully and effectively. Only when the local churches take their mission seriously in their given context and seek to develop forms and structures that are suitable for carrying it out, they become the true embodiment of the Church of Christ in a given context. The unity that we seek must make room for legitimate diversities that are necessary because of the context- relatedness of the Church and its mission. The new model must emerge as a result of the constant interaction between the biblical witness, historical in- sights, ecumenical deliberations, dialogue with people of other faiths and ideologies, recognition of contextual needs as well as possibilities and the guidance of the Holy Spirit. As the Church has a sociological dimension, the question of exercising power in the Church needs to be taken into account, so that it would not be let to degenerate into oppressive power, but would consciously be made participatory in such a way that it would be rendered humane and would stand in the service of the divine mission for a fuller and more meaningful life for all.

The importance of the ecclesial unity, however, should be affirmed unequivocally. The question here is not whether there should be unity, but what kind of union.[40] It is encouraging to see that the Central Committee of the WCC in 1991 it was acknowledged that the term "visible unity" is ambivalent and how it should be structurally realised is a matter of further discussion.[41] Even more important is the fact that the official discussion paper at the Fifth World Conference of Faith and Order held at Santiago de Compestela in 1993 has recognised that "the concept of *koinonia/* communion offers the biblical framework and theological foundation for different models of unity, such as "conciliar fellowship," "reconciled diversity," "organic unity," and so on. It is "not a new model added to them."[42] This shows a new openness on the part of the Faith and Order Commission as regards the concept of unity and model of union at the ecumenical level.

c) Ministerial and Ecclesiastical Structure

The ministerial and ecclesiastical structure of the church is another important topic of current concern both in the ecumenical and the Indian contexts. In connection with the BEM process, it was noted at the WCC Central Committee Meeting in 1991 that the question of the understanding and structures of ministries of the Church was still unresolved and further work needed to be done in this area.[43] The churches' response to the BEM process has shown that it is more difficult for the churches to arrive at a consensus on Ministry than on Baptism and Eucharist.[44] The Lima document (1982), however, has not taken seriously the cultural diversities and contextual needs in connection with the concept and patterns of Christian ministry.[45] The question of the teaching authority of the Church is yet to be adequately addressed at the ecumenical level.[46]

In India, irrespective of the confessional traditions, all the churches inherited the concepts as well as patterns of ministry from their respective "mother" churches. Generally speaking, one- pastor-one-congregation pattern of ministry has become the norm. Especially in the village context, this pattern becomes a financial burden on the poor congregations. Most of the income is spent on the meagre salaries of the pastors, and the Indian churches continue to be heavily dependent on outside financial help for projects, especially for the socio-economic projects. The more serious problem, however, is that in this pattern of ministry the *laos*, who form more than 99% of the congregation, are reduced to a passive mass of people. This makes the Christian ministry and mission largely ineffective, especially outside the four walls of the church. The present concept and pattern of ministry cannot take the calling of the whole people of God seriously, as envisioned by the Lima document. The N.T. points to diversified ministries in order to meet the various needs of the people, on the one hand, and to make room for exercising the manifold charismata in the church, on the other. This has not been taken seriously so far.

Though the needs of the people are changing with the changing situations; the pattern of ministry has remained the same, without being contextual, contemporary, forward-looking and reaching-out into the world effectively. No serious efforts have been made in the Indian context to develop a more effective pattern of ministry in light of the Christian vision of reality and the mission of the Church, on the one hand, and critically as well as creatively informed by the religio-cultural and socio-political ethos and insights of India, on the other. In view of the ministerial and ecclesiastical structure, the following questions arise:

a) What is the mission and ministry of the whole Church in the present-day context? How can we effectively express today both structurally and functionally that the entire congregation as *laos* is a minister of God for the world in a given context?

b) What is the relationship between the Church and the Christian ministry? Are they equally primordial? Or, is the one prior to the other? Or, are they mutually dependent on each other? What is their mutual relationship?

c) How to relate the special or ordained ministry in a helpful way to the ministry of the whole people of God and vice versa, as well as to relate ordination to baptism?

d) Should the ordained ministry, full-time ministry, and the theologically trained ministry necessarily be identical?

e) How to hold together charisma and office, on the one hand, and ordained office and the non-ordained office, on the other, in a healthy and helpful way?

f) What are the relative merits and demerits of one-pastor-one- congregation pattern of ministry? What are the other possibilities? Is some kind of collegiate ministry, preferably of a voluntary nature, possible as well as desirable?

g) What are the prospects and problems of the three-fold ministry, which in practice works as a two-fold ministry (the office of the deacon being seen only as a preparation for that of a presbyter!), that the Indian church has inherited? Does it require modifications? Would it be more helpful to think of the office of the Bishop in terms of an added function to that of the presbyter as seems to be the case in the N.T. and not as a separate order in itself, that is, Bishop as one among the college of presbyters, who, preferably in turn, does the work of exercising pastoral and missional oversight? Or, would it be possible to develop new forms of *episcope* (oversight) without necessarily tying it with episcopacy?[47]

h) If diversified ministry is both necessary and helpful, how can we give structural expression to the diversified ministry?

i) What can we learn from the Indian religio-cultural and socio- political heritage, ethos and insights, with regard to developing an effective pattern of ministry in the present-day Indian context?

j) What are the essential marks that may be regarded as *sine qua non* of the Christian ministry that would enable mutual recognition of each other's ministry ecumenically, and, at the same time, would be effective locally?[48]

V

After having considered three important aspects of ecclesiology, namely the Christian identity, ecclesial unity and ministerial and ecclesiastical structure, we shall now make an attempt to understand afresh the nature and function of the Church briefly.

In the light of the N.T. data, we can agree with Hans Küng that "in the *pre-Easter period,* during his lifetime, Jesus did not found a church: ... *In the pre-Easter period,* Jesus, by his preaching and ministry, laid the foundations for the emergence of a post-resurrection Church."[49] According to Leonardo Boff, Jesus established the Twelve as a messianic community gathered around Jesus and his Spirit, which was then broadened and gave rise to other apostolic communities.[50] This would mean, as we said at the beginning of this paper, that the church in some sense is constitutive to the Christian faith.

As regards the question, "What is the Church," some of the new insights that have come to the fore in the ecumenical discussions are helpful: The Church can be seen as a "sacrament for the world (*sacramentum mundi*)," as the Second Vatican Council put it, which gives and spends itself for the well-being of the world by being an effective sign and instrument of God's reign of love, that is, the Kingdom of God. This understanding will be complemented and enriched by the idea of the Church as a "prophetic sign." For the Church seeks to be in the service of the transformation of the whole cosmos in the *eschaton*. This understanding can be expressed by saying that the Church is meant to be the "vehicle of life for the world."[51]It is important that we understand the term "life" in its biblical depth and richness. What is meant here is not merely *bios,* though *bios* is integral to it. It is the new life, life eternal, that is, participating in the vivifying and transforming life of God. It is life lived in fellowship with God. Jesus could, therefore, summarise the main purpose of his ministry in terms of offering life in all its fullness.[52] It is life here and hereafter. While it firmly holds on to the trans-historical, eschatological and transcendental dimensions of life, it takes the life on earth equally seriously. For in Christianity creation, incarnation and resurrection of the body are all held together, integrating into its own being the tragedy of death-death on the cross.

This means that life in all aspects has to be taken seriously, since the historical well-being is an integral aspect of a Christian understanding of ultimate salvation, without ignoring the tragic aspects of our life here and now. This, then, clearly means that this new life has to manifest itself as liberating and transforming life in social, economic, and political realms as well. Jesus understood his mission as mission of bringing good news to the poor.[53] While the economically poor form an important part of the recipients of this good news, the poor in the Bible also include the socially excommunicated and marginalised, the lonely, the oppressed, the handicapped, the needy, the sick, the helpless, and the like.

In India, several theologians have taken the life-orientation of the Christian faith seriously. For example, P. Chenchiah understood Christianity in terms of a "a *sui generis* pattern of life."[54] P. D. Devanandan understood 'the Church as part of the new creation as demonstrating the life of the Kingdom of God here and now, as a healing, serving, transforming *koinonia,* the family of God."[55] In M. M. Thomas' theology the concepts of "new humanity," and "common humanity" play an important role.[56]

It is worth noting that in the ecumenical deliberations the Church is now being understood more and more in terms of *koinonia*. The advantage of this term is that, it gives expression to the inter-personal and the communitarian dimension of life, since *Koinonia,* also means participation, partaking, sharing, fellowship and community.[57] While this is a helpful term, care should be taken so that it would not be used just to emphasise the inner life of the Church, which may lead to a communal misunderstanding of it. The Faith and Order document does seek to avoid such introverted and narrow perception by pointing out clearly that this *koinonia* in the first instance belongs to the Triune God, who seeks to offer it to the whole of creation. And the Church's mission is understood in terms of manifesting, by the power of the Holy Spirit, "the divine life holding out to the world the possibility of being enfolded within that divine life." In this, the Church responds to the humanity's search for a better life. The attention is also drawn to the truth that the life and destiny of humanity and creation are inseparably bound together.[58] In this light, two things become important: Firstly, the *koinonia,* which is rooted in the Triune God, must remain open to all people-including people of other faiths and ideologies. Secondly, the *koinonia* itself should be understood as a foretaste, sign and instrument of the God-intended fellowship for the whole of humanity and the cosmos.

Interacting theologically with the religio-cultural heritage of India, A. J. Appasamy interpreted the Church as a body that Christ assumed. What is important in this regard is to note that Appasamy understood Creation, Incarnation, Church and the Eucharist as four bodies that belong to the Lord as bodies that he assumed.[59] While Appasamy did not work out the details of the nature of these bodies in their inter-relatedness, this "analogy," derived from the body-soul analogy of Ramanuja, may be found fruitful in our understanding of the Church, if the analogy is used thoughtfully.

VI

The Church finds its true identity in critical and creative interaction with the world, while participating in God's mission in and for the world, in seeking to bring fullness of life that God offers for all, especially for those who are the "lost," the "last' and the "least" in today's world. The Church's mission has a specific and irreducible dimension, namely that of bearing witness in word, deed and life-style to the self-giving, forgiving and transforming love of God as revealed in the incarnation, death and the resurrection of the Lord Jesus Christ. At the same time, it is also called to join hands with others in the wider mission of God, that is concerned with the preservation of the integrity of God's creation, justice and peace and in pointing to the reality of God as the ground, meaning and goal of all that there is. In this the Church is called to be on the way with the crucified and the risen Lord, by the power of the Holy Spirit, as His "iconic", "prophetic" and "sacramental" presence in every given context for the fuller life of the world.

Endnotes:

This article was earlier published as O. V. Jathanna, "Ecclesiology in Context: Reflections from an Indian Perspective in the Light of Current Ecumenical Deliberations," *Bangalore Theological Forum* 28, nos. 3-4 (September-December 1996): 3-11. Used with permission of the author and publishers of *Bangalore Theological Forum.*

[1] Robin Boyd, *An Introduction to Indian Christian Theology* (New Delhi: ISPCK, 1991 [reprint]), 82-85. A selection of Upadhyaya's writings on 'The Church and her Mission" is found as Chapter 9 of Julius Lipner and George Gispert-Sauch, eds., *The Writings of Brahmabandhab Upadhyay*, vol. 2 (Bangalore: The United Theological College, 1991).

[2] *The World Mission of the Church: Tambaram 1938* (London and New York: IMC, 1939).

[3] O. V. Jathanna, *The Decisiveness of the Christ-event and the Universality of Christianity in a World of Religious Plurality: With Special Reference to Hendrick Kraemer and Alfred George Hogg as well as to William Ernest Hocking and Pandipeddi Chenchiah* (Berne, Frankfurt: Peter Lang, 1981), 503-7.

[4] Mathai Zachariah, ed. *The Church: A People's Movement* (Nagpur: NCCI, 1975).

[5] Ibid., 1.

[6] Gerwin Van Leeuwen, ed. *Searching for an Indian Ecclesiology* (Bangalore: Asian Trading Corporation, 1984). See further: M.M. Thomas, *A Diaconal Approach to Indian Ecclesiology* (Rome: CIIS and Tiruvalla: CSS, 1995); and Kanichikattil Francis, *Church in Context: Essays in Honour of Mathias Mundadan, CMI* (Bangalore: Dharmaram Publications, 1996).

[7] *BEM* stands for the *Baptism, Eucharist and Ministry* text of the *Faith and Order Commission,* which is also called, *The Lima Document* (1982).

[8] Thomas F. Best, ed. *Faith and Order 1985-1989: The Commission Meeting at Budapest (Geneva:* WCC, 1990), 3, 5, 147-148.

[9] Ibid., 219, 27. *Minutes of the Meeting of the Faith and Order Standing Commission: 4-11 January, 1994: Cret-Berard, Switzerland,* 28.

[10] *Baptism, Eucharist, Ministry: 1982- 1990,* 147-151.

[11] *Information: Faith and Order,* March 1994, 1.

[12] *Minutes of the Meeting of the Faith and Order Standing Commission: 4-11 January, 1994: Cret-Berard, Switzerland,* 28-29.

[13] Ibid., 29. The question was, however, raised whether the ecclesiology study should become a much broader "umbrella study," covering a number of specific studies on issues related to *BEM,* on authority, universal ministry of unity, Scripture -Tradition- Context, ecclesiology and ethics. Ibid.

[14] *World Council of Churches Central Committee: Minutes of the Forty-fifth Meeting, Johannesburg, South Africa, 20-28 January 1994,* 106. In this connection, we may also note that Unit III: Justice, Peace and Creation has a programme called, 'Theology of Life: Justice, Peace, Creation," which seeks to articulate the theological foundation and integration of justice, peace as well as creation and to enrich and renew ecumenical social ethics and social thought. Ibid., 105. We can see here an attempt to bring together the concerns of Faith and Order and Life and Work movements. The Faith and Order had recognised that the question of the unity of the churches cannot be an

end in itself. This is reflected in its earlier major study project, "Unity of the Church and Renewal of Human Community." In the words of John Deschner: "The aim of the study is quite simply to ask us to pay more attention to the broader location of our church unity work: not simply to our location among divided churches, but to the location of our churches in a divided world." *Towards Visible Unity: Commission on Faith and Order: Lima 1982,* vol. 1 (Geneva: WCC, 1982), 112. The concerns of this study now continue under the new study programme, "Unity of the Church and Nationalism and Ethnic Identity." *Information,* March 1994, 2.

[15] *Information: Faith and Order,* July 1994, 2.

[16] Ct. Clodovis Boff's phrase, used as the title of his book, *"Feet-on-the-Ground-Theology"* (Maryknoll, New York: Orbis, 1987).

[17] *Baptism, Eucharist and Ministry* (Geneva: WCC, 1982), paragraphs 2-7.

[18] *Information, Faith and Order,* July 1995, 2.

[19] On this see: O. V. Jathanna, "Christen in lndien: Aspekte einer indischen Ekklesiologie," *Die Zeichen der Zeit* 4, no. 95 (49/4, 1995), 149-151.

[20] Raimundo Panikkar, "Prolegomena to the Problem of Universality of the Church," in *Unique and Universal. Fundamental Problems of an Indian Theology,* ed. J. B. Chethimattam (Bangalore: Centre for the Study of World Religions, Dharmaram Publications, 1972), 155.

[21] Hans Küng, *Christ Sein* (Zurich: Ex Libris, 1996), 545-594.

[22] See: T. M. Philip, *The Encounter Between Theology and Ideology: An Exploration into the Communicative Theology of M.M. Thomas* (Madras: CLS, 1986), 67-70, 114-116.

[23] Cf. John Webster, 'The Identity of Indian Christians," in *Church in Context: Essays in Honour of Mathias Mundadan, CMI,* ed. Kanichikattil Francis (Bangalore: Dharmaram, 1986), 65: "Historically, the Dalit mass movements gave the Christian Church and community a new identity. Since the number of Dalits who converted was so large in most parts of India the mass movements changed the Christian community from a tiny, literate and 'progressive' urban community into a much larger but predominantly poor, illiterate and 'backward' rural community. In India as a whole, at least a majority but probably between two- thirds and a three-quarters of all Christians are Dalits. In some areas, the percentage would be well above ninety percent. Thus, in most of the country, Indian Christian identity is, in fact, Dalit identity." In this article, Webster presents the studies made by A. M. Mundadan, Susan Bayly, John G.B. Webster and Frederick F. Downs with regard to the issue of Christian identity in India, 56-71.

[24] Pandipeddi Chenchiah, "Community or Movement?," *Guardian* (Madras), 1942, 28-29. Reproduced in: D. A. Thangasamy, *The Theology of Chenchaiah* (Bangalore: CISRS and YMCA, 1966), 307-311.

[25] While this is by and large true, there were notable exceptions.'

[26] I am grateful to Mr. M. E. Prabhakar, a Christian Dalit leader, who pointed out, during the discussion after the presentation of this paper, that there would have been no need for the Christian Dalits to ask to be included in the governmental reservation, if the Church had done its part in bringing justice to them. One important point, we 1eed to note is that the reservation, by the very nature of the case, is something provisional, and it has achieved very little thus far. While the entire Church must stand in solidarity with the brothers and sisters from the Dalit background within its own fold, and join hands with their struggle to be included in the reservation as a matter of

justice to be done in the present context, the Church has to seriously think of better alternatives that would be more effective in the long run. Further, while the Church has a special responsibility for "Christian Dalits," it must also be concerned with the Dalit cause in general.

[27] Hans Staffner, "Baptism and the Law of Inheritance," *Vidyajyothi* 48, no. 2 (1984), 75-81. *Idem,* "Evangelisierung in lndien heute: 1st es moeglich, ein christlicher Hindu zu sein? *Zeitschrift feur Missionswissenschaft* 72, no. 3 (1989): 163-184. O. V. Jathanna, 'Taufe imindischen Kontext," *Darurn* 1, no. 93 (1993): 18-19.

[28] K. Baago, "Honestly Speaking," *The United Church Review,* July 1967, 148. *Idem,* "Church, Mission, and Other Religions, 7- 8. R. Panikkar, "A Dream of an Indian Ecclesiology," in *Searching for an Indian Ecclesiology*, ed. Gerwin Van Leeuwen, (Bangalore: Asian Trading Corporation, 1984), 33.

[29] A. Karokaran, "Mission, Conversion, Baptism," in A *Call to Discipleship,* ed. Godwin Singh (New Delhi: ISPCK, 1985), 159-160

[30] Godwin Singh, ed. A *Call to Discipleship,* (New Delhi: ISPCK, 1985), 206-09.

[31] Ibid., 4.

[32] J. R. Chandran, "Baptism," *Aikyatha,* December 1991, 10.

[33] M. M. Thomas, A *Diaconal Approach to Indian Ecclesiology* (Rome: CIIS and Tiruvalla: CSS, 1995), 60. For the meaning of Christian Mission, see the concluding section of this paper, No. VI.

[34] T. M. Philip, *The Encounter Between Theology and Ideology: An Exploration into the Communicative Theology of M. M. Thomas* (Madras: CLS, 1986), 87-88.

[35] Bengt Sundkler, *Church of South India, The Movement Towards Union: 1900-1947* (London: Lutterworth Press, 1954). C.B. Firth, *An Introduction to Indian Church History* (Madras: CLS, 1976). Hugald Grafe[hrsg.], *Die evangelisishe Kirche in lndien* (Erlangen: Verlag der ev. Luth. Mission, 1981). *Church of South India After Thirty Years: Report to the Special Committee appointed by the Church of South India Synod to study the Life and Work of the Church* (Madras: CLS, 1978).

[36] K. C. Abraham, "Church of South India Ecclesiology," *Jeevadhara* 19, no. 112 (July 1989), 251-254.

[37] *After Thirty Years,* 49-51.

[38] For a Bishop's understanding of Episcopacy in the CSI, see: Ananda Rao Samuel, "Episcopacy in the Church of South India," *Episcope and Episcopate in Ecumenical Perspective,* Faith and Order Paper 102 (1980), 43-50.

[39] This is just to indicate that enthusiasm for organizational-organic union largely seems to have d1m1n1shed 1n India at present. While personal and property matters do come in the way, keeping the people away from coming together in Church Union it should, at the same time, be pointed out that the kind of unity that has been achieved in the united churches, that is, CSI and the CNI, has not inspired other churches that are still outside the union to earnestly seek wider unity.

[40] See further: O. V. Jathanna, "Review Article" on *Living Today Towards Visible Unity,* ed. by Thomas Best," *Bangalore Theological Forum,* 20, no. 4 (1988), 65-73.

[41] *World Council of Churches Central Committee: Minutes of the Forty-Third Meeting, Geneva, Switzerland, 20-27 September 1991,* 53.

[42] Thomas Best and Guenther Gassmann eds. *On the Way to Fuller Koinonia* (Geneva: WCC, 1994), 271.

[43] *WCC Central Committee: Minutes of the Forty-Third Meeting, Geneva, Switzerland, 20-27 September 1991,* 49.

[44] *Baptism, Eucharist & Ministry: 1 982-1990: Reports on the Process and Responses,* Faith and Order Paper No. 149, 1990, 74-88.

[45] M. M. Thomas' critique of the Lima Document is that it does not give the central place to *diakonia.* He uses the term *diakonia* in its broader sense. M. M. Thomas, *A Diaconal Approach to Indian Ecclesiology,* 10.

[46] See the Report of the Odessa Consultation held in 1977, *How Does the Church Teach Authoritatively Today?* Lukas Vischer, "How does the Church Teach Authoritatively Today?" *Concilium,* no. 148 (1981): 1-10.

[47] For the ecumenical discussion on *episcope* and *episkopos,* see: *Episcope and Episcopate in Ecumenical Perspective* (Geneva: WCC, 1980).

[48] For a feminist view of the nature of the Church, its structure and ministry, see: Letty M. Russell, *Church in the* Round (Louisville, Kentucky: Westminster/John Knox Press, 1993). Elisabeth Schüssler Fiorenza, *In Memory of Her: A Feminist Theo logical Reconstruction of Christian Origins* (London: SCM Press Ltd., 1983). Russell uses the imagery of a common round table for the Church, emphasizing partnership and sharing for all members. Fiorenza seeks to reconstruct Christian origins. The second part of her book deals with women's history as the history of the discipleship of equals, in the light of the "world" of Jesus and those who followed him (97-241). The Third part takes up the issue of patriarchy and ministry (245-351).

[49] Hans Küng, *The Church* (London: Burns & Oates, 1968), 72- 74. Leonardo Boff agrees with Küng's view. L. Boff, *Ecclesiogenesis: The Base Communities Reinvent the Church,* (Maryknoll: Orbis Books, 1986), 50.

[50] Boff, *Ecclesiogenesis: The Base Communities Reinvent the Church,* 28. See also 60.

[51] Elizabeth Templeton, "Towards the Realisation of Common Life," in *On the Way to Fuller Koinonia,* eds., Thomas Best and G. Gassmann (Geneva: WCC, 1994), 2.

[52] John 10:10.

[53] Luke 4:18.

[54] Jathanna, *The Decisiveness of the Christ-event and the Universality of Christianity in a World of Religious Plurality: With Special Reference to Hendrick Kraemer and Alfred George Hogg as well as to William Ernest Hocking and Pandipeddi Chenchiah,* 379.

[55] Boyd, *An Introduction to Indian Christian Theology,* 199.

[56] T. M. Philip, *Theology and Ideology,* 67-70, 114, 116.

[57] Best and Gassmann eds., *On the Way to Fuller Koinonia,* 271.

[58] Ibid., 273-275.

[59] R. Boyd, *An Introduction to Indian Christian Theology,* 140-143.

Chapter 15
Towards 'People' (*Laos*) Ecclesiology for Mission

Simon Pinto

Introduction

"The image of the Church I like," said Pope Francis to Father Spadaro,

> [I]s that of the holy, faithful people of God.... There is no full identity without belonging to a people. No one is saved alone, as an isolated individual, but God attracts us looking at the complex web of relationships that take place in the human community. God enters into this dynamic, this participation in the web of human relationships.[1]

It was in the early 1960s that the Roman Catholic Church met to deliberate on its own self. It recognized that the formulations of the Council of Trent in the 16th century were no longer appropriate. Therefore, prompted by the Holy Spirit the Church reformulated its ecclesiology. The nuance of this reformulation is still being worked out, as the Church pursues its effort to find meaning for its existence. And the present pope is stressing on the communion of the people of God who believe in and form one body in Christ. They all enjoy fundamental equality as by baptism they form one 'people' even though they may have a legitimate functional diversity. This insists an open inclusive ecumenical church.

One of the major ecclesiological principles adopted by the Second Vatican Council is embodied in its teaching that the Church is the whole *People of God*.[2] In other words, the Church is not only the hierarchy, the clergy, and/or members of religious communities. It is the whole community of the baptized. This 'people' is not only marked by a rich diversity of gender, class, education, social status, race, ethnicity, culture and so on but have been bestowed with a variety of charisms. So there is enormous energy that is to be channelized in sharing the one responsibility of the Church's mission to the world.

"United we stand divided we fall." This phrase can be taken to refer to the churches and the mission today. Our commitment to mission is one though we are many churches. Then why cannot it be executed as one. Our efforts towards it are to be amplified as we hope with Pope John Paul II that the third millennium is of Asia[3] in regard to mission.

1. Indian Mission Context

India is the largest democracy in the world and a Democratic Society of equals. Every one equally enjoys freedom, rights and duties. As such democracy is a form of government in which all eligible citizens participate equally—either directly or through elected representatives. According to *Merriam-Webster Dictionary*, it is "an organization or situation in which everyone is treated equally and has equal rights."[4]

In this line Indian multi-religious context can throw challenges to the Church in India. Michael Amaladoss, a renowned Indian dialogue theologian speaks of a community model for dialogue mission. According to him, certain inclusivistic approaches in the Christian theology of religions and modern *advaitic* approaches to other religions tend to be transcendental. But India proposes to build a secular society according to a democratic constitution that has positive attitudes towards the religions in the presence of all great and other small religions.[5] This approach is different and new towards building community of the kingdom through dialogue with other religions.

However, as the Church takes her origin not in the common will of a group of people but through God's call, how can it call itself a democratic community? On the other hand, how can the Church in India not be influenced by the democratic Indian community? Or how far can it imbibe the values of democracy to make itself more participatory in carrying out the mission of Christ? Can the Church recognize and insist equal rights and duties of all its members for its running and being in mission? We shall answer these and more questions as we go by.

It is essential to note that the Church in India is not one people of God. We are divided and in this divided church, common witness is at stake. Can the Church see all the churches as equals? Can it bring in the ideals of equal rights and duties in the running and mission of all the churches? How could this be realized in concrete? These and more questions also are discussed in the following pages.

2. Towards an Indian Contextual Ecclesiology

What is Indian Church? As K. Pathil puts it,

> Indian Church is a local Church on the basis of our common cultural and political unity. But all the same, Indian Church is a communion of many local/individual churches which are diverse due to their historical, socio-cultural and other differences.[6]

This concept of a regional church is pluralistic in the sense that it is a communion of many local or individual churches so much so it is essentially an inculturated church having Indian political unity as the background.

According to Kurien Kunnumppuram the Indian Church of the Future is an inculturated, Autonomous and a Church of the People.[7] All these aspects are derived from the Second Vatican Council. Thanks to this 'Great Ecumenical Council, that we have a new church in India, rather a new blueprint with some orientations regarding the mission and the future shape of the new Church. This is what we can gather from the Council: a God-centred and a people-centred church rooted in a deep experience of God. We proceed to venture towards an Indian Contextual Ecclesiology basing on the suggestions of Kunnumpuram. What else shall we name it but 'People' (*Laos*) Ecclesiology?

3. Five Pillars of a new Indian Ecclesiology

First, I would like to propose five pillars that would support this '*Laos*' Ecclesiology. They could be spelled out in the following:

3.1. The first Pillar is the Common priesthood and communion of all the baptized with a functional difference in the service of the community.

3.2. The second Pillar is Ecumenical one, which takes into itself the democratic elements like liberty, equality and fraternity; common decision making and participatory church elements from the brethren churches in India.

3.3. The third Pillar is the Catholic Church's Contribution of a participatory church. The Church is the assembly, where all are equal in their dignity and the difference is only in their ministry and service. This ideal is not in practice in India, except where the SCCs have been hyper active.

3.4. The fourth Pillar is the Kingdom Communion as centre for all humanity and human community formation. It is the phenomenological approach to community rather than transcendental. The Church, as part of this Kingdom Communion, is the sign and sacrament of the Kingdom of God.[8]

3.5. The fifth Pillar is the Personal salvific relationship between God and every human person.[9] The Church invites all through it for a salvific communion of the Trinitarian God. "The Church's first purpose then is to be the sacrament of the inner union of the human person with God" (*EA* 24).

Therefore, 'People' Ecclesiology is basically built on the people of God Ecclesiology from above and has people's movements to support from the base. Both People of God Ecclesiology and the Communion Ecclesiology of the Council have been collectively taken together to bring forth this new Ecclesiology.

4. The Ingredients of 'People' Ecclesiology

The first ingredient is *Ad-Intra* ingredient. This is well explained by Pope Benedict XVI. He words it Co-responsibility and Participation of every member of the Community in the mission of communion.[10] "It has pleased God, however, to make humans holy and save them not merely as individuals without any mutual bonds, but by making them into a single people which acknowledges Him in truth and serves him in holiness" (*LG* 9; *AG* 2).

The second ingredient is the *Ad-Extra* ingredient. It is well said that the Church is

> [A] lasting sure seed of unity, hope and salvation for the whole human race.... God has gathered together as one all those who in faith look upon Jesus as author of salvation and source of unity and peace, and has established them as the Church, that for each and all she may be the visible sacrament of this saving unity (*LG* 9).

It denotes Ecumenical and Interreligious dialogical dialoguing. It calls for Respect, Support and fight for religious freedom of every person. Being the 'pioneer in dialogue', the Church brings other churches and religions together in the task of realizing the Kingdom of God in complete, in all the people and in whole of the universe. Accordingly, Wesley Ariarajah, in his book, *Not Without My Neighbour*, outlines dialogue as a paradigm for ecclesiology. He asks the pertinent question: 'Why are we in mission? Is it because God is present with our neighbour or because God is absent?'[11] Furthermore, there is a growing awareness in the Church that God is at work everywhere in the world. He has been offering the whole humankind, his mercy and saving love. Hence it is possible that we call the humanity the people of God in a broader sense.[12]

The third ingredient is the Need for Radicalization in theologizing to find an apt Ecclesiology because new way of thinking of the Vatican II has not gone deep into the working of the Church.

The fourth ingredient is the Need to connect itself deeply to the Ecclesiological Tradition. Here it is Roman Catholic Tradition of a People of God Ecclesiology[13] of Vatican II, a clear shift from Institution to Mystery; from Papal Monarchy to Episcopal collegiality; from Hierarchy to People; from universal Church to Local churches; from Roman Catholicism to Christian Churches; from the one True Religion to many religions; from church to the World.[14] According to Veli-Matti Kärkkäinen, "Perhaps the most important development of Vatican II was the replacement of the old *societas perfecta* institutional-hierarchic ecclesiology, with the dynamic people of God."[15] Therefore, *Lumen Gentium* in its opening words defined Church as "sacrament or as a sign and instrument both of a very closely knit union with God and of the unity of the whole human race" (*LG* 1). This inclusiveness in understanding the Church is noteworthy. Further the dogmatic constitution spoke of the Church as the new People of God. "Christ instituted this new covenant, the New Testament, that is to say, in His Blood, calling together a people made up of Jew and gentile, making them one, not according to the flesh but in the Spirit. This was to be the new People of God" (*LG*9).

Therefore, 'People' ecclesiology is conceived to make progress in the new way of thinking of the Council. It tilts more towards people, community, co-responsibility participatory working of the Church and the like. It is surely God who is centre but this ecclesiology answers the felt need of a People-centred *Ekklesia*.

5. People (*Laos*) Ecclesiology: A Blend of Communion And Mission Charisms And Participation

For that matter 'People' Ecclesiology is a composite of Communion, Mission, Charisms and participatory Church concepts and their implications at best. It is the result of a dialogue with Communion Ecclesiology, Ecclesiology of Mission, Charismatic Ecclesiology and Participatory Ecclesiology.

The Church as Mystical Communion consists of people of faith who are united by their common participation in God's Spirit through Christ. The ties that bind are not institutional but pneumatological, communal, and personal. "The Church, from this point of view, is not in the first instance an institution or a visibly organized society. Rather it is a communion of men [*sic*], primarily interior but also expressed by external bonds of creed, worship, and ecclesiastical fellowship."[16] The experience of ecclesiastical community differs from any other community in that it has both a horizontal *and* vertical dimension.

The emphasis here is on the shared life of mutual fellowship in loving community. However, the Church is more than a friendly family of like-minded believers. There is built in this mystical communion a certain tension between the Church as a network of friendly interpersonal relationships and the Church as a mystical communion of grace. The term *koinonia* (communion) is used ambiguously to cover both, but it is not evident that the two necessarily go together. Is the Church more importantly a friendly fellowship among people or a mystical communion that has its basis in God?[17]

Obviously, friendly fellowship and mystical communion are not antithetical to one another, but neither are they the same. The appropriate metaphor for church relationships is not lovers within the same home, but travellers on the same journey. "Christians commonly experience the Church more as a companionship of fellow travellers on the same journey than as a union of lovers dwelling in the same home."[18]

5.1. Ecclesiology of Communion

Communion Ecclesiology is an approach to understanding the Church. Vatican II defines Church as communion (*LG*1, 4, 9). This means that it is community of persons. And therefore Communion Ecclesiology "focuses on relationships, whether among the persons of the Trinity, among human beings and God."[19]

Until now the term 'communion' was associated with hierarchical or ecumenical discussions. But now it is used to bringing its dynamism to spiritual sphere calling it a 'Spiritual path' (*NMI* 43). Unless we follow this *spiritual path,* external structures of communion will serve very little purpose. They would become mechanisms without a soul, 'masks' of communion rather than its means of expression and growth (*NMI* 43).

Still further, the same letter says that the Church should become *a home and school of communion* in the Third Millennium (*NMI* 43). A *home* is a place where we live and a *school* is a place where we learn. We live and learn and *vice versa*. Though *living* and *learning* as such are personal and intra-personal processes, they are essentially inter-personal realities. This Christian relationship is of double dimension; relationship with God and with my neighbour. In this way the communion lessons are learnt and lived in the Church. So, Christian life is one of intimate union with God, the Father in Jesus Christ, through the Holy Spirit and a union among the whole of humanity as the children of God in the Church.[20]

The horizons of Communion Ecclesiology extend to the communion among the bishops of world and also the dynamic relationship between the church universal and the local churches, diocese and parishes, small faith communities and parish community. As Communion Ecclesiology is popular also among the Protestants and among the Eastern Orthodox churches, it has an ecumenical facet too.

The original Ecclesiology which existed in the second and third centuries was Eucharistic. Later, Nicholas Afanassieff, a Russian priest-theologian, rediscovered this Ecclesiology. In support of this, Pope John Paul II said, "Just as the Church 'makes the Eucharist' so 'the Eucharist builds up the Church'."[21] While we find St. Paul speaking of the Eucharist as communion in the tenth, eleventh and twelfth chapters of his first letter to the Corinthians, we see Ignatius Antioch supporting unity of the Church in his writings.[22]

The Universal Ecclesiology constructed by St. Cyprian holds the local church as part in the whole. So, he is read as the fountainhead of the Universal Ecclesiology. Opposed to this Universal Ecclesiology, Eucharistic Ecclesiology holds the local church to be a complete church by itself. Here the part is not less than the whole. As a consequence *autonomy and independence of the local churches is strongly upheld by this Ecclesiology.* Here comes the question of the unity of the universal church. Unity is an intrinsic quality, for Nicholas. His Eucharistic Ecclesiology has the potential for ecumenical communion or unity.[23]

The Church is a Church of churches, a communion of communions. The bishop presiding over the Eucharist in the local church expresses the unity of love and it is true of every local church. The communion among all the Catholic bishops of the world, with the Pope as their head, symbolizes this unity of love on the level of the Church universal.[24] Then the Church is well understood as communion of communions.

The same is true with regard to the Small Christian Communities in the parish-church. The Small Christian Communities gathered in unity of love are communions in communion with the parish-church.

Such an understanding of communion extends to the Church's mission of dialogue.

> The Synod therefore renewed the commitment of the Church in Asia to the task of improving both ecumenical relations and interreligious dialogue, recognizing that building unity, working for reconciliation, forging bonds of solidarity, promoting dialogue among religions and cultures, eradicating prejudices

> and engendering trust among peoples are all essential to the Church's evangelizing mission on the continent. All this demands of the Catholic community a sincere examination of conscience, the courage to seek reconciliation and a renewed commitment to dialogue. At the threshold of the Third Millennium it is clear that the Church's ability to evangelize requires that she strive earnestly to serve the cause of unity in all its dimensions. Communion and mission go hand in hand (EA 24).

Therefore we proceed further to understand ecclesiology of mission that puts us in perspective.

5.2. Ecclesiology of Mission

Communion and mission are connected. To put it in the words of *Christi Fideles Laici,*

> Communion and mission are profoundly connected with each other, they interpenetrate and mutually imply each other, to the point that *communion represents both the source and the fruit of mission: communion gives rise to mission and mission is accomplished in communion.* It is always the one and the same Spirit who calls together and unifies the Church and sends her to preach the Gospel "to the ends of the earth" (Acts 1:8) (*CL* 32).

This 'people' is marked by a rich diversity of gender, class, education, social status, race, ethnicity, culture and so on. And this people communicate their communion to become a community. The more they "communicate from their inner being, the more personal communion becomes." Communion thus "underscores the personal and charismatic basis of communion." On the other hand it extends to the peoples who live in a socially and economically polarized situation.[25]

Communion and mission is one of the frame works of ecclesiology. The communion and mission of the Trinity is the source of the Church's communion and mission. While communion is the bond of life in the Church, the Father the Son and the Holy Spirit are a life of perfect communion. We are invited to share in God's life of communion. And still ahead there is the communion among the members of the Church like:

- The Parish – communion of households
- The Diocese – communion of parishes

- The Universal or Catholic Church – communion of Local Churches.

Then we have the communion beyond the visible Church and it is here that we accept the Church to be the communion of disciples.

Accordingly we see the mission of the Church. Though it takes many forms, the ultimate goal of the Christian mission is to widen and enrich the communion of the human family to make it completely inclusive. Therefore, the goal is to broaden the eucharistic assembly just as every gathering (communion) leads at some point to sending forth (mission). So, the purpose of going forth is to build up, to enhance the experience of communion.[26]

After Vatican II, there is a growing agreement that communion is the category that best explains the essential nature of the Church. So, there has been a flourishing of communion ecclesiologies. Perhaps there has been a less prominence to mission which is an equally important category of understanding the Church.[27]

The enlargement of the apostolate of Jesus found in the parallel gospels of Mt. 15:21-28 and Mk. 7:24-30 is significant.

Mt. 15:21-28	Mk. 7:24-30
Jesus left that place and went away to the district of Tyre and Sidon.	From there he set out and went away to the region of Tyre. He entered a house and did not want anyone to know he was there. Yet he could not escape notice,
Just then a Canaanite woman from that region came out and started shouting, "Have mercy on me, Lord, Son of David; my daughter is tormented by a demon."	But a woman whose little daughter had an unclean spirit immediately heard about him, and she came and bowed down at his feet. Now the woman was a gentile, of Syro-Phoe nician origin. She begged him to cast the demon out of her daughter.

But he did not answer at all. And his disciples came and urged him, saying, "send her away, for she keeps shouting after us." He answered, "I was sent only to the lost sheep of Israel." But she came and knelt before him saying, "Lord help me."	
He answered, it is not fare to take the children's food and throw it to the dogs." She said, "Yes, Lord, yet even the dogs eat the crumbs that fall from their masters' table."	He said to her, "Let the children be fed first, it is not fare to take the children's food and throw it to the dogs." But she answered him, "Sir, even the dogs under the table eat the children's crumbs."
Then Jesus answered her, "Woman, great is your faith! Let it be done for you as you wish." And her daughter was healed instantly.	Then he said to her, "For saying that, you may go – the demon has left your daughter." So she went home, found the child lying on the bed, and the demon gone.

It is the episode of Canaanite woman. At first Jesus replies her saying, "I was sent (the verb is *apostellein* – meaning apostolate-mission) only to the lost sheep of the house of Israel" (Mt. 15:24). He does not hesitate to make use of the derogatory remark to demarcate the Jews to be the recipients of his own apostolate. So he says, "It is not fare to take the children's bread and throw it to the dogs" (Mt. 15:26). Then the woman is confronted with a choice either to withdraw offended by Jesus' position or risk everything for the cure of her daughter. She does not care if she be considered a dog, because she does not belong to the chosen people; she does not claim for herself the bread destined for the children of Israel but only the crumbs that fall from the master's table are enough for her. Then comes the significant fact, on which we intend to place the emphasis. It is the woman's faith, in a certain sense, forcibly extends the apostolate of Jesus. And in the apostolic consciousness of Jesus there is a change that clearly states that the salvific dimension of mission is universal.[28]

Heb. 3:1 calls Jesus the apostle in the absolute sense. "Therefore, brothers and sisters, holy partners in a heavenly calling, consider that Jesus, the apostle and high priest". The same theme runs in Jn. 3:17, 34-36; 6:29, 39, 57; 8:42; 10:36 and 11:42. And so, the person and mission in Jesus is the fundamental axiom of Christology and consequently, of Christian Anthropology.[29]

Vocation, person and mission in Jesus are interlinked so much so that "Vocation expresses the person, and the person's face is fully defined only by mission."[30] In the same way we cannot understand Mother Mary, apostles Peter or Paul outside this bond between person and mission made evident by vocation. In the same way we understand our own person and our mission in the light of our vocation as Christians.

> [T]he theology of the laity re-proposes the New Testament terms decisive for the character of the Christian, i.e., of the disciple and witness of Christ, called to communicate his fascination, in the vast field of the world. In this mission the Christian's person is wholly fulfilled. Responding to the Father's loving – kindness, the person discovers, by the power of the spirit of the Risen Lord, his true face.[31]

Should we preach Jesus or should we preach the Christ? The question is not easy as it looks to be. The event of historical Jesus with his vocation and mission attested by both the Catholic tradition and the Bible is as much the content of mission as the resurrected Christ, the divine person of the Holy Trinity.

5.2.1. Essential features of an Ecclesiology of Mission

The first essential feature is the individual personal mission. The question answered here is 'who is the Church?' The Church is the communion of personal missions grouped round the mission of Mary. The second feature is the Church defined as a dual relation. First, her relation with the person-mission of Jesus Christ as her inseparable origin and second, her relation with the world to which she is constantly sent till its completion in glory. The third feature is that the Church is essentially sacramental and Eucharistic. The individual historically situated, meets his form of inclusion in Christ, at the Eucharist. Eucharist is a place, in which the event of Christ is donated to the believer and accepted by him in an act of freedom.[32]

Ecclesiology of mission is thus focused on the subject and permits the freedom of each member of the Church to be realized. It implies personal witness, which is the missionary emergency of our time.

5.2.2. The Implications

The missionary implications of communion and mission can be summed up in the words of Ecclesia in Asia. It says that the Church's evangelizing mission essentially upholds the work of communion and unity among all.

> The Synod therefore renewed the commitment of the Church in Asia to the task of improving both ecumenical relations and interreligious dialogue, recognizing that building unity, working for reconciliation, forging bonds of solidarity, promoting dialogue among religions and cultures, eradicating prejudices and engendering trust among peoples are all essential to the Church's evangelizing mission on the continent. All this demands of the Catholic community a sincere examination of conscience, the courage to seek reconciliation and a renewed commitment to dialogue. At the threshold of the Third Millennium it is clear that the Church's ability to evangelize requires that she strive earnestly to serve the cause of unity in all its dimensions. Communion and mission go hand in hand (*EA* 24).

Looking at the Church as Mystery of Communion brings in the idea of a fundamental equality of all in the community. Communion looked at from the perspective of mission would take us to the idea of everyone's participation in the mission. The expression of these would evolve a community that is informed enough to freely express its opinion publicly. And collegiality, dialogue and co-operation are also promoted.

In the spirit of the renewal of Vatican II there is a need of enhancing greater participation of the all in the pastoral administration through the participatory structures like vibrant Parish Pastoral councils, Parish Finance Committees, Diocesan Pastoral Councils and Diocesan Finance Committees.

5.3. Hans Küng – Charismatic Ecclesiology

Hans Küng, although continues to trouble the hierarchy about his criticism of the infallibility of the Pope, made a significant contribution to the Vatican II in regard to the theology of the Church as the People of God. He sees the Church as "the people of God," the whole ecclesia, and the whole fellowship of the faithful. All the faithful belong to the people of God and therefore there must be no clericalization of the Church.

> If we see the Church as the people of God, it is clear that the Church can never be merely a particular class or caste, a group of officials or a clique within the fellowship of the faithful. The Church is always and in all cases the *whole* people of God, the *whole* ecclesia, the *whole* fellowship of the faithful. Everyone belongs to the chosen race, the royal priesthood, the holy nation.[33]

Therefore, according to Küng there cannot exist the unhealthy distinction between clergy and laity which attempts to remove the decision making activity and initiative away from the lay faithful in the Church. He further adds that the "legalistic mind basically mistrusts the free operation of God's spirit in the Church because the Spirit blows where it wills and does not wait for official permission."[34] He observes that exegetically the word *Laos* does not refer to a distinction within the community between priests and people but between the people of God and the "non-people," those outside of faith.[35]

The Church, a priestly people derives its priestly function from the one continuing and eternal high priest (*LG* 10). And the place of this true priestly function is not only in a sanctuary but also in the world in the middle of everyday life, the loving service of God.[36]

On the other hand, discussing the charismatic structure of the Church, Küng is critical about the failure of Church's ecclesiology to express the pneumatic nature of the Church's structure mentioned by 1 Corinthians.[37] Charism "is God's call to the individual person in view of a specific service within the community, including the ability to perform this service."[38] There is a variety in charisms. As we see in 1 Cor. 12:28-31, charisms are not limited to the special group of persons. The clergy is near the end of the list of Church hierarchy in this passage, where it is stated that the Spirit gifts the Charisms. As also not one person possesses all charisms. Charisms are given in the service of the community. Since the needs of the community are many, there is correspondingly a variety of charisms. From here he draws support for an ecclesiology that would back the theology of the lay faithful.[39]

All what is said above could be also seen in the words of Pope John Paul II in his *Tertio Millennio Adveniente.* It reads:

> In the universal Church and in the particular Churches, is the ecclesiology of communion described in *Lumen Gentium* being strengthened? Does it leave room for charisms, ministries, and different forms of participation by the People of God, without adopting notions borrowed from democracy and sociology which do not reflect the Catholic vision of the Church and the authentic spirit of Vatican II? Another serious question is raised by the nature of relations between the Church and the world. The Council's guidelines—set forth in *Gaudium et Spes* and other documents—of open, respectful and cordial dialogue, yet accompanied by careful discernment and courageous witness to the truth, remain valid and call us to a greater commitment (*TMA* 36).

The charisms are from the Spirit, from above. However, the Spirit gives them not to isolated individual persons but to 'people'. In other words charisms are given for the good of the whole community in time and space. The prospects for a more democratized church are to be fostered by applying the principles of democracy inherent in the law of the Church itself. Even then we are not to fail to exercise restraint in the exaggeration of the same.

5.4. Miroslav Volf – Participatory Ecclesiology

Croatian Protestant theologian Miroslav Volf (Yale professor) "seeks to suggest a viable understanding of the Church in which both person and community are given their proper due."[40] This concept of participatory ecclesiology got its publicity in Volf's *After Our Likeness: The Church as the Image of the Trinity*. Volf rejects what he brands the 'episcopocentric' ecclesiology of Ratzinger and Zizioulas in favour of a 'polycentric community'.[41] According to him Paul seems to envision such a model of ecclesial life with a polycentric participative structure when he tries to re-establish peace within the enthusiastic and chaotic congregation in Corinth. "For you can all prophesy one by one, so that all may learn and all be encouraged. And the spirits of prophets are subject to the prophets, for God is a God not of disorder but of peace" (1 Cor. 14:33).[42]

According to Volf, mediation of salvation occurs not only through office-holders, but also through all other members of the church. He links this to the notion of a 'polycentric community'. This in turn leads us to a 'polycentric participative' model. Therefore, the Church does have soteriological significance but not of the sort associated with Magisterial Christianity.[43]

Ratzinger and Zizioulas understand the Trinity hierarchically and they ground the hierarchical relations within the Church basing on this understanding. Volf says,

> In following Jürgen Moltmann,[44] I by contrast take as my premise the symmetrical relations within the Trinity.... Relations between charismata, modelled after the Trinity, are reciprocal and symmetrical, all members of the Church have charismata, and all are to engage their charismata for the good of all others.[45]

This paradigm allows Volf to speak of Free Church ecclesiology. For Volf

> diachronic plurality is even more important than synchronic...the charismata with which these members serve in the congregation can change, certain charismata come to the fore at certain times, while others become unimportant. Members who are "passive" are not truly "charismatic" even though "there are no members without charisma".[46]

In the final analysis of Volf's ecclesiology, we can sympathize with his point that too much is given away to ordained ministers. However, we cannot dismiss the concept of leadership that goes beyond the local church that has been held dear by Roman Catholics. What we can take in dialogue with this ecclesiology is the participation of 'People'. 'People' both as person and community cannot be passive. Each member of the Church has charism and is called to engage his/her charism for the good of all others. Likewise is each church.

6. Papal Interventions

The Popes have time and again made statements in regard to the 'People' issues in the Church. Their vision is enlarged by the years in line with the new way of thinking of the Council. With regard to the relationship between clergy and the lay faithful, their vocabulary moves from collaboration to co-responsibility recognizing everyone a 'missionary disciple'.

6.1. Pope John Paul II- Collaboration of the Faithful

The 1997 instruction from the Holy See entitled "On Certain Questions Regarding Collaboration of the Lay Faithful in the Ministry of Priests" is singled out for it well represents the predominant thinking of the magisterium on the relation of the laity and ordained within the Church's unity. With the weight of papal authority, the instruction seeks to reinforce the essential difference between the clergy and laity in the light of a perceived blurring of the boundaries in ministry that risks "serious negative consequences" including damage to a "correct understanding of true ecclesial communion." While affirming the common priesthood of all the baptised and setting the ministerial priesthood within that context and recognising a legitimate diversity in ministerial functions, the instruction nevertheless promotes a theology of the laity.

6.2. Pope Benedict XVI - Call to Co-Responsibility

Pope Benedict XVI in his address to diocese of Rome on 26 May 2009 spoke of 'co-responsibility' as an appropriate hermeneutic through which to understand the role of the lay faithful in the Church.

> [I]n such a way that the co-responsibility of all the members of the people of God in their entirety is gradually promoted with respect to vocations and for the respective roles of the consecrated and lay people. This demands a change in mind set, particularly concerning lay people. They must no longer be viewed as 'collaborators' of the clergy but truly recognized as 'co-responsible' for the church's being and action, thereby fostering the consolidation of a mature and committed laity.[47]

He adds the following remarks:

> It is therefore important that a mature and committed laity be consolidated that can make its own specific contribution to the ecclesial mission with respect to the ministries and tasks that each one has in the life of the church and always in cordial communion with the bishops.[48]

6.3. Pope Francis – Missionary Discipleship of All the Members of the People of God

Pope Francis in his apostolic exhortation *Evangelii Gaudium* insists on the missionary responsibility of all the members of the people of God. He says:

> In virtue of their baptism, all the members of the People of God have become missionary disciples (cf. Mt. 28:19). All the baptized, what-ever their position in the Church or their level of instruction in the faith, are agents of evan-gelization, and it would be insufficient to envis-age a plan of evangelization to be carried out by professionals while the rest of the faithful would simply be passive recipients. The new evangeli-zation calls for personal involvement on the part of each of the baptized. Every Christian is chal-lenged, here and now, to be actively engaged in evangelization; indeed, anyone who has truly ex-perienced God's saving love does not need much time or lengthy training to go out and proclaim that love. Every Christian is a missionary to the extent that he or she has encountered the love of God in Christ Jesus: we no longer say that we are "disciples" and "missionaries", but rather that we are always "missionary disciples." (*EG* 120).

The words like co-responsibility, the people of God, disciples and missionary disciples are a welcome step towards understanding and accepting the Church as a 'People' and its complete implications. We may expect much more from the present pope, who called himself 'Bishop of Rome' on his election to the office.

7. The Church as Radical Democratic Assembly of Equals?

Coming to the discussion on the Church as radical democratic assembly of equals, we find the clergy-laity divide and the consequent lack of power-sharing in the Church is observed today. The reasons could be the apathy and inertia in the bulk of the clergy.

> There is, to be sure, a small but a growing number of lay people who are clamouring for a say in the decision making process in the Church.... This is in stark contrast to what is happening in the secular society. A large number of Catholics are making significant contributions in the professions, the media, the civil services, the police and the armed forces.[49]

All initiative and power is thus in the hands of a priest. Therefore, there is a need for empowering the laity in the right sense in the Church.

In the New Testament vocabulary we do not find any distinction between the clergy and the lay people. Such a distinction came about in the 1st century with Clement of Rome, who spoke about '*Laikos*' who are distinguished from the high priest, the priests and the Levites. This distinction was based on the functions and did not go against the communion of the then Corinthian community. Despite the new term there was actually no clergy-laity divide during the patristic period. However some significant change took place during the Middle Ages. There developed a view that clergy are spiritual and the laity are carnal, worldly. The Council of Trent stressed the hierarchical structure of the Church, while totally ignoring the universal priesthood of the believers. By the 19th century the idea prevalent that priests possessed sacred power aggravated the clergy-laity divide. But by the first half of the 20th century 'Catholic Action', which was described as the collaboration of the laity in the apostolate of the hierarchy, emerged strongly. This meant that the laity had no apostolate of their own.[50]

This changed with the great Council. And today the laity are longing for a truly participatory Church, a democratic rule in the Church. The readymade answer would be that the Church is not a democracy. However, *Gaudium et Spes* wants that the structures of the Church must be enriched keeping in view the signs of the times.

> Since the Church has a visible and social structure as a sign of her unity in Christ, she can and ought to be enriched by the development of human social life. The reason is not that the constitution given her by Christ is defective, but so that she may understand it more penetratingly, express it better, and adjust it more successfully to our times (*GS* 44).

Rudolf Pesch finds the New Testament Church built on a democratic form of life that is, "a life of liberty, equality and fraternity."[51] Joining him is Raymond Brown agrees that participative decision-making was prevalent in the early Church. According to Brown, in Acts 6:1-6 and 15:1-12, Luke has described the collective decision making on major issues.[52]

Talking about the same in the post-New Testament period, Yves Congar states that when he was preparing his book on the Laity in 1950-52, "I discovered everywhere in each generation and in four spheres of faith, worship, the apostolate and the Church's social life, a union between the hierarchical structure and the communal exercise of all Church activities."[53] It was St. Cyprian of 3rd century, who declared:

> I have made it a rule, ever since the beginning of my episcopate, to make no decision merely on the strength of my own personal opinion without consulting you (the presbyters and the deacons), without the approbation of the people.[54]

And when we come to the 13th century, even the authoritarian popes adhered to the principle of the Roman law which says, "Whatever affects everybody ought to be corporately approved by everybody."[55]

The Catholic Bishop's Conference of India (CBCI) general body meeting of 1996 at Thiruvananthapuram, in its response of the CBCI evaluation report declared:

> We reiterate our sincere desire to improve and perfect the movements towards a truly participatory Church where all sections of the People of God, revitalizing their baptismal grace, fulfil their vocation and mission.... In this context we emphasize the importance of involving all sections of the Church, especially the laity, and reposing greater confidence in them, in order to bring about a mature, participatory Church.[56]

A participatory Church, is in the practice of non-dominating leadership "which is most effective in bringing out the best in others." It requires in the leaders "an attitude of trust in our people, appreciating their reliability and competence."[57] The CBCI strongly recommends the establishment of parish and diocesan pastoral councils restructuring the Catholic Council of India, a body that represents all sections of the Catholic community.[58] Parish and diocesan finance councils are already mandatory. The diocesan priests' council is another democratic structure of participatory decision making.

Pope John Paul II identifies the selection of community leaders to be part of a democratic principle (c.147, 1752). Consultations provide more realistic channel for increasing the participation of the whole Church.

Accountability is another added principle of democracy in the running of the Church. This ensures the seriousness of the accountability of the Church leaders and the participation of the members of the Church in their selection.

Conclusion

If the Church has to be called a democratic assembly, it is possible only in the matter of administration and not in the matters of faith. It is possible to apply the idea of democracy to the Church by way of the equal status of the whole people of God in the Church. It is because of their one baptism. It brings in the beautiful picture of a participatory Church that sees all its members co-responsible for its mission and running of the *whole* Church.

Endnotes:

[1] Antonio Spadaro, "A Big Heart Open to God: The Exclusive Interview with Pope Francis," *America: The National Catholic Review* 30 September 2013, http://americamagazine.org/pope-interview, (accessed December 12, 2013). Antonio Spadaro is the editor in chief of *La Civiltà Cattolica,* a journal published in Rome by the Society of Jesus since 1850.

[2] Cf. *Lumen Gentium,* Chapter 2.

[3] "Just as in the first millennium the Cross was planted on the soil of Europe, and in the second on that of the Americas and Africa, we can pray that in the Third Christian Millennium *a great harvest of faith* will be reaped in this vast and vital continent," said Pope John Paul II in his Address to the Sixth Plenary Assembly of the Federation of Asian Bishops' Conferences (FABC), Manila (15 January 1995), 11: *Insegnamenti* XVIII, 1 (1995), 159, Quoted in *Ecclesia in Asia,* no.1.

[4] "Democracy," http://www.merriam-webster.com/dictionary/democracy, (accessed December 12, 2013).

[5] Michael Amaladoss, *Making All Things New: Mission in Dialogue* (Maryknoll: Orbis Books, 1989), 132.

[6] Kuncheria Pathil, "Theology of the Local Church," *Jeevadhara* 28 (1998): 278.

[7] Kurien Kunnumpuram, *The Indian Church of the Future* (Mumbai: St. Pauls, 2007), 7.

[8] Cf. Simon Pinto, *Theology of Interreligious Dialogue for a Multi-Religious Context in India* (Rome: Urbaniana, 2013), 134-144.

[9] Ibid., 134f.

[10] Benedict XVI, "Address to Diocese of Rome," 26 May 2009, available at http://www.vatican.va/holy_father/benedict_xvi/speeches/2009/may/documents/hf_ben-xvi_spe_20090526_convegno-diocesi-rm_en.html, (accessed December 01, 2013).

[11] S. Wesley Ariarajah, *Not Without My Neighbour: Issues in Inter-Faith Relations* (Geneva: WCC, 1999), 129.

[12] Kunnumpuram, *The Indian Church of the Future,* 119.

[13] Veli-Matti Kärkkäinen, *An Introduction to Ecclesiology: Ecumenical, Historical and Global* Perspectives (Downers Grove: Inter Varsity Press, 2002), 26.

[14] Kunnumpuram, *The Indian Church of the Future,* 81-108.

[15] Kärkkäinen, *An Introduction to Ecclesiology: Ecumenical, Historical and Global Perspectives,* 22.

[16] Avery Dulles, *Models of the Church: Expanded Edition* (New York: Image Books, 1987), 55.

[17] Ibid., 60f.

[18] Ibid., 61.

[19] M. Dennis Doyle, *Communion Ecclesiology: Visions and Versions* (Maryknoll: Orbis Books, 2000), 12.

[20] Anthony Kochalumakal, "Growing Together and Going Together: At the Source of Spirituality of Communion," *Third Millennium* 9, no. 2 (2006): 79f.

[21] John Paul II, *Dominicae Cenae.*

[22] Cf. John Kudiyiruppil, "The Ecumenical Potential of Eucharistic Theology," *The Living Word* 108, no. 5 (2002): 296-302.

[23] Ibid., 305f.

[24] Ibid., 307.

[25] Michael Nai-Chiu Poon, "Communicating Communion: Contextualising in a Globalising Asia-Pacific," *Asia Journal of Theology* 27 (2013): 179-80.

[26] Pelzel Morris, *Ecclesiology: The Church as Communion and Mission* (Chicago: Loyola Press, 2001), 4.

[27] Ibid., 5.

[28] Angelo Scola, "The Mission of the Church at the Dawn of the Third Millennium," in *Laity Today*, ed. Pontifical Council for the Laity (Vatican: Libreria Editrice Vaticana, 2002), 94f.

[29] Ibid., 95f.

[30] Ibid., 96.

[31] Ibid., 97.

[32] Ibid., 101-107.

[33] Hans Küng, *The Church* (New York: Image Books, 1976), 169.

[34] Hans Küng, "The Charismatic Structure of the Church," in *The Church and Ecumenism, Concilium*, ed. Hans Küng, vol. 4 (New York: Paulist Press, 1965), 41.

[35] Küng, *The Church,* 170.

[36] Ibid., 478.

[37] Küng, "The Charismatic Structure of the Church," 47.

[38] Ibid., 59; Küng, *The Church*, 247.

[39] Ibid., 55-57; Küng, *The Church*, 239-246.

[40] Kärkkäinen, *An Introduction to Ecclesiology*, 134.

[41] Miroslav Volf, *After our Likeness: The Church as the Image of the Trinity* (Grand Rapids: William B. Eerdmans Publishing Company, 1998), 224.

[42] Ibid., 224f.

[43] Ibid., 227, 236.

[44] Jürgen Moltmann, presents a stirring vision which every Christian community could well ponder. With a missionary emphasis, he seeks to help the reader face the question of the church's identity in the light of the contemporary political, economic, and social scene. He calls his ecclesiology Messianic Ecclesiology. Ref. Jürgen Moltmann, *The Church in the Power of the Spirit: A Contribution to Messianic Ecclesiology* (Minneapolis: Augsburg Fortress Press, 1993).

[45] Volf, *After our Likeness: The Church as the Image of the Trinity,* 236.

[46] Ibid., 227.

[47] Benedict XVI, "Address to Diocese of Rome," 26 May 2009, available at http://www.vatican.va/holy_father/benedict_xvi/speeches/2009/may/documents/hf_ben-xvi_spe_20090526_convegno-diocesi-rm_en.html, (accessed December 12, 2013).

[48] Ibid.

[49] Kunnumpuram, *The Indian Church of the Future,* 147.

[50] Ibid., 148-153.

[51] Rudolf Pesch, "The New Testament Foundation of a Democratic Form of Life in the Church," *Concilium* 3 (1971): 48f.

[52] Raymond E. Brown, *Priests and* Bishop (London: Geoffrey Chapmann, 1971), 58f.

[53] Yaves Congar, *Lay People in the Church* (London: Geoffrey Chapmann, 1965), 43.

[54] Ibid.

[55] Ibid., 35.

[56] CBCI, "Response of the General Body to CBCI Evaluation Report," *Catholic India* (1996): 24.

[57] Ibid., 25.

[58] Ibid., 24F.

Chapter 16
The Significance of Communication in *Ekklesia*

Tinumeren Ozukum

Introduction

Communication today is so intimately related to the life and mission of the church and has become so indispensable a dimension of apostolate that there does not exist anymore question whether church should pay attention to communication. Rather the question today is why and how should church get involved in social communication.[1] This is one single reason among many why communication today becomes a matter of deep theological concern and church responsibility.

While on the other hand, *ekklesia* has originated in the Trinitarian communication that overflowed into the world through many and varied ways and finally the word-became-flesh. Church is by nature a community of communicators. From the moment of its origin, church has always used the best means of communication at its disposal. The scripture and the many manuscripts, liturgies, sacraments and rituals, art and architectures are all clear examples of how church was the leading communicator in all centuries. Even in modern times, church was the first one to use the mass media of printing and radio.[2]

On the basis of the New Testament conception of the church that is from *ekklesia,* the following constitutive elements may be said to belong essentially to it:[3]

a) the word of God, which initially calls men/women to faith and subsequently builds them up into truly Christian communities,

b) the activity of the Holy Spirit which vivifies the community from within,

c) faith in Christ sealed and externally manifested in baptism,

d) the Eucharistic fellowship of the worshipping community,

e) the officially designated special ministry of the word and the sacraments and,

f) the communion of all local congregation in a closely knit fellowship of mutual concern and service. These are the massive blocks that build up the church of Jesus Christ.

With this assumption I would like to discuss the common features of communication and *Ekklesia*, that is community building and equal participation for which the new forms of communication has been discussed to bring out the new understanding of the nature of *Ekklesia* from the communication perspective.

Common Features of Communication and *Ekklesia*

The definition of communication and *ekklesia* go parallel because both have same purpose, that is, to bring together for common purpose. The word *ekklesia* in a simple way means a local congregation of Christians. Although we often speak of these congregation collectively as the New Testament church or the early church, no New Testament writer uses *ekklesia* in this collective way. An *ekklesia* was a meeting or assembly. Its most common use was for the public assembly of citizens.

One of the major objectives of communication is to bring people together or assemble for fellowship. In which, group communication has its unique way, because group is not just any collection or aggregate of persons. Groupness emerges from the relationship among the people involved. A group traditionally has been defined as "an assemblage of persons who communicate, in order to fulfil a common purpose and achieve a goal.[4] These bring the meaning of *ekklesia* of Jn. 13:34-35 and Jn. 17:20-26! The Divine unity enjoyed eternal fellowship. The Son is beloved by the Father and the Father is loved by the Son. The Spirit is one with the Father and Son. They had a shared life in absolute unity.

It is true that, *ekklesia* was introduced since the time God created Adam and Eve's family, it was the beginning of fellowship. Because a family is an assemblage of people who have legally been declared a group, in fact it is one of the primary groups in which most of us participate. Families are group operating system by the very nature of their purpose and functions, decision making, interpersonal relationship, and mutual dependency. The Gospels tell us that Jesus chose 12 disciples who became the foundation of this new people. The correspondence to the 12 tribes of Israel is clear, and shows that the church was understood both as grounded in Judaism and as the fulfilment of God's intention in calling Israel to become "a light to the nations, that my salvation may reach to the end of the earth" (Isa. 49: 6; Rom. 11: 1-5). It is this recognition that allows Paul to call this new Gentile-Jewish community, this new creation, "the Israel of God" (Gal. 6: 15, 16).

In this new community the traditional barriers of race, social standing and sex- barriers that divided people from one another and categorized them into inferior and superior classes- are seen to be shattered (Gal. 3: 28).[5] The internal, cohesive force of the young Christian community is expressed in the New Testament by the word *Koinonia* used by Paul for the religious fellowship or participation of the believers in Christ. Christians, through faith in Christ, are called to fellowship in the Son (1 Cor. 1:9); when gathered together as an *ekklesia* for worship they all share the same body and blood of the Lord (1 Cor. 10:16), they enjoy the fellowship of the spirit (2 Cor. 13:13). And it is precisely this vertical fellowship with God that brings about the horizontal fellowship among Christians. The union and communion of the faithful among themselves stem from their communion with God, their *Ekklesia* is deeply rooted in God.

Christian communities are congregations of men and women, but at the same time they form the church of God. The origin of the church does not lie with human but with God. Christians accept in faith the divine summons to fellowship but they have no control over God's call which necessarily precedes their response in faith.[6] This is exactly the principles of communication; Communication is one of God's gifts to humanity, the gift that binds individuals together into communities, and communities into one human family. It is the gift that exists from the beginning of the universe. The capacity for sharing the love with God and with one another is the foundation of our human community.

Communication Method for *Ekklesia*

Schramm's[7] understanding of communication is deeply rooted in his notion of society, and he affirms that communication is the tool that makes societies possible. Society, for him, is a sum of relationships in which information of some kind is shared. He adds:

> Human communication is something people do. It has no life of its own. There is no magic about it except what people in the communication relationship put into it. There is no meaning in a message except what people-relating to one another and to their groups, organizations, and societies; influencing one another; being influenced; informing and being informed; teaching and being taught; entertaining and being entertained. To understand humancommunication, we must understand how people relate to one another.[8]

The core of Schramm's renewed understanding recognizes communication as relationship, a sharing, rather than something someone does to someone else. When this relationship works effectively, it results in what he calls a kind of "in tune-ness". On the contrary, when it works poorly it bears disunity, misunderstanding and sometimes hostility. However it works, Schramm concludes, "this is the process that allows us to form the images in our heads that map our environments and guide our behaviour."[9]

This method of communication offered a clear objective for any organization and committee, because communication always takes place for building community and for the common purpose and goal. *Ekklesia* is also the place where people come together as community with same attitude to communicate and share a common purpose.

In 1986 the World Association for Christian Communication (WACC) under the leadership of its General Secretary Hans W. Florin adopted the Christian Principles of Communication. Through the Christian Principles, WACC challenged the secular ethos of the age by insisting that communication is a function of transcendence. The introduction of the Christian Principles observes that "Communication remains God's great gift to humanity, without which we cannot be truly human."[10]

Communication Creates Community of *Ekklesia*

The most important New Testament term for Christ-confessing communities is the Greek word *ekklesia*; it is applied to individual house churches, to the area churches that perhaps consist of several house churches, and to all believers in Christ.[11] The Christ confession *ekklesia* is an assembly in which its members come together, and it is a community or group whose members are bound together even outside their actual meetings through reciprocal social interaction.[12] However, in the history of the church, we see that it has accommodated itself rather easily to poverty, slavery, racism, oppression of women, casteism, etc. we have often been catering to their victims with charity, without challenging the structures.[13]

Philip Lee while defining that, 'Communication creates community' states that, "A Community of people and nations, as well as a community of different churches and religions, has to emerge and cooperate if the world's pluralistic and multicultural societies are to survive."[14] Hence, "Genuine communication can revitalize a sense of belonging and rekindle community spirit, because the model for such communication is participatory and inclusive, rather than one-way and exclusive,"[15] says Philip Lee. Thus genuine communication builds trust, that in the building of trust, communities are strengthened and that when communities are strengthened the participants find themselves in communion, building trust and this creates and further strengthens the community. It also further helps to develop a spirit of togetherness, mutual help and concern for each other.

It is clear from the New Testament as a whole that the Christian community understood itself as the community of the end time, as the community called into being by God's end-time act of revelation and divine presence in Jesus of Nazareth. So, Paul tells the Christians in Corinth that they are those "upon whom the end of the ages has come" (1 Cor. 10:11). That is, God had visited his creation, had called out of both Judaism and the Gentile world a new people, empowered by his Spirit to be present in the world, sharing the good news of his radical, unconditional love for his creation (Eph. 2:11-22).[16] Therefore, it appears that like most of the Jews, the evangelist and his Christian Jewish community did not dare mix freely with the Gentiles for fear of a breach of the dietary and purity laws. This may explain the small number of

Gentiles in the community of Matthew. Yet the negative attitude of the community towards the Gentiles is not sufficiently explained by the minimal contacts that existed due to religious adherence. This makes us think of another possibility that the Matthean community should have suffered even persecution at the hands of the Gentiles.[17]

As Community of the Spirit

Luke-Acts presents the church as that community of people in which and through which the Spirit of God is working. As Jesus is empowered for his mission by the Spirit (Lk. 4:1-13, 28-30), so the early Christian community is empowered for its witness to the world (Acts 1:8). As Jesus, empowered by the Spirit, proclaims the good news and touches the lives of people with reconciliation, release, and restoration (Lk. 4:18, 19), so the church is empowered by the Spirit to become a community of caring and sharing (Acts 2: 43-47; 4: 31-37). As Jesus, the man of the Spirit, reaches out to the weak, poor and rejects of the Palestinian society, a special emphasis throughout Luke's Gospel, so the community of Spirit is concerned with concrete human need (Acts 6:1-6). These parallels could be multiplied; they illustrate Luke's understanding of the oneness of Jesus' ministry with that of the church. The latter is the extension of the former, yet is impossible without that foundation provided in Jesus' own ministry.[18]

***Ekklesia* is Participatory**

WACC's documents on the Principles of Christian Communication, brings out the fact that, "Mass communication tend to be organised along one-way lines; it flows from top to bottom, from the centre to the periphery, from the few to the many, and it trickles down from the "information rich" to "information poor". To some extent, and depending on the context, the mass media are exclusive in their choice of subjects and the way they are treated.[19] Participatory communication is fundamentally inclusive. It is multi-directional, opens dialogue, exchange of ideas, flexibility of thought. Participation also leads to transparency and mutual accountability as people understand their responsibilities in the context of the welfare of their communities. Moreover, participatory communication is a core in *ekklesia* to hold the promise of empowering people to gain greater control over their context and the enjoyment of a fuller life.

However, the emergence of a truly participatory church in India will have great witnessing power for a country that has a history of a priestly caste that for centuries has oppressed and dominated over dalits and of a rich and powerful elite that has exploited the poor. Evils of discrimination are all pervasive. Thus, while the church raises her prophetic voice against such evils, *ekklesia* in modern term "church" is equally called to build an egalitarian society where there is no place for power and domination but only a participative community.[20]

New forms of Communication

The church today is witnessing the emergence of new forms of communication within the Christian community, which takes into consideration not only the power of reason but also the realm of emotions, feelings and perceptions. The great appeal of charismatic movements, Christian communities, spiritual conventions, cultural celebrations of faith, sharing of faith in affinity groups, etc., are some examples for this.[21] At the same time today, with the growth of the web, new forms of communication are becoming dominant. Old methods of communication are impacted by this change. Technology's growth creates behavioural and organizational change in deep ways. Organizations need to see that the impact from the web is larger than the technology itself because it reflects a new worldview. There has been a change in how new generations see the world. In his 1993 book, *Post-Capitalist Society*, the late Peter Drucker worded it this way:

> Every few hundred years in Western history, there occurs a sharp transformation... within a few short decades, society rearranges itself – its worldview; its basic values; its social and political structure; its arts; its key institutions.... Fifty years later, there is a new world and the people born then cannot even imagine the world in which their grandparents lived and into which their own parents were born. We are currently living through just such a transformation.[22]

Communication is unitive, it brings what is 'mine' and 'yours' into 'ours', so that not only what we share become common, we ourselves also become a community. The nature of the community (or communion) clearly depends on what we share and holds in common. The more we communicate from our inner being, the more personal communion becomes. The well-being of a community depends on how well its members communicate. Therefore, communication is not only about technique; it is what it is to be human.[23] The Christian faith tells us that communication and communion are God's gift for humanity. In fact, communication and communion are central to God's own being. So, the triune God is ground of our being; and Christian life is the communion of the Holy Spirit.[24]

New understanding of the nature of the *Ekklesia*

The realization that the church is above all a community called to communion, has to bring changes in the leadership style. The leaders of the church have to take the teachings of the church on social communication seriously and mould themselves and those whom they train for *ekklesial* leadership in effective communication skills. Jesus is their model communicator in this process of communicating in the cultural idioms of the people they serve. Every new medium especially those available in the cyberspace must be used to communicate God's love.[25]

Development reveals some of the ways cultural territories diversify and expand in a world where people and images move about at breakneck speed. In truth, culture and tradition have never been motionless; they are always reinvented by subsequent generation. But the cultural environment we live in today are changing in unprecedented ways and in greater measure than ever before. Immigration, urbanization, and technology all fuel the turmoil. Cultural categories, contexts, assumptions, allegiances and relevancies are all shifting madly about. World cultures are being continuously re-contextualized into new provinces of meaning.[26] As such, the information highway is the promise of a renewed sense of community and in many instances, new types and formations of community. It appears likely that computer-mediated communication can happen by way of electronic path-ways that cement roads were unable to do. Such a communication must connect us rather than atomize us, put us at the control of a "vehicle" and yet not detach us from the rest of the world.[27]

Conclusion

The society we live in is an age of media technological revolution and this has become vital for the effective operation of life in its various spheres. Today, information technology of communication have become determining factors in shaping peoples cultural, social, religious and ethical spheres. On the other hand, *Ekklesia* is also very much concerned with itsprinciples on equal participation and building community, the platform for which is provided by these new forms of communication. Defne Sabanes Plou points out rightly that "Human communication is interactive, and technology should be a tool to aid that interactivity. It should not be used to exploit or subordinate people."[28] Communication which is the core of *ekklesia* fulfils the interactive elements of human communication.

As discussed above the new forms of communication has laid the foundation for *ekklesia* which can be understood as a continuation and strengthening of the participatory communication. The aim of this participatory approach is to build awareness, consciousness, facilitate conscientisation and mobilisation of people for sharing common as well as divergent ideas. There is a direct connection between communication and *ekklesia* that enable us to participate actively of all in the social, religious, economic, cultural and political life of the community.

Endnotes:

[1] Joseph Palakeel, *Towards Communication Theology* (Bangalore: Asian Trading Corporation, 2003), 10.

[2] Ibid., 9.

[3] Luis M. Bermejo, *Church Conciliarity & Communion* (Gujarat: Gujarat Sahitya Prakashan, 1990), 38.

[4] Roy M. Berko, Andrew D. Wolvin, and Darlyn R. Wolvin, *Communicating a Social and Career Focus*, ninth ed. (Boston: Houghton Mifflin Company, 2004), 236.

[5] Manfred T. Brauch, "Church," in *Baker Encyclopaedia of the Bible*, ed. Walter A. Elwell, vol. 1, (Grand Rapids: Baker Books House Company, 1988), 459.

[6] Bermejo, *Church Conciliarity & Communion*, 38.

[7] Wilbur Schramm (1907-1987) is considered one of the key proponents of communication research in the 20th century for his remarkable contribution to a better understanding of human communication theory and interpersonal communication, knowledge, paradigm and curriculum development.

[8] Jacob Srampickal, *Communications Can Renew the Church* (Kochi: Karunikan Books, 2009), 177.

[9] Ibid., 177f.

[10] Dennis A. Smith, "A Latin American Pilgrimage : Personal Reflection on Ecumenism and the Christian Principles of Communication," in *Christian Communication: Ecumenical Challenges in the 21st Century*, ed. Samuel Meshack (Yogyakarta: WACC, 2011), 13.

[11] Ekkehard W. Stegemann and Wolfgand Stegemann, *The Jesus Movement: A Social History of Its First Century*, trans. O. C. Dean Jr. (Minneapolis: Augusburg Fortress Press, 1999), 262.

[12] Ibid., 264.

[13] Michael Amaladoss, *A Call to Community* (Gujarat: Gujarat Sahitya Prakashan, 1994), 119.

[14] Philip Lee, "Communication for Ecumenism Building Living Bridges," in *Christian Communication: Ecumenical Chanllenges in the 21st Century*, ed. Samuel Meshack (Yogyakarta: WACC, 2011), 43.

[15] Ibid.

[16] Brauch, "Church," 459.

[17] Stanislas Savarimuthu, *A Community in Search of Its Identity* (Delhi: ISPCK, 2007), 31f.

[18] Brauch, "Church," 459.

[19] WACC Document on "Christian Principles of Communication."

[20] Antony D'Cruz O. Praem, "Towards a New Humanity: Kurien Kunnumpuram Revisited," in *Commited to the Church and the Country*, ed. Kuruvilla Pandikattu, James Ponniah, and Thomas Kuriacose (Delhi: ISPCK, 2013), 9.

[21] Srampickal, *Communications Can Renew the Church*, 259.

[22] Drew Goodmanson, "Communication 3.0 Trends That Will Impact Your Ministry," http://www.goodmanson.com/category/church-technology/ekklesia/ (accessed February 26, 2014).

[23] Michael Nai-Chiu Poon, "Communicating Communion: Contextualising in a Globalising Asia-Pacific," *The Asia Journal of Theology* 27, no. 2 (2013): 179.

[24] Ibid., 180.

[25] Srampickal, *Communications Can Renew the Church*, 259.

[26] James Lull, *Media, Communication, Cultural: A Global Approach* (Cambridge: Cambridge Polity Press, 1996), 145.

[27] Steven G. Jones, "Understanding Community in the Information Age," in *Cyber Society*, ed. Steven G. Jones (New Delhi: SAGE Publication, 1995), 10.

[28] Defne Sabanes Plou, *Global Communication: Is There a Place for Human Dignity?* (Geneva: WCC, 1996), 73.

Chapter 17
Towards a New *Ecclesia*: Re-Reading the Concept of 'Ecclesia' in the Bible; A Few Pointers

Roger Gaikwad

Pierre Berton published a book in 1965 entitled, *The Comfortable Pew: A Critical Look at Christianity and the Religious Establishment in the New Age.* In a nutshell, the author accuses the Church of forgetting its main identity and what it first stands for. Broadly speaking, there are two main issues with the church. Firstly, the Church has become institutionalized in the sense that it is more concerned about conformity and keeping the *status quo*. Secondly, the Church is in danger of being fossilized because of its inability to say relevant to the people and the society at large. Both of these contribute to the crisis of the Church. **Who is killing the churches?** is the thought-provoking title of another book. **The answer is rather shocking. It says that God, yes is killing the churches,** because they have ceased to serve the purpose for which they were established. Remember the judgment on the *ecclesia* in Laodicea, "I know your works: you are neither cold nor hot...I will spew you out of my mouth (Rev. 3:15-16) and the warning of Jesus: "I tell you, many will come from east and west and will eat with Abraham and Isaac and Jacob in the kingdom of heaven, while the heirs of the kingdom (the self- righteous Jews who claimed to be the ecclesia of God) will be thrown into the outer darkness" (Mt. 8:11-12).

Hence it is but essential for us to examine our understanding of the nature and the purpose of the Church afresh. Let us begin by looking at a popular understanding of the concept of "*ecclesia*" in the Bible. Christians have usually related the word *ecclesia* with a body of believers in Jesus Christ. For example, J. B. Norris identifies five main uses of the word *ekklçsia* in the New Testament.[3] First, the term refers to the original body of believers in Jerusalem (Acts 5:11); secondly, it is used of various communities of believers, like those subsequently formed in the different cities of the Roman

Empire (1 Thess. 1: 1); thirdly (but rarely), it is used of a partial assembly of a larger group of believers (3 Jn. 6); fourthly, it refers to the community of believers throughout the world, the body of Christ, (Eph. 1: 22); and lastly, it is sometimes used of a house-meeting, as in Philemon verse 2 or Col. 4: 15.

In the sense of being a united body of believers, any religious community could be dais to be an *ecclesia*. For example, a Buddhist prayer states: "We are solemnly gathered in the presence of the Buddha of External Light and Life to sing his praises and to hear his Words of Wisdom so that our lives may be brightened in the knowledge of his presence and that the Path of Truth may be revealed before us. May his great Compassion embrace us all. *Namu Amida Butsu*." Similarly the Adi Granth declares, "*Sat Sangat* (holy congregation) is the treasury of Divine Name; There we meet God; Through the Grace of Guru, One receives there Light and all darkness is dispelled."[4] So also the Mishnah declares: "If two sit together and the words between them are of Torah, then the Shechinah is in their midst." In like fashion, in Islam, Forty Hadith of an-Nawawi 36 observes: "And when a company meets together in one of themselves, the Shechinah comes down to them and mercy overshadows them, the angels surround them, and God remembers them among them that are Hits."

Such understandings of the term *ecclesia* conjure traditional images of churches or religious bodies as being sacred gatherings of devout God-fearing people who read the Scriptures, enjoy times of fellowship together, and engage in meritorious acts of service while they live in a society that functions according to its own structures and practices. When such gatherings become routine, the cutting edge of the life and witness of *ecclesia* is blunted and the *status quo* in society is hardly changed. The impact of the Church which is called to be the salt of the earth and the light of the world (Mt. 5:13-14) is minimized.

In an endeavour to relevantly and dynamically interpret the concept of *ecclesia,* an attempt is made here to look at three important perspectives for our reflection.

Ecclesia: A Secular yet Spiritual calling! (An Activist Perspective)

In its day to day usage in ancient society, "ecclesia" stood for the political assembly of citizens of a Greek state. According to the *Encyclopedia Britannica, ecclesia* was the name given to the governmental assembly of the city of Athens, duly convoked (called out) by proper officers and possessing all political power including ever juridical functions. Even the *Oxford Universal English Dictionary* states that the term 'ecclesia' originates from Medieval Latin and Greek words meaning "summoned," and so the term "ecclesia" in its original historical context denoted a regularly convoked assembly, especially the general assembly of Athenians. We find indications of this usage in Acts 19, where the term "ecclesia" occurs three times (Acts 19: 32, 39, 41). In all these usages, "ecclesia" refers to a town council: a civil body in Ephesus.

Yet this term *ecclesia* came to be used for the Christian Church or congregation. What, then, did the writers of the New Testament mean when they used the word "ecclesia" to describe a Christian body of People? It could be assumed, as one article puts it[5] that they intended to convey the original Greek meaning of the word: **a body of Christians called out of the Roman and Judean system to come together into a separate civil community.** It meant a politically autonomous body of Christians under no king but Jesus; under no other jurisdiction but that of Jesus. No other ruled them! Only Christ! And that was the reason these same Christians ran into trouble with kings and rulers; they were arrested, crucified and martyred.

In Acts 17, verses 1- 6 we see that Paul and Silas had a reputation that preceded them. They were "turning the world (system) upside down." What was their inflammatory message? The answer is found in verse 7: "Whom Jason has received them (into his house): and these all do contrary to the decrees of Caesar, saying that there is another King, one Jesus." They were announcing another King! Not Caesar! This was a king who was bigger that Caesar. **They were forming civil bodies that no longer looked to Caesar as their King.** Paul and Silas were not "church builders" like preachers today claim. They were not proselytizing people from one church or synagogue to another. They were 'kingdom' builders! They were dethroning rulers in the minds of the people and alienating them from the mental hold Caesar had upon them through his "empire" government. They were teaching the principles of Christian government they were putting forth the call of God to whoever would hear and obey, and those whose hearts responded to the call became citizens of Christ's kingdom and joined themselves to the *ecclesia,* or community of believers.

When you consider the fact that an "*ecclesia*" was "a civil body politic," this is a strong proof that the Christian *ecclesia* we read about in the New Testament were independent civil bodies of Christians- independent from worldly kings and governors, ruled by the theocratic government of God's Spirit. They wanted freedom to serve King Jesus. They weren't building and attending churches! The pattern laid down in the New Testament bears no resemblance to what we know today as "church." God's people are meant to live by the *ecclesia* pattern- together in communities, holding all things common, under the government of God through the anointed servant-leaders.

It is significant that Paul's Epistles were circulating prior to the publication of the Gospels and they mention the word "church" 43 times. (The book of Acts mentions "church" 17 times). Jesus is reported to have instead used the word "kingdom (of heaven)" in all the four Gospel over 100 times. In other words the reign of God was the focus of Jesus' Gospel, and not the Church. At best the Church (meaning a body of disciples) was only an instrument to facilitate the reign of God.

However we need to take note of what Brian Kingslake says in *Out of This World: Lay-bys on the Road to Heaven* about the Christian kingdom,

> The Emperor Constantine, whose mother Helena was a Christian woman (perhaps from Britain), declared Christianity to be the official religion of the whole Roman Empire! The Christian community hailed this as a magnificent triumph for their faith. God's reign on earth had begun! Ironically, however, Constantine's well-meant action just about brought the Church to an end. It could survive persecution, but not this! Christianity became fashionable.[6]

What implications does the activist perspective of ecclesia have for us today?

Ecclesia: A Religious Community connotation (An Ecclesial Perspective)

According to another perspective[7] the Old Testament uses two different words of the religious gathering of God's people. The first is *qahal*. This word means "assembly" and is used for nearly any kind of gathering, even gathering in rebellion against God. However, in connection with Israel, it is especially the assembly for religious purposes such as the giving and receiving of the Law (see Deuteronomy 9: 10). There is another Hebrew word, *'edah*, which also generally means "assembly" and is often translated "congregation." *Qahal* focuses on the event of experience with God. *'Edah* focuses on the unity of the whole people whom God appoints.

In Greek, as mentioned earlier, *ekklçsia* was used to describe any convened assembly of citizens for social and legal purposes. Ekklesia was never used for a religious gathering. What this means is that the use of *ekklçsia* in the New Testament cannot be based in classic Greek. The meaning of *ekklçsia* must be derived from the Hebrew background implicit in Paul's orientation – as an assembly for the purpose of religious expression. When we point in this direction, we realize that there is an element in the Hebrew idea that is not present in the Greek word *ekklçsia*. This element is *'edah*– the unity of the gathered assembly.

In other words, the "church" is a unity, a single body (remember Paul's body language) where every individual fades into the whole, an integrated unity, where no single member is any more valuable than any other and where every member is vital to the functioning of the whole. ***'Edah* is a body without hierarchy, without "professionals," without status-seekers and without individual glorification. It is the one assembly, doing all together what God commands.**

Such a perspective calls for a rethinking about the status and role of the ordained ministry in the *ecclesia*. The ordained minister does not have powers, spiritual powers, which unordained Christians lack. The *ecclesia* may for the sake of its smooth functioning and to facilitate meaningful expression of its life and witness appoint servant leaders. It is 'delegated' authority and responsibility. **Therefore there is no place for a sacerdotal hierarchical structure in the *ecclesia*.** The Pastoral Epistle in the Bible do not make mention of any such power or authority structured hierarchy. Rather they imply that there are different kinds of service ministries in the administration of the *ecclesia*.

In this connection one is reminded of the dictum: Priesthood of all believers. It implies, among other things, that the daily work done by Christians, done with integrity, done conscientiously, done so as to given expression to God's reign, has the same spiritual significance as the work of the clergy, monk, or nun. The term 'Full-time Christian service' should not be given exclusively to pastoral, administrative and institutional services in the Church. **All the work done by all the members of the *ecclesia*, whether in the field or in the factory, in the house or in the larger society is 'full-time service.'** The *ecclesia* is not the congregation worshipping together in a place on Sunday, separating its act from the day concerns of life, focusing upon another world. Rather **the *ecclesia* is the body of the disciples of Jesus Christ who with commitment and solidarity seek to give expression to the reign of God in society from Sunday to Saturday, every week**. Remember Paul's Exhortation: "And whatever you do, in word or deed, do everything in the name of the Lord Jesus, giving thanks to God the Father through him" (Col. 3:17). **Working for the cause of the Gospel brings them together for worship; work, witness and worship are integrated**.

What directions begin to emerge? If the Bible's view of the Church is an event called for a purpose operating as a single, completely unified body, a lot of things will have to change.

Ecclesia: A Liberating Movement (A Theological Perspective)

The text "Follow me and I will make you fish for people" (Mt. 4:19) has over the years become so interpreted that the church instead of being an out-going community of service, has become an inward looking self-complacent communal organization of the saved, interested in increasing its numbers. Christians have tended to become keepers of aquariums rather than fishers of people. Texts such as 1 Cor. 9:20-22 could be easily misconstrued to mean that objective of the Church is to increase its numbers: "And to the Jews I became as a Jew, that I might gain Jew; to them that are under the law, as under the law, not being myself under the law, that I might again them that are under the law; to them that are without law, as without law, not being without law to God, but under law to Christ, that I might gain them that are without law."

The metaphor of fishing for human beings (or using a hook to catch them) is relatively rare in the Bible. When it occurs, it always has a hostile sense of capturing or killing human beings (Jer. 16:16: "Behold I am sending for many fishers, says the LORD and they shall catch them"; Am. 4:2: "Behold the days are coming upon you, when they shall take you away with hooks; even the last of you with fish hooks"; see also Ezek. 29:4-5; Hab. 1:14-17). The metaphor occurs at a time in the Qumran literature, likewise in a negative context destruction or judgment. The metaphor of "catching men" is also found with a negative sense in later Rabbinic literature.

However, Jesus was giving a positive, salvific meaning to this metaphor in the Jewish tradition. The episode of calling Peter and Andrew to be fishers of people, and of the call of the two other fishermen (James and John) is followed by the text: "And he went about all Galilee, teaching in the synagogues and preaching the gospel of the kingdom and healing every disease and every infirmity among the people" (Mt. 4: 23). The disciples were called and commissioned to bring succor and salvation to those on the margins, the neglected ones. That was the positive meaning of fishing for people. It was not primarily to set up an institutional church, but to cultivate a movement which would proclaim the Gospel of love and hope for the neglected and condemned one.

Mark 2: 16-17 records: "And the Scribes of the Pharisees, when they saw that he was eating with sinners and tax collectors said to his disciples, 'Why does he eat with tax collectors and sinners?' And when Jesus heard it he said to them, 'Those who are well have no need of a physician, but those who are sick; I came not to call the righteous, but sinners'." Jesus' parable of the invitation to the great banquet (Lk. 14: 15-24) emphasizes that the poor, the maimed, the blind and the lame, lying in the streets and the lanes are welcomed by the host (God). **Indeed fishing for people is not so much a matter of counting how many are added to the church as it is of the Church reaching out in liberating love and empowering dignity to those on the margins.**

Once again let me quote Brian Kingslake,

> In Protestant Britain, after the Industrial Revolution, the Church became equated with Big Business. Wealthy factory owners supported and attended the parish church and were accepted as Christians, even though in many cases their life-style ran counter to all the teachings of the Sermon on the Mount, Jesus had said: "Blessed are the poor, the mourners, the meek, those who hunger and thirst after righteousness, the merciful, the pure in heart, the peacemakers." Big Business countered with: "Blessed are the rich, the unscrupulous, those who elbow their way to the top and lavishly satisfy their hunger and thirst and all their appetites and desires![8]

One could repeat the same quote, substituting the Industrial Revolution with Globalization, and Protestant Britain with Developed Countries and Multi-National Corporations.

M. M. Thomas, in his Chavara Lectures (1994), emphasized,

> A diaconal approach to Indian Ecclesiology aimed at the re-structuring of the church of Christ in modern religiously and ideological pluralistic India in ways more relevant to the discharging of its humanizing mission.[9]

Athyal points out that:

> [T]he underlying concern in these attempts to re-articulate the identity and role of the church, is the growing awareness that the traditional understanding of the functions of the church as teaching the Word of God and administering the sacraments, is in urgent need of revision.[10]

The ecclesia has to be discovered afresh in the groaning of the masses, whose cries draw out God's liberating activities (like the suffering and cries of the Hebrews in Egypt and God's response), in the campaigns of Moseses and Mordecais, in the "crosses" and "resurrections" of the disciples of Jesus Christ, and in lives and activities of all those beyond our religionized Christianity – "those who are not against us in the cause of the gospel are for us and should not be forbidden" (cf. Lk. 9: 49-50).

Endnotes:

[1] This article was earlier published as Roger Gaikwad, "Towards a New Ecclesia: Re-Reading the Concept of 'Ecclesia' in the Bible: A Few Pointers," *Religion and Society* 56, no. 2 (June 2011): 12-20. Used with permission of the author and the publisher of *Religion and Society*.

[2] Rev. Dr. Roger Gaikwad is the General Secretary of NCCI, Nagpur.

[3] cf. http://www.testimony-magazine.org/back/Special_Issues/Sept91/art3.htm (accessed June 13, 2011).

[4] *Sarang ki Var, Mohalla* 1, 1244.

[5] Cf. http://www.aggressivechristianity.net/articles/ecclesia.htm (accessed June 13, 2011).

[6] Brian Kingslake, *Out of This World. Lay-bys on the Road to Heaven* (England: James Evesham Worc., 1978) available at http://www.swedenborg digitallibrary.org/ootw/ootw24.htm (accessed June 13, 2011).

[7] cf. http://skipmoen.com/tag/qahal/ (accessed February 13, 2011).

[8] Kingslake, *Out of This World. Lay-bys on the Road to Heaven.*

[9] M. M. Thomas, *A Diaconal Approach to Indian Ecclesiology* (Tiruvalla: CIIS & CSS, 1995), 8.

[10] cf. http://jmathyal.tripod.com/id19.html (accessed June 13, 2011).

BIBLIOGRAPHY

Books

"Church." In *Mounce's Complete Expository Dictionary of the Old and New Testament Words*. Edited by William D. Mounce, D. Matthew Smith and Miles V. Van Pelt, 100. Grand Rapids: Zondervan Publishing House, 2006.

"καλεω." Walter Bauer. *A Greek-English Lexicon of the New Testament and Other Early Christian Literature.* 3rd ed. Chicago: University of Chicago Press, 2000.

"קָרָא." *The Brown-Driver-Briggs Hebrew and English Lexicon*, 896. Peabody: Hendrickson Publishers, 2004.

"קָהַל." Wilhelm Gesenius & S. P. Tregelles, *Gesenius' Hebrew and Chaldee Lexicon to the Old Testament Scriptures,* 726. Bellingham: Logos Research Systems, Inc. 2003.

Adams, Edward. "First-Century Models for Paul's Churches: Selected Scholarly Developments since Meeks." In *After the First Urban Christians: The Social-Scientific Study of Pauline Christianity Twenty-Five Years Later*. Edited by Todd D. Still and David G. Horrell, 60-78. Edinburgh: T&T Clark, 2009.

Alberigo, Giuseppe, and Joseph A. Komonchak, eds. *History of Vatican II*. 5 vols. Maryknoll: Orbis Books, 1995, 1997, 2000, 2003, 2006.

Amaladoss, Michael. *A Call to Community*. Gujarat: Gujarat Sahitya Prakash, 1994.

________. *Making All Things New: Mission in Dialogue*. Maryknoll: Orbis Books, 1989.

Ambrose. "Epistles 20:19." In *Nicene and Post-Nicene Series II*. Vol. 10. Edited by Philip Schaff and Henry Wace. Edinburgh: T&T Clark, ND.

Amin, S., and François Houtart, eds. *Globalization and Alternatives*. Geneva: CETIM/AAJ/LIDLIP/WILPF, 2000.

Anand, Subhash. *Hindu Inspiration for Christian Reflection, Towards Hindu-Christian Theology*. Gujarat: Gujarat Sahitiya Prakash, 2004.

Antoine, R. "Rituals and Worship." In *Religious Hinduism*. Edited by R. De Smet and J. Neuner, 200-209. Mumbai: St. Pauls Press, 1996.

Appasamy, A. J. *Christianity as Bhakti Marga: A Study of the Johannine Doctrine of Love*. Madras: CLS, 1928.

________. *The Gospel and India's Heritage*. London: SPCK, 1942.

Ariarajah, S. Wesley. *Not Without My Neighbour: Issues in Inter-Faith Relations*. Geneva: WCC, 1999.

Baago, Kaj. *The Movement Around Subba Rao: A Study of the Hindu-Christian Movement around K. Subba Rao in Andhra Pradesh*. Madras: CLS, 1968.

Bacani, Teodora C. *The Church and Politics*. Philippines: Claretian Publications, 1987.

Baptism, Eucharist and Ministry, Faith and Order Paper No. 111. Geneva: WCC, 1982.

Barabas, Steven. "Sacrament." In *New International Bible Dictionary*. Edited by J. D. Douglas and Merrill C. Tenney, 878-79. Grand Rapids: Zondervan Publishing House, 1987.

Barclay, William. *New Testament Words*. London: SCM Press Ltd., 1964.

________. *The Mind of St. Paul*. New York: Harper and Row, 1958).

Bauckham, Richard. *God and the Crisis of Freedom*. Louisville: Westminster John Knox Press, 2002.

Bauer, Walter, W. F. Arndt and F. W. Gingrich. *A Greek-English Lexicon of the New Testament and Other Early Christian Literature*. 2nd rev. ed. Chicago: University of Chicago Press, 1957.

Beed, C. and C. Beed. *Alternatives to Economics*. Lanham, MD: University Press of America, 2006.

Beisner, E. C. *Prosperity and Poverty*. Westchester: Crossway, 1988.

________. *Where Garden Meets Wilderness*. Grand Rapids, Acton Institute, 1997.

Berko, Roy M., Andrew D. Wolvin and Darlyn R. Wolvin. *Communicating a Social and Career Focus*. Ninth ed. Boston: Houghton Mifflin Company, 2004.

Berman, Joshua A. *Created Equal How the Bible Broke with Ancient Political Thought*. New York: Oxford University Press, 2008.

Bermejo, Luis M. *Church Conciliarity & Communion*. Gujarat: Gujarat Sahitya Prakash, 1990.

Best, Thomas and Guenther Gassmann, eds. *On the Way to Fuller Koinonia*. Geneva: WCC, 1994.

Bettenson, Henry. *Documents of the Christian Church*. 2nd ed. Oxford: Oxford University Press, 1967.

Bhavya. "Indian Women and the Experience of Inculturation." In *The Church and Culture in India, Inculturation: Theory and Praxis*. Edited by Paul Pulikkan and Paul M. Collins, 202-216. Delhi: ISPCK, 2010.

Blomberg, C. *Neither Poverty nor Riches*. Leicester: Apollos, 1999.

Blue, Bradly. "Acts and the House Church." In *The Book of Acts in its First Century Setting*, edited by David W. J. Gill and Conrad Gempf, 2, 119-222. Grand Rapids: William B. Eerdmans Publishing Company, 1994.

Boer, Harry R. *A Short History of the Early Church*. Grand Rapids: William B. Eerdmans Publishing Company, 2001.

Boff, Clodovis. *Feet-on-the-Ground- Theology*. Maryknoll: Orbis Books, 1987.

Boff, Leonardo. *Ecclesiogenesis: The Base Communities Reinvent the Church*. Maryknoll: Orbis Books, 1986.

Boice, James Montgomery. *Expositor's Bible Commentary: Galatians*. Vol. 10. Grand Rapids: Zondervan Publishing House, 1976.

Bonhoeffer, Dietrich. *Letters and Papers from Prison*. Edited by Eberard Bethge. New York: Macmillan Publishing Co., 1972.

Bowden, John, ed. *Christianity: The Complete Guide*. London: Continuum, 2005.

Boyd, Robin H. S. *An Introduction to Indian Christian Theology*. New Delhi: ISPCK, 1994.

Brauch, Manfred T. "Church." In *Baker Encyclopaedia of the Bible*. Edited by Walter A. Elwell. Vol. 1, 458-461. Grand Rapids: Baker Books House Company, 1988.

Bright, John. *A History of Israel*. 4th ed. Louisville: Westminster John Knox Press, 2000.

Brown, Raymond E. *Priests and Bishop*. London: Geoffrey Chapmann, 1971.

________. *The Church Apostles Left Behind*. New York: Paulist Press, 1984.

Brown, Schuyler. *The Origins of Christianity: A Historical Introduction to the New Testament*. Revised ed. Oxford: Oxford University Press, 1993.

Brueggemann, Walter E. *Abingdon Old Testament Commentaries: Deuteronomy*. Nashville: Abingdon Press, 2001.

Brunner, Emil. *The Misunderstanding of the Church*. Translated by Harold Knight. London: Lutterworth Press, 1952.

Bultmann, Rudolf. *Theology of the New Testament*. Vol. 1. London: SCM Press Ltd., [1952], 1959.

Burgess, Stanley M., and Eduard M. van der Mass, eds. *The New International Dictionary of Pentecostal and Charismatic Movements*. Grand Rapids: Zondervan Publishing House, 2002.

Cairns, Earle E. *Christianity Through the Centuries*. Grand Rapids: Zondervan Publishing House, [1954] 1977.

Cairns, Ian. *Word and Presence: A Commentary on the Book of Deuteronomy*. Grand Rapids: William B. Eerdmans Publishing Company, 1992.

Campbell, Alastair V. *Paid to Care? Limits of Professionalism in Pastoral Care*. London: SPCK, 1985.

Chadwick, Henry. "The Early Christian Community." In *The Oxford Illustrated History of Christianity*. Edited by John McManners, 21-60. Oxford: Oxford University Press, 1992.

Charles, Robert Henry. *Pseudepigrapha of the Old Testament*. Bellingham: Logos Research Systems, Inc., 2004.

Chester, Andrew. "The Pauline Communities." In *A Vision for the Church: Studies in Early Christian Ecclesiology*. Edited by Markus Bockmuehl and Michael B. Thompson, 105-120. Edinburgh: T&T Clark, 1997.

Chirichigno, C. Gregory. *Debt-Slavery in Israel and the Ancient Near East*. Sheffield: Journal for the Study of the Old Testament Press, 1993.

Chittister, Joan. *Women, Ministry and the Church*. New York: Paulist Press, 1983.

Church of South India after Thirty Years: Report to the Special Committee appointed by the Church of South India Synod to study the Life and Work of the Church. Madras: CLS, 1978.

Cloke, Gillan. "Women, Worship, and Mission: The Church in the Household." In *The Early Christian World.* Edited by Philip F. Esler, 1, 422-451. London: Routledge, 2000.

Codina, Victor. "Sacraments." In *Systematic Theology: Perspectives from Liberation Theology.* Edited by Jon Sobrino and Ignacio Ellacuría, 216-32. Maryknoll: Orbis Books, 1996.

Coenen, Lothar. "Church." In *The New International Dictionary of the New Testament Theology.* Edited by Colin Brown. Vol. 1, 291. Grand Rapids: Zondervan Publishing House, 1975.

Congar, Yves Marie. *Lay People in the Church. A Study on the Theology of Laity.* Westminster: Newman Press, 1957.

Conzelmann, Hans. *An Outline of the Theology of the New Testament.* New York: Harper & Row, 1969.

Coppes, Leonard J. "קָרָא." *Theological Wordbook of the Old Testament.* Edited by R. Laird Harris, Gleason L. Archer and Bruce K. Waltke, 810-811. Chicago: Moody Press, 1999.

Craddock, Fred B. *Luke: Interpretation, a Bible Commentary for Teaching and Preaching.* Louisville: John Knox Press, 1990.

Craigie, Peter C. *The New International Commentary on the Book of Deuteronomy.* Grand Rapids: William B. Eerdmans Publishing Company, 1976.

Crichton, J. D. "Sacramental Theology." In *The Westminster Dictionary of Christian Theology.* Edited by Alan Richardson and John Bowden, 515-16. Philadelphia: The Westminster Press, 1983.

Currid, John D. *A Study Commentary on Exodus.* Vol. 2. Darlington, NY: Evangelical Press, 2001.

Daughrity, Dyron B. *Changing World of Christianity: The Global History of a Borderless Religion.* Bern: Peter Lang, 2010.

De Lubac, Henry. *Catholicism.* London: Burns, Oates & Washbourne, 1950.

De Vaux, Roland. *Ancient Israel: Its Life and Institutions.* Grand Rapids: William B. Eerdmans Publishing Company, 1967.

Devanandan, Paul D. *Christian Concern in Hinduism.* Bangalore: CISRS, 1961.

Devasahayam, V. "Doing Dalit Theology: Basic Assumptions." In *Frontiers of Dalit Theology.* Edited by V. Devasahayam, 270-282. Madras: Gurukul Lutheran Theological College, 1997.

Dever, G. William. "How to Tell a Canaanite from an Israelite?" In *The Rise of Ancient Israel.* Edited by Hershel Shanks, 27-56. Washington: Biblical Archaeology Society, 1992.

Dietrich, Gabriele, and Bas Wielenga. *Towards Understanding Indian Society*. Tiruvalla, India: CSS, 1998.

"Dogmatic Constitution on the Church." In *Vatican Council II: The Conciliar and Post Conciliar Documents*. Edited by Austin Flannery, 350-426. Dublin: Dominican Publication, 1975.

Dowley, Tim. *The History of Christianity*. Oxford: Lion Publishing House, 1990.

Doyle, M. Dennis. *Communion Ecclesiology: Visions and Versions*. Maryknoll: Orbis Books, 2000.

Dulles, Avery. "The Church as Sacrament." In *Models of the Church*, 55-67. New York: Image Books, 2002.

________. *Models of the Church*. Garden City: Doubleday and Company, Inc., [1974], 1987.

________. *Models of the Church: Expanded Edition*. New York: Image Books, 1987.

Dunn, James D. G. *Baptism in the Holy Spirit*. London: SCM Press Ltd., 1977.

________. *Jesus, Paul, and the Gospels*. Grand Rapids: William B. Eerdmans Publishing Company, 2011.

________. *The Theology of Paul the Apostle*. Grand Rapids: William B. Eerdmans Publishing Company, 2006.

________. *Word Biblical Commentary: Romans 1-8*. Vol. 38A. Dallas: Word Book Publisher, 1988.

Ellingworth, P. "Leprosy." In *Dictionary of Jesus and the Gospels*. Edited by Joel B. Green, Scot McKnight, and I. Howard Marshall, 463-464. Downers Grove: InterVarsity Press, 1992.

Elliott-Binns, L. E. *The Beginning of Western Christendom*. London: Lutterworth Press, 1948.

Ellis, E. E. *Pauline Theology: Ministry and Society*. Grand Rapids: William B. Eerdmans Publishing Company, 1989.

Episcope and Episcopate in Ecumenical Perspective. Geneva: WCC, 1980.

Fager, Jeffrey A. *Land Tenure and the Biblical Jubilee: Uncovering Hebrew Ethics through the Sociology of Knowledge*. Sheffield: Journal for the Study of the Old Testament Press, 1993.

Fernando, D. R. S. *Contextual Theology in Sri Lanka*. Leuven: Katholieke Universiteit Leuven, 1987.

Fiorenza, Elisabeth Schüssler. *In Memory of Her: A Feminist Theological Reconstruction of Christian Origins*. London: SCM Press Ltd., 1983.

________. *But She Said: Feminist Practices of Biblical Interpretation*. Boston: Beacon Press, 1992.

________. *Discipleship of Equals: A Critical Feminist Ekklesia-logy of Liberation*. New York: Crossroad, 1993.

________. *Bread not Stone: The Challenge of Feminist Biblical Interpretation*. Boston: Beacon Press, 1995.

________. *Rhetoric and Ethics: The Politics of Biblical Studies*. Minneapolis: Augsburg Fortress Press, 1999.

________. *Wisdom Ways: Introducing Feminist Biblical Interpretation*. Maryknoll: Orbis Books, 2001.

________. "Wo/men, Mission and the Catholicity of Theology." In *The Church in Mission: Universal Mandate and Local Concerns*. Edited by Thomas Malipurathu and L. Stainslaus, 147-180. Gujarat: Gujarat Sahitya Prakash, 2002.

________. *The Power of the Word: Scripture and the Rhetoric of Empire*. Minneapolis: Augsburg Fortress Press, 2007.

________. "Introduction: Exploring the Intersections of Race, Gender, Status, and Ethnicity in Early Christian Studies." In *Prejudice and Christian Beginnings: Investigating Race, Gender, and Ethnicity in Early Christianity*. Edited by Laura Nasrallah and Elisabeth Schüssler Fiorenza, 1-23. Minneapolis: Augsburg Fortress Press, 2009.

Firth, C. B. *An Introduction to Indian Church History*. Madras: CLS, 1976.

Flannery, Austin, ed. *Vatican Council II: The Conciliar and Post Conciliar Documents*. New York: Costello, 1984.

Forrester, Dunncan. *On Human Worth: A Christian Vindication of Equality*. London: SCM Press Ltd., 2001.

Francis, Kanichikattil. *Church in Context: Essays in Honour of Mathias Mundadan, CMI*. Bangalore: Dharmaram Publications, 1996.

Funkenstein, Amos, and Adin Steinsaltz. *The Sociology of Ignorance*. Tel Aviv: Ministry of Defense, 1987.

Gee, Donald. *Concerning Spiritual Gifts*. Springfield: Gospel Publishing House, 1972.

Geisler, Norman. *Systematic Theology (Church, Last Things)*. Vol. 4. Bloomington, Minnesota: Bethany House, 2005.

Gonzalez, Justo L. *A History of Christian Thought*. Vol. 1. Nashville: Abingdon Press, 1970.

Goppelt, Leonhard. *Theology of the New Testament*. Vol. 1. Grand Rapids: William B. Eerdmans Publishing Company, 1981.

Gottwald, Norman K. "The Prophetic Critique of Political Economy: Its Ground and Import." In *The Hebrew Bible in Its Social World and Ours*. Edited by Norman K. Gottwald. Atlanta: Scholars Press, 1993.

________. *The Tribes of Yahweh*. London: SCM Press Ltd., 1979.

Grafe[hrsg.], Hugald. *Die evangelisishe Kirche in Indien*. Erlangen: Verlag der ev. Luth. Mission, 1981.

Grassi, Joseph A. "Child, Children." In *The Anchor Bible Dictionary*. Edited by David Noel Freedman. Vol. 1, 905. New York: Doubleday & Company Inc., 1996.

Graybill, John B. "Temple." In *The New International Dictionary of the Bible*. Edited by J. D. Douglas and Merrill C. Tenney, 990-997. Grand Rapids: Zondervan Publishing House, 1994.

Greenslade, S. L. ed. *Early Latin Theology: Selections from Tertullian, Cyprian, Ambrose, and Jerome.* Louisville: Westminster Press, 1956.

Greenstein, Edward L. "Biblical Law," In *Back to the Sources: Reading the Classical Jewish Texts.* Edited by Barry W. Holtz, 83-103. New York: Summit, 1984.

Grudem, Wayne. *Business for the Glory of God.* Wheaton: Crossway, 2003.

Guelich, Robert A. *Mark 1-8:26: Word Biblical Commentary.* Vol. 34a. Dallas: Word Book Publisher, 2002.

Guthrie, Donald. *New Testament Theology.* Secunderabad: OM Books, 1992.

Hage, Wolfgang. *Syriac Christianity in the East.* Moran Etho. Kottayam: St. Ephrem Research Institute, 1997.

Hagner, Donald A. *Matthew 14-28: Word Biblical Commentary.* Vol. 33B. Dallas: Word Book Publishers, 2002.

Hares, W. P. *A History of the Christian Church of the First Six Centuries.* 2nd ed. Madras: The Christian Literature Society for India, 1952.

Harnack, Adolf. *Outlines of the History of Dogma.* Translated by Edwin Knox Mitchell. Boston: Beacon Press, 1959.

Harrison, R. *The Wycliffe Exegetical Commentary: Numbers.* Chicago: Moody Press, 1990.

Hartley, John E. *Word Biblical Commentary: Leviticus.* Vol. 4. Dallas: Word Book Publisher, 1992.

Hendriksen, William, and Simon J. Kistemaker. *Exposition of the Gospel According to Luke: Baker New Testament Commentary.* Grand Rapids: Baker Book House, 1953-2001.

Hess, K. "Serve." *New International Dictionary of the New Testament Theology.* Edited by Colin Brown. Vol. 3, 544-549. Grand Rapids: Zondervan Publishing House, 1978.

Hessert, Paul. *Introduction to Christianity.* New Jersey: Prentice-Hall, 1958.

Hewitt, Emily C. *Women Priests: Yes or No?* New York: The Seabury Press, 1995.

Hill, Edmund. "Church." In *New Dictionary of Theology.* Edited by Joseph A. Komonchak, Mary Collins and Dermot A. Lane, 185-201. Bangalore: Theological Publication in India, 1996.

Hinson, E. Glenn. *The Early Church: Origins to the Dawn of the Middle Ages.* Nashville: Abingdon Press, 1996.

Hnuni, R. L. "Patriarchal Cultures and Traditions in the Bible." In *Feminist Hermeneutics.* Edited by Lalrinawmi Ralte and Evangeline Anderson Rajkumar, 79-85. Delhi: ISPCK for IWIT, 2002.

Hodgson, Peter C., and Robert C. Williams. "The Church." In *Christian Theology: An Introduction to Its Traditions and Tasks.* Edited by Peter C. Hodgson and Robert H. King, 249-273. Philadelphia: Fortress Press, 1982.

Hollenweger, Walter J. *Pentecostalism: Origins and Developments Worldwide.* Peabody: Hendrickson Publishers, 1997.

Homrighausen, Elmer G. *I Believe in the Church*. Nashville: Abingdon Press, 1954.

Horsley, Richard A. "1 Corinthians: A Case Study of Paul's Assembly as an Alternative Society." In *Paul and Empire: Religion and Power in Roman Imperial Society*. Edited by Richard A. Horsley, 242-252. Harrisburg, Pennsylvania: Trinity Press International, 1997.

Houtart, François, *The Eleventh Hour: The Explosion of a Church*. New York: Sheed and Ward, 1968.

________. "Religion and Development." *Religion and Development in Asia, Baguio Feres Seminar Report*, 2-25. N.p: n.p., 1976.

________. "Religious Identity." In *How to Conquer the Barriers to Intercultural Dialogue: Christianity, Islam and Judaism*, edited by Christiane Timmerman and Barbara Segaert, 105-116. Bern: Peter Lang, 2007.

________. "The Church and the Developing Nations: Some Questions for Theologians." In *Theology of Renewal*. Edited by L. K. Shook. Vol. II. Toronto: Palm Publishers, 1968.

________. *Challenge to Change*. New York: Sheed and Ward, 1964.

________, et. al. *A Socio-Religious Analysis of the East Ramnad District, Tamilnadu*. Louvain: KUL, n. d.

________. *Size and Structures of the Catholic Church in India: The Indianization of an Exogeneous Religious Institution in a Society in Transition*. Louvain la Neuve: C.R.S.R. Université Catholique de Louvain, 1982.

________, and André Rousseau. *The Church and Revolution: From the French Revolution of 1789 to the Paris Riots of 1968, from Cuba to Southern Africa, from Vietnam to Latin America*. Maryknoll: Orbis Books, 1971.

________, and Emile Pin. *The Church and the Latin American Revolution*. New York: Sheed and Ward, 1965.

________. "The Roman Catholic Church and Social Change in Latin America." In *The Church and Social Change in Latin America*, edited by Henry A. Landsberger, 113-133. Notre Dame: University of Notre Dame Press, 1970.

Hultgren, Arland J. *The Rise of Normative Christianity* (Minneapolis: Fortress Press, 1994), 50.

Ignatius of Antioch, "The Epistle of Ignatius to The Trallians." In *The Ante-Nicene Fathers: Translations of the Writings of the Fathers down to A.D. 325*. Edited by Alexander Roberts and James Donaldson. Vol. 1. Buffalo, NY: Christian Literature Publishing, 1885.

Information: Faith and Order, July 1994, 2.

Information: Faith and Order, March 1994, 1.

Inrig, Gary. *Life in His Body*. Wheaton: Harold Shaw Publishers, 1975.

Irvin, Dale T., and Scott W. Sunquist, *History of the World Christian Movement: Earliest Christianity to 1453*. Vol. I. Bangalore: Theological Publications in India, 2004.

Jathanna, O. V. *The Decisiveness of the Christ-event and the Universality of Christianity in a World of Religious Plurality: With Special Reference to Hendrick Kraemer and Alfred George Hogg as well as to William Ernest Hocking and Pandipeddi Chenchiah.* Berne: Peter Lang, 1981.

Jenson, Robert W. *Visible Words: The Interpretation and Practice of Christian Sacraments.* Philadelphia: Fortress Press, 1978.

Jeremias, Joachim. *Jerusalem in the Time of Jesus.* London: SCM Press Ltd., 1969.

MacArthur Jr., John. *Body Dynamics.* Wheaton: Victor Books, 1982.

John, Stackhouse G. *Finally Feminist: A Pragmatic Christian Understanding of Gender.* Grand Rapids: Baker Books, 2005.

Johns, Cheryl Bridges. "Pentecostal Formation-A Pedagogy among the Oppressed." *Journal of Pentecostal Theology.* Supplement Series-2. Sheffield: Sheffield Academic Press, 1993.

Johnson, Luke Timothy. "Paul's Ecclesiology." In *The Cambridge Companion to St. Paul.* Edited by J. D. G. Dunn, 199-211. Cambridge: Cambridge University Press, 2003.

Johnston, Philip S. *Deuteronomy: The People's Bible Commentary.* Oxford: The Bible Reading Fellowship, 2005.

Jones, Steven G. "Understanding Community in the Information Age." In *Cyber Society.* Edited by Steven G. Jones, 10-35. New Delhi: SAGE Publication, 1995.

Kärkkäinen, Veli-Matti. *An Introduction to Ecclesiology: Ecumenical, Historical and Global Perspectives.* Downers Grove: Inter Varsity Press, 2002.

Karokaran, A. "Mission, Conversion, Baptism." In A *Call to Discipleship.* Edited by Godwin Singh, 159-160. New Delhi: ISPCK, 1985.

Kelly, J. N. D. *Early Christian Creeds.* London: Longmans, Green & Co. Ltd., 1964.

________. *Early Christian Doctrines.* San Francisco: Harper & Row, [1948] 1978.

Kittel, Gerhard. "ἀββα." In *Theological Dictionary of the New Testament Theology.* Edited by Gerhard Kittel. Translated by Geoffrey W. Bromiley. Vol. 1, 5-6. Grand Rapids: William B. Eerdmans Publishing Company, 1964.

Kümmel, W. G. *Introduction to New Testament.* Nashville: Abingdon Press, 1975.

Küng, Hans. "The Charismatic Structure of the Church." In *The Church and Ecumenism, Concilium.* Edited by Hans Küng. Vol. 4, 41-61. New York: Paulist Press, 1965.

________. *Christ Sein.* Zurich: Ex Libris, 1996.

________. *The Church.* Translated by Ray and Rosaleen Ockenden. New York: Shed and Ward, 1967.

Kunnumpuram, Kurien. *The Indian Church of the Future.* Mumbai: St. Pauls, 2007.

Ladd, George Eldon. *A Theology of the New Testament*. Grand Rapids: William B. Eerdmans Publishing Company, [1974] 1993.

Latourette, Kenneth Scott. *A History of Christianity*. New York: Harper & Row Publishers, 1953.

Lee, Philip. "Communication for Ecumenism Building Living Bridges." In *Christian Communication: Ecumenical Chanllenges in the 21st Century*. Edited by Samuel Meshack, 33-51. Yogyakarta: WACC, 2011.

Lennan, Richard. *The Ecclesiology of Karl Rahner*. Oxford: Clarendon Press, 1995.

Lewis, Jack P. "קָהָל." In *Theological Wordbook of the Old Testament*. Edited by R. Laird Harris, Gleason L. Archer and Bruce K. Waltke, 790. Chicago: Moody Press, 1999.

Lichtheim, Miriam. *Ancient Egyptian Literature: A Book of Readings*. Vol. 1. Berkeley: University of California, 1975.

Lipner, Julius, and George Gispert-Sauch, eds. *The Writings of Brahmabandhab Upadhyay*. Vol. 2. Bangalore: The United Theological College, 1991.

Lohse, Eduard. "σαββατον, σαββατισμος, παρασκευς." In *Theological Dictionary of the New Testament*. Edited by Gerhard Kittel, 7, 1-35. Grand Rapids: William B. Eerdmans Publishing Company, [1971] 2006.

Longenecker, Bruce W. "Socio-Economic Profiling of the First Urban Christians." In *After the First Urban Christians: The Social-Scientific Study of Pauline Christianity Twenty-Five Years Later*. Edited by Todd D. Still and David G. Horrell, 36-59. Bloomsbury: T&T Clark, 2009.

Louw, Johannes. P., and Eugene A. Nida. *Greek-English lexicon of the New Testament: Based on Semantic Domains*. Vol. 1. New York: United Bible Societies, 1989-1996.

________. *Lexical Semantics of the Greek New Testament: A Supplement to the Greek-English Lexicon of the New Testament Based on Semantic Domains*. Edited by David E. Aune. Atlanta: Scholars Press, 1992.

Lull, James. *Media, Communication, Cultural: A Global Approach*. Cambridge: Cambridge Polity Press, 1996.

Lust, Johan. "ἐκκαλεω." *Greek-English Lexicon of the Septuagint*. Stuttgart: Deutsche Bibelgesellschaft, 2003.

Manikaraj, D. "Mission, Evangelism and Conversion." In *Frontiers of Dalit Theology*. Edited by V. Devasahayam, 457-476. Madras: Gurukul Lutheran Theological College, 1997.

Marshall, I. Howard. *The Gospel of Luke: A Commentary on the Greek Text; The New International Greek Testament Commentary*. Exeter: Paternoster Press, 1978.

Martin, Dale B. "Patterns of Belief and Patterns of Life: Correlations in *The First Urban Christians* and Since." In *After the First Urban Christians: The Social-Scientific Study of Pauline Christianity Twenty-Five Years Later*. Edited by Todd D. Still and David G. Horrell, 116-133. Bloomsbury: T&T Clark, 2009.

Martos, J. "Sacrament." In *The Westminster Dictionary of Christian Theology.* Edited by Alan Richardson and John Bowden, 514-515. Philadelphia: The Westminster Press, 1983.

Martyr, Justin *Apology* II, 3.

McConville, J. Gordon. *Apollos Old Testament Commentary: Deuteronomy.* Leicester: Apollos, 2002.

McGee, Garry B. *Selected Documents on the Early History of the Assemblies of God in India.* Springfield, Massachusetts: AGTS, 1991.

McKelvey, R. J. "Temple: Temple in the New Testament." In *The New Bible Dictionary.* Edited by J. D. Douglas, 1247-1250. Grand Rapids: William B. Eerdmans Publishing Company, 1970.

McNutt, Paula M. *Reconstructing the Society of Ancient Israel.* London: SPCK, 1999.

Meeks, Wayne A. *The First Urban Christians: The Social World of the Apostle Paul.* New Haven: Yale University Press, 1983.

________. *The Moral World of the First Christians.* Philadelphia: The Westminster Press, 1986.

Meggitt, Justin J. *Paul, Poverty and Survival.* The Studies of the New Testament and its World. Edinburgh: T&T Clark, 1998.

Meyers, Carol. *The New Cambridge Bible Commentary: Exodus.* Cambridge: Cambridge University Press, 2002.

Michell, George. *The Hindu Temple: An Introduction to Its Meaning and Forms.* Chicago: University of Chicago Press, 1977.

Migliore, Daniel L. *Faith Seeking Understanding: An Introduction to Christian Theology.* Grand Rapids: William B. Eerdmans Publishing Company, 1993.

Milgrom, J. *Numbers: The JPS Torah Commentary.* Philadelphia: The Jewish Publication Society, 1990.

Miller, D. *Principles of Social Justice.* Cambridge, MA: Harvard University Press, 1999).

Minear, Paul. *Images of the Church in the New Testament.* Philadelphia: Westminster Press, 1960.

Moltmann, Jürgen. *The Church in the Power of the Spirit: A Contribution to Messianic* Ecclesiology. Minneapolis: Augsburg Fortress Press, 1993.

Monteiro, Evelyn. *Church and Culture: Communion in Pluralism.* Delhi: ISPCK, 2004.

Morris, Pelzel. *Ecclesiology: The Church as Communion and Mission.* Chicago: Loyola Press, 2001.

Mott, S., and R. Sider. "Economic Justice: A Biblical Paradigm." In *Toward a Just and Caring Society.* Edited by D. Gushee, 15-45. Grand Rapids: Baker Books, 1999.

Muffs, Yochanan. *Love and Joy: Law, Language, and Religion in Ancient Israel.* New York: Jewish Theological Seminary of America, 1992.

Mundadan, A. Mathias. *History of Christianity in India*. Vol. 1. Bangalore, Theological Publication of India, 1984.

Murry, Ezamo. *An Introduction to Pastoral Care and Counselling*. Delhi: ISPCK, 2005.

Nagel, T. "Equality." In *The Oxford Companion to Philosophy*. Edited by T. Honderich, 248-49. Oxford: Oxford University Press, 1995.

Neelankavil, Tony. "From Inculturation to Interculturality: A Methodological Move in Asian Churches' Encounters with Cultures." In *The Church and Culture in India, Inculturation: Theory and Praxis*. Edited by Paul Pulikkan and Paul M. Collins, 11-24. Delhi: ISPCK, 2010.

Nelson, Richard D. *Deuteronomy: A Commentary*. Louisville: Westminster John Knox Press, 2002.

Neusner, Jacob. *The Mishnah: A New Translation*. New Haven: Yale University Press, 1988.

O'Connor, O. David. "The Social and Economic Organization of Ancient Egyptian Temples." In *Civilization of the Ancient Near* East. Edited by J. Sasson, 1, 319-329. New York: Scribner, 1995.

Oepke, Albrecht. "γυνη." In *Theological Dictionary of the New Testament*. Edited by Gerhard Kittel. Vol. 1, 776-789. Grand Rapids: William B. Eerdmans Publishing Company, [1964] 2006.

Orr, J. Edwin. *Evangelical Awakening*. Madras: CLS, 1970.

Osberg, L. "Inequality." In *Encyclopedia of the Social and Behavioral Sciences*. Edited by N. Smelser and P. Baltes, 73-76. Amsterdam: Elsevier, 2001.

Palakeel, Joseph. *Towards Communication Theology*. Bangalore: Asian Trading Corporation, 2003.

Pamphili, Eusebius. *Ecclesiastical History*, Books 1-5. Translated by Roy J. Deferrari. Washington: Catholic University of America Press, 1953.

Panikkar, Raimundo. "Prolegomena to the Problem of Universality of the Church." In *Unique and Universal. Fundamental Problems of an Indian Theology*. Edited by J. B. Chethimattam, 155-164. Bangalore: Centre for the Study of World Religions, Dharmaram Publications, 1972.

________. "A Dream of an Indian Ecclesiology." In *Searching for an Indian Ecclesiology*. Edited by Gerwin Van Leeuwen, 24-54. Bangalore: Asian Trading Corporation, 1984.

Pannenberg, Wolfhart. *The Church*. Translated by Keith Crim. Philadelphia: Westminster Press, 1983.

________. *Systematic Theology*. Vol. 3. Grand Rapids: William B. Eerdmans Publishing Company, 1998.

Patterson, J. O. ed. *Holy Convocation*. N. p.: n.p., 1969.

Pathil, Kuncheria. *Theology of the Church New Horizons*. Bangalore: Dharmaram Publications, 2006.

Patton, J. "Pastoral Counselling." In *Dictionary of Pastoral Care and Counselling*. Edited by Rodney J. Hunter, 849-854. Nashville: Abingdon Press, 2005.

Paul, Shalom M. *Studies in the Book of the Covenant in the Light of Cuneiform and Biblical Law*. Eugene, Ore: Wipf & Stock, 2006.

Pelikan, Jaroslav. *The Emergence of Catholic Tradition (100-600)*. Vol. 1 of *The Christian Tradition: A History of the Development of Doctrine*. Chicago: University of Chicago Press, 1971.

Philip, T. M. *The Encounter between Theology and Ideology: An Exploration into the Communicative Theology of M. M.* Thomas. Madras: CLS, 1986.

Pinto, Simon. *Theology of Interreligious Dialogue for a Multi-Religious Context in India*. Rome: Urbaniana, 2013.

Plou, Defne Sabanes. *Global Communication: Is There a Place for Human Dignity?* Geneva: WCC, 1996.

Prabhakar, M. E. "Christology in Dalit Perspectives." In *Frontiers of Dalit Theology*. Edited by V. Devasahayam, 402-432. Madras: Gurukul Lutheran Theological College, 1996.

Praem, Anthony D'Cruz O. "Towards a New Humanity." In *Committed to the Church and the Country*. Edited by Kuruvilla Pandikattu, James Ponniah, and Thomas Kuriacose, 3-20. Pune: Jnana-Deepa Vidyapeeth, 2013.

Rao, Kalagara Subba. *Retreat Padre*. Second ed. Machilipatnam: n. p., 1972.

________. *Translations of the New Songs*. Vijayawada: n. p., n. d.

Rao, M. Edwin. *The Glorious Fifty Years of the Epiphany Cathedral*. Hyderabad: Pragathi Printers and Publishers, 1988.

Richards, Lawrence O. *Expository Dictionary of Bible Words*. Grand Rapids: Zondervan Publishing House, 1985.

Richardson, Alan. *An Introduction to the Theology of the New Testament*. London: SCM Press Ltd., [1958], 1969.

Ridderbos, Herman. *Paul: An Outline of His Theology*. Grand Rapids: William B. Eerdmans Publishing Company, 1992.

Robinson, D. W. B. "Church." In *The New Bible Dictionary*. Edited by J. D. Douglas, 228-231. Grand Rapids: William B. Eerdmans Publishing Company, 1970.

Roloff, J. "ἐκκλησια." In *Exegetical Dictionary of the New Testament*. Edited by Horst Balz and Gerhard Schneider. Vol. 1, 410-415. Grand Rapids: William B. Eerdmans Publishing Company, 1990.

Rouse, Ruth, Stephen Neill, and Harold E. Fey, eds. *A History of the Ecumenical Movement: 1517-1968*. 4th revised edition ed. Geneva: WCC Publications, 1993.

Russell, Letty M. *Church in the Round: Feminist Interpretation of the Church*. Louisville: Westminster John Knox Press, 1993.

Sabanes, Julio R. "Biblical Understanding of Community." In *Man in Community: Christian Concern for the Human in Changing Society*. Edited by Egbert de Vries, 168-174. New York: Association Press, 1966.

Sahi, Jyoti. "'Inculturation' From the Perspective of an Artist." In *Renewed Efforts at Inculturation for and Indian Church*. Edited by Erasto Fernandes and Joji Kunduru, 73-86. Bangalore: Dharmaram Publications, 2002.

Samuel, Ananda Rao. "Episcopacy in the Church of South India." *Episcope and Episcopate in Ecumenical Perspective*, Faith and Order Paper 102 (1980), 43-50.

Sarna, Nahum M. *Exodus: The JPS Torah Commentary*. Philadelphia: Jewish Publication Society, 1991.

Savarimuthu, Stanislas. *A Community in Search of Its Identity*. Delhi: ISPCK, 2007.

Schaff, Philip. *History of the Christian Church: Apostolic Christianity; A.D. 1-100*. Vol. I. Grand Rapids: William B. Eerdmans Publishing Company, 1985.

________. *History of the Christian Church: Ante-Nicene Christianity; A.D. 100-325*. Vol. II. Grand Rapids: William B. Eerdmans Publishing Company, 1985.

Schattenmann, Johannes. "Fellowship." In *New International Dictionary of the New Testament Theology*. Edited by Colin Brown. Vol. 1, 635-644. Grand Rapids: Zondervan Publishing House, 1975.

Schmidt, Karl Ludwig. "καλεω, κλησις, κλητος κτλ." In *Theological Dictionary of the New Testament*. Edited by Gerhard Kittel. Vol. 3, 487-536. Grand Rapids: William B. Eerdmans Publishing Company, 1964-1976.

Schnackenburg, Rudolf. *The Church in the New Testament*. New York: Herder & Herder, 1965.

Schneider, John R. *The Good of Affluence: Seeking God in a Culture of Wealth*. Grand Rapids: William B. Eerdmans Publishing Company, 2002.

Schnelle, Udo. *Apostle Paul: His Life and Theology*. Translated by M. Eugene Boring. Grand Rapids: Baker Academic, 2003.

Schreiner, Thomas R. *Baker Exegetical Commentary on the New Testament: Romans*. Grand Rapids: Baker Books, 1998.

________. *Paul Apostle of God's Glory in Christ: A Pauline Theology*. Secunderabad: OM Books, 2001.

Scola, Angelo. "The Mission of the Church at the Dawn of the Third Millennium." In *Laity Today*. Edited by Pontifical Council for the Laity. Vatican: Libreria Editrice Vaticana, 2002.

Sebastian, J. Jayakiran. "Baptism and the Unity of the Church in India Today." In *Baptism and the Unity of the Church*. Edited by Michael Root and Risto Saarinen, 196-207. Grand Rapids: William B. Eerdmans Publishing Company, 1998.

Singh, Godwin R., ed. *A Call to Discipleship: Baptism and Conversion*. Delhi: ISPCK, 1985.

Singh, Sunil Kumar. *Church Management in the Indian* Context. Delhi: ISPCK, 1998.

Smith, Dennis A. "A Latin American Pilgrimage: Personal Reflection on Ecumenism and the Christian Principles of Communication." In *Christian Communication: Ecumenical Challenges in the 21st Century*. Edited by Samuel Meshack, 7-16. Yogyakarta: WACC, 2011.

Snell, C. Daniel. *Life in the Ancient Near East: 3100-332 B.C.E.* New Haven: Yale University Press, 1997.

Snyder, Howard A. *Liberating the Church*. Downers Grove: Inter-Varsity Press, 1983.

Soetens, Cl. "Les Archives Vatican Ii a Louvain-La-Neuve." In *Sources Locales De Vatican II*. Edited by Cl. Soetens and J. Grootaers. Louvain-La-Neuve: Leuven, Bibliotheek van de Faculteit der Godgeleerdheid, 1990.

Song, C. S. *Third-Eye Theology: Theology in Formations in Asian Settings*. Maryknoll: Orbis Books, 1990.

________. "Oh, Jesus Here With Us!" In *Asian Faces of Jesus*. Edited by R. S. Sugirtharajah, 131-148. Maryknoll: Orbis Books, 1993.

Srampickal, Jacob. *Communications Can Renew the Church*. Kochi: Karunikan Books, 2009.

Stegemann, Ekkehard W., and Wolfgand Stegemann. *The Jesus Movement: A Social History of Its First Century*. Translated by O. C. Dean Jr. Minneapolis: Augsburg Fortress Press, 1999.

Sterner, R. Eugene. *Healing and Wholeness*. Indiana: Warner Press, 1978.

Stott, John. *Issues Facing Christians* Today. Bombay: Gospel Literature Service, 1986.

Strong, James. *The Exhaustive Concordance of the Bible: Showing Every Word of the Text of the Common English Version of the Canonical Books, and Every Occurrence of Each Word in Regular Order*. Nashville: Abingdon Press, [1894] 1965.

Sundkler, Bengt. *Church of South India, The Movement Towards Union: 1900-1947*. London: Lutterworth Press, 1954.

Swift, Louis J. "Ambrose." In *Encyclopedia of Early Christianity*. Edited by Everett Ferguson, 30-32. New York: Garland Publishing Company, 1990.

Tanner, Norman. *The Church and the World: Gaudium Et Spes, Inter Mirifica*. New York: Paulist Press, 2005.

Tanner, R. E. S. *Religious Experience and Culture: An Enduring Reciprocity*. Bangalore: Dharmaram Publications, 2012.

Tellenbach, Gerd. *Church, State and Christian Society*. Translated by R. F. Bennett. New Jersey: Humanities Press, [1940] 1970.

Templeton, Elizabeth. "Towards the Realisation of Common Life." In *On the Way to Fuller Koinonia.* Edited by Thomas Best and G. Gassmann, 117-122. Geneva: WCC, 1994.

Thangasamy, D. A. *The Theology of Chenchaiah.* Bangalore: CISRS and YMCA, 1966.

The Lima Document (1982).

The World Mission of the Church: Tambaram 1938. London: IMC, 1939.

Theissen, Gerd. *Sociology of Early Palestinian Christianity.* Translated by John Bowden. Philadelphia: Fortress Press, 1978.

Thomas, M. M. "Manilal C. Parekh." In *Towards an Indian Christian Theology: Life and Thought of Some Pioneers.* Edited by M. M. Thomas and P. T. Thomas, 159-163. Tiruvalla: Christava Sahitya Samithi, 1998.

Thomas, M. M. *A Diaconal Approach to Indian* Ecclesiology. Rome: CIIS, 1995.

Thottakara, Augustine. *Indian Spirituality: Hindu Spiritual Traditions, A Christian Interpretation.* Bangalore: Dharmaram Publications, 2010.

Tidball, Derek. *An Introduction to the Sociology of the New Testament.* Exeter: Paternoster Press, 1983.

Tillich, Paul. *A Complete History of Christian Thought.* Edited by Carl Braaten. New York: Harper and Row Publishers, 1968.

Torrance, Thomas F. "Foundation of the Church." In *Theological Foundations for Ministry: Selected Readings for a Theology of the Church in Ministry.* Edited by Ray S. Anderson, 199-215. Edinburgh: T. & T. Clark, Ltd., 1979.

Towards Visible Unity: Commission on Faith and Order: Lima 1982. Vol. 1. Geneva: WCC, 1982.

Troeltsch, Ernst. *The Social Teaching of the Christian Churches.* Translated by Olive Wyon. Vol. 1. New York: The Macmillan Company, [1931] 1949.

Turner, Denis. "Christian Activity in the World." In *The Church in the World.* Edited by Denis Turner, 56-71. Dublin: Scepter Books, 1968.

Uffenheimer, Benjamin. "Myth and Reality in Ancient Israel." In *The Origins and Diversity of Axial Age Civilizations.* Edited by S. N. Eisenstadt, 135-168. Albany, New York: State University of New York Press, 1986.

Van Leeuwen, Gerwin, ed. *Searching for an Indian Ecclesiology.* Bangalore: Asian Trading Corporation, 1984.

Vandana. *Waters of Fire.* Madras: Christian Literature Society, 1981.

________. *Find Your Roots and Take Wing: Spiritual Formation for the East and the West: Three Essays.* Bangalore: Asia Trading Corporation, 1991.

________. *Nâma Japa: The Prayer of the Name.* Delhi, Motilal Banarsidass, 1995.

________. "Water Symbolism in the Gospel of St. John in the Light of Indian Spirituality." In *Readings in Indian Christian Theology.* Edited by R. S. Sugirtharajah and Cecil Hargreaves, 200-13. Delhi: ISPCK, [1993] 2004.

Viswanathan, Gauri. "Coping with (Civil) Death: The Christian Convert's Right of Passage in Colonial India." In *After Colonialism: Imperial Histories and Postcolonial Displacements.* Edited by Gyan Prakash, 183-210. Princeton: Princeton University Press, 1995.

Volf, Miroslav. *After our Likeness: The Church as the Image of the Trinity.* Grand Rapids: William B. Eerdmans Publishing Company, 1998.

Vorländer, H. "Woman, Mother, Virgin, Widow." In *New International Dictionary of the New Testament Theology.* Edited by Colin Brown. Vol. 3, 1055-1068. Grand Rapids: Zondervan Publishing House, 1981.

Webster, John C. B. 'The Identity of Indian Christians." In *Church in Context: Essays in Honour of Mathias Mundadan, CMI.* Edited by Kanichikattil Francis, 56-71. Bangalore: Dharmaram, 1986.

________. *The Dalit Christians: A History.* Delhi: ISPCK, 2009.

Weeks, Noel. *Admonition and Curse: The Ancient Near Eastern Treaty/Covenant Form as a Problem in Inter-Cultural Relationships.* Edinburgh: T & T Clark, 2004.

Wenham, Gordon J. *The Book of Leviticus: The New International Commentary on the Old Testament.* Edited by R. K. Harrison and Jr. Robert L. Hubbard. Vol. 3. Grand Rapids: William B. Eerdmans Publishing Company, 1979.

Wilson, Viju. *Ecclesiology of Prophetic Participation.* Delhi: ISPCK, 2012.

Wright, Christopher J. H. *Walking in the Ways of the Lord: The Ethical Authority of the Old Testament.* Leicester: Apollos, 1995.

Yarnold, E. J. "Sacramental Theology." In *The Westminster Dictionary of Christian Theology.* Edited by Alan Richardson and John Bowden, 516. Philadelphia: The Westminster Press, 1983.

Yonge, Charles Duke. *The Works of Philo: Complete and Unabridged.* Peabody: Hendrickson Publishers, 1996.

Young, William G. *Handbook of Source Materials for Students of Church* History. Delhi: ISPCK, 2009.

Zachariah, Mathai, ed. *The Church: A People's Movement.* Nagpur: NCCI, 1975.

Journals and Magazines

Plessis, David du. "Pentecost." *A Quarterly Review of World-wide Pentecostal Activity* 30 (Dec. 1954): 17.

"Editorial." *Religion and Society* 19, no. 1 (March 1972): 4-5.

"How Does the Church Teach Authoritatively Today?" *The Ecumenical Review* 31, no. 1 (January 1979): 77-93.

Abraham, K. C. "Church of South India Ecclesiology." *Jeevadhara* 19, no. 112 (July 1989): 251-254.

Alex, John. "Origin and Transition of the Church in the First Five Centuries." *New Life Theological Journal* 2, no. 1 (Jan.-June, 2012): 41-56.

Baago, K. "Honestly Speaking." *The United Church Review* (July 1967): 148.

Barclay, John M. G. "Poverty in Pauline Studies: A Response to Steven Friesen." *Journal for the Study of the New Testament* 26, no. 3 (2004): 363-366.

Barrett, David B. and Todd M. Johnson. "Annual Statistical Table on Global Mission: 1999." *International Bulletin of Missionary Research* 23, no. 1 (January 1999): 24-25.

Bartling, Walter J. "A Ministry to Ministers: An Examination of the New Testament *Diakonia*." *Concordia Theological Monthly* 33, no. 6 (1962): 325-336.

Baum, Gregory. "Sociology and Theology." *Concilium* 1 (1971): 22-31.

Beed, Clive, and Cara Beed. "Economic Egalitarianism in Pre-Monarchical Israel." *Faith and Economics* 54 (2009): 83-105.

Berman, Joshua A. "God's Alliance with Man." *Azure* 25 (Summer 2006): 79-113.

________. "The Biblical Origins of Equality." *Azure* 37 (2009): 57-69.

Brunner, Emil. "One Holy Catholic Church." *Theology Today* 4, no. 3 (October 1, 1947): 318-331.

Campbell, J. Y. "Κοινωνια and its Cognates in the New Testament." *Journal of Biblical Literature* 51, no. 4 (1932): 352-380.

Carroll, John T. "Children in the Bible." *Interpretation* 55, no. 2 (April 2001): 121-134.

CBCI. "Response of the General Body to CBCI Evaluation Report." *Catholic India* (1996): 24.

Chandran, J. R. "Baptism." *Aikyatha* (December 1991): 10.

Chenu, Marie-Dominique. "The Church's 'Social Doctrine.'" *Concilium* 10 (1980): 71-75.

Cross, M. Frank. "Reuben, First Born of Jacob." *Zeitschrift Fur Die Altetstamentliche Wishenschaft* 100 (1988): 46-65.

Das, Jogesh. "Women's Human Rights in North-East India." *Journal of Humanities and Social Science* 3, no. 4 (Sep.-Oct. 2012): 34-37.

Easley, Kendell H. "The Pauline Usage of PNEUMATI as a Reference to the Spirit of God." *Journal of the Evangelical Theological Society* 27, no. 3 (September 1984): 299-313.

Elliott, John. "Jesus Was Not an Egalitarian: A Critique of an Anachronistic and Idealist Theory." *Biblical Theology Bulletin* 32 (2002): 75-91.

Faust, Avraham. "Early Israel: An Egalitarian Society." *Biblical and Archaeological Review* 39, no. 4 (July-Aug 2013): 45-63.

Fiorenza, Elisabeth Schüssler. "Discipleship and Patriarchy: Early Christian Ethos and Christian Ethics in a Feminist Theological Perspective." *Annual of the Society of Christian Ethics* (1982): 131-172.

Friesen, Steven J. "Poverty in Pauline Studies: Beyond the So-called New Consensus." *Journal for the Study of the New Testament* 26, no. 3 (2004): 323-361.

Gaikwad, Roger. "Towards a New Ecclesia: Re-Reading the Concept of 'Ecclesia' in the Bible: A Few Pointers." *Religion and Society* 56, no. 2 (June 2011): 12-20.

George, Roji T. "'Body Politics of Paul' in Corinth: Temple and the Rules of Purity in Constructing Identity in 1 Cor. 5:9-13." *Bible Bhashyam* 37, no. 1 (2011): 74-99.

________. "Divine Grace in the Making of Paul, the *Yesu Bhakta*: Reclaiming the Role of Grace in the Self-Consciousness of Paul as a *Bhakta* in the Light of St. Tukaram's *Bhakti* Thought." *Bangalore Theological Forum* 45, no. 1 (2013): 74-96.

Gottwald, Norman K. "Social Class as an Analytic and Hermeneutical Category in Biblical Studies." *Journal of Biblical Literature* 112, no. 1 (1979): 6-10.

Graafland, J. "Market Operation and Distributive Justice: An Evaluation of the Accra Confession." *Journal of the Association of Christian Economists U. K* 38 (2008): 1-21.

Hiebert, D. Edmond. "Behind the Word 'Deacon': A New Testament Study." *Bibliotheca Sacra* 140, no. 558 (1983): 151-162.

Horton, Walter Marshall. "The Christian Community: Its Lord and Its Fellowship; The Biblical Basis for Christian Ethics." *Interpretation* 4 (October, 1950): 387-400.

Houtart, François. "Attitude toward Development among Catholics in Sri Lanka." *World Development* 8 (1980): 603-612.

________. "The Cult of Violence in the name of Religion: A Panorama." *Dialogue* 29 (2002): 1-10.

________. "The Point of View of a Sociologist: The Crisis of Authority in the Church," *Convergence* 5 (1969).

________. "The Pope in Cuba: A Visit Which Aimed at Being a Turning Point and May Have Been But a Parenthesis." *COELI – Centre Oecumenique de Liaisons Internationales,* 82-83 (1997): 29-32.

________. "Traditional Christian Ethics and the Social Reality: A Critique." *Dialogue* 30 (2003): 93-103.

Jathanna, O. V. "Review of *Living Today Towards Visible Unity*, by Thomas Best." *Bangalore Theological Forum* 20, no. 4 (1988): 65-73.

________. 'Taufe imindischen Kontext." *Darurn* 1, no. 93 (1993): 18-19.

________. "Christen in Indien: Aspekte einer indischen Ekklesiologie." *Die Zeichen der Zeit* 4, no. 95 (49/4, 1995): 149-151.

________. "Ecclesiology in Context: Reflections from an Indian Perspective in the Light of Current Ecumenical Deliberations." *Bangalore Theological Forum* 28, nos. 3-4 (September-December 1996): 3-11.

Kloha, Jeffrey. "Koinonia and Life Together in the New Testament." *Concordia Journal* 38, no. 1 (2012): 24-36.

Kochalumakal, Anthony. "Growing Together and Going Together: At the Source of Spirituality of Communion." *Third Millennium* 9, no. 2 (2006): 79-92.

Kudiyiruppil, John. "The Ecumenical Potential of Eucharistic Theology." *The Living Word* 108, no. 5 (2002): 294-317.

Levenson, Jon D. "Poverty and the State in Biblical Thought." *Judaism* 25, no. 2 (1976): 232-235.

Lillie, Betty Jane. "*Koinonia* in the New Testament: Integral Dynamic of the Christian Life," *Proceedings- Eastern Great Lakes and Midwest Biblical Societies* 28 (2008): 55-66.

Vischer, Lukas. "How does the Church Teach Authoritatively Today?" *Concilium,* no. 148 (1981): 1-10.

Ma, Wonsuk. "Toward an Asian Pentecostal Theology." *Asian Journal of Pentecostal Studies* 1, no. 1 (January 1998): 15-41.

Mason, John. "Biblical Teaching and Assisting the Poor." *Transformation* 4 (1987): 1-14.

Abrams, Minnie F. "How Pentecost came to India." *Pentecostal Evangel* May 1945, 6.

Mott, Stephen Charles, and Ronald J. Sider. "Economic Justice: A Biblical Paradigm." *Transformation* 17, no. 2 (2000): 50-63.

Neal, M. Soss. "Old Testament Law and Economic Society." *Journal of the History of Ideas* 34, no. 3 (July-Sept., 1973): 323-344.

Oakes, Peter. "Constructing Poverty Scales for Graeco-Roman Society: A Response to Steven Friesen's 'Poverty in Pauline Studies." *Journal for the Study of the New Testament* 26, no. 3 (2004): 367-371.

Omanson, Roger L. "The Role of Women in the New Testament Church." *Review & Expositor* 83, no. 1 (Winter 1986): 15-25.

Pathil, Kuncheria. "Theology of the Local Church." *Jeevadhara* 28 (1998): 257-278.

Pesch, Rudolf. "The New Testament Foundation of a Democratic Form of Life in the Church." *Concilium* 3 (1971): 48-59.

Piana, George La. "The Roman Church at the end of the Second Century: the Episcopate of Victor, the Latinization of the Roman Church, the Easter Controversy, Consolidation of Power and Doctrinal Development, the Catacomb of Callistus." *Harvard Theological Review* 18, no. 3 (July, 1925): 201-277.

Poon, Michael Nai-Chiu. "Communicating Communion: Contextualising in a Globalising Asia-Pacific." *The Asia Journal of Theology* 27, no. 2 (2013): 172-184.

Roberts, J. W. "The Meaning of *Ekklesia* in the New Testament." *Restoration Quarterly* 15, no. 1 (1972): 27-36.

Schaefer, Kurt C. and Edd S. Noell. "Contract Theory, Distributive Justice, and the Hebrew Sabbatical." *Faith and Economics* 45 (Spring 2005): 1-19.

Skaggs, Rebecca. "The Challenge of Diversity: Chaos or Community." *Pneuma: The Journal of the Society for Pentecostal Studies* 21, no. 2 (Fall 1999): 173-179.

Spitaler, Peter. "Welcoming a Child as a Metaphor for Welcoming God's Kingdom: A Close Reading of Mark 10.13-16." *Journal for the Study of the New Testament* 31, no. 4 (2009): 423-446.

Staffner, Hans. "Baptism and the Law of Inheritance." *Vidyajyothi* 48, no. 2 (1984): 75-81.

_________. "Evangelisierung in Indien heute: Ist es moeglich, ein christlicher Hindu zu sein? *Zeitschrift feur Missionswissenschaft* 72, no. 3 (1989): 163-184.

Steele, Elizabeth. "The Role of Women in the Church." *Currents in Theology and Mission* 13, no. 1 (1986): 13-21.

Synan, Vinson. "Pentecostalism, Varieties and Contributions." *Pneuma: The Journal of the Society for Pentecostal Studies* 9, no. 1 (Spring 1987): 31-49.

Talbott, Rick. "Imagining the Matthean Eunuch Community: *Kyriarchy* on the Chopping Block." *Journal of Feminist Studies in Religion* 22, no. 1 (2006): 21-43.

Taylor, Mark Lewis. "Challenging Theological Studies: Critical Feminism and Liberating Interpretation." *Theology Today* 66, no. 2 (July 2009): 234-240.

Ward, Roy Bowen. "Ekklesia: A Word Study." *Restoration Quarterly* 2, no. 4 (1958): 164-179.

Wright, Christopher J. H. "The Use of the Bible in Social Ethics." *Transformation* 1 (1984): 3-10.

Zachariah, George. "Church without Walls: Church Happening in the Street." *Masihi Sevak: Journal of Christian Ministry* 38, no. 3 (April 2013): 17-23.

Newspaper

The Hindu (Visakhapatnam), August 31, 2012, 11.

Deccan Chronicles (Visakhapatnam), November 11, 2012, 4.

Los Angeles Daily Times (Los Angeles), 18 April 1906, 2

The Hindu (Visakhapatnam), August 31, 2012, 5.

Catholic India (1996): 24.

Guardian (Madras), 1942, 28-29.

The New York Times, April 3, 1987.

Theses

Abrahams, Lutasha Ann-Louise. "A critical comparison of Elizabeth Schüssler Fiorenza's notion of Christian ministry as a 'Discipleship of Equals' and Mercy Amba Oduyoye's notion as a 'Partnership of both Men and Women'." Master's thesis, University of the West Cape, 2005.

Hivner, Richard Leroy, Jr. "Exploring the Depths of the Mystery of Christ: The Life and Work of K. Subba Rao of Andhra Pradesh, South India, with Special Reference to His Songs." Master's thesis, University of South Africa, 2004.

Minutes and Proceedings

Best, Thomas F., ed. *Faith and Order 1985-1989: The Commission Meeting at Budapest*. Geneva: WCC, 1990.

Minutes of the Meeting of the Faith and Order Standing Commission: 4-11 January, 1994: Cret-Berard, Switzerland, 28.

WACC Document on "Christian Principles of Communication."

Wallerstein, Immanuel. *The Catholic Church and the World* (2005).

WCC Central Committee: Minutes of the Forty-Third Meeting, Geneva, Switzerland, 20-27 September 1991, 49.

World Council of Churches Central Committee: Minutes of the Forty-fifth Meeting, Johannesburg, South Africa, 20-28 January 1994, 106.

World Council of Churches Central Committee: Minutes of the Forty-Third Meeting, Geneva, Switzerland, 20-27 September 1991, 53.

Webpages

"Democracy." http://www.merriam-webster.com/dictionary/democracy (accessed December 12, 2013).

"Education." http://www.unicef.org/india/education.html (accessed December 11, 2013).

"Pontifical Council for Promoting Christian Unity, Peace in the World: Dialogue among Christians and Other Religions," 6. http://www.vatican.va/roman_curia/pontifical_councils/chrstuni/documents/rc_pc_chrstuni_doc_20020107_peace-kasper_en.html (accessed May 12, 2007).

"Reading Paul in the Context of Empire: Roman Imperialism, Pauline Resistance, and Contemporary Implications." http://miketodd.typepad.com/files/paul-the-politics-of-empire.pdf (accessed January 21, 2014).

"The Nature and Purpose of the Church: A Stage on the Way to a Common Statement Faith and Order Paper No. 181 - November 1998." http://www.wcc-coe.org/wcc/what/faith/nature1.html (accessed August 20, 2006).

Abrahams, Lutasha Ann-Louise. "A Critical Comparison of Elizabeth Schüssler Fiorenza's Notion of Christian Ministry as a 'Discipleship of Equals' and Mercy Amba Oduyoye's Notion as a 'Partnership of both Men and Women'." http://etd.uwc.ac.za/usrfiles/modules/etd/docs/etd_gen8Srv25Nme4_7804_1181886366.pdf (accessed August 26, 2013).

Benedict XVI, "Address to Diocese of Rome," 26 May 2009, available at http://www.vatican.va/holy_father/benedict_xvi/speeches/2009/may/documents/hf_ben-xvi_spe_20090526_convegno-diocesi-rm_en.html, (accessed December 12, 2013).

Burke, B. *The Encyclopaedia of Informal Education*, s.v. "Antonio Gramsci, schooling and education," (1999, 2005) http://www.infed.org/thinkers/et-gram.htm (accessed December 27, 2007).

Dager, Albert James. "What Is 'The Church?' With Whom Did God Make His New Covenant?" *Media Spotlight: A Biblical Analysis of Religious & Secular Media*. http://www.mediaspotlight.org/pdfs/What%20Is%20The%20Church.pdf (accessed March 23, 2014).

Dager, Albert James. "What is 'the Church'?: With whom did God make His New Covenant?" *Media Spotlight: A Biblical Analysis of Religious and Secular Media*. https://www.yumpu.com/en/document/view/10258417/what-is-the-church-media-spotlight (accessed January 07, 2014).

Darko, Daniel. "A book review on, *Transforming Vision: Explorations in Feminist The*logy*, by Elisabeth Schüssler Fiorenza." http://www.bookreviews.org/pdf/8348_9131.pdf (accessed February 28, 2014).

"Dialectical Interaction of Religion and Society: A Dialogue with François Houtart." *Australian E-Journal of Theology* no. 10 (Pentecost 2007); http://aejt.com.au/ (accessed January 22, 2012).

Ditzel, Peter. "Ekklesia or Church, Does It Matter?" http://www.wordofhisgrace.org/ekklesia.pdf (accessed January 20, 2014).

Ecclesia in Asia, no.1, http://www.vatican.va/holy_father/john_paul_ii/apost_exhortations/documents/hf_jp-ii_exh_06111999_ecclesia-in-asia_en.html (accessed January 21, 2013).

Edwards, Dennis. *Resurrection of the Body and Transformation of the Universe in the Theology of Karl Rahner*. http://www.krs. stjohnsem.edu/Edwards Dennis 2005.pdf (accessed May 27, 2007).

Evans, Graham G. B. "The Mission of the Church" http://chesterrep.openrepository.com/cdr/bitstream/10034/97541/4.htm, (accessed January 27, 2014).

Fiorenza, Elisabeth Schüssler. "A Critical Feminist Spirituality of Struggle." http://www.womenutc.com/elisabeth.htm (accessed August 06, 2013).

________. "Equality: A Radical Democratic Ekklesial Vision." http://www.cta usa.org/reprint11-98/fiorenza.html (accessed August 06, 2013).

________. "We Are Church-A Kindom of Priests." *WOW* (July 22, 05). http://women-churchconvergence.org/WOW%20anniversary%20addresses/WE%20ARE%20CHURCH%20%20A%20KINDOM%20OF%20PRIESTS%20by%20Elisabeth%20Schussler%20Fiorenza.pdf (accessed August 26, 2013).

________. "Wo/men of the Word: Reclaiming Our Power of Memory." http://www.futurechurch.org/watw/btg/schusslerfiorenza.htm (accessed August 06, 2013).

________. "Wo/men of the Word: Reclaiming Our Power of Memory." http://www.futurechurch.org/watw/btg/schusslerfiorenza.htm (accessed August 06, 2013).

Goodmanson, Drew. "Communication 3.0 Trends That Will Impact Your Ministry." http://www.goodmanson.com/category/church-technology/ekklesia/ (accessed February 26, 2014).

Hays, Richard B. "Ecclesiology and Ethics: In 1 Corinthians." http://cpcnewhaven.org/documents/Ecclesiology%20and%20ethics.pdf (accessed January 16, 2014).

http://christadelphians.wordpress.com/what-and-why-ecclesia/ (accessed July 14, 2013).

http://feministphilosophers.wordpress.com/2008/05/01/word-of-the-day-kyriarchy/ (accessed August 08, 2013).

http://jmathyal.tripod.com/id19.html (accessed June 13, 2011).

http://sanskaramvatika.com/why.html (accessed February 12, 2014).

http://skipmoen.com/tag/qahal/ (accessed February 13, 2011).

http://timesofindia.indiatimes.com/city/thane/In-laws-booked-for-dowry-harassment/articleshow/23664542.cms (accessed December 10, 2013).

http://womenchurchconvergence.org/WOW%20anniversary%20addresses/The%20Church%20as%20Liberation%20Community%20by%20Rosemary%20RR.pdf (accessed January 27, 2014).

http://www.aggressivechristianity.net/articles/ecclesia.htm (accessed June 13, 2011).

http://www.binghamton .edu/fbc/159en-corrected.htm (accessed May 27, 2007).

http://www.britannica.com/EBchecked/topic/177746/Ecclesia (accessed August 08, 2013).

http://www.testimony-magazine.org/back/Special_Issues/Sept91/art3.htm (accessed June 13, 2011).

Kingslake, Brian. *Out of This World. Lay-bys on the Road to Heaven.* England: James Evesham Worc., 1978. http://www.sweden

borgdigitallibrary.org/ootw/ootw24.htm (accessed June 13, 2011).

McCabe, Michael. "The Role of the Church in Civil Society: Some Theological Orientations." http://www.africamission-mafr.org/mccabe_gb.doc (accessed May 12, 2007).

Mohan, Vasundhara. "Status of Women in India: Problems and concerns." Centre for Study of Society and Secularism, 20 http://www.csss-isla.com/Status%20of%20Women%20in%20India%20Internees%20report[1].pdf (accessed December 10, 2013).

Martin, Diarmuid. "Companion to the Compendium of the Social Doctrine of the Church." http:// www.dublindiocese.ie/index.php?option=com_content&task=view&id=745&Itemid=37. (December 12, 2013).

Pieris, Aloysius. "Vatican II: A *Crisigenic* Council with Unwritten Agenda," *East Asian Pastoral Review* 42, no. 1-2 (2005): 7-24. http://eapi.admu.edu.ph/content/crisigenic-council-unwritten-agenda (accessed January 25, 2014).

Ruether, Rosemary Radford. "The Church as Liberation Community from Patriarchy: The Praxis of Ministry as Discipleship of Equals."

Sahabandhu, Jerome. "Portraying the Person and Work of François Houtart." *Australian E-journal of Theology* (2006). http://dlibrary.acu.edu.au/research/theology/ejournal/aejt_8/index.html (accessed January 25, 2014).

______. "Dialectical Interaction of Religion and Society: A Dialogue with François Houtart." *Australian E-Journal of Theology* no. 10 (Pentecost 2007); http://aejt.com.au/ (accessed January 22, 2012).

Spadaro, Antonio. "A Big Heart Open to God: The Exclusive Interview with Pope Francis." *America: The National Catholic Review* 30 September 2013. http://americamagazine.org/pope-interview, (accessed December 12, 2013).

Springett, Ron. "The Spirit and the Church." https://adventistbiblicalresearch.org/sites/default/files/pdf/Springett-Spirit_and_the_church_0.pdf (accessed January 18, 2014).

Vatican, *Populorum Progressio*, [Encyclical of Pope Paul VI on the development of people, March 26, 1967], 57-60. http://www.vatican.va/holy_father/paul_vi/encyclicals/documents/hf_p-vi_enc_ 26031967_populorum_en .html (accessed May 15, 2007).

Vatican. *Deus Caritas Est*, 28. http://www.vatican.va/holy_father/benedict_xvi/encyclicals/documents/hf_ben-xvi_enc_20051225_deus-caritas-est_en.html (accessed May 12, 2007).

Vatican. *Evangelii Nuntiandi*, 33 – 35. http://www.vatican.va/holy_father/paul_vi/apost_ exhortations/documents/hf_p-vi_exh_19751208 evangelii-nuntiandi_en.html (accessed May 12, 2007).

Index